# Getting Started with IBM FileNet P8 Content Manager

Install, customize, and administer the powerful FileNet Enterprise Content Management platform

William J. Carpenter

BIRMINGHAM - MUMBAI

# Getting Started with IBM FileNet P8 Content Manager

Copyright © 2011 Packt Publishing

All rights reserved. No part of this book may be reproduced, stored in a retrieval system, or transmitted in any form or by any means, without the prior written permission of the publisher, except in the case of brief quotations embedded in critical articles or reviews.

Every effort has been made in the preparation of this book to ensure the accuracy of the information presented. However, the information contained in this book is sold without warranty, either express or implied. Neither the author, nor Packt Publishing, and its dealers and distributors will be held liable for any damages caused or alleged to be caused directly or indirectly by this book.

Packt Publishing has endeavored to provide trademark information about all of the companies and products mentioned in this book by the appropriate use of capitals. However, Packt Publishing cannot guarantee the accuracy of this information.

First published: January 2011

Production Reference: 1210111

Published by Packt Publishing Ltd.
32 Lincoln Road
Olton
Birmingham, B27 6PA, UK.

ISBN 978-1-849680-70-7

www.packtpub.com

Cover Image by David Guettirrez (bilbaorocker@yahoo.co.uk)

# Credits

**Author**
William J. Carpenter

**Reviewers**
Philip Hirschi
Raffaele Manfellotto
Ian Story

**Acquisition Editor**
Amey Kanse

**Development Editor**
Susmita Panda

**Technical Editor**
Arani Roy

**Indexers**
Monica Ajmera Mehta
Rekha Nair

**Editorial Team Leader**
Gagandeep Singh

**Project Team Leader**
Ashwin Shetty

**Project Coordinator**
Zainab Bagasrawala

**Proofreader**
Aaron Nash

**Graphics**
Geetanjali Sawant

**Production Coordinators**
Arvindkumar Gupta
Alwin Roy

**Cover Work**
Arvindkumar Gupta

# About the Author

**William J. Carpenter** is an ECM architect working with IBM in the Seattle area. Bill has experience in the Enterprise Content Management business since 1998, as a developer, as a development manager, and as an architect. He is the co-author of the books *IBM FileNet Content Manager Implementation Best Practices and Recommendations* and *Developing Applications with IBM FileNet P8 APIs*, is a contributing author on IBM developerWorks, and is a frequent conference presenter. He has experience in building large software systems at Fortune 50 companies and has also served as the CTO of an Internet startup. He has been a frequent mailing list and patch contributor to several open source projects. Bill holds degrees in Mathematics and Computer Science from Rensselaer Polytechnic Institute in Troy, New York.

# Acknowledgement

I could not have written this book without the mountains of direct and indirect help I've received over the years in learning the lore of ECM. That help came from two primary places. First, my many colleagues at IBM (and at FileNet in the days before IBM) have taught me most of what I know about ECM (before, I couldn't even spell ECM, and now...). Thanks to those in product development, support, field engagements, and to others that I have known over the years; and, especially, I thank my fellow architects for our many patient, professional, and detailed discussions on countless topics. Second, I have learned a lot about ECM from our customers, partners, and the IBM colleagues who work most closely with them. Although P8 is a platform, most of our work is driven by use-cases. Hearing about new use-cases is always a delight and an education (even if the discussion is about features we don't have).

My special thanks to the technical reviewers. They worked long hours reading and commenting on all of the chapters of the book, as evident by the many comments and suggestions they sent my way. The book is significantly better for it. Thanks also to the editors and staff at Packt Publishing for giving me the writing opportunity and guiding me along the path to publication. Ultimately, of course, any remaining errors in the text are fully my responsibility.

Finally and most of all, I'd like to thank my wife, daughter, and son for patiently enduring my lack of attention over these past months. Despite my absence from many household activities, projects, and duties, they gave me constant encouragement for my work on this book. (I know what you are thinking, but I'm not going to be thanking the family cat. As it turns out, he was not that helpful for the writing part. Also, his technical ideas were just plain nonsense.)

— WJC, Seattle, December 2010

# About the Reviewers

**Philip Hirschi** has written about FileNet's P8 ECM product for close to ten years, with a special emphasis on security. In his previous career, he worked at UNICEF HQ in New York City. Before that he was cellist in John McLaughlin's groundbreaking fusion band The Mahavishnu Orchestra, featuring Jean-Luc Ponty, and still plays in various bands in Seattle's fertile indie rock scene. Phil says, "Bill Carpenter is one of the smartest and funniest guys I know. My main editorial suggestion was to add more jokes."

**Raffaele Manfellotto** is a highly skilled, well-qualified information technology consultant with a clear understanding and appreciation of the demands and expectations of working within customer environments. He has a B. Sc. Hons in Computer Science and an M. Sc. in Computer Networks. He has more than five years experience within the Enterprise Content Management (ECM) industry working for large companies in North America and the EMEA regions.

**Ian Story** has worked in the field of Enterprise Content Management since 1998, in a variety of technical and management roles, for firms that include Weyerhaeuser, Washington Mutual, and JPMorgan Chase & Co. He holds undergraduate degrees in both Computer Science and business from Pacific Lutheran University and resides on the outskirts of Seattle, Washington. He is extremely active within the ECM community, as the president of the Pacific Northwest IBM ECM UserNet, member of the Americas IBM ECM Board, member of the IBM ECM Technical Advisory Council, and an IBM Information Champion. Ian is also the co-founder of Bucket2, a privately held software research and development firm specializing in mobile applications; he can be reached via the Bucket2 website at `http://www.bucket2.com`.

---

I'd like to thank the author, Bill Carpenter, for the opportunity to review and provide commentary on this book, and to everyone in the ECM ecosystem—customers, partners, and IBM themselves—for their friendship throughout the years.

---

# www.PacktPub.com

## Support files, eBooks, discount offers, and more

You might want to visit www.PacktPub.com for support files and downloads related to your book.

Did you know that Packt offers eBook versions of every book published, with PDF and ePub files available? You can upgrade to the eBook version at www.PacktPub.com and as a print book customer, you are entitled to a discount on the eBook copy. Get in touch with us at service@packtpub.com for more details.

At www.PacktPub.com, you can also read a collection of free technical articles, sign up for a range of free newsletters and receive exclusive discounts and offers on Packt books and eBooks.

http://PacktLib.PacktPub.com

Do you need instant solutions to your IT questions? PacktLib is Packt's online digital book library. Here, you can access, read, and search across Packt's entire library of books.

## Why Subscribe?

- Fully searchable across every book published by Packt
- Copy and paste, print and bookmark content
- On demand and accessible via web browser

## Free Access for Packt account holders

If you have an account with Packt at www.PacktPub.com, you can use this to access PacktLib today and view nine entirely free books. Simply use your login credentials for immediate access.

## Instant Updates on New Packt Books

Get notified! Find out when new books are published by following *@PacktEnterprise* on Twitter, or the *Packt Enterprise* Facebook page.

# Table of Contents

**Preface** ... 1
**Chapter 1: What is ECM?** ... 7
  **ECM in three sentences** ... 8
  **Use cases** ... 9
    Central Document Repository ... 9
    Compliance and governance ... 10
    Document-centric workflow ... 11
  **Things to look for in an ECM platform** ... 12
    Safe repository ... 13
    Strong security features ... 13
    Platform support ... 13
    Scalability ... 14
    Extensibility and add-ons ... 14
    Vendor and partner ecosystem ... 14
    Enterprise interoperability ... 14
    Strong APIs ... 15
    Notifications and triggers ... 15
    Traditional document management features ... 15
      Versioning and history ... 15
      Workflow integration ... 16
      Search and navigation ... 16
      Auditing and reporting ... 16
      Metadata ... 16
  **ECM and standards** ... 16
    AIIM: DMA and ODMA ... 17
      DMA ... 17
      ODMA ... 18
    WebDAV ... 18
    JCR ... 19

| | |
|---|---|
| CMIS | 19 |
| **What ECM is not** | **19** |
| ECM is not CMS | 19 |
| ECM is not a database | 20 |
| ECM is not source code management | 21 |
| **A bit of FileNet history** | **22** |
| **Summary** | **23** |
| **Chapter 2: Installing Environmental Components** | **25** |
| **Some important IBM documents** | **25** |
| Plan and prepare your environment | 27 |
| Fix Pack Compatibility Matrix | 28 |
| **Environmental components** | **28** |
| Hardware and software requirements | 29 |
| Tailored planning and installation guides | 30 |
| **Our target environment** | **31** |
| **Configuring the environmental components** | **33** |
| User and group accounts | 34 |
| Red Hat Enterprise Linux | 36 |
|     Network addresses | 37 |
|     System clocks | 37 |
|     File storage area | 38 |
|     Firewalls | 39 |
| Installing DB2 | 40 |
|     Create a new database | 42 |
|     Drop default user tablespace | 42 |
|     Create a buffer pool definition | 42 |
|     Create tablespaces | 43 |
|     Add a user to the database | 44 |
|     Set DB2 parameters | 45 |
|     Repeat for OSTORE1 | 45 |
| WebSphere Application Server | 45 |
|     Profiles and ports | 46 |
|     WAS process attributes | 48 |
|     WAS performance tweaks | 50 |
|     WAS and DB2 | 51 |
| Installing Tivoli Directory Server | 52 |
| Using the directory | 54 |
|     Populating the directory | 55 |
|     TDS web console setup | 56 |
|     Server-side sorting | 59 |
|     The suffix | 59 |
|     Users | 60 |
|     Groups | 62 |
|     CE-specific entries | 63 |
|     Manual TDS queries | 64 |

| Scripts and desktop shortcuts | 64 |
| Summary | 67 |

## Chapter 3: Installing the Content Engine — 69
### An aside about some names — 69
### P8 platform architecture — 70
- Content Engine (CE) — 71
- Other components — 73
  - Application Engine (AE) — 73
  - Content Search Engine (CSE) — 74
  - Process Engine (PE) — 74
  - Rendition Engine (RE) — 74

### Installing the CE — 75
- Getting the software — 75
- Running the CE server installer — 76
- Configuration Manager — 76
- WAS console tweaks — 81
- Installing FEM — 83
- Bringing up the P8 Domain — 88
- Create an ObjectStore — 90

### Summary — 92

## Chapter 4: Administrative Tools and Tasks — 93
### Domain and GCD — 94
- Topology levels — 98
- Using topology levels — 100

### Exploring Domain-level items — 100
- AddOns — 102
- Fixed Content Devices — 103
- Server Cache configuration — 103
- Content configuration — 105
- Trace logging — 106
- Content cache — 109

### Exploring Object Store-level Items — 109
- Content Access Recording Level — 110
- Auditing — 111
- Checkout type — 111
- Text Index Date Partitioning — 112
- Cache configuration — 113
- Metadata — 114
  - Property templates — 114
  - Choice lists — 115
  - Classes — 116
  - Subclassing example — 117

[ iii ]

*Table of Contents*

| | |
|---|---|
| Object Browse and Query | 124 |
| **Summary** | **126** |
| **Chapter 5: Installing Other Components** | **127** |
| **Content Search Engine (CSE)** | **129** |
| The CSE user | 130 |
| Running the CSE installer | 130 |
| Command line configuration steps | 133 |
| Configuring CSE via the K2 Dashboard | 134 |
| Configuring CE for CSE via FEM | 136 |
|     Configuring the P8 Domain | 137 |
|     Configuring an Object Store | 138 |
| **Process Engine server (PE server)** | **141** |
| Users and groups | 142 |
| Database configuration | 143 |
|     DB2 database and tablespaces | 143 |
|     DB2 user permissions | 144 |
|     DB2 client software | 144 |
| PE server installation and configuration | 145 |
|     PE server installation | 146 |
|     CE client installation | 146 |
|     PE server configuration | 147 |
|     Shared memory | 149 |
|     Test the connections | 150 |
| CE configuration for PE | 150 |
| PE client software | 151 |
| **Application Engine (AE)** | **151** |
| **Workplace XT (XT)** | **151** |
| Configure LDAP | 152 |
| Trust relationships and LTPA | 154 |
| Run the installer | 155 |
| CE and PE client software | 156 |
|     CE client | 156 |
|     PE client | 157 |
| XT pre-deployment configuration | 157 |
| Deploying XT | 158 |
|     Classloader configuration | 159 |
|     Map special subjects | 160 |
|     ORB uniqueness | 160 |
| Running XT the first time | 160 |
| **IBM System Dashboard for ECM (SD)** | **162** |
| **Rendition Engine (RE)** | **163** |
| **Summary** | **164** |

## Chapter 6: End User Tools and Tasks — 165
### What is Workplace XT? — 166
- Browsing folders and documents — 167
- Adding folders — 167
- Adding documents — 168
- Viewing documents — 170
### Entry templates — 171
### Workflow interactions — 172
- One-time isolated region setup — 173
- Approval workflows — 174
- Tasks in XT — 175
### Versioning — 176
### Properties and security — 179
### Searches — 180
- Simple Search — 181
- Keyword Search — 182
- Advanced Search — 182
- Stored Searches and Search Templates — 183
### Summary — 185

## Chapter 7: Major CM Features — 187
### Documents — 188
- Content — 188
  - Multiple content elements — 189
  - Content transfer and content reference — 189
  - Content element numbering — 190
- Versioning — 191
  - Checkout and checkin — 192
  - Freeze — 193
  - Major and minor versions — 194
- Document lifecycles — 195
- Autoclassification — 196
- Compound documents — 197
- DITA publishing — 198
- Rendition Engine — 198
### Search — 199
- Merge mode — 200
- Selectable and searchable properties — 201
- Property searches and full-text searches — 201
- JDBC provider — 202
- Search Templates and Stored Searches — 203
### Folders and containment — 204

[ v ]

*Table of Contents*

| | |
|---|---|
| Referential containment | 204 |
| Filing | 205 |
| Containment names | 207 |
| The decision to file documents | 208 |
| **Custom properties and classes** | **209** |
| Properties of Class Definitions | 210 |
| Properties of Property Definitions | 210 |
| **Custom objects** | **212** |
| **Annotations** | **213** |
| **Links** | **214** |
| **Subscriptions, events, and auditing** | **215** |
| What is an event? | 216 |
| Subscriptions | 217 |
| Audit logging | 219 |
| Content Access Recording Level | 219 |
| Event handlers | 220 |
| Workflow launch | 220 |
| **AddOns** | **221** |
| AddOn components | 222 |
| Creating and installing AddOns | 222 |
| Authoring an AddOn | 223 |
| **Summary** | **224** |
| **Chapter 8: Security Features and Planning** | **225** |
| **Authentication or authorization?** | **225** |
| **Authentication in CM** | **226** |
| Java Authentication and Authorization Service (JAAS) | 227 |
| Where authentication actually happens | 230 |
| Application Server trust relationships | 230 |
| Thick EJB clients | 231 |
| CEWS clients | 232 |
| Single Sign-on | 235 |
| Anonymous and guest access | 236 |
| Impersonation and run-as | 237 |
| **Enterprise directories** | **239** |
| **Authorization in CM** | **240** |
| Discretionary and Mandatory Access Control | 240 |
| Access Control Lists | 241 |
| User and group access | 243 |
| Rights | 243 |
| Levels | 244 |
| Unused bits | 245 |
| Implicit rights | 245 |

| | |
|---|---|
| Object Owner | 246 |
| Object Store administrator | 246 |
| Special query right | 247 |
| **Extra access requirements** | **247** |
| Modification Access Required | 247 |
| Target Access Required | 248 |
| **Default instance security** | **249** |
| **#CREATOR-OWNER** | **250** |
| **Security policy and document lifecycle policy** | **250** |
| Security Policy and Security Templates | 251 |
| Document lifecycle policy | 252 |
| **Dynamic security inheritance** | **252** |
| Inheritable depth | 253 |
| Parent and child security objects | 253 |
| System-defined inheritance | 255 |
| Roles and adapters | 256 |
| Project team example | 256 |
| Project team adapters | 257 |
| Folders as adapters | 259 |
| **Marking sets** | **259** |
| A marking set example | 261 |
| **The final veto** | **262** |
| **A hypothetical scenario** | **263** |
| The players | 263 |
| The business requirements | 263 |
| The strategy | 265 |
| The implementation | 265 |
| The test | 267 |
| **Summary** | **268** |
| **Chapter 9: Planning Your Deployment** | **269** |
| **Distributed deployments in functional tiers** | **270** |
| Web browsers | 270 |
| Web servers | 271 |
| CE, PE, and friends | 272 |
| Databases and filesystems | 272 |
| **Custom applications** | **273** |
| **Parallel environments** | **273** |
| Pre-production | 274 |
| Development and testing | 274 |
| **How many domains?** | **275** |
| **How many Object Stores?** | **277** |
| **Network security** | **278** |
| TLS/SSL | 278 |
| Firewalls | 279 |

| | |
|---|---|
| **Supported platforms** | **280** |
| **Integrating content with workflow** | **281** |
| **Content storage** | **281** |
| Database Storage Area | 282 |
| File Storage Area | 282 |
| Fixed content devices | 283 |
| Content Federation Services (CFS) | 283 |
| **Clustering, High Availability, and Disaster Recovery** | **284** |
| Clustering | 284 |
| High Availability | 285 |
| Disaster Recovery | 285 |
| **Distributed deployments** | **286** |
| CE topology | 287 |
| PE considerations | 288 |
| CSE considerations | 288 |
| CE distributed deployment features | 289 |
|     Content cache | 289 |
|     Request Forwarding | 290 |
| Typical distributed deployments | 291 |
|     Remote application tier | 291 |
|     Remote application and CE tier | 292 |
| **Summary** | **292** |
| **Chapter 10: Included and Add-On Components** | **293** |
| **Standard CM components** | **294** |
| Server components | 294 |
| Applications and connectors | 295 |
| Environmental components | 296 |
| **Initiatives and scenarios** | **297** |
| **Compliance management** | **297** |
| **IBM Enterprise Records (IER)** | **298** |
|     Declaration | 298 |
|     Classification | 299 |
|     Protection | 299 |
|     Disposition | 299 |
|     Audits and reporting | 301 |
| IBM eDiscovery | 301 |
|     IBM eDiscovery Analyzer (eDA) | 302 |
|     IBM eDiscovery Manager (eDM) | 303 |
| IBM Content Collector | 303 |
|     ICC for File Systems | 304 |
|     ICC for Microsoft SharePoint | 304 |
|     ICC for Email | 304 |
|     Task connectors | 304 |

## Table of Contents

| | |
|---|---|
| IBM Classification Module | 305 |
| **Smart Archive Strategy** | **306** |
| Ingestion | 307 |
| Infrastructure | 307 |
| Management | 307 |
| **IBM FileNet Business Process Manager** | **308** |
| IBM FileNet Business Process Framework | 308 |
| IBM Enterprise Content Management Widgets | 309 |
| **Other components** | **309** |
| IBM FileNet System Monitor | 309 |
| IBM FileNet Image Services | 309 |
| IBM FileNet Capture and Datacap | 310 |
| Content Management Interoperability Services | 310 |
| Darwin Information Typing Architecture | 311 |
| IBM Content Analytics | 311 |
| **Summary** | **312** |
| **Chapter 11: A Taste of Application Development** | **313** |
| **The Content Engine APIs** | **314** |
| Don't bypass the APIs | 314 |
| Reading | 314 |
| Updating | 315 |
| API transports | 316 |
| CEWS transport | 316 |
| EJB transport | 317 |
| User transactions | 318 |
| JAAS context | 319 |
| Transport-specific coding | 319 |
| CE .NET and Java APIs | 320 |
| CEWS protocol | 321 |
| Attachment formats | 322 |
| Compatibility layers | 323 |
| Java Compatibility Layer | 324 |
| COM Compatibility Layer | 325 |
| CEWS 3.5 protocol | 325 |
| **Other APIs** | **326** |
| PE APIs | 326 |
| CMIS | 326 |
| ECM Widgets | 327 |
| AE/XT customization and integration | 328 |
| **Development environments** | **328** |
| CE Java API in Eclipse | 329 |
| The project | 330 |
| CE API dependencies | 332 |

[ ix ]

| | |
|---|---|
| The application code | 333 |
| Running the application | 335 |
| Some things we didn't show | 336 |
| CE .NET API in VS C# Express | 337 |
| The project | 337 |
| CE API dependencies | 339 |
| The application code | 340 |
| Running the application | 342 |
| Some things we didn't show | 342 |
| **Summary** | **342** |
| **Chapter 12: The DUCk Sample Application** | **343** |
| **Business requirements** | **344** |
| Restricted quantity documents | 344 |
| Restricted circulation documents | 345 |
| **Design of end-user view** | **345** |
| Common login screen | 346 |
| Find documents | 347 |
| Content download | 348 |
| Adding a document | 349 |
| Viewing details for a document | 350 |
| Restricted quantity documents | 351 |
| Restricted circulation documents | 352 |
| Modifying a document | 352 |
| Enterprise mandates | 354 |
| Navigational overview | 354 |
| **Data model and security model** | **356** |
| Document properties | 356 |
| Restriction indicators | 357 |
| Restricted circulation | 357 |
| Access logging | 358 |
| Access control | 359 |
| Requests for access | 359 |
| Restricted Quantity | 361 |
| **Technical implementation details** | **363** |
| CE metadata changes | 363 |
| The annotation subclass | 364 |
| Custom document properties | 364 |
| Custom events | 364 |
| Audit logging configuration | 365 |
| Deploying the event handler code module | 366 |
| The DuckRQB project | 367 |
| New code module | 368 |
| Modifying a code module | 368 |
| Debug logging | 370 |
| The Duck project | 371 |

| | |
|---|---|
| Exporting and deploying Duck.war | 374 |
| Deployment descriptor | 375 |
| Deploying to WAS | 376 |
| Selecting the JSF Runtime | 376 |
| Configure role mapping | 377 |
| Starting the application | 377 |
| **Summary** | **378** |
| **Chapter 13: Support, Fix Packs, and Troubleshooting** | **379** |
| **Resources** | **379** |
| Documentation | 380 |
| Information center | 380 |
| Standalone documents | 381 |
| Other links | 382 |
| IBM Redbooks | 383 |
| IBM developerWorks | 384 |
| Worldwide IBM ECM Community | 384 |
| Online support resources | 385 |
| Support portal | 385 |
| PMRs and APARs | 385 |
| Technotes | 385 |
| Personalized notifications | 386 |
| Fix Central | 386 |
| Information on demand conferences | 387 |
| **Releases and fixes** | **387** |
| Product releases | 387 |
| Interim fixes | 389 |
| Fix packs | 391 |
| Installing fix packs | 393 |
| Supporting components | 393 |
| CM components | 394 |
| CE 4.5.1.4 server | 395 |
| CSE 4.5.1.1 client | 396 |
| CSE 4.5.1.1 server | 397 |
| Redeploying the updated CE server | 398 |
| CE 4.5.1.4 clients | 401 |
| XT 1.1.4.8 | 402 |
| **Troubleshooting** | **404** |
| Prevention | 404 |
| Configuration Control | 404 |
| Snapshots | 405 |
| Backups | 405 |
| Looking for trouble | 406 |
| Initial configuration | 406 |
| Authentication | 407 |
| WAS bootstrap information | 409 |
| Performance | 409 |

| | |
|---|---:|
| Trace logging | 410 |
| Isolation | 410 |
| Database tuning | 411 |
| **Summary** | **412** |
| **Index** | **413** |

# Preface

Beginning with an overview of Enterprise Content Management, the book moves quickly to the matter of getting a real Content Manager system up and running. You learn key Content Manager applications that are demonstrated to show you the major concepts that matter to you as a developer, administrator, or as an end-user. There are separate chapters that describe major platform features, security-related features, and integrations with other commonly used software components. A realistic sample application, designed right in front of you unfolds the genius in IBM FileNet P8 Content Manager. Finally, you take an in-depth look at troubleshooting, support sites, and online resources to help yourself meet your ongoing needs.

## What this book covers

*Chapter 1*, *What is ECM?*, provides background on the meaning and history of Enterprise Content Management (ECM). If you are just getting started with ECM, this chapter will give you some interesting context with which to approach both the rest of the book and your upcoming ECM experiences.

*Chapter 2*, *Installing Environmental Components*, concerns itself with installing what we call the environmental components, which are pre-requisite components, not a part of IBM FileNet Content Manager (CM) itself. We'll cover an example of configuring environmental components, a database, a directory server, and a J2EE application server, upon which the IBM FileNet software depends.

*Chapter 3*, *Installing the Content Engine*, sets about actually installing the Content Engine (CE) software. Besides the CE itself, you will also install the FileNet Enterprise Manager administrator tool and perform the steps needed to initialize a Domain and create your first Object Store. You will have a working, minimal system by the end of this chapter.

*Preface*

*Chapter 4, Administrative Tools and Tasks*, takes a brief tour of some common administrative features of CM. Many administrative concepts are described in this chapter and FileNet Enterprise Manager is used to illustrate the exploring and configuring of most of them.

*Chapter 5, Installing Other Components*, resumes the installation adventures by installing a few additional components that are a part of the CE environment. In particular, it'll cover installation of the Content Search Engine. You will also be installing the Process Engine and the Workplace XT application, and exploring more of the CM ecosystem.

*Chapter 6, End User Tools and Tasks*, is an exploration, mainly via Workplace XT, of common things done not by administrators, but by ordinary users. It includes such things as browsing, searching, and manipulating documents.

*Chapter 7, Major CM Features*, explores most of the features of Content Manager (CM) and discusses the major component architecture. These explanations are from the viewpoint of how the features are designed to work within the Content Engine and not with any specific application in mind. Thus, this material is applicable to both custom and out of the box applications.

*Chapter 8, Security Features and Planning*, addresses the many aspects of CM security. CM's comprehensive security features are one of its major strengths. You've seen security in other chapters, in little pieces, here and there. It's now time to take a more comprehensive look at things.

*Chapter 9, Planning Your Deployment*, moves from discussing individual features to looking at the big picture of how you would plan for and deploy the components of an ECM platform to a real environment.

*Chapter 10, Included and Add-On Components*, surveys the most popular of those other components that are frequently used with the base CM platform to build an ECM solution.

*Chapter 11, A Taste of Application Development*, provides a short overview of application development for IBM FileNet Content Manager (CM). It provides a high-level overview of various APIs available with CM, and discusses a bit of development methodology and philosophy.

*Chapter 12, The DUCk Sample Application*, contains a complete, self-contained sample application that demonstrates several CM features. The chapter is written as a hypothetical case study in application development, starting with business requirements and progressing all the way through a working prototype of the final application.

*Chapter 13, Support, Fix Packs, and Troubleshooting,* describes online and other resources to help you stay informed about product features, fixes, and updates. It also discusses some common troubleshooting situations and techniques and application of CM fix packs.

# What you need for this book

This book provides extensive discussion of the installation and operation of IBM FileNet Content Manager 4.5.1. You will get more out of those discussions if you have the installation files for the P8 components on-hand. Details of exactly which components we will use are given starting in *Chapter 2*.

Although it is not necessary to exactly match the versions of FileNet and the supporting software, you will have fewer adjustments to make the more closely you do match it. Our environment uses Red Hat Enterprise Linux for all components except the Process Engine and FileNet Enterprise Manager (Windows Server is used for those). We will use Tivoli Directory Server, DB2 Universal Database, and WebSphere Application Server. The precise components used matter most in the early chapters where we install and configure the software. Once the software is running, the functional features are essentially identical for all platforms. To follow our steps and bring up a working system for educational or demonstration purposes, you don't necessarily need high-end server hardware, but things may be sluggish if you don't have a liberal amount of memory.

You can benefit from reading this book without having a P8 system, but you will be benefitted more if you have a system available so that you can try things we have described and also experiment on your own. This system can be the one that you install as you read the early chapters or it can be a system that has been set up separately.

# Who this book is for

If you are a CIO, an IT manager, an IT staff engineer, or perhaps a business leader, business analyst, or even an end-user who wants to better understand the role that Content Manager plays in your enterprise, irrespective of any previous knowledge of IBM FileNet P8 Content Manager or Enterprise Content Management in general, then this book is a must-have for you.

If you are someone who is just starting to work with Content Manager or who is facing a decision about whether to use Content Manager or another solution, be assured, you will not find a better guide. Even if you have years of experience, you can still enrich your knowledge with the clear, practical explanations of basic and advanced features. Although it is not a developer's guide, per se, the API overview and sample application will help you as an enterprise developer or architect to get your bearings in Content Manager technologies.

# Conventions

In this book, you will find a number of styles of text that distinguish between different kinds of information. Here are some examples of these styles, and an explanation of their meaning.

Code words in text are shown as follows: "In that case, any CE updates will be a part of your `UserTransaction` and will be committed or rolled back based on J2EE transaction calls your application makes."

A block of code is set as follows:

```
import com.filenet.api.collection.ObjectStoreSet;
import com.filenet.api.constants.PropertyNames;
import com.filenet.api.core.Connection;
import com.filenet.api.core.Domain;
```

Any command-line input or output is written as follows:

```
$ cd /home/db2inst1/sqllib/java
$ java -cp db2jcc.jar com.ibm.db2.jcc.DB2Jcc -version
```

**New terms** and **important words** are shown in bold. Words that you see on the screen, in menus or dialog boxes for example, appear in the text like this: "From the toolbar, navigate to **Window | Open Perspective | Java**".

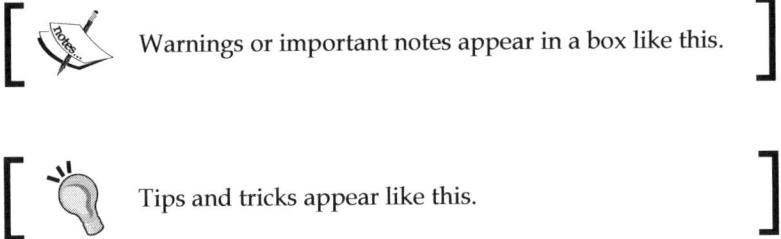

Warnings or important notes appear in a box like this.

Tips and tricks appear like this.

# Reader feedback

Feedback from our readers is always welcome. Let us know what you think about this book—what you liked or may have disliked. Reader feedback is important for us to develop titles that you really get the most out of.

To send us general feedback, simply send an e-mail to `feedback@packtpub.com`, and mention the book title via the subject of your message.

If there is a book that you need and would like to see us publish, please send us a note in the **SUGGEST A TITLE** form on www.packtpub.com or e-mail suggest@packtpub.com.

If there is a topic that you have expertise in and you are interested in either writing or contributing to a book, see our author guide on www.packtpub.com/authors.

# Customer support

Now that you are the proud owner of a Packt book, we have a number of things to help you to get the most from your purchase.

**Downloading the example code for this book**

You can download the example code files for all Packt books you have purchased from your account at http://www.PacktPub.com. If you purchased this book elsewhere, you can visit http://www.PacktPub.com/support and register to have the files e-mailed directly to you.

# Errata

Although we have taken every care to ensure the accuracy of our content, mistakes do happen. If you find a mistake in one of our books — maybe a mistake in the text or the code — we would be grateful if you would report this to us. By doing so, you can save other readers from frustration and help us improve subsequent versions of this book. If you find any errata, please report them by visiting http://www.packtpub.com/support, selecting your book, clicking on the errata submission form link, and entering the details of your errata. Once your errata are verified, your submission will be accepted and the errata will be uploaded on our website, or added to any list of existing errata, under the Errata section of that title. Any existing errata can be viewed by selecting your title from http://www.packtpub.com/support.

# Piracy

Piracy of copyright material on the Internet is an ongoing problem across all media. At Packt, we take the protection of our copyright and licenses very seriously. If you come across any illegal copies of our works, in any form, on the Internet, please provide us with the location address or website name immediately so that we can pursue a remedy.

Please contact us at copyright@packtpub.com with a link to the suspected pirated material.

We appreciate your help in protecting our authors, and our ability to bring you valuable content.

## Questions

You can contact us at questions@packtpub.com if you are having a problem with any aspect of the book, and we will do our best to address it.

# 1
# What is ECM?

This chapter provides background on the meaning and history of **Enterprise Content Management (ECM)**. If you are just getting started with ECM, this chapter will give you some interesting context with which to approach both the rest of the book and your upcoming ECM experiences. The chapter is short enough that we suggest you read it straight through (if you are an old hand at ECM in general, then we probably don't have to tell you what parts you can read over lightly in this chapter).

When we joined FileNet in 1998, there was no such term as ECM. Every vendor and analyst had his or her own terminology, generally some sort of variation of document management. These days, it seems like every experienced IT professional must be conversant in ECM terminology. Sometimes the familiarity is genuine, and sometimes it's merely a blizzard of buzzwords. Although ECM is a standard industry term these days, it's not always clear what it means except by example. By the end of this chapter, you will be able to explain it in simple terms.

This chapter contains the following topics:

- Introductory definition of ECM
- Some motivating use cases for using ECM
- Most important ECM product features
- Historical and emerging ECM-related standards
- Things commonly confused with ECM
- FileNet history

*What is ECM?*

# ECM in three sentences

Okay, that section title was a bit of a trick. We don't think we can explain ECM in three sentences. Let's see if we can explain it in three paragraphs.

ECM is automation for providing essential control of access to information, vital to the operation of an organization. Control isn't just about limiting access, though that's an important part of it. It's more about being organized in your approach to finding, collecting, storing, and retrieving content, regardless of the specific applications you eventually choose to use for those aspects. It's called *enterprise* content management because its scope is not limited to a single department or division. It is not merely an application, but a complete platform for supporting disparate applications, information sources, and processes. In this case, *content* means so-called unstructured content—documents and objects of various sorts that don't have the easy-parse luxury of highly-structured data. There certainly are important structured data aspects to unstructured content, as we'll see in later chapters, but the emphasis is to move beyond transactional business data.

> The term "enterprise" does not have to mean a commercial business organization. ECM solutions are also widely deployed in local, national, and international government organizations, and volunteer and non-profit organizations. What all of these enterprises have in common is a need to manage their content, usually at scale, to meet organizational objectives. Whether those objectives are called business objectives, compliance requirements, or something else, it is clear that they translate to the same things at a technical level.
>
> We will use the terms "enterprise" and "business" interchangeably in this book. ECM concepts are seldom limited to commercial entities.

The vision of ECM is to use a strong IT infrastructure to harness content that is already in use throughout an organization. Once content is under centralized control, it must then be made available for use by a variety of users, technical and non-technical, for both ordinary and extraordinary needs of the organization. You must have both halves of this picture. The business cannot reliably use content if it is incomplete, incorrect, or not readily available. On the other hand, locking content into an IT fortress is of limited value if business users cannot access it for the legitimate needs of the enterprise.

Over the years, precursors to ECM moved gradually from nothing at all, to local groups managing content, to departmental point solutions, and on to enterprise roll-outs of true ECM platforms. The goal of ECM is to do for unstructured content what relational databases long ago did for structured content.

Before the widespread use of general purpose database software, applications devised their own means for storing transactional data. An enterprise might develop a reusable software component to serve the needs of multiple applications, but this still left the data isolated. The development of application data storage containers is not the core business of most enterprises. When relational databases came along, it was easy to see the benefits of using them as a standardized platform component. New applications, utilities, reports, and so on, could be easily written without disruption to the existing body of applications because the storage and retrieval aspects were delegated to the database.

Though databases are an important component of ECM platforms, unstructured content has additional challenges that an ECM platform addresses. For example, there are often more elaborate referential integrity constraints and more fine-grained security requirements that lie outside the design "sweet spot" of a relational database.

# Use cases

To get an immediate feel for some of the problems that ECM can solve, let's look at a few typical use cases. These are just examples of popular scenarios to give you some concrete idea of what ECM is all about. There are certainly many more that are not covered here.

## Central Document Repository

It seems pretty obvious these days that there is a benefit to centrally managing business documents, but it was not always so. Early systems for centralized management tended to also mean giving up control of your documents to that central authority, and it isn't always obvious whether that's a good idea. Modern ECM systems focus on centralized technical control (secure storage, reliable backups, high availability, and so on) while leaving business control of the information in the hands of the appropriate users.

In the early days of electronic documents, if you needed to see the latest copy of a document, you tracked down the author and asked for it. That system had a couple of weaknesses. You couldn't get a document from Floyd if Floyd was out sick or on an airplane or just unavailable (Floyd might also just get tired of being asked). You also couldn't get a document from Floyd if Floyd himself lost track of his document or if Floyd's hard drive failed.

## What is ECM?

File sharing was among the first techniques for overcoming these problems. Someone, perhaps IT or perhaps the local computer-savvy user, set up a widely-accessible shared directory. Various users could "publish" documents by placing them in the shared directory. Although this solved some of the original problems, it brought with it other problems. Beyond the use of a few users, the organization of the shared directory tree could become quite chaotic. This is especially problematic if there are multiple versions of the "same" document in the shared directory. Some of these copies could come about from the master copy of the document being revised by the author; others would come from different users making their own safe copies in the shared directory. Conventions for subfolders and file-naming are easy to invent, but it takes a lot of user discipline to keep up with those conventions over time. Perhaps the biggest problem with this technique is that metadata (properties that describe content) is limited to what the underlying filesystem provides, and that is usually limited to simple creation and modification bookkeeping.

The early techniques for content management may have lacked finesse, but the motivation behind them was sound. An organization of any size needs a reliable system for maintaining a "single version of the truth". That is, you should be able to get the information you need and be confident that you are not using an out-of-date copy, an unpublished draft, or an otherwise unofficial version. An ECM system helps in two major ways:

- First, it facilitates your technical ability to access the information whenever you decide and from wherever you decide
- Second, it facilitates the bookkeeping for current, past, and in-process versions

When these two major factors are reliably provided, users readily acknowledge that the ECM repository holds the master copy of content. They see immediate benefits for themselves and for the enterprise, and their willing surrender of local content to the repository multiplies the benefit over time.

## Compliance and governance

It would be nice if you could decide what documents were important to your organization. You'd identify them, give them the proper attention, and waste no resources on other things. Today, few organizations can take that approach. Laws and regulations require businesses and other organizations to keep more and more information about the decisions they make (or fail to make). Even if you are not subject to formal regulatory compliance, you probably find it necessary to exercise control over business documents as a necessary contingency for the possibility of court proceedings.

It may seem sufficient to simply institute some sort of best practices for the handling of various kinds of documents. Perhaps you could also institute an annual employee sign-off that they were aware of those best practice requirements. Unfortunately, in most cases, that approach is no longer acceptable. In the eyes of regulators, auditors, court judges, and other outsiders, you must not only do proper record-keeping but also be able to prove that you did it properly. Leaving things up to individual responsibility sounds great, but it leaves you with a lot of risk.

The primary risk in compliance and litigation cases is that your enterprise has acted inappropriately. There is a secondary risk—that you have not followed rules or best practices for keeping records of what your enterprise has done. An ECM solution can reduce this secondary risk by automatically doing a large part of your record-keeping. Not only will your repository securely hold your master copy of some particular document, but it will also hold a tamper-proof copy of the entire revision history of the document. Security access can be adjusted as the document moves through various phases of its life cycle. Finally, when the document has reached the end of its usefulness, it can be automatically and definitively purged from the repository.

## Document-centric workflow

An early scenario for content repositories was to streamline business procedures for handling the documents put into those repositories. That may sound a bit circular, but what we mean is "An enterprise has business processes that are central to its operation". Automated handling of those processes, **Business Process Management (BPM)**, that is related to a piece of content is only reliable if the content itself is reliably available. A content repository serves that role nicely.

A common example is that of a mortgage broker processing a large number of applications for loans. In a typical loan processing scenario, dozens of separate documents, some seen by the applicant, some purely internal, must be gathered from different sources before the final decision can be made to grant the loan. Those documents include property appraisals, income verification documents, title insurance policies, and various internal documents supporting the underwriting process.

It is a daunting task just to keep track of the status of the comings and goings of those documents, a great number of which are faxed or scanned images. Add to that the assembly of those documents into packages for various decision-making steps and you start to see a very busy highway of information flow. The applicant might call at any time to supply information or inquire about status. It is completely unrealistic for a customer service agent to track down physical copies of documents. It is often the case that the people using the documents are in different physical locations, separated by anything from alleyways to oceans.

Document-centric workflow is an industry term for that part of BPM concerned with routing and processing documents. The documents are typically part of some decision-making flow, as in the mortgage example. In an ECM solution, the document itself lives in a repository, and the workflow system contains a link to it. This maintains the advantage of the master copy concept described in the first use case, and it also allows fully-electronic and automated handling of the business process itself. The actual document is accessed as needed, and the workflow will typically update properties of the content in the repository with the results of decision-making or processing steps.

# Things to look for in an ECM platform

There are a lot of different notions about what specific things go into ECM and what are merely "something else". Every vendor has its own prioritized list, generally based on what its own product's strengths are. This section is a list of things that we would absolutely look for if we were selecting an ECM system (and please pay no attention to the fact that we might have an IBM employee discount). Except for the first item, the list is not in any specific order of importance. All of these things are important for any ECM platform. There are dozens of additional features that could be mentioned which are important for particular scenarios.

This section might seem to border on salesmanship because most of these points are strengths of FileNet products. Have we selected them on that basis? We prefer to think of it as having made sure the products have the features that we independently think are important.

There are several other players in the ECM arena, most of them, by definition, FileNet and IBM competitors. We'll let them speak for themselves (and write their own books). We will note, however, that some of those vendors offer point solutions rather than a comprehensive platform. A point solution is optimized for some particular task, use case, or scenario, but it does not necessarily have what it takes when your needs grow beyond that. Sometimes the answer is to stitch together a constellation of point solution components in the hope of making a well-running whole. Other vendors may offer products with a wider range of features but which suffer in scalability or usability as more and more applications are added or more and more parts of the organization participate in ECM. We'll get off our sales soapbox now and let you come to your own conclusions.

## Safe repository

The number one priority has to be a well-constructed repository that will not lose anything put into it. This may seem like a blindingly obvious requirement for any modern IT system, but there still exist solutions whose guarantees in this area bear scrutiny. To protect against loss of information, an ECM repository will provide things like system-enforced referential integrity checks, fully-transactional updates, and mechanisms to prevent one user's changes from accidentally overwriting another user's changes. We're obviously talking about things well beyond healthy hard drive platters.

## Strong security features

Access to the ECM repository must support authentication that is comparable to the best authentication mechanisms used elsewhere in your organization. Likewise, it must support authorization checks at the level of individual items and types of operations. For example, giving someone the authority to update a document should not automatically give them the authority to delete it. Having the authority to delete a document should not automatically mean you have the authority to delete other documents.

Permissions for items in the repository must be settable with enough granularity that you can accommodate unique situations, but it must also have a workable defaulting mechanism so that the mere setting of permissions doesn't become a burden. The security aspects of the ECM system must not only keep the bad guys away, but it must also avoid putting up a barrier to the good guys.

## Platform support

It's tempting to say that the ECM system must run on a wide range of hardware and software platforms, but it's more realistic to say that it must run on the platforms that are important to you. Unless you already plan to use a variety of different platforms, then support for a variety of platforms only matters directly in providing you choices as you might evolve your infrastructure over time. Indirectly, support for many platforms is one of the factors that can help you develop a feel for whether a particular vendor has a breadth of technical expertise.

## Scalability

Anyone can build a solution that performs adequately in a development environment by banging a couple of rocks together. A real test, and the real requirement, is that it performs well under the production load you expect to have and beyond that. Up to a certain point, you will be able to add more load by using faster servers, adding more memory, and so on. There will definitely come a point, however, where the "bigger and faster hardware" approach will reach its limits. How can your ECM system cope beyond that point? You will need an architecture, in the product and in your own deployment, that scales across multiple servers. In the ideal case, there should be no architectural factors that limit scaling in any practical sense; you should, for example, be able to add servers into clusters to scale to any arbitrary load that you might someday encounter.

## Extensibility and add-ons

It's an easy bet that the ECM needs you have today will not be the same as the ECM needs you have in a year or two. It's a common phenomenon that organizations like the benefits of their first tastes of ECM so much that they want to expand their early efforts into wider and wider areas. You want an ECM system that is ready to grow when you are.

## Vendor and partner ecosystem

Look for an ECM system from a vendor who actively fosters a rich partner and third-party ecosystem. Partners can provide unique applications, integration services, and specific knowledge about particular business scenarios. Sometimes this complements the vendor's own capabilities and sometimes it even competes with them. For someone who is using an ECM system, it pays to have options.

## Enterprise interoperability

Your ECM system should interoperate well with the rest of your enterprise infrastructure. That means things like using your enterprise directory for authentication, supporting the way you run your datacenters, perform backups, and operate high-availability and disaster recovery configurations. If your enterprise has IT infrastructure in multiple geographical areas, the ECM system must adequately support a distributed deployment.

## Strong APIs

Even if you do not plan to develop any custom applications yourself, you want an ECM system with feature-rich, well-supported, well-documented APIs with a record of stability. You or a third party might need to write some "glue" code to integrate other enterprise systems, or you might someday decide to augment out-of-the-box applications with something that is unique to your organization. In any case, the existence of strong APIs indicates at least two things—the vendor is willing to provide a mechanism for the necessary customization and integration of its product, and the vendor understands that they are providing a platform. There are ideas for applications and implementations that go beyond those that the vendor provides. Even if you never plan to use them directly, the quality of the APIs tells you something about the nature of the overall ECM system. It is also an important factor in the vendor and partner ecosystem mentioned above.

## Notifications and triggers

Would you like to know when certain types of documents are created or updated? Maybe you have automated follow-up steps that you want to perform in such cases, or maybe you just need someone to take a look. If you only had one application talking to your content repository, you would have no need for the ECM system to provide notifications or triggers when things happened. Your application would simply pay attention and make the notifications itself. You will have many applications as your use of ECM grows, and it's not good design to keep rebuilding notification logic into all those applications. Instead, you should look for that sort of feature from the ECM solution itself, and it should be suitably configurable for your specific needs.

## Traditional document management features

There are several traditional document management features that you will want your ECM system to have. Here are a few of them.

### Versioning and history

As documents are revised, you want to be able to keep track of changes that have been made. You want to be able to retrieve a past version. You want to be able to find out who made the change, when it was made, and so on. It should be your decision about how many past versions are kept, and your needs may vary from document to document or from type to type.

## Workflow integration

There are many scenarios for applying a workflow to a document, launched perhaps on document creation or update. It should be easy to make such calls to your workflow system. This should not only be functionally easy, but it should be highly performant. A tight integration promotes both.

## Search and navigation

There should be features to search for content on arbitrary criteria. Given one item that you have already located by whatever means, it should be easy to navigate to related items. The meaning of "related" can be different in different contexts. It will sometimes be determined by applications and sometimes by individual users. You don't want a system that only supports predefined relationships.

## Auditing and reporting

For regulatory and other compliance reasons, as well as for plain old good stewardship, you may need to be able to say who had certain access when. Perhaps just as importantly, you need to be able to tell who tried to do something but was turned back by security access checks.

## Metadata

Different ECM platforms have different terminology for metadata. It means the accumulated data about the content—who owns it, when was it last changed, how big it is, and so on. You should be able to extend the built-in metadata with your own, and there should be various handy data types available (for example, integers, dates, strings).

# ECM and standards

There have been many attempts to create standardized interfaces and APIs for ECM systems over the years, including several that predate the term ECM. ECM is no different from other areas of the computer industry in that the availability of standards helps customers and independent software vendors create applications and add-on components that will work with more than a single vendor's products. The downside is that cross-vendor standards often cater to only a core set of common features or (worse) provide for a wide range of optional features that vendors may freely choose to implement or not. This can place a burden on application writers when they want to exploit a feature not available in every supported ECM product.

This is a brief survey of some of the standards you may see mentioned, but it is not meant to be exhaustive. Although having a longer list of implemented standards is generally better than having fewer, what really matters is whether an ECM solution implements standards that are important to you.

> Several of these standards are of only historical and contextual interest. We haven't given web links to them, but have tried to use precise terminology and document titles so that you can readily track them down for yourself if you are interested in more detail.

All of the standards on this list were born of high hopes, but those hopes have not always borne fruit. As a disclaimer, we should mention that we personally participated in some of these efforts. As we prepared this list, it was striking to us how many different standards organizations have touched this area.

## AIIM: DMA and ODMA

Perhaps the most widely-known industry organization related to ECM is the **Association for Information and Image Management (AIIM)**. The predecessor organization that became AIIM was founded in 1943. AIIM's mission is to promote standards, provide education, foster best practices, and generally serve as a clearinghouse for ECM-related matters. It also hosts several recurring ECM-related conferences.

Starting in the mid-1990s, AIIM served as the secretariat coordinating the development of two related standards—DMA and ODMA.

## DMA

The **Document Management Alliance (DMA)** was the name of a group of cooperating organizations that developed an AIIM-sponsored standard. All major players in the document management industry at the time participated to one degree or another in DMA.

The standard, released in 1997, was also named DMA and was intended to provide two major things—an architectural model for how a document management system would interact with other components, and a set of standardized interfaces. Although DMA compliance is seldom mentioned in requirements specifications these days, it continues to have influence in many current ECM products in terminology and architectural concepts.

## ODMA

The **Open Document Management API (ODMA)** was a set of standardized conventions and APIs, and a software development kit allowing desktop document management applications to manipulate documents from multiple vendor repositories. The intent was to make the user's view of repository document access as simple as accessing documents on a local filesystem. ODMA 1.0 was published in 1994, and ODMA 2.0 was published in 1997. Today, ODMA is pretty much of only historical interest. Other, more modern, application integration technologies are in reasonably-wide use. As with DMA, it has a legacy that lives on in some vendor products as commonly used terminology and architectural concepts.

## WebDAV

RFC-2518, *HTTP Extensions for Distributed Authoring -- WEBDAV*, was published as a standards track document by the **Internet Engineering Task Force (IETF)** in February 1999. The "V" in WebDAV stands for "versioning", but the first standardization effort was scaled back and did not include it. Versioning was addressed by a subsequent effort. RFC-2518 has since been made obsolete by RFC-4918, *HTTP Extensions for Web Distributed Authoring and Versioning (WebDAV)*, published in June 2007.

You can tell from the name that WebDAV was an HTTP-specific access mechanism. It defined protocol-level extensions for resource access. Many scenarios are possible, but the first use case people think of for WebDAV is desktop applications accessing a document repository (the other motivating use case, source code management, drove many features in the WebDAV specification, but it wasn't really feasible to realize it with the first version of WebDAV since it lacked versioning support).

Early WebDAV implementations were plagued with incompatibilities between vendors. Things have mostly settled down these days, but if you have a requirement for WebDAV support, you would be wise to ask your ECM vendor about support for the specific client applications you are using. If you have a need for versioning support in the WebDAV implementation, you should ask about that too. Some WebDAV implementations do not provide it.

## JCR

*Content Repository for Java Technology API* was published in 2005 as JSR 170 under Sun's Java Community Process. It is commonly referred to as Java Content Repository (JCR). A follow-on version of JCR was published in 2009 as JSR-283, *Content Repository for Java Technology API Version 2.0*. JCR is (obviously) Java-specific technology. It specifies a set of standard interfaces that a repository vendor can implement to provide JCR access to a repository.

## CMIS

A cross-vendor initiative, **Content Management Interoperability Services (CMIS)**, was announced publicly in September 2008. Many ECM solution vendors announced, then or since, intentions to implement CMIS access to their repositories. In fact, there are already many CMIS implementations available. CMIS itself underwent standardization at the **Organization for the Advancement of Structured Information Standards (OASIS)**. The final standard was ratified in May 2010, and we can expect to see several more vendor implementations (or updates).

CMIS exposes access to content repositories as a collection of related RESTful APIs and web services for common ECM needs. That makes it technology-neutral for the calling clients. It's also well-suited to a modern design paradigm of calling into an adapter layer for a specific repository. The hope is that CMIS can serve as that repository-specific adapter layer for most everyday purposes and need only be supplemented for truly unusual operations. We're far from the first to say that CMIS hopes to be for ECM what SQL is for databases.

## What ECM is not

Let's digress into a discussion of a few things that ECM is not. We're making this digression because these are common points of confusion.

## ECM is not CMS

There are a lot of software products available, both open source and commercial, that fall into the category of **Content Management Systems (CMS)**. You can find references to hundreds or thousands of them with a simple web search. There's a good chance that you are already familiar with one or more of these, and there is even a good chance that you think one or more of them is fantastic. We won't disagree with that. We've used a few open source and commercial CMS implementations, and some of them are really quite good at what they do.

*What is ECM?*

CMS is not ECM, although it is not unusual for an ECM platform to have components very similar to those of a CMS. In such cases, you might be able to use your ECM platform as a CMS, but you will not generally be able to use a CMS as an ECM platform.

A typical CMS consists of a single or small collection of applications and a backing database. Almost all are self-contained systems aimed at organizations who want to have a secure and controlled process for publishing material on websites. The applications consist of web-based content editors and page layout engines. There will be built-in collaborative workflow for a content approval cycle, typically with some kind of role-based permissions system.

The most well-known examples of CMS are highly-tuned applications for managing the lifecycles of web content with a minimum of technical knowledge for the assorted writers, editors, and approvers. The difference between these CMS applications and an ECM platform is in those very words—a CMS is often more like a single application than a system of anything. There may or may not be points of integration with other applications.

## ECM is not a database

It's not a particularly unusual reaction for someone to look at all the things that make up a typical ECM platform and conclude that they could do it faster, simpler, cheaper, or better by just creating a relational database with pointers to content files in a filesystem and a few web pages to act as the frontend application. It often seems to them that much of the complexity and size of ECM is self-induced. If only things were limited to the simple things actually needed, the whole thing would be a lot smaller and tidier. Perhaps you, the reader, are thinking that very thing.

Well, why should you not do that? If you are something of an ECM visionary with enough like-minded colleagues, you very well might find success in doing it. Otherwise, you are statistically very likely to spend a lot of effort building things that are eventually replaced by an ECM system when the maintenance burden and backlog of things to do become too much to bear. If you're a stubborn person, please don't take this as a challenge! Our real aim is to get you to your goals as soon as possible without making you travel through the purifying fire of a gnarled custom implementation.

If you have no other document management system in your organization, this sort of database application will be greeted warmly. The first thing you know, someone will ask you to add a feature for keeping track of multiple versions of a document as it gets revised from time to time. Someone else will ask you for a mechanism for sharing a particular document with a specific set of people. Yet another someone will ask if they can organize the documents in something that looks like a folder structure so that they are easier to find. Someone will ask if you can automatically notify someone when certain kinds of documents are modified. Early success will lead to quite an imaginative list of features to implement. Although you may have thought of some of them at the beginning, you probably didn't have time to implement them, so they just went onto your "to do" list. Sooner or later, the same people who were slapping you on the back to congratulate you for your early efforts will be ready to wring your neck for not yet implementing the things they asked for.

This custom approach is certainly possible and relatively straightforward for almost any given single document management task. In fact, it's quite educational to do so because it can help you understand your own needs more clearly. For example, it's easy to write a web application that allows many people to upload document content for storage in a secure location and with which they can later download those documents. A single database table with only a few columns can do all of the bookkeeping of document ownership, keywords, on-disk location, and so on.

Just as most organizations would not seriously contemplate creating their own relational database system from scratch, the ECM landscape is rich enough that it seldom makes sense to build it yourself. Of course, once you have a target ECM platform, it often makes sense to develop your own custom applications on top of it, just as it is routine to implement database applications on top of an off-the-shelf DBMS.

# ECM is not source code management

It's hard to escape the parallels between some fundamental ECM platform features and those offered by **source code management** (**SCM**) systems. The feature of a secure, centralized repository of multiple-versioned documents comes immediately to mind, as do several others. Software development organizations certainly regard the management of source files as critically as business users regard the management of spreadsheets (in our experience, experienced professional software developers tend to regard it even more critically, perhaps because they understand the impact of making colossal mistakes).

Is it feasible to build ECM out of SCM? It's probably technically possible, assuming you select an SCM system that has the scalability, security, and other features you are looking for. It's probably also a lot of work, though.

The design centers for the two types of systems are different. For most organizations, the volume of documents handled by an ECM system will be orders of magnitude larger than those handled by SCM. Tools available from the vendor or third parties for an SCM system will be well-suited to the lifecycles of software development artifacts, but they may be non-existent or poorly suited for use by typical business users. For example, an SCM is likely to have reasonable integration with **integrated development environment** (IDE) tools used by developers and testers, but it's unlikely to have any integration at all with office productivity applications.

Once again, you will find yourself creating or customizing tools and features from scratch. It's not impossible to implement ECM on top of SCM, but it's not really the right tool for the right job. In the same way, it would probably be quite a bit of work to implement SCM on top of an ECM platform because a lot of the features of SCM are in the applications (or what would look like an application to ECM).

# A bit of FileNet history

Because you're reading a book about a FileNet product, we thought you might be interested in a bit of background on the company itself.

FileNet was founded in 1982, and the first product was an imaging solution that capitalized on newly-available optical disk technologies. Because of the state of the industry at that time, FileNet's first offerings were more complete and self-contained than seems imaginable in today's environment. They included custom hardware for the scanners, the storage modules, and the user workstations. They also included custom operating system software, custom network protocols to connect the various components, and an innovative application called **WorkFlo** that eventually evolved into what we now know generically as workflow.

As the industry evolved, so did FileNet's products. While maintaining its heritage of industry leadership in imaging solutions, the company moved into the area of document management. In 1995, FileNet acquired document management company Saros and, in the late 1990s, launched Panagon, an integrated suite of products that included classic imaging, document management, and workflow. In contrast to the early years, these products did not rely specifically on proprietary hardware and low-level software.

In 2001, FileNet announced a new product line called Brightspire. Brightspire was a completely new technology stack with a **Content Engine (CE)** based entirely on Microsoft platforms and technologies, though it did also include Java APIs. Within a couple of years, the platform component was renamed to P8 and the content-related product was renamed to FileNet Content Manager. The CM 4.0 release was significant in introducing **Content Engine Multiplatform (CEMP)**, a rewrite of the CE as a J2EE-based application.

FileNet was acquired by IBM in 2006, and the product line became known as IBM FileNet Content Manager. As you can see, with only a few turns, CM is a mature product that evolved in-house and is not an amalgam of unrelated parts from opportunistic acquisitions.

As of this writing, the prevalent release in the field is IBM FileNet Content Manager 4.5.1, and the remainder of this book is based on that release. CM 5.0 has just been released, and we will mention some of its features throughout later chapters.

# Summary

In this chapter, we gave you a whirlwind tour of ECM, including dispelling popular misconceptions. We covered some historical underpinnings of document management along with past and present standardization efforts. We covered the essential features that you should look for in any ECM platform.

From this point, we will be moving immediately into the practical matter of getting your FileNet system up and running. *Chapters 2* through *6* will guide you through installing a complete, standalone CM system and give you an overview of the main applications.

# 2
# Installing Environmental Components

This chapter concerns itself with installing what we call environmental components. These are pre-requisite components, not part of IBM FileNet Content Manager (CM) itself. We'll cover an example of configuring environmental components – a database, a directory server, and a J2EE application server – upon which the IBM FileNet software depends.

This chapter covers the following topics:

- Configuration of a Red Hat Linux server
- Installation and configuration of a DB2 database server
- Installation and configuration of a IBM WebSphere Application Server
- Installation and configuration of a IBM Tivoli Directory Server *uses LDAP for authentication*

If you follow the installation steps, you will have a platform ready for the actual CE installation and configuration in *Chapter 3, Installing the Content Engine*.

## Some important IBM documents

IBM publishes a huge amount of documentation about both the CM product and the P8 platform. The documentation is aimed at a variety of different audiences—enterprise decision makers, administrators of various kinds, security officials, developers, and end users. The sheer amount of documentation can be a little disorienting. This section will introduce you to the documentation that is most interesting to someone installing a new CM site.

*Installing Environmental Components*

Most P8 documentation is readily available via IBM's website. The gateway into this is the *IBM FileNet P8 Version 4.5.1 information center* at http://publib.boulder.ibm.com/infocenter/p8docs/v4r5m1. The infocenter (as it is commonly called) is one-stop shopping for all aspects of official P8 product documentation and should definitely have a spot on your bookmarks list. You can also find your way there by using your favorite Internet search engine to look for p8 information center. *Chapter 13, Support, Fix Packs, and troubleshooting* contains information about how to locally install a copy of the infocenter.

An interesting aspect of the infocenter (and much of IBM's online documentation) is that you can narrow down the things you see according to the software environment that you actually have. We strongly encourage you to do this, especially for the installation-related information. Click the information filter icon and select the specific items applicable to your environment.

The table of contents in the left-hand portion of the infocenter page dynamically adjusts to show only the topics relevant to the selected filter choices. Most of our examples will be using the applicable IBM components, but P8 is supported with a variety of combinations of application servers, databases, and directory servers.

In addition to the online infocenter information, many P8 documents are also available for download in **Portable Document Format** (**PDF**) or other formats. The starting point for finding those downloadable variants is the web page *Product Documentation for FileNet P8 Platform*. You can get to it from the infocenter start page, but here is a direct link to it: http://www-01.ibm.com/support/docview.wss?uid=swg27010422. Because it includes documentation for all supported releases, make sure you select the appropriate release when you download things from that web page. It's possible to download from the same page a deployable WAR file containing searchable P8 documentation. It was more useful before the infocenter was published. If you are working with the current P8 release and have reasonable Internet access from your environment, you may find access to the infocenter to be more convenient.

> Unless noted otherwise, all of the documents mentioned from now on are available via links from the infocenter. Although we could give specific links here, the most stable link is the link to the infocenter itself, and we think navigating from there to the individual documents is the most reliable strategy.

## Plan and prepare your environment

*Plan and Prepare Your Environment for IBM FileNet P8* should be one of your first stops in preparing for your own installation. It's available both as part of the infocenter and as a downloadable PDF document. It's a comprehensive backgrounder on the many supported deployment scenarios, roles performed during installation, types of accounts, and other required information. For brevity, we'll refer to this document as the planning and preparation guide (PPG).

People often ask why there cannot be a simple setup program that asks a couple of questions and then installs the product like a typical Microsoft Windows, Linux, or Apple Mac consumer application. It would be possible to create that sort of simple installer for a demo environment, but it would not be correct for almost anybody's real environment. There are just too many choices in enterprise environments and they can't be readily guessed or assumed. Instead, the P8 installation process consists of a planning step, where information about the environment and planned deployment is gathered, and an installation step where the software is actually installed using that information. It is definitely true that the people who skip over parts of the planning step tend to pay a price in effort and confusion during the installation step. With proper attention in the planning step, the actual installation is fairly short, though you can judge that for yourself.

An important concept introduced in the planning guide is the *Installation and Upgrade Worksheet*. This is an actual spreadsheet that will help your gather the required information in an organized fashion for your own installation. It has macros that allow you to generate a customized spreadsheet specific to the software you will be installing. We will be using figurative names from the worksheet throughout the actual installation procedure.

Both the PPG and the worksheet can be downloaded directly from the documentation link provided above.

## Fix Pack Compatibility Matrix

If this is your first P8 installation, you will undoubtedly choose the most recent releases and fix packs of your components. Later, however, when you are applying fix packs or upgrading components individually, it is important that you check the *FileNet P8 4.5.x Fix Pack Compatibility Matrix* to make sure you are not creating unsupported combinations. It is almost always the case that, if you upgrade everything to the latest release and fix pack, then the combination is supported. Always check the matrix to be sure.

## Environmental components

The CE runs under a J2EE application server, but it also uses other enterprise environmental components. We call these environmental components because most enterprises have already selected them and use them for other applications before installing CM. Here is how CE uses the database and directory components:

- All CE metadata is stored in a relational database, though the conceptual model presented to applications is object-oriented. That's why the architecture we'll discuss in *Chapter 3* shows separate data and object tiers. The CE takes care of the bookkeeping details of mapping relational data to and from objects, so the only people who are typically interested in the low-level database details are the database administrators in an organization.

- The CE expects to use an enterprise directory for both authentication (proving who you are) and authorization (determining what rights you have). Although it is not technically correct, it is common to refer to the directory as an LDAP directory because that is the protocol used for directory interactions. Of course, strictly speaking, it doesn't have to be an enterprise directory. You could set up a specialized directory just for use with the CE (in fact, most application servers have a built-in directory). Except for a few special cases, the use of some other directory (other than your enterprise's directory) is not especially useful in production environments, and it has a certain amount of maintenance bother associated with it. The CE only reads information from the directory; it never updates the directory.

CM includes limited use licenses for IBM WebSphere Application Server and IBM DB2 Universal Database. The license in CM includes use of those components only in CM and not for general use. Further, the license applies to specific versions of WebSphere and DB2. These versions are great for development environments, prototyping, proofs of concept, and so on. They are also fine for production applications within certain scalability limits. If you plan to rely on these versions for production use rather than separately licensing them, be sure to check their features to make sure they cover your production needs. In particular, the WebSphere license does not include the **Network Deployment** (**ND**) edition, which you will almost certainly need in order to do clustering for high availability and scaling.

## Hardware and software requirements

The list of environments where P8 is supported is long, but it's not infinite. The document *IBM FileNet P8 Version 4.5 Hardware and Software Requirements* is the official guidance on supported hardware, operating systems, databases, directory servers, application servers, and other non-P8 components. Given the Java technology behind most of P8, it's no surprise that most of this hardware/software guide is devoted to the software environment.

> Pointers to official P8 documentation and other resources are covered comprehensively in *Chapter 13*.

The most important thing to check in that document is whether the specific things you want to use are supported, but you will also want to pay attention to the section on P8 component collocation. **Collocation** means the ability for software to be installed together without causing problems. The collocation rules for P8 components are pretty relaxed and easy to meet, but there are important exceptions sometimes called out in the documentation. In a production environment, you will often want to separate things onto different servers for performance and scalability reasons. In a development or demo system, you might choose to collocate many components for simplicity; be sure to check the hardware/software guide to avoid functional problems.

If you are setting up a new environment and have the freedom to choose whatever components you want, then the best advice we can give you is to choose a fairly recent release of each component. The IBM support matrix typically covers the current release of a component and one or more older releases. Time, inevitably, marches on, and later releases of CM will likely obsolete older versions of other components as newer versions are added.

*Installing Environmental Components*

Let's look briefly at the supported components. We'll avoid specific release numbers because the hardware/software guide is the best place to check on something that specific. Our listing is just to give you a feeling for the breadth of coverage. Also, not every individual component is supported on each platform combination.

- Operating systems: IBM AIX, Microsoft Windows (server editions), Sun Solaris, HP-UX, Red Hat Enterprise Linux, Novell SUSE Linux Enterprise Server
- Application servers: IBM WebSphere, Oracle WebLogic, JBoss by Red Hat
- Databases: IBM DB2, Oracle, Microsoft SQL Server
- Directory servers: IBM Tivoli Directory Server, Novell eDirectory, Sun Java System Directory Server, Microsoft Active Directory, Microsoft ADAM, Oracle Internet Directory
- Storage devices: Operating system native file systems, IBM System Storage DR550, IBM Tivoli Storage Manager, EMC Centera, Network Appliance, and IBM N-series SnapLock

Not all combinations of components are supported. The hardware/software guide gives detailed charts and notes on the supported combinations.

## Tailored planning and installation guides

Earlier, we described how the infocenter could be filtered for a specific software environment. There are single-document versions of the planning guide and the installation guide that cover all supported software components and combinations. By their very nature, those documents have much redundancy and are impressively long.

The P8 team also produces tailored planning and installation guides for the most common configurations. If your environment matches one of those configurations, you will find it much easier to use a tailored guide. As of this writing, there are over a dozen distinct guides available at `http://www-01.ibm.com/support/docview.wss?rs=3278&uid=swg27016206`, and more combinations will be produced from time to time.

[ 30 ]

If you look at our list of supported software components above, you will see over 300 combinations of operating system, application server, database, and directory. That's without even considering release number variations for those components. If your particular combination is not among the tailored guides, our advice is to use both the tailored guide that most closely matches your environment and the single-document guide. Use the tailored guide to read cover to cover, and use the single-document guide as a reference when the tailored guide discusses a component that doesn't match your software environment. Once you get into the rhythm of the tailored guide, you will find it much easier to pick out isolated sections of information from the single-document guide.

## Our target environment

With all of the hundreds or even thousands of possible combinations of configurations, it's not feasible for us to describe them all. Instead, our plan is to pick a configuration and show how to install it in what we call an all-in-one configuration. An all-in-one configuration means that we will be installing everything on a single server. This is a great way to set up an isolated system for developers and testers or for demo purposes. As it turns out, it's pretty common to use a virtual server image instead of a physical server, so it's also a handy way to give someone a copy of an environment (assuming that the licensing you have for everything permits that).

> We're calling it an all-in-one configuration, but it will turn out to be two servers. Not every component runs on every operating system. We're choosing to use Linux for most things, but there are a couple of things that we will run on a Windows server. Calling it an all-in-two configuration doesn't have the same zing.

Even if you have completely different requirements for the software components in the environment, you should find this chapter handy because the installation process is very similar for most combinations. If you are new to P8, you might like to try installing exactly the combination that we use just to make sure you get quickly to a working environment. From there, you can branch out to the target environment you plan to actually use.

For the examples that we show in this chapter, we will be using the following software components:

- Red Hat Enterprise Linux (RHEL) 5.5
- Microsoft Windows Server 2003 (W2K3)
- IBM WebSphere Application Server (WAS) 7.0 for FileNet Content Manager 4.5.1

- IBM DB2 Workgroup Server Edition (DB2) 9.5 for FileNet Content Manager 4.5.1
- IBM Tivoli Directory Server (TDS) 6.2

Of course, we know just what you are thinking: that we are using mostly IBM software because we are IBM shills. Well, it may or may not be true that we are IBM shills, but our reason for selecting these components is a bit different. As we mentioned, the CM license includes limited use licenses for both WebSphere and DB2. You can also download evaluation copies of RHEL and TDS from the vendor websites (http://www.redhat.com/rhel/server and http://www.ibm.com/tivoli, respectively). If you are that unusual user who has a copy of CM but hasn't yet selected the other software components, feel free to mention our name when you buy the additional IBM pieces. It won't get you any kind of discount, but we never object to having the IBM sales force buy us lunches for sending customers their way.

> We'd like to make clear that we did not choose all IBM components because the P8 platform works better with those components or favors them in some way. P8 tries its best to support all application servers, databases, directories, and operating systems equally. Competing products in each of those categories are not equal, but each has its own strengths and weaknesses independent of P8's integration with them. As IBM employees and shareholders, we'd like you to buy and use as much IBM hardware and software as you can manage. As P8 software architects and authors of this book, we expect you to choose those elements of your platform based on your own requirements and selection criteria.

There is one small exception to the all-in-one configuration—the administrative tool, **FileNet Enterprise Manager** (**FEM**), runs only on Microsoft Windows. We'll install that in *Chapter 3*, and we'll be installing additional components on the W2K3 server in *Chapter 5, Installing Other Components*. If you want to delay configuring that machine, you can install FEM on a Windows desktop environment that you have already since FEM is not invasive.

For the hardware, whether you are using a physical server or a virtual machine image, your most precious resource will be memory. You'll be running a couple of J2EE application servers, a database system, and a directory server. Those things will take as much memory as you will give them, so give them all you can get. We would suggest at least 2 gigabytes of memory as the bare minimum, though things will sometimes feel sluggish with that minimum. When we can, we try to use at least 4 gigabytes for this kind of setup. You may also need 10–15 gigabytes of disk space to begin with, depending on what other things you have installed, and you will probably need another gigabyte or so of scratch space while you are installing things. If you can't get all the memory you need, things may be pretty slow. If you can't get all the disk space you need, you will be spending some housekeeping time shuffling things around, deleting old files, and so on. We configured our RHEL server with 30 gigabytes of disk and things fit quite comfortably with plenty of room to spare.

# Configuring the environmental components

We are aware that we have an entire chapter about installing things before we even get to the chapter about installing the CE. That's because installing the CE is actually pretty straightforward once you have the environmental components running the way you want them. If it's your first time, though, you may be installing or configuring those components without much enterprise guidance on the many settings. It's pretty natural to conclude that the CE installation is pretty complicated. It's an almost unavoidable blurring of the lines, but most of the effort is not in the CE itself.

We're assuming you already have or can easily obtain all of the components in the bullet list in the previous section. If you have versions that are slightly different from those listed, you may find the occasional dialog box that's different or a slightly different step, but the overall procedure should be quite similar. If you are installing those things from scratch, you can take the defaults for pretty much everything. For the things that should or must be different from the defaults, we'll be modifying those in this section. If you're installing entirely different pieces for some or all of those components, this section should still be useful as a guide to the overall procedure, and you can fill in any gaps using CM's voluminous installation-related documentation (described above in the section *Some important IBM documents*).

Naturally, you need to have the operating system before you can do anything else. The other components can probably be installed in pretty much any order. We chose to install them with DB2 first, WAS second, and TDS last. TDS needs a database for the directory data, and TDS 6.2 will be happy to use the already-installed DB2 9.5. If it doesn't find a version of DB2 that it likes, TDS will install and use an embedded copy of DB2. TDS also needs an application server, but TDS 6.2 wants to use WAS 6.1. As we will be using WAS 7.0, TDS will instead use its own embedded copy of WAS.

## User and group accounts

The PPG lists several user and group accounts that are needed to perform the installation tasks and operate the installed system. These accounts can be operating system accounts, database accounts, or enterprise directory accounts (the PPG sometimes calls these "directory accounts" and sometimes calls them "LDAP accounts"; they mean the same thing in this context). A quick way to get an overview of all these accounts of various types is to look at the installation worksheet and scan the column labeled **User or Group Account**. If you are looking at the generic tab on the worksheet, you'll see many accounts that are irrelevant, but on a customized worksheet (which you can create by running the customization macro from the **Instructions** tab), the list should be what you will actually be using.

It's worth noting that in most places the guide says that you have to create such an account or pick an existing account. This is important because the list of individual accounts is quite long. It's long because, when the guide talks about various accounts, it is really talking about roles for which those accounts are used. For example, you will see both the **CE application server installation account** and the **CE installation account**. Although they sound like almost the same thing, those are two different roles for different tasks during installation. The guide defines each account and describes it (and the privileges it needs) so that you can know the differences. Many times, you will decide to use a single account to fulfill more than one role.

In your production environment, you will certainly use accounts that are consistent with your enterprise administrative and security policies. For example, you might have a policy that dictates that members of certain directory or operating system groups must be used to perform certain functions. Perhaps you have a database administrator group, and database maintenance must be performed by a member of that group. We certainly urge you to follow your established policies.

In this discussion, however, where we are creating an all-in-one installation for the purpose of experimentation, we're going to make it easy on all of us and use the `root` account for all operating system operations that require higher privileges. For "ordinary user" operations, we'll use the `ecmuser` account described later in the chapter. You'll see similar generic choices for directory accounts.

Of course, this leaves our all-in-one installation with potentially different characteristics than any ultimate production environment you might use. Once you have some experience with this easy-to-install setup, it would probably be a good idea to do another installation specifically to go through the steps of picking users and groups that you will be using in production. This can sometimes uncover permission problems with processes or files.

> Yes, we must confess it. Despite good security habits in other parts of our working lives, we often log onto our virtual server images using the `root` account. For a production server, we would never do that. We're big fans of the model used in some Linux distributions where logins to the `root` account are completely disabled.
>
> In a non-critical virtual server image, especially one running Linux, the greatest danger is that we will make a blunder that destroys the image. That represents only an inconvenience and not a disaster. We're not using the images for random web surfing, or downloading Internet media files, or even reading e-mail. Because we often have images running for weeks at a time, we do enable all of the security monitoring software available (even though our images are generally running inside two nested firewalls).
>
> The only excuse we have for using the `root` account this way is this lame advice given by parents and bosses around the world: *Do as we say, not as we do.*

In our examples, we will be using the figurative user and group names from the installation worksheet where such names exist. There are also a few cases where an environmental component asks us to create or select accounts. Even with the help of the installation worksheet, it's possible to lose track of some of these. You might like to make a table where you record the figurative name we use, the actual name you use (if different), and the passwords.

*Installing Environmental Components*

# Red Hat Enterprise Linux

We use a fairly vanilla installation of RHEL 5.5 and we accept almost all of the defaults from the installation process. Database installation procedures will often suggest that you modify shared memory configuration or other kernel parameters. That did not happen for our DB2 9.5 installation, so we left all those things at the default values.

Besides the superuser, root, you will be creating at least one non-privileged account as part of the installation process. You can use whatever you'd like for that account user ID, but we typically use something both generic and suggestive (in case we give a copy of the image to someone else who might not like a user ID of slimy-mud-puppy or whatever). For the image we're using here, we chose user ID ecmuser. During or after installation, create an operating system group ecmgroup and make ecmuser a member of that group.

We also need an operating system account that will receive some DB2 privileges and which the CE will use for communicating with the database via WAS datasources. The RHEL control panel for root has an applet for conveniently adding this user at the operating system level. You can do that before or after adding the user to the database, but we suggest you do it now so it's not forgotten. Create a new user called cedbuser (this user is referred to with the figurative name ce_db_user in the PPG and the installation worksheet, but DB2 doesn't like user names with underscores, so we removed them). We suggest choosing a login shell that prohibits actual operating system logins since this user ID is only used for software-controlled database operations. We'll cover the database privileges in the DB2 section below.

[ The fully-qualified name we chose for our RHEL system is wjc-rhel.example.net. Our W2K3 system is wjc-w2k3.example.net. The domain example.net is reserved for use in examples by RFC 2606, *Reserved Top Level DNS Names*. You will probably choose different names for your systems as you follow along, and you will definitely use different names for your production environment. To avoid constantly pointing this out, we will just use our system names in various examples and screenshots and will assume you can make the mental translation to your system names. ]

## Network addresses

If you intend to access any of the CM servers from outside the machine where you are installing it, you will probably want to get a static IP address for the machine and register it in your local **Domain Name Service (DNS)**. Neither of these is strictly necessary for the software components we're using here, and they are only for your convenience. We will be installing at least one component on a different machine, but it may be sufficient for you to use dynamically assigned IP addresses when connectivity is needed.

> We often use dynamic IP addresses for our virtual servers. Our network infrastructure tends to assign our servers the same IP address for long periods of time. Instead of registering the server names in DNS, we manually modify the local host file whenever we notice an interesting change. On Linux, that file is `/etc/hosts`. On Windows, that file is `C:\Windows\system32\drivers\etc\hosts`. Both files have the same format and consist of lines with IP addresses followed by one or more host names. In a normal configuration, the systems will consult the hosts file before consulting DNS. On the other hand, if your organization makes it easy to get static IP addresses and put server names into DNS, you might as well save yourself some trouble and do it that way. It might save you from one or two troubleshooting mysteries down the road.

## System clocks

It is a requirement that all P8 servers have synchronized system clocks. That wouldn't matter in an environment where there was only one physical server, but it's a good habit to get into. Strictly speaking, it is only required that the various clocks agree with each other. It's not actually required that they be correct. To keep yourself from going crazy, though, the simplest course is to have your operating system clocks synchronized to the real world time by using **Network Time Protocol (NTP)** or a similar technique.

The problems that arise when clocks for various servers are out of sync can be quite mysterious and hard to isolate. That's why it's one of the first questions support is likely to ask if you have a really odd problem. Also, when looking at logfiles and trying to correlate entries from different servers, it can be quite confusing if the system clocks are different by even a few seconds. For fully detailed logging, it is not unusual to see literally thousands of lines of logging within a single clock second.

## File storage area

A *storage area* is CE jargon for the place where actual content bits for documents will be stored (as opposed to the properties; those are always stored in the database). To make our CM installation somewhat realistic, we will be using a file storage area. A file storage area resides on a operating system filesystem. In a normal production environment, you would likely have a dedicated file server where the disks actually reside, and multiple CE servers would see folders shared via a supported file sharing protocol (for example, NFS). All CE servers in a domain must be able to reach all storage areas. We don't really need that complexity for an all-in-one image. The disks will also be local. However, you can still configure it that way if you want things to more closely match a production environment.

We create a single file storage area in the local filesystem and arrange it so that only `ecmuser` has access (because, as described later, we will be running the WAS profile that holds our CE as `ecmuser`). The following commands, to be run as the `root` user, can be used to create and configure the top-level directories that will be needed:

```
# mkdir /p8filestores
# mkdir /p8filestores/fs1
# chown -R ecmuser /p8filestores
# chmod -R 770 /p8filestores
```

The names are arbitrary, but we will need to remember them later. If you were using file sharing, you would instead be creating a mount point for the parent of the filestore directories (`/p8filestores` in this example).

# Firewalls

If your server has a software or hardware firewall, you will have to configure it to allow connections on various ports if you want to interact with your CM installation from outside the server itself. Here is a list of all the port numbers that we will be using along with a brief note for each one. You might decide that you do not need to open all these ports in your environment.

| Port | Note |
| --- | --- |
| 9080 | AE WAS instance, http, non-secure |
| 9443 | AE WAS instance, https, secure |
| 9081 | CE WAS instance, http, non-secure |
| 9444 | CE WAS instance, https, secure |
| 2809 | AE WAS instance, EJB |
| 9100 | AE WAS instance, EJB |
| 2810 | CE WAS instance, EJB transport |
| 9101 | CE WAS instance, EJB transport |
| 9060 | AE WAS console, non-secure |
| 9043 | AE WAS console, secure |
| 9061 | CE WAS console, non-secure |
| 9044 | CE WAS console, secure |
| 9990 | CSE K2 dashboard |
| 12100 | TDS web console, non-secure |
| 12101 | TDS web console, secure |
| 55000 | DB2 instance db2inst1 connections |
| 3801 | DB2 instance db2inst1 connections |

> If you are using a virtual server image with snapshot capability, now is a good time to take a snapshot. In fact, we recommend that after each of the major installation steps described later in this chapter. If something goes wrong in a later step, you can recover back to the snapshot point to save yourself the trouble of starting over.

## Installing DB2

The DB2 database installation is straightforward, and you should do it as `root`. The DB2 installer offers both server and client options; select the server option. If you do a "typical" installation, you can accept the defaults offered unless you have your own reason to make different choices. We're using DB2 9.5 because that's the version included with the CM licensing. The latest version is DB2 9.7, and there are only a few small differences in the installation. We've noted those in the steps that follow.

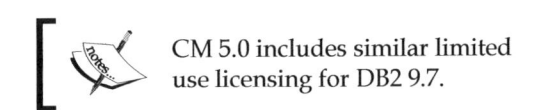

> CM 5.0 includes similar limited use licensing for DB2 9.7.

Some specific points to watch during the DB2 installation:

- Java support should be enabled by default and is required; do not disable it.
- The installer will offer you a choice of creating an instance as part of the installation or creating it later. We suggest you create it as part of the installation.
- There will also be a choice to install the IBM Tivoli System Automation for Multiplatforms Base Component (SA MP Base Component). Unless you plan to use SA MP Base Component and know that your Linux server meets the prerequisites and licensing entitlements, we suggest you choose to not install it.
- At the end of the installation, the installer will inform you that the default instance is listening on port `55000`. We'll use that information later (so make a note of it, especially if for some reason the installer tells you a different port number). You should also find an entry for it near the end of your `/etc/services` file.

As part of the installation, DB2 will use or create a handful of operating system accounts. If you have taken the installer defaults, you will have these operating system users and groups:

- user `dasusr1`, group `dasadm1`: The DB2 Administration server user.
- user `db2inst1`, group `db2iadm1`: The DB2 instance owner for the default instance `db2inst1`.
- user `db2fenc1`, group `df2fadm1`: The DB2 fenced user.

You can consult DB2 documentation (`http://publib.boulder.ibm.com/infocenter/db2luw/v9/`) for more details about the uses for each of these users and groups. Notice that the last character in each name is the digit 1, which may not be obvious in every font.

Immediately after installation, there are some DB2 configuration parameters to set for this instance. While logged on as the user `db2inst1`, use the `db2set` command line tool and set these additional parameters (the first of these only applies if you are using DB2 9.7 and does not apply for DB2 9.5):

```
$ db2set DB2_WORKLOAD=FILENET_CM
$ db2set DB2_OPTPROFILE=Yes
```

Our next step is to create a database for use by CM in the default instance, `db2inst1`.

> Database vendor terminology for this step varies a little bit, and everyday terminology for things can be a little lax, all of which can lead to some confusion over exactly what things are needed. When using DB2, it's a bit of a subjective matter whether to create all CE Object Stores within the same database or to create a distinct database for each Object Store. Using separate databases gives you separate possibilities for security, backups, and other database administration matters. Once they are created, tablespaces within a single database can be more convenient for some database administration tasks when that previously mentioned flexibility isn't needed. For our example, we'll use multiple databases because it's conceptually easier to understand.

Perform the following steps via the DB2 Control Center. Log in with the user ID `db2inst1`. Run the command `db2cc` to launch the DB2 Control Center. Start the database manager. In the DB2 Control Center, navigate to the node for instance `db2inst1`, right-click, and select **Start**.

*Installing Environmental Components*

## Create a new database

Select the **Databases** node under instance `db2inst1`, right-click, and select **Create Database**. We suggest you create your database with **automatic maintenance**. You (or the enterprise database administrator) might make a different choice for a large production site, but automatic maintenance is simplest for this all-in-one system. This will be the database for the CE's Global Configuration Database (GCD). You can give it any name you want, but GCD is logical and memorable. You can accept the defaults for any questions as you work through the wizard. A new entry **GCD** will appear under the **Databases** node.

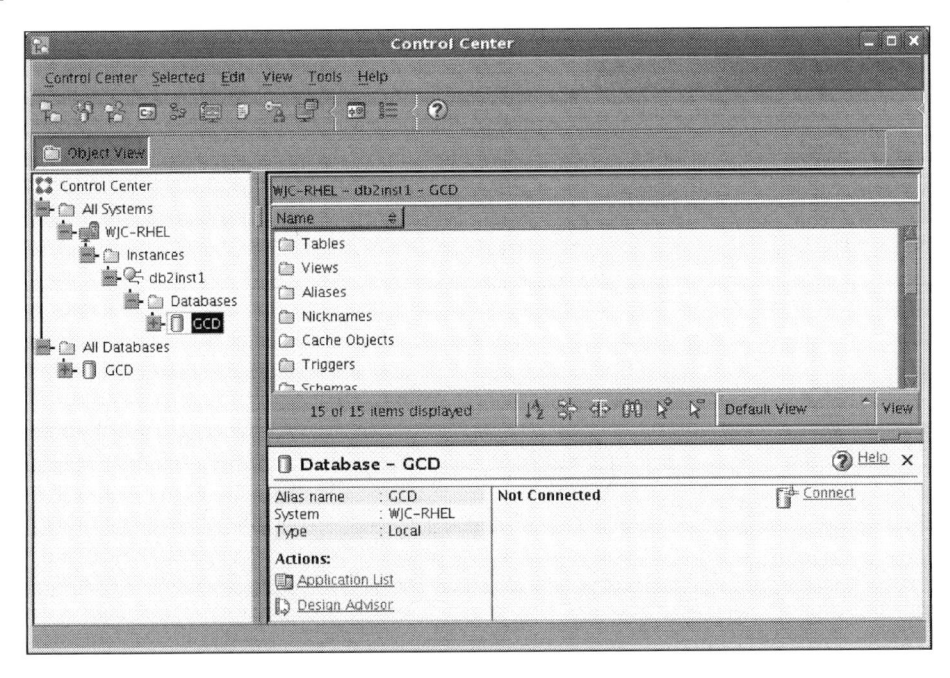

## Drop default user tablespace

If there is a default user tablespace, you can drop it since its configuration will not be suitable for our use here. Expand the GCD node and select the **Table Spaces** folder. In the main panel, select **USERSPACE1**, right-click, and select **Drop**.

## Create a buffer pool definition

All tablespaces must use a 32 KB page size (this is a CE requirement). The defaults in DB2 9.5 and 9.7 are 4 KB. That means you will have to create a new buffer pool definition. Select the **Buffer Pools** node under **GCD**, right-click, and select **Create**. Make sure the new buffer pool has a **Page size** of 32 and give it a meaningful name. We call ours **WJC32K**.

# Create tablespaces

We'd suggest selecting **automatic storage** for all tablespaces. The tablespace wizard is launched by selecting the **Table Spaces** folder, right-clicking, and selecting **Create**. Then create the tablespaces as follows:

1. Create a tablespace of type **User temporary**. We called ours CEUSRTEMP, but the name is not important. When asked for the type, select **User temporary**.

2. On the panel where the buffer pool is configured, do not accept the default buffer pool with 4 KB page size; instead, select the buffer pool created above with a 32 KB page size (**WJC32K**, if you used the name we used). After selecting your buffer pool definition for this tablespace, you can click through the rest of the panels taking the defaults for all questions.

3. Create a tablespace of type **System temporary**. We called ours CESYSTEMP. Again, use the buffer pool definition you created so that the tablespace has a 32 KB page size.

4. As usual, use the buffer pool definition that gives a 32 KB page size. We called ours CEDATA. Create a tablespace of type **Large** to hold the actual tables for the GCD.

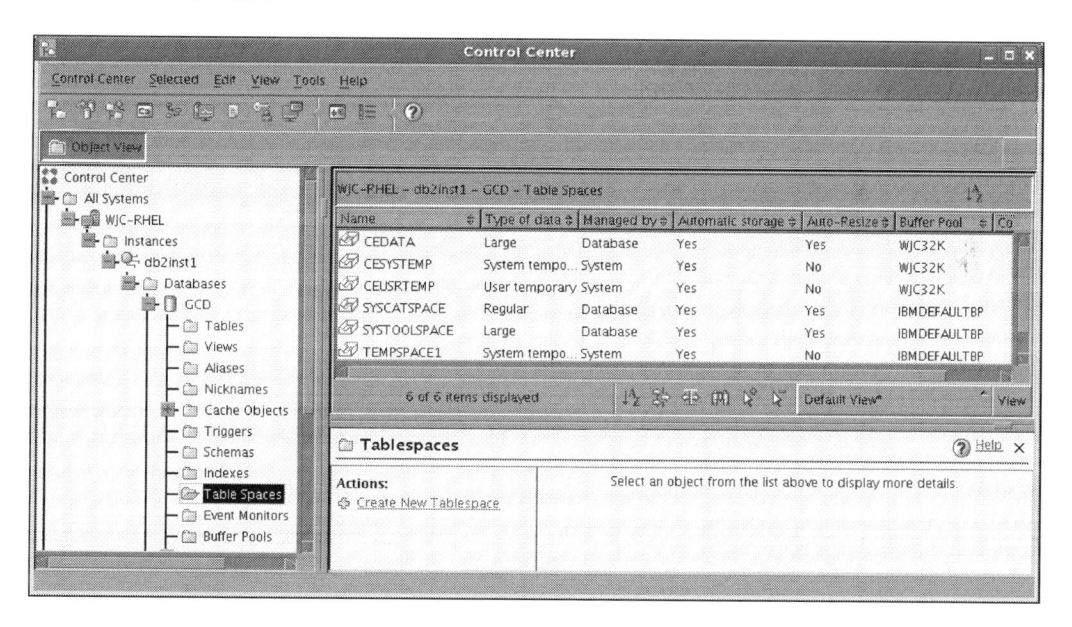

## Add a user to the database

This database user will be used in configuring the datasources within the J2EE application server. Select the database **GCD** and then navigate to **User and Group Objects | DB Users**. Add user `cedbuser` by selecting it from the dropdown menu. This is the same user we added at the operating system level earlier; we're just giving it database privileges now. This user must be given the authority to:

- **Connect to database, Create tables,** and **Create schemas implicitly** (all set on the **Database** tab)
- Use the **User temporary (CEUSRTEMP)** and **Large (CEDATA)** tablespaces that we created above (set via the **Table Space** tab)
- **SELECT** for tables `SYSIBM.SYSTABLES` and `SYSIBM.SYSCOLUMNS` (set via the **Table** tab), and view `SYSCAT.DATATYPES` (set via the **View** tab)

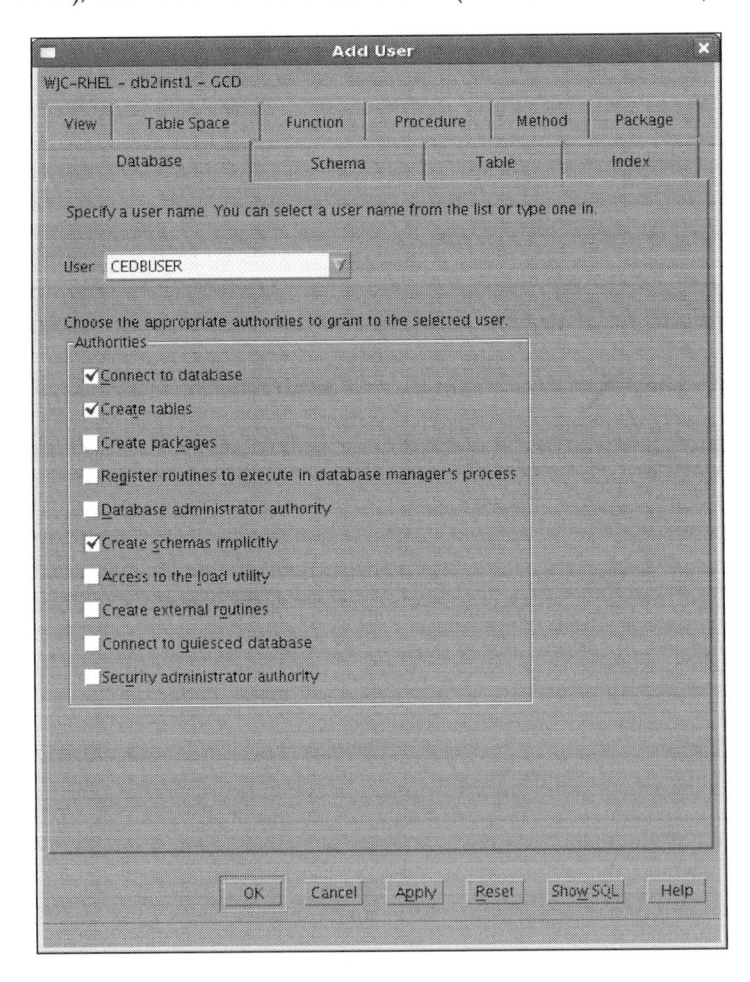

> The permissions we just described don't have anything to do with the privileges of CM users. Remember, all access to the database is mediated by the CE server. This database user and these permissions are what the CE needs to do its low-level database work.

## Set DB2 parameters

Some DB2 configuration parameter settings are recommended or required when using the database for CM. You set these parameters by selecting the database GCD, right-clicking, and selecting **Configure Parameters** from the context menu. Set **APPLHEAPSZ** to a minimum of 2560; if you are using DB2 9.7, set **CUR_COMMIT** to On.

## Repeat for OSTORE1

Repeat all of the above steps to create a database named OSTORE1 for our first Object Store. If you are feeling adventurous, you can create additional databases (OSTORE2, OSTORE3, or whatever you'd care to call them) for additional ObjectStores while the procedure is fresh in your mind. Even for a development system like this, we like to have at least two ObjectStores. We use one for all sorts of *ad hoc* activity and another for more structured exploration.

> If you know your way around DB2, you can save yourself a little configuration trouble by cloning database GCD to create database OSTORE1. It's beyond our scope to describe it here, but the essence is to create a backup of database GCD and then restore it into a new database OSTORE1. You can do all of that from the DB2 Control Center. If you use this technique, you want to do it now, while the GCD database has yet to be populated for CE use.

Since the last few steps are a slightly tricky list of privileges and configuration parameter settings, you should double-check the P8 product documentation for updates. Check both the PPG and the *FileNet P8 Performance Tuning Guide*.

## WebSphere Application Server

The actual installation process for WAS, though lengthy, is straightforward and mostly self-driving, so we won't step through it. You can accept the defaults for all panels. You will be asked to supply a WAS administrator username and password. This is only temporary and will be replaced by the was_admin account we will configure in TDS later in this chapter. For now, we suggest you specify username admin and whatever password you'd like.

## Profiles and ports

The WAS installation process creates a default profile, `AppSrv01`, pre-configured with many TCP/IP port assignments. These assignments include the port numbers for the administrative console application, the web container, the JNDI provider, various security services, and so on. There is a CM requirement that the **Application Engine (AE)** and the Content Engine cannot run in the same WAS profile (for other application servers, there is a similar rule, but profiles are a WAS-specific notion). Different profiles on the same server must have different port assignments for similar functions so that you can connect to them all via a single host address. This would not ordinarily even be a factor because you would be installing the AE and the CE on different servers, but we have to plan for it for our all-in-one configuration.

The AE is a more user-facing component, so we'll choose, strictly as a matter of preference, to have the AE use the standard WAS port numbering. That means it gets installed into the default WAS profile. Before installing the CE, we'll create a new WAS profile to hold it, accepting the default name of `AppSrv02`. The CE ends up in the second WAS profile even though we are installing the CE first. When the components communicate with each other, the names of the WAS profiles are irrelevant. It is only the administrators who have to keep track of them.

If you are installing the 32-bit version of WAS 7, the graphical Profile Management Tool normally runs as part of the WAS installation process. You can run it separately to create the second profile using the following command (assuming the default install path for Linux):

```
# /opt/ibm/WebSphere/AppServer/bin/ProfileManagement/pmt.sh
```

This graphical tool is not available for the 64-bit version of WAS 7 for Linux. Instead, run the following commands to create a new profile with the default name of `AppSrv02`:

```
# cd /opt/ibm/WebSphere/AppServer/bin
# ./manageprofiles.sh -create -templatePath profileTemplates/default
```

Here are the contents of `logs/AboutThisProfile.txt` of the `AppSrv01` profile (created automatically when the profile was created):

```
Application server environment to create: Application server
Location: /opt/IBM/WebSphere/AppServer/profiles/AppSrv01
Disk space required: 200 MB
Profile name: AppSrv01
Make this profile the default: True
Node name: localhostNode01
```

```
Host name: localhost
Enable administrative security (recommended): True
Administrative console port: 9060
Administrative console secure port: 9043
HTTP transport port: 9080
HTTPS transport port: 9443
Bootstrap port: 2809
SOAP connector port: 8880
Run application server as a service: False
Create a Web server definition: False
```

Here are the contents of the same file for the profile `AppSrv02`:

```
Application server environment to create: Application server
Location: /opt/IBM/WebSphere/AppServer/profiles/AppSrv02
Disk space required: 200 MB
Profile name: AppSrv02
Make this profile the default: False
Node name: localhostNode02
Host name: localhost
Enable administrative security (recommended): False
Administrative console port: 9061
Administrative console secure port: 9044
HTTP transport port: 9081
HTTPS transport port: 9444
Bootstrap port: 2810
SOAP connector port: 8881
Run application server as a service: False
Create a Web server definition: False
```

A profile will also have a `properties/portdef.props` file that deals more specifically with port numbers.

As you can see, the default port numbers for profile `AppSrv02` are one higher than those for the default profile, `AppSrv01`. At this point, it's not too important to know what each port is for, but you will eventually have to enter some of these port number values elsewhere.

*Installing Environmental Components*

For a given WAS profile, you can also find these port numbers via the WAS admin console for that profile. If you used the default port numbers for the WAS admin consoles, you can connect to `AppSrv01` or `AppSrv02` using the URL `http://wjc-rhel.example.net:9060/ibm/console` or `http://wjc-rhel.example.net:9061/ibm/console`, respectively. From there, navigate to **Servers | Server Types | WebSphere application servers | server1 | Configuration | Ports**. The following screenshot is for `AppSrv02`:

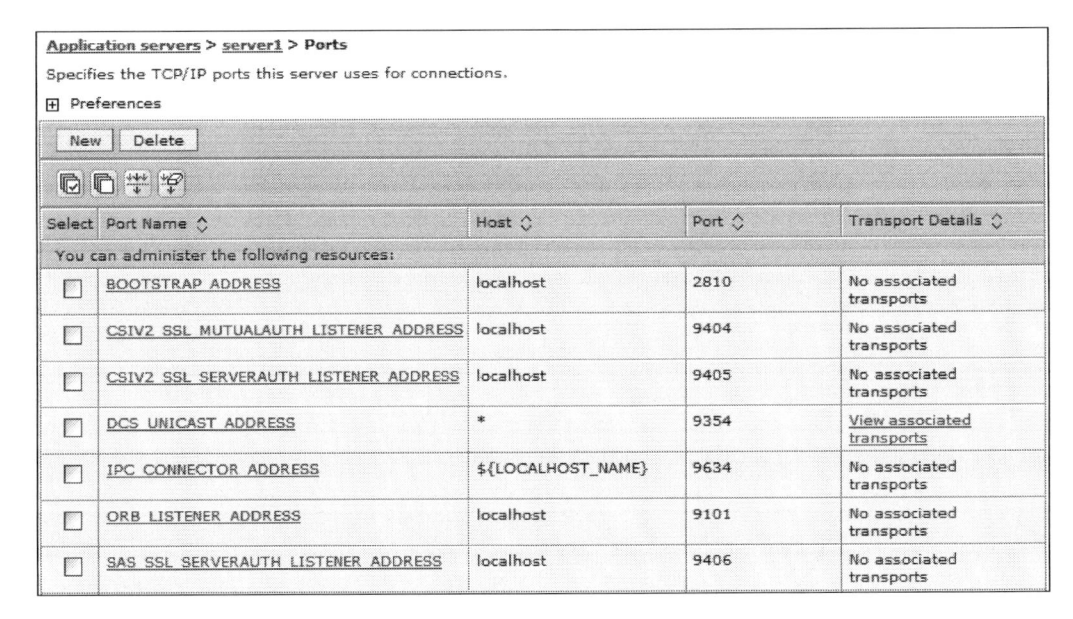

| Select | Port Name | Host | Port | Transport Details |
|---|---|---|---|---|
| ☐ | BOOTSTRAP_ADDRESS | localhost | 2810 | No associated transports |
| ☐ | CSIV2_SSL_MUTUALAUTH_LISTENER_ADDRESS | localhost | 9404 | No associated transports |
| ☐ | CSIV2_SSL_SERVERAUTH_LISTENER_ADDRESS | localhost | 9405 | No associated transports |
| ☐ | DCS_UNICAST_ADDRESS | * | 9354 | View associated transports |
| ☐ | IPC_CONNECTOR_ADDRESS | ${LOCALHOST_NAME} | 9634 | No associated transports |
| ☐ | ORB_LISTENER_ADDRESS | localhost | 9101 | No associated transports |
| ☐ | SAS_SSL_SERVERAUTH_LISTENER_ADDRESS | localhost | 9406 | No associated transports |

## WAS process attributes

The preparation guide calls out a UMASK setting for the CE Java process. On Unix-like operating systems, UMASK controls the default permissions for files created by a process.

> UMASK is sometimes thought of as the default permission for files created by a user, but it's technically a setting for a running process. It gets set on a user's login shell process and is inherited by other processes.

For our installation, this corresponds to the process running the JVM for profile `AppSrv02`. So, again, use the WAS console, but this time navigate to **Servers | Server Types | WebSphere application servers | server1 | Java and Process Management | Process execution**. Change the value in the **UMASK** field to `007` (all permissions for the process user and group, no permissions for anyone else).

```
Application servers > server1 > Process execution
Use this page to configure additional process executi[on]
platform.

Configuration

General Properties
    Process Priority
    [20]

    UMASK
    [007]

    Run As User
    [ecmuser]

    Run As Group
    [ecmgroup]

    Run In Process Group
    [0]

    [Apply]  [OK]  [Reset]  [Cancel]
```

This same form is used to specify an alternate user and group for the JVM process, and we will run our CE as operating system user `ecmuser` and group `ecmgroup`, as you can see in the previous screenshot. At the operating system level, this user and group have relatively low privilege levels, and it saves us from the bad security practice of running a piece of software as complex as WAS as the `root` user.

If we were to use the `ecmuser` account to install the application server, things would probably "just work", but we took the lazy approach and installed it using the `root` account. The procedure we have found to be simplest for changing the "run as" user and group is:

- Change the user or group in that WAS console form and commit the changes
- Shut down that WAS profile (we would ignore errors that sounded like they were related to permissions)

*Installing Environmental Components*

- Change all of the files for that WAS profile to the user and/or group that we put on the form
- Start up that WAS profile (from the `root` account or the user account that we configured for the profile)

In this case, we are running both the AE and CE profiles as user/group `ecmuser`/`ecmgroup`. We also set the **UMASK** value to `007` on the AE profile just for consistency. We could just leave those fields blank and always start WAS from the `ecmuser` account, but doing this bit of configuration is a little protection against our making a mistake. We can start WAS from the `root` account and it will still run as `ecmuser`.

Run these commands to fix up the ownership of files under the AE and CE WAS profiles:

```
# cd /opt/ibm/WebSphere/AppServer/profiles
# chown -R ecmuser:ecmgroup AppSrv01 AppSrv02
```

## WAS performance tweaks

There is a small amount of performance tuning configuration to be done for WAS from the administrative console for the CE profile. Navigate to **Servers | Server Types | WebSphere application servers | server1 | Java and Process Management | Process definition | Java Virtual Machine**. Specify an initial heap size of at least 512 MB and a maximum heap size of at least 1024 MB. Depending on your available RAM, you may find it beneficial for performance to specify larger values.

The planning and preparation guide has a note about optionally increasing the WAS transaction timeout. There are only a few update operations that run the risk of hitting the transaction timeout such as the creation of an ObjectStore and subsequent installation of AddOns into an ObjectStore. The WAS default is 300 seconds, and you can leave it at that value unless you run into trouble in one of those operations.

Finally, there is one important detail of WAS configuration that often trips people up. It's one of the few things that is more likely to be a problem in a test or demo environment than in a production environment. Earlier, we showed a screen capture from the WAS admin console showing the bootstrap address. We were interested in the port numbers then, but now let's look at the host part of the address. The WAS installation did its best to work out the name of our host, but it could only come up with `localhost`. That will work fine for connecting from the same server, but to connect to that WAS instance from any other machine, the bootstrap host name must be resolvable in DNS from the client machine. For our system, we will enter `wjc-rhel.example.net` for at least the bootstrap address. That's usually sufficient for CM purposes, but you can change all of the other `localhost` entries if you are so inclined.

> Depending on your DNS environment, you might have to merely imagine entering the server name. The domain name might not resolve in your DNS. In that case, enter the IP address for that server instead.

## WAS and DB2

It's now time to marry our WAS and DB2 components. This consists of two separate items. We must make sure that WAS is using a CE-compatible JDBC driver to talk to DB2, and we must configure WAS datasources to be used by the CE to talk to the GCD and ObjectStores. All CE communication with databases is mediated by a J2EE application server.

The P8 hardware/software guide gives the acceptable JDBC drivers for each supported database and platform. This is typically stated in terms of a minimum release level, but there are occasionally specific driver versions to avoid. Because we made sure to specify Java support when we installed DB2, JDBC drivers were installed as part of the default instance in default location `/home/db2inst1/sqllib/java/`. The file `db2jcc.jar` contains the actual JDBC provider in which we are interested. To find the exact version number for the provider in that file, we use Java to interrogate the driver itself. The following command executes the `DB2Jcc` class in the JAR file and passes an argument to it asking for version info. The line immediately following is typical output.

```
$ cd /home/db2inst1/sqllib/java
$ java -cp db2jcc.jar com.ibm.db2.jcc.DB2Jcc -version
IBM DB2 JDBC Universal Driver Architecture 3.53.95
```

As of this writing, the P8 hardware/software guide specifies a minimum version of 3.53.95 for DB2 9.5 (3.57.82 for DB2 9.7), so we can use this already-installed driver. If that were not the case, driver software is available for download from the DB2 support site. That's typical for all the supported databases.

To make WAS aware of this particular DB2 driver, log onto the WAS console for the CE profile, and navigate to **Environment | WebSphere variables**. Set the value of variable **DB2UNIVERSAL_JDBC_DRIVER_PATH** to `/home/db2inst1/sqllib/java`. Be sure to save your change.

*Installing Environmental Components*

We could manually configure the necessary JDBC datasources for connecting to the GCD and ObjectStore databases, but we'll let the P8 Configuration Manager application take care of those details when we install the actual CE software in *Chapter 3*. If you are interested in how to set up datasources manually, you can find detailed instructions in the WAS documentation. If you do it manually, be sure to check P8 documentation for necessary settings for both performance and functional aspects.

## Installing Tivoli Directory Server

TDS uses a database (for storing directory and configuration data) and an application server (for hosting its web-based administration tool). The installation program will try to detect already installed versions that it can use. If none are found, it will use embedded versions of DB2 and WAS laid down by the installer.

By now, the story should sound familiar—Install TDS using the "typical" path, and take default suggestions for various things. That's almost the case. The steps we show next use DB2 9.5 and the "typical" install path. For our installation, TDS 6.2 is able to use DB2 9.5. For some early versions of TDS 6.2, there is a bug that can prevent things from starting up properly. We'll show you how to work around that bug next. However, when using DB2 9.7, the "typical" path works smoothly, as it does when using DB2 9.5 and later fix packs of TDS 6.2.

TDS 6.2 will not use WAS 7.0, so it installs its own embedded copy of WAS 6.1. If you accept the defaults, you will find the embedded copy of WAS under `/opt/ibm/ldap/appsrv/`.

> TDS 6.2 is the latest version supported by CM 4.5.1. CM 5.0 may eventually support TDS 6.3. TDS 6.3 can, in turn, use WAS 7.0 as its embedded application server. In that case, WAS 7.0 would be automatically detected and used by the TDS installer.

In the "typical" installation path, TDS creates a separate DB2 instance, `dsrdbm01`, and an operating system user account of the same name. It also creates a directory administrative operating system user, `idsldap`.

Before you launch the TDS installer:

- Make sure the DB2 administrative server is running. This is needed so that TDS can create its own DB2 instance and database.
- Set an environment variable to tell TDS which DB2 instance to use. We're doing that now, even though the instance doesn't yet exist, just so that the installation runs smoothly.

*Chapter 2*

From a command-line window, and while situated in the directory containing the TDS installation files, run the commands shown as follows. Although we are running them from the command line, the TDS installer launches a GUI.

```
# su - dasusr1 -c "db2admin start"
# DB2INSTANCE=dsrdbm01
# export DB2INSTANCE
# ./install_tds.bin
```

The first line starts the DB2 administrative server. The second and third lines set and export the DB2INSTANCE environment variable. Because of the bug we mentioned earlier, TDS can get confused about which DB2 instance to use, and setting that environment variable eliminates the confusion. You'll see later that we included the same thing in the script we use to start TDS running. The last line above launches the TDS installer. All of these should be done as the root user.

When you take the "typical" installation path, you will end up with a screen with a **Finish** button. That will be followed by the automatic launching of the **IBM Tivoli Directory Server Instance Administration Tool**. The main panel will show an already created directory service instance dsrdbm01. The instance will be in a **Stopped** state. Click the **Start/Stop** button on that summary panel to start the directory instance.

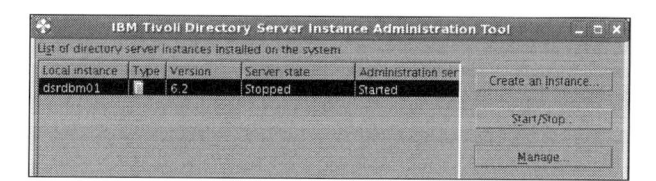

Close all the nested wizard panels, dialog boxes, and other TDS-related on-screen flotsam and jetsam. Your directory is installed, running, and waiting to be filled with data. By default, the directory administrator account was created as cn=root, which we will use below.

If you're a little lost in what happened with all of the mentions of dsrdbm01 that you may have seen flash by, here is a short list of what happened:

- We've created a new TDS instance to hold our enterprise directory. It doesn't really have a name, but it's owned by dsrdbm01 and is stored in that user's home directory, so it implicitly takes that name.

- We've created a new DB2 instance that was named `dsrdbm01`. For DB2 administrative purposes, it's separate from the instance `db2inst1` that we created when we installed DB2 and which we will use for holding ObjectStore databases.
- We've created a DB2 database within DB2 instance `dsrdbm01`. The database is also called `dsrdbm01` and is stored in that user's home directory. The operating system user account `dsrdbm01` will be used by TDS when it accesses the database.

## Using the directory

Directory information can be used for a mind-bogglingly large number of different purposes, and many of these considerations add complexity to the data itself. For CM purposes, however, the uses are straightforward and standard.

- **Basic user information**: Used mainly to uniquely identify an individual for various purposes.
- **User authentication**: CM delegates this to the J2EE application server, and it could theoretically not consult the directory at all. In practice, directory-based password authentication is still the most common technique. Even when password authentication is not used, the directory is almost always part of the picture.
- **Group memberships**: Membership in some particular group can be used to control authorization (that is, permissions to access various things).

There is common confusion about the concepts of authentication and authorization, perhaps because the words are so similar. Authentication is proving who you are to the system. Authorization is the system deciding what you are entitled to do. Authentication is a natural prerequisite for authorization (we'll come back to making a big deal about this in *Chapter 8, Security Features and Planning* when we talk about security features). CM does not use the directory or J2EE for authorization. It has an internal access control system, but it does depend on the directory for user identity and group membership purposes.

## Populating the directory

If you have just installed TDS, you will have essentially an empty directory in the sense that it doesn't have any real users or groups in it. TDS does come with a file of sample data that you can import into the directory, and you can certainly do that if you would like to see some realistic data or follow some of the TDS tutorial material. It won't interfere with the directory data we add below for use with CM.

> If you are already familiar with the directory schema conventions used in your enterprise, you can do similar things in the isolated directory that we have just created. You'll have to make a few corresponding adjustments later in this chapter when we configure WAS and the CE for directory interactions.

Let's go through the process of manually adding a few users and groups. Some specific directory user and group roles are needed for the CM environment. Most people who work around enterprise software have at least an intuitive feel for the notion of users and groups, but knowing the ins and outs of an enterprise directory structure is a much more specialized kind of knowledge. We'll walk you through the steps that we use.

We'll be using a scheme that may or may not closely match your enterprise's conventions, but it will be fine for operating the all-in-one environment, and it's an easy way to get things up and running.

- The first few top layers of our directory naming follow the common pattern of Domain Components, where elements of an organization's DNS domain name are mapped into the top level of the directory hierarchy. Our enterprise is a fictitious organization and so secretive that it doesn't even have a name. However, its DNS domain name is `example.net` (taken from a list of domains reserved for examples by RFC-2606).

- In one isolated leg of the directory naming hierarchy, we'll make a flat list of individual users.

- Each user will have a unique tag as one of his/her common name attributes for the directory entries. Not only will that uniquely (and permanently) identify each user within the flat list, but it will also serve as the login user ID (the **short name**, in directory jargon).

- In a separate leg of the directory naming hierarchy, we'll put the groups. Groups can be nested within groups, but we won't be exploiting that feature.

*Installing Environmental Components*

> We could use the TDS Realms interface to construct our users and groups. If you use TDS in your enterprise, that's a good way to go. It offers several user interface niceties for directory administration, and it also offers partial referential integrity for the entries. We're using the simpler and slightly more laborious effort described here because you can use it with any LDAP directory.

## TDS web console setup

There are some one-time actions for configuring the TDS web console. We'll go through these here.

First, start the WAS instance embedded with TDS by running the following command as `root`. This is needed any time you want to use the web console as the web console runs as a servlet under that WAS profile.

```
/opt/ibm/ldap/V6.2/appsrv/profiles/TDSWebAdminProfile/bin/startServer.sh server1
```

> The above command is all one line, and the only space is just before the word `server1`.

Connect to the web-based administration tool with a web browser at `http://wjc-rhel.example.net:12100/IDSWebApp/`. At the login prompt, you will be tempted to enter the directory service administrator account and password configured earlier. That's not what it's asking for. It is asking for the *console* login. This is always defaulted to user `superadmin` and password `secret`. The password is literally the word "secret".

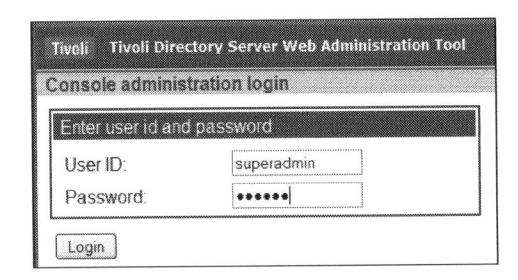

> Unless you do frequent work with this TDS tool, we guarantee that, sooner or later, you will forget the user ID and password you are supposed to use for the console login. We've already forgotten and re-learned it several times.

[ 56 ]

You can either live with that (and have a little chuckle every time you forget), or you can use the provided options of **Console administration | Change console administrator login** and **Change console administrator password** to something you will remember and that is possibly a little more secure. Although the default credentials don't get you very far, they get far enough that some prankster could change them and lock you out.

> As we will manage only a single directory from this console, we changed the credentials to the same as the directory server administrator, `cn=root`.

At this point, we have a functioning TDS console server, but it doesn't know about any actual directories to administer. The next step is to tell it there is a directory running on the same server. Navigate to **Console administration | Manage console servers**. Click the **Add** button.

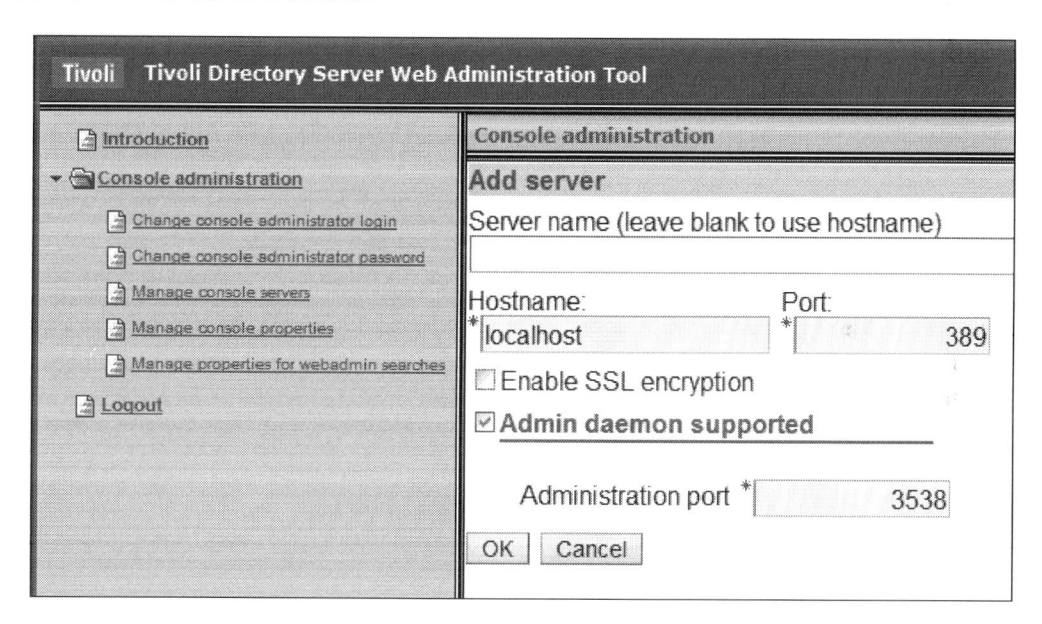

We used the **Hostname** `localhost` because the directory server is running on the same server as the console server. For the same reason, we left the **Enable SSL encryption** option unchecked. That's for communication between the console and the directory server. If you were remotely managing directory servers, you would probably want to enable TLS/SSL.

*Installing Environmental Components*

Click **OK** to apply the change. Log out of the console administration tool and then return to the login page. You will find it transformed into something more expected.

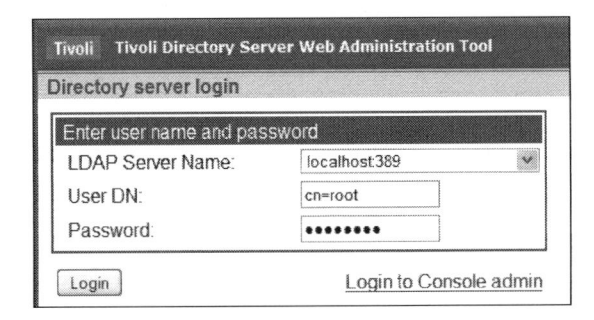

You can now log in to the directory administration tool (not the console configuration tool) by providing the credentials we configured earlier, cn=root. If you ever need to go back to the console configuration tool, you can just click the **Login to Console admin** link.

If you click the **Login** button, you will be taken to the **Tivoli Directory Server Web Administration Tool**, from which all of our directory configuration and data entry will be done.

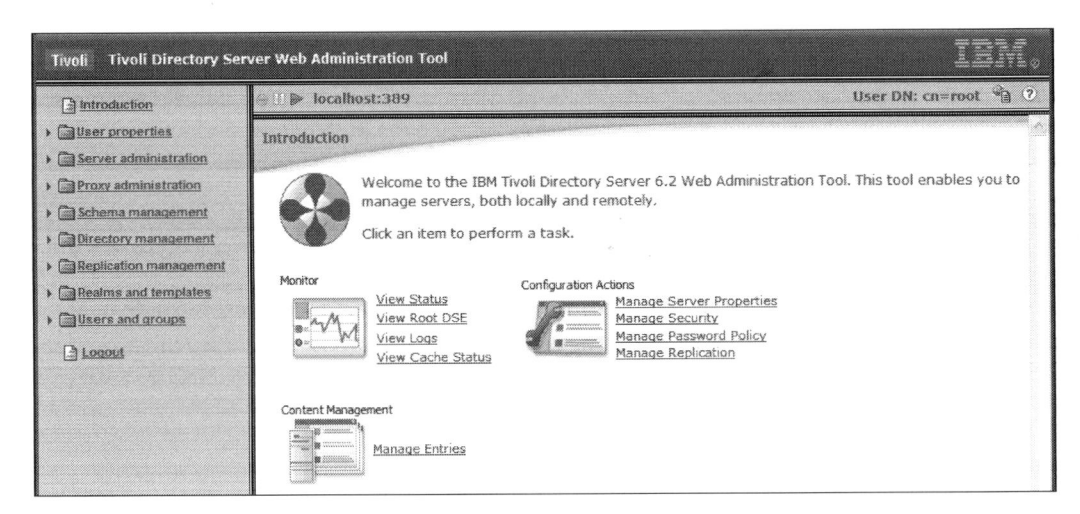

## Server-side sorting

It is a CE requirement to configure TDS to allow server-side sorting of search results. This is usually enabled by default, but you can check it via the TDS web administration application. Navigate to **Server administration | Manage server properties | Search settings** and make sure that the checkbox for **Allow only administrators to perform sort searches** is *not* checked. You don't want to restrict it to administrators; you want to allow anyone to do sorted searches.

## The suffix

TDS can hold arbitrarily many logical partitions of data, each falling within a unique **suffix**. A suffix is just a collection of attribute values under which all other entries fall. Our organization refers to the enterprise directory as "WhoZit?", so we will make our suffix be `dc=whozit,dc=example,dc=net`.

> Directory concepts and notation can seem pretty odd. Most people don't encounter them every day. There is a lot of material available on the web to explain both the concepts and the notation. Here is one example that is clearly written and oriented toward directory novices: `http://www.skills-1st.co.uk/papers/ldap-schema-design-feb-2005/index.html`.

You can add a suffix to TDS via the web-based administration tool. Navigate to **Server administration | Manage server properties | Suffixes**. Type the full suffix into the **Suffix DN** box and click the **Add** button. Be sure to also click the **OK** or **Apply** button to commit the change (it's easy to miss).

> You might also have to restart the directory server before the new suffix will show up in the directory. Navigate to **Server administration | Stop/start/restart server**.

*Installing Environmental Components*

## Users

A good practice in directory administration is to add all of the entries for individual people in a flat structure and then reference those entries from groups, organizational entities, and other structures that can change over time. The idea is to keep the Distinguished Name for users constant regardless of what other changes are needed in the directory. We'll define a node called `cn=people` to hold all the people entries, regardless of organizational or other affiliations. Navigate to **Directory management | Add an entry**. From the list of structural object classes, select **groupOfNames** and click **Next**. We're using the `groupOfNames` class because it triggers some conveniences in the TDS administrative tool user interface for us later; be careful that you don't accidentally select **groupOfUniqueNames**. For this simple container node, we don't need any additional attributes, so click **Next** to move past the **auxiliary object classes** panel. This will bring you to the **Required attributes** panel.

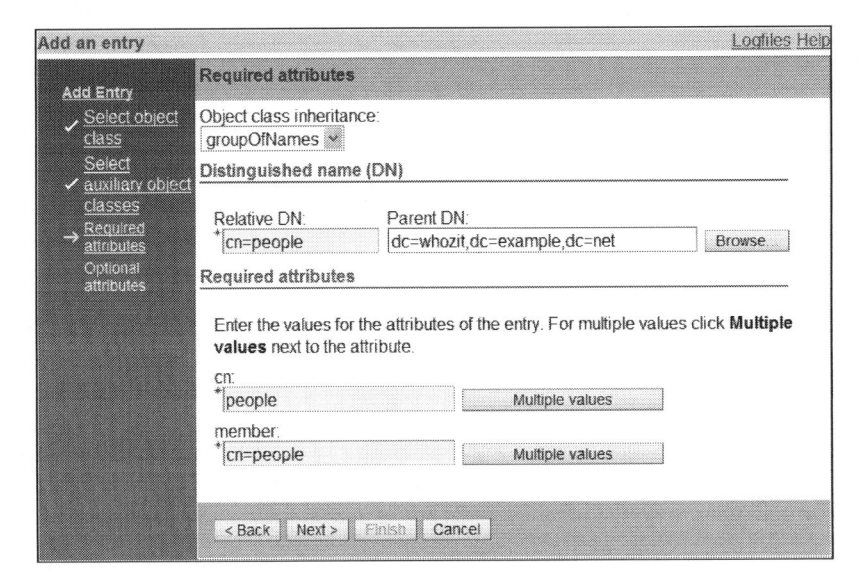

Enter the name of our new container `cn=people` as the **Relative DN** and also enter `people` as the **cn** attribute value. Because a **groupOfNames** must have at least one member, add the node itself in that field. You can browse to select the LDAP suffix we chose for the **Parent DN**.

> It is a quirk of some versions of the TDS administration tool that a newly-created LDAP suffix won't show up in some places until it has at least one entry under it. If that happens to you, simply type the value `dc=whozit,dc=example,dc=net` into that field; it will be available via the **Browse** button for all future operations.

You can leave blank the optional attribute fields that appear on the next screen. After you click **Finish** to commit the change, TDS will ask if you'd like to add a similar entry. You can save yourself a little work by clicking **Yes**. Make another container to hold group definitions, and give it the **Relative DN** of cn=groups. We now have our two special-purpose directory nodes—cn=people,dc=whozit,dc=example,dc=net for the users and cn=groups,dc=whozit,dc=example,dc=net for the groups.

To add individual users, return to **Directory management | Add an entry**. This time, select the structural object class **person**. Another popular choice is **inetOrgPerson** because it has many more additional optional attributes, but for our purposes the class person is simpler and will be sufficient. The important thing is that the user entries have the userPassword attribute because that will be the login password for CM and for various other things.

For the **Relative DN**, supply a value which is unique to a given user. This would typically be something like an employee ID number or e-mail address. It will also be the login user ID, so it should be a value that is meaningful to the users and not confidential. In the next screen, we used initials (which is OK for an example but probably terrible if your enterprise has more than a couple of people in it). It's important that the value be permanently unique as the combination of the **Relative DN** and the **Parent DN** comprises the full **Distinguished name** for a user. The directory will not allow you to create entries with duplicate values, a safeguard which was one of the beneficial ideas behind using a flat list of users.

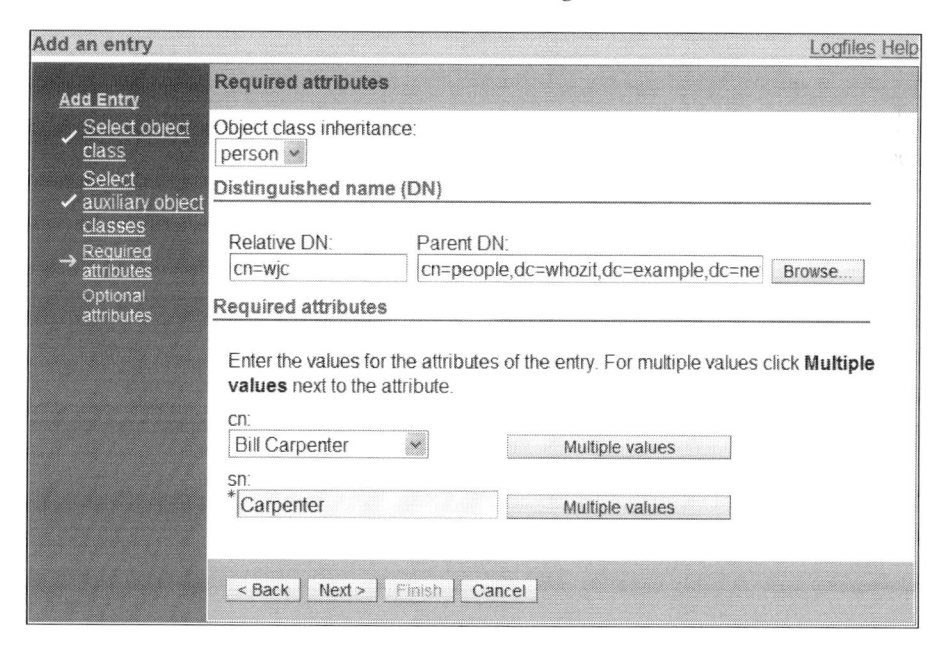

*Installing Environmental Components*

Although it's defined as optional, be sure to supply a value for the `userPassword` attribute for each entry. In a true enterprise directory, you would probably customize things to make the `userPassword` attribute required.

Go ahead and create one or two entries for individual users. Feel free to experiment with the tool; you can always delete entries later. We'll return to populating the directory with CM-specific information a little bit later in this section.

## Groups

Let's make at least one directory group to see how it's done. We added the node `cn=groups,dc=whozit,dc=example,dc=net` earlier. Navigate to that node, check the box next to **cn=groups**, and select **Add** from the drop-down menu to put a new entry directly under that node. Make the new entry a **groupOfNames** and give it a **Relative DN** of `cn=vampires`. (Someone told us that we would sell a lot more books if we mentioned vampires, but we think that will only work if they are young, attractive, and moody. We shall see.) Again, add the new entry as a member of itself. When you have completed this and committed the change, you should be able to navigate to the new node `cn=vampires,cn=groups,dc=whozit,dc=example,dc=net`. Select that node from the list of groups, as shown in the next screenshot. From the **Select Action** dropdown, choose **Manage Members** and click **Go**.

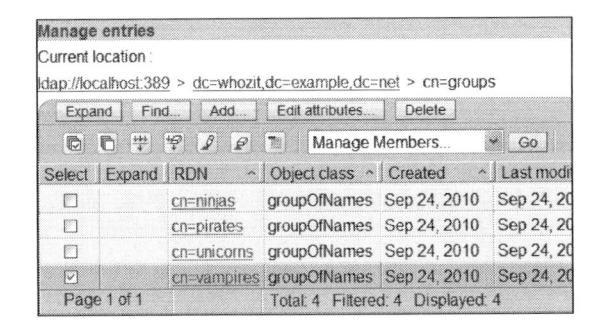

You'll be brought to a screen where you can add members to the group by entering their Distinguished names or browsing for them in the directory. As you would expect, you could instead navigate to an individual person's entry and select **Manage Memberships** to manage things from that point of view. Feel free to experiment before moving on to the next subsection.

## CE-specific entries

For the installation and initial configuration of the CE, a small number of users and groups are required. It would be reasonably common to designate existing directory entries to be used for these things, but for our all-in-one environment we'll create new, dedicated entries. This will help you to see what accounts are used for which purposes.

The following table summarizes the users and groups that you should create now using the procedures just described. The specific user or group IDs shown are merely suggestions and match the figurative names used in the PPG and in the installation worksheet. You can use different names if you feel like it. Be sure to keep track of the passwords you assign to these accounts. Although it is not required for CE purposes, you might like to assign these special accounts to a descriptively-named group for simple bookkeeping purposes. For example, we sometimes use a group named `pseudousers` in our set ups.

| User | Group | Comment |
| --- | --- | --- |
| `ce_bootstrap_admin` | | Make this a dedicated account not used for anything else and with a password that doesn't expire. Used by the CE for initial access to the GCD. |
| `gcd_admin` | | Domain administrator. |
| `object_store_admin` | `object_store_admin_group` | ObjectStore administrator(s). |
| `ce_service_user` | | Used by the CE to do LDAP directory lookups. |
| `was_admin` | | Use this user ID to logon to the WAS admin console after we have changed it to use TDS for authentication. |

If you are following the pattern described in this section, you will have users with distinguished names like `cn=ce_bootstrap_admin,cn=people,dc=whozit,dc=example,dc=net`. Don't forget to place user `object_store_admin` into group `object_store_admin_group`.

[ 63 ]

*Installing Environmental Components*

These are the only directory entries needed for CE installation, but we will return to the directory when we install additional CM components. Since this is a development system, you might add some additional users to represent non-administrator users in your environment. For example, we often make users called `poweruser` and `unpriv` that we use for different roles in security configuration experiments.

## Manual TDS queries

For troubleshooting purposes, or for any other reason, you can manually query TDS from the command line using the `/opt/ibm/ldap/V6.2/bin/ldapsearch` command. We won't attempt to give a tutorial on LDAP query syntax, but the following two commands query for all of the people and groups, respectively, in the directory data we defined above:

```
$ cd /opt/ibm/ldap/V6.2/bin
./ldapsearch -b "cn=people,dc=whozit,dc=example,dc=net" "cn=*"
./ldapsearch -b "cn=groups,dc=whozit,dc=example,dc=net" "cn=*"
```

## Scripts and desktop shortcuts

There are a lot of moving parts in an all-in-one server, and even an experienced person can have trouble remembering all the possible commands and locations. On a development or demo system, you may find yourself starting and stopping various things on a regular basis.

In our architecture role, we deal with a substantial library of virtual server images with different configurations. The procedures for doing even routine tasks vary a lot from vendor to vendor and sometimes even from release to release of the same vendor product. We find it handy to create a series of desktop shortcuts for starting and stopping our DB2 instance, starting and stopping the TDS instance, and starting and stopping both of the WAS profiles. We do the WAS profiles separately from each other because we often find ourselves fiddling with our CE without needing the AE to be running.

For our own convenience, we also gather up many of those same commands into scripts that we can run from the `root` account to make sure everything is running or to make sure everything is shut down.

> These scripts are also available with other downloadable material from the Packt Publishing website: http://www.packtpub.com/support.

Here's the first script, which we call up.sh. It brings up all the servers in a logical order that satisfies dependencies (some of those dependencies will only arise after we have installed and configured a few more things in *Chapters 3* and *5*). We start the databases first, then the directory, then the application server profiles. Some of the individual commands use the Linux su command to become a different user in cases where it matters. The command-line hyphen is important to pick up the environment of that other user.

```sh
#!/bin/sh

# up.sh: Script to bring up all the components.
# Handy after reboot.  Run as root.

set -v

### applications/default DB2 instance
su - db2inst1 -c "db2 db2start"
#echo "Press enter..."; read x

### TDS admin service.
## Normally started via inittab.  We have it here
## just in case we shut it down via the down.sh
## script and need to bring it back up.
/opt/ibm/ldap/V6.2/sbin/ibmdiradm -I dsrdbm01
#echo "Press enter..."; read x

### TDS DB2 instance
## Normally started automatically by TDS, but
## we start it manually just to make sure.
su - dsrdbm01 -c "db2 db2start"
#echo "Press enter..."; read x

### TDS directory instance
## We set DB2INSTANCE to TDS knows which instance to use
DB2INSTANCE=dsrdbm01; export DB2INSTANCE
/opt/ibm/ldap/V6.2/sbin/idsslapd -I dsrdbm01
#echo "Press enter..."; read x

### TDS directory admin console server
/opt/ibm/ldap/V6.2/appsrv/profiles/TDSWebAdminProfile/bin/startServer.sh server1
#echo "Press enter..."; read x

### WAS CE instance
```

## Installing Environmental Components

```
/opt/ibm/WebSphere/AppServer/bin/startServer.sh server1 -profileName
AppSrv02
#echo "Press enter..."; read x

### WAS AE instance
/opt/ibm/WebSphere/AppServer/bin/startServer.sh server1 -profileName
AppSrv01
#echo "Press enter..."; read x

### CSE
rm -f /tmp/k2start.log
su - k2_os_user -c /opt/IBM/FileNet/ContentEngine/verity/k2/_ilnx21/
bin/k2adminstart > /tmp/k2start.log
#echo "Press enter..."; read x

## This is done so the window doesn't disappear
echo "Press enter..."; read x
```

The second script, which we call down.sh, is pretty much just the reverse of up.sh (it's available along with up.sh in the downloadable material from the Packt Publishing website). It brings things down in the opposite order from which they were started. For both scripts, there can be occasions where a given server is already started or stopped. In that case, there are harmless errors printed. After a few times of running these scripts, it's easy to see what's important and what is a routine and expected error.

If your environment is similar to ours, you can make your own shortcuts for individual items by copying lines from up.sh and down.sh. There are a few things that are "shortcut worthy" but which don't appear in those scripts. Here's a brief catalog of those, once again assuming that you are running them from the root account and that you have used the default values for user account and filesystem locations:

- To start the DB2 admin server (needed to do most things in the DB2 control center): /opt/ibm/db2/V9.5/das/bin/db2admin start.
- To run the DB2 control center GUI for DB2 instance db2inst1: /bin/su - db2inst1 -c db2cc. The command begins with switching to user db2inst1 before running the DB2 control center. If you get X Window System connection errors, you may have to adjust the permissions you give for someone to connect to your X display. The easiest (but also most security risky) way to do this is to first run the command xauth +localhost (only allows connections from the same host) or xauth + (turns access checks completely off).

- To run the DB2 control center GUI for instance `dsrdbm01` used by TDS: `/bin/su - dsrdbm01 -c db2cc` (see the note about X display errors in the previous bullet).
- To connect to the admin console for WAS profile `AppSrv01` (which will become our AE): `http://wjc-rhel.example.net:9060/ibm/console`.
- To connect to the admin console for WAS profile `AppSrv02` (which will become our CE): `http://wjc-rhel.example.net:9061/ibm/console`.
- To connect to the TDS web-based admin tool: `http://wjc-rhel.example.net:12100/IDSWebApp`. To use TLS/SSL, it's `https://wjc-rhel.example.net:12101/IDSWebApp`.

In the URLs above, you could optionally use a server name of `localhost` if you were connecting from the server itself.

## Summary

In this chapter, we successfully installed the CE prerequisite environmental components for an all-in-one environment. This included setting up the operating system, and installing and configuring a database system, a directory server, and a J2EE application server.

Now that all those things are in place and we made and recorded a number of decisions in the installation worksheet, we're ready to install the CE itself in *Chapter 3*.

# 3
# Installing the Content Engine

In this chapter, we set about actually installing the **Content Engine** (CE) software. Some things in this chapter assume you have an environment similar to that described in *Chapter 2*. If your environment differs from that, you may need to make some adjustments as you go through the configuration steps.

This chapter contains the following topics:

- Orientation for the CM product, the P8 platform, and the various components
- Installation of the CE itself
- Immediate post-installation tasks up through the creation of your first Object Store

If you follow the installation steps, you will have a working CE server by the end of this chapter.

## An aside about some names

What's the difference between Content Manager and Content Engine? Where does P8 fit into all of this? If you are mainly used to consumer-oriented commercial software or open source software, it may seem odd to have so many different names for what sounds like the same thing. Let's sort it out now so that you will have no trouble understanding the terminology for the rest of the chapter and the book. We will use these terms correctly throughout the book so that you will always know precisely what we mean.

*Installing the Content Engine*

IBM FileNet Content Manager (CM) is a product name. It is a specific combination of things that you can license from IBM. Because it is a fairly complex product, there are many individual software components that make up CM. P8 (in case you are wondering, it doesn't stand for anything in particular; it's just a name, though there is a small mythology about its origins) refers to a family of software components. Although the IBM FileNet development teams are hard at work every day building and enhancing P8 components, you don't buy or license a thing called P8. You license CM, and that includes the right to use several P8 components, among other things.

> There is another product called **IBM Content Manager**, or IBM CM (often referred to as CM8). The naming can be slightly confusing when it's compared to **IBM FileNet Content Manager**. Although these two products are both ECM products, and therefore both have the same general product goals, they have different development histories and technical architectures. Both are under active development (in fact, within the same larger development organization in IBM) and both are likely to be around for a long, long time. Except for right here, we won't be talking about IBM Content Manager at all in this book. Whenever we say Content Manager or just CM, we'll mean IBM FileNet Content Manager.

We'll have a lot to say about the CE in this chapter and the chapters that follow. For now, we just want to make the clear distinction that it is a specific, tangible software component within the CM product.

## P8 platform architecture

In this section, we'll look at a typical deployment architecture for a CM installation. The following figure shows such a deployment diagram. For the moment, we won't say too much about the cloud of applications (we'll come back to it in chapters 5 and 6). It includes the P8 **Application Engine** (**AE**) and most of the CE administrative tools created and shipped by the CE team. All of the components in the object and data tiers of the figure will be described in this section.

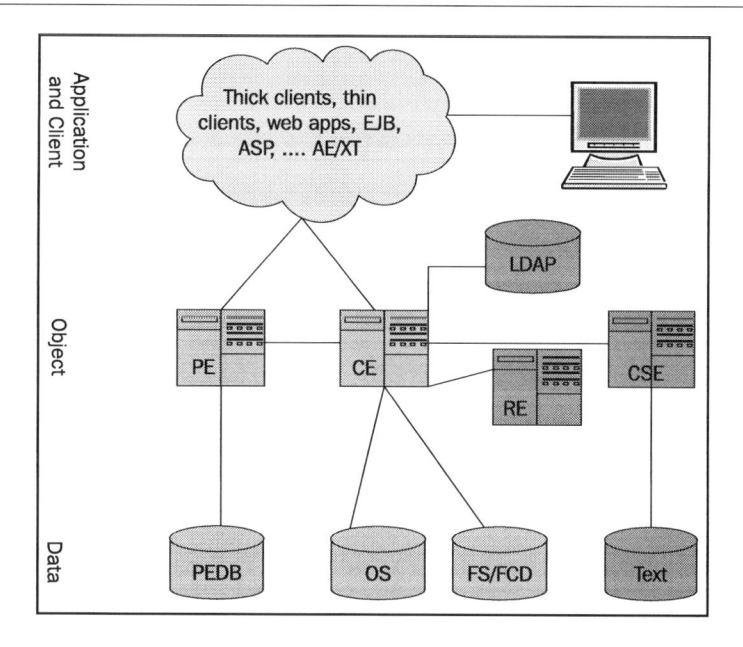

## Content Engine (CE)

The centerpiece of the CM product is the P8 **Content Engine**. It mediates all activity between applications and the actual content. The CE provides security, referential integrity, a sophisticated object-oriented data model, and many other features that go into managing content. We'll be drilling down into most of those features in *Chapter 7*; security gets its own treatment in *Chapter 8*. For now, you can think of the CE managing content and related objects in a way that is analogous to how a database server manages database tables, rows, and columns, and the features built on top of them.

> You'll sometimes see the Content Engine called "the P8CE" and sometimes just "the CE". You'll sometimes see it called "the CE server" and sometimes the word "server" will be left out. Sometimes the same author will mix and match these terms. All these usually mean the same thing. We'll use the simpler term "the CE" most of the time, but we will occasionally have to distinguish the server piece from some other thing that belongs to the CE (for example, the CE APIs). This should always be clear from the context.

*Installing the Content Engine*

The CE concerns itself with three broad categories of persistent data:

- **Content**: This is what most people traditionally think of as the actual documents or other pieces of managed content. It is the actual collection of raw bits that an office productivity or other application works with. Except for a few special cases, the CE does not look inside the content itself. While under CE control, content can be stored in a filesystem, in an Object Store database, or in a variety of specialized storage devices from several vendors. The component labeled "FS/FCD" in the previous figure represents either a filestore (storage in a filesystem) or a fixed content device (one of several specialized storage devices).

- **Metadata**: This represents data about content or other objects. For example, the date that a document was last modified is metadata. The CE data model has a rich set of system metadata supporting CE features, and it also allows very flexible extensions in custom metadata. Regardless of where content might be stored, metadata is always stored in a repository called an **Object Store** implemented atop a relational database. The component labeled "OS" in the diagram is an Object Store database. For a document, its metadata plus its content make up a document object. There are many other types of objects that reside within an Object Store. For example, each folder in the Object Store's folder hierarchy is actually an object.

- **Global Configuration Database (GCD)**: This is a special database that holds definitions and configuration for objects that reside outside of any Object Store. The GCD corresponds to a P8 **Domain** and is the key to all Object Stores, CE server instances, filestores, and other top-level objects. A Domain can have a large number of Object Stores, but a specific P8 installation always has exactly one Domain.

What, then, is a Domain? Besides being the collection of all the top-level objects in an installation, it is also a requirement that most components in a Domain have network connectivity with all other Domain objects. So, for example, every CE server must be able to reach every Object Store directly. All of the components of a Domain share a common user and group directory infrastructure. Many, perhaps most, applications can only work with a single Domain and are unaware of the possibilities of multiple Domains. That's due in part to the arrangement whereby the connection URL used to configure the CE APIs also implicitly selects the Domain, but we'll return to that point later.

> The database tables used by Object Stores and by the GCD do not overlap. It is technically possible to house the GCD in the database used by one of the Object Stores. Whether that is a good idea or not is mainly a matter of operational convenience. For example, the size of a GCD is fairly small, and it might be easier to do frequent, complete backups of it if it resides in a separate database.

The CE is a sophisticated J2EE application that makes use of an application server's web, EJB, and Resource Adapter containers. The good news is that the CE spends most of its time waiting for and servicing application requests that arrive via one of the CE APIs. Despite the CE's internal architectural complexity, you can generally just regard it as a black box J2EE application and not worry too much about what specific J2EE services it uses for its implementation.

> When we use the term *application server* throughout this book, we will always mean a J2EE application server unless we specifically say otherwise (we use the term J2EE because we're "old school" and haven't gotten in the habit of calling it by the newer name Java EE).

## Other components

We'll briefly mention a couple of other P8 software components that are included with the CM product bundle. You may wish to refer to the deployment architecture diagram above.

## Application Engine (AE)

The P8 **Application Engine** (**AE**) represents most of the out-of-the-box application tier shipped with CM. Most notably, it includes Workplace and Workplace XT, both of which are full-featured web applications suitable for end user use for general document management tasks. We'll have more to say about AE in chapters 5 and 6.

> Technically, the AE and Workplace XT are different components, as evidenced by them being installed separately. However, they do mostly fulfill the same roles that we just mentioned. AE is a platform including Workplace and other pieces. Workplace XT is an application.

## Content Search Engine (CSE)

The P8 **Content Search Engine (CSE)** is a full-text search engine that can be used to index CE string properties and the content of most commonly found business document types. The component labeled "Text" in the diagram is the text index data managed by CSE. It is currently filesystem based.

> Notice that there is no direct interaction between applications and the CSE. All interaction (indexing and searching) is between the CSE and the CE.

For CM 4.5.1 and earlier, the CSE is based on an embedded copy of the Autonomy K2 search engine (you might recognize this as the Verity K2 search engine; Verity was acquired by Autonomy a few years ago). Although K2 is included in the licensing of CM as the CSE component, the license does not include using K2 for other purposes. CM 5.0 includes an IBM-developed text search engine, but support for the K2-based CSE will continue for some time. Details had not been announced as of this writing.

## Process Engine (PE)

The P8 **Process Engine (PE)** is an enterprise-grade, fully-featured **Business Process Management (BPM)** system. The PE is integrated with the CE for processing documents and other objects as workflow attachments. The bookkeeping for the workflows themselves is maintained in separate databases managed by PE (labeled "PEDB" in the diagram). Interestingly, in a normal configuration, the PE server acts as a CE client, and the CE server acts as a PE client. The CM license includes a limited license to use the PE for a couple of pre-defined workflows included with the AE.

## Rendition Engine (RE)

The P8 **Rendition Engine (RE)** is a server for transforming commonly-used business document types into HTML or PDF formats. In this sense, the term "rendition" means the target document is merely a transformed copy of the source document. It does not include any material content or formatting changes. You may sometimes hear the RE called the publishing engine. RE is separately licensed and based on an embedded copy of Liquent Vista software. Although Liquent Vista is included in the licensing of RE, the license does not include using Liquent Vista for other purposes.

# Installing the CE

Well, we have certainly gone through a lot since the beginning of *Chapter 2*, and we are only now getting to the actual CE installation. Why was it so much trouble just to get here?

There's an important fact to remember—we set up all the supporting infrastructure from scratch, and we described various configuration decisions you might make and various procedures for performing configuration steps. In many large enterprises, someone in the organization will already be the database expert, or the application server expert, or the directory expert. In fact, the larger the organization, the less negotiating and deciding you are likely to do. It will be more a case of the responsible party telling you how things are going to be configured, or perhaps even doing it instead of allowing you to do it.

We covered a lot of ground to help you get your all-in-one environment going, but we don't think you would be doing it the same way when setting up a production environment (or a pre-production environment intended to mirror the production environment). You would be more likely to merely spend time gathering the necessary information and a lot less time installing supporting software components. Time you spend with the PPG and the installation worksheet will pay off in smoother sailing in the steps that follow here for actually installing and configuring the CE software.

# Getting the software

As of this writing, there is no freely-downloadable version of IBM FileNet Content Manager. Most of the supporting components described in earlier sections are available in at least a trial version from the respective vendors. With CM, arrangements are made to deliver the software to you when a licensing agreement is reached. That can be in the form of physical media, or you might get it via electronic download.

If you are not the person in your organization who received the software, you'll have to find that out internally. One thing that might help in your quest is asking around for the person who has the login to the IBM Passport Advantage or Passport Advantage Express account. Those are common pathways to licensed IBM software downloads.

In the rest of this section, we will assume that you have the CM software in hand, either as a set of physical disks or as downloaded (and unpacked) files.

*Installing the Content Engine*

## Running the CE server installer

Whether on physical media or an unpacked download, the name of the CM 4.5.1 installer for the CE on Linux is `P8CE-4.5.1-LINUX.BIN`. Start by running the program as the `root` user. After typical installer start-up, splash screen, welcome, and license acceptance panels, you will be asked to accept or provide an installation location. We recommend accepting the default of `/opt/IBM/FileNet/ContentEngine`. There are some additional choices to make if you are installing on Microsoft Windows, but those do not apply for a Linux installation.

The basic installation will complete, and you will be offered the chance to immediately launch the Configuration Manager. Leave the box unchecked and click **Done** to finish the installer. We'll run Configuration Manager manually.

The CE installer also suggests that you install **Content Search Engine** (CSE) and **Process Engine** (PE) client software before running the Configuration Manager. That only matters if fix packs are released for either of those components. We'll be installing just the base 4.5.1 releases of all CM components now and cover fix packs and upgrades in *Chapter 13*.

## Configuration Manager

The CE installer has merely copied the CE and related software to a local disk location. Most of the work of setting configuration options and actually deploying the CE into the application server is done in the Configuration Manager. You could certainly configure all necessary items by hand in each software component, but the Configuration Manager understands the relationships between the components and performs some validity checks along the way in addition to cheerfully taking care of a lot of clerical work. The CE WAS profile, the DB2 instance, and TDS must be running when you are working in the Configuration Manager.

Assuming you used the default location during the CE installation, launch the Configuration Manager by running the following command:

```
# /opt/ibm/FileNet/ContentEngine/tools/configure/configmgr
```

*Chapter 3*

> For the specific combination of CM 4.5.1 and WAS 7.0, there is a small known issue that occurs at a certain point in the application server configuration panel. The issue is described at `http://www-01.ibm.com/support/docview.wss?uid=swg21415627`. You must modify the Configuration Manager's configuration file so that it uses the WAS JRE. Do this before launching Configuration Manager. If you instead launch the Configuration Manager and run into the problem, you can merely exit the tool, make the correction, and relaunch the tool.
>
> (The problem occurs with the base version of the CE 4.5.1 Configuration Manager and may be addressed by a fix pack by the time you are attempting this.)

The Configuration Manager is a thick client application with a graphical user interface. On first launch, you will be greeted with a welcome screen where you can read a little bit about the role and functions of the Configuration Manager. When you are ready, close the welcome screen, and you will find yourself in a rather empty-looking workbench screen.

Since this is an all-new installation, your first step will be to navigate to **File | New Installation Profile**. That brings up the profile creation wizard. A Configuration Manager profile (which should not be confused with a WAS profile) is a collection of all of the configuration choices that you make. Configuration Manager can keep track of many distinct in-progress and completed profiles, so the first required field in the wizard is a name for the new profile. We called ours `wjc-rhel`, the same as the simple hostname of the CE server machine, but the name is arbitrary and is for your own use should you create more than one.

The first choices you will make will be for the application server. Select **WAS 7.0** and remember to change the profile from the default `AppSrv01` to `AppSrv02`. Likewise, use port `8881` for the SOAP field instead of the WAS default of `8880`. The field for the **Application server cell** is a drop-down menu that should be populated automatically if you have supplied the correct information for the earlier fields. The administrator username and password are the credentials you use to logon to the WAS administrative console. Use the credentials you created when you installed WAS (we suggested `admin`), not the `was_admin` user ID that we will be using later.

This panel is also the place where you might encounter the Java problem mentioned above. When you have filled in all of the required fields, it's a good idea to use the **Test Connection** button before leaving the panel.

[ 77 ]

*Installing the Content Engine*

> If you want to make sure you configure `AppSrv02` and don't accidentally configure `AppSrv01`, you can shut down profile `AppSrv01` while you are doing this. If testing the connection works, you'll be confident you are connecting to the right place.

As seen in the following screenshot, the Configuration Manager does not save any passwords into files by default. That's the most secure behavior. You can change that via a tool preference in **Windows | Preferences**.

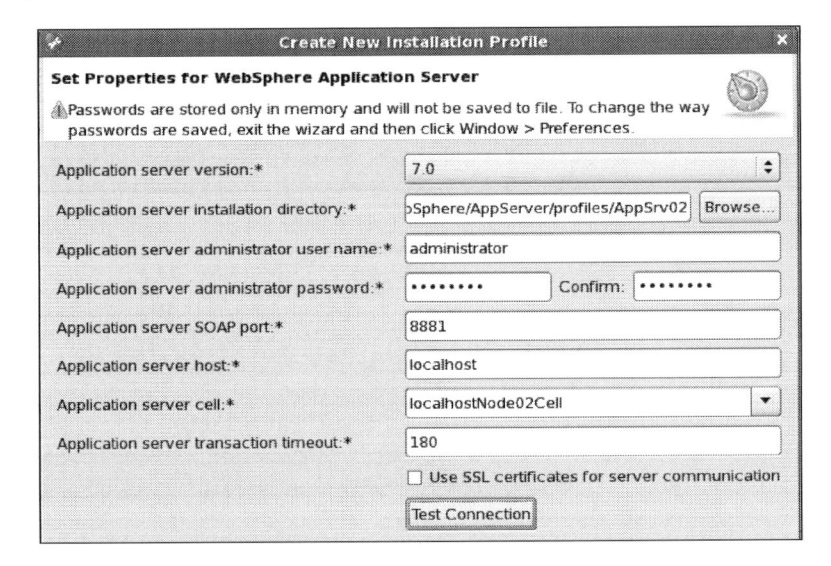

The panel that follows lists a series of checkboxes for tasks to include in the configuration. You want to select them all and click the **Finish** button. The wizard closes and your workbench will show your profile with a list of tasks under it in the **Content Engine Task View**.

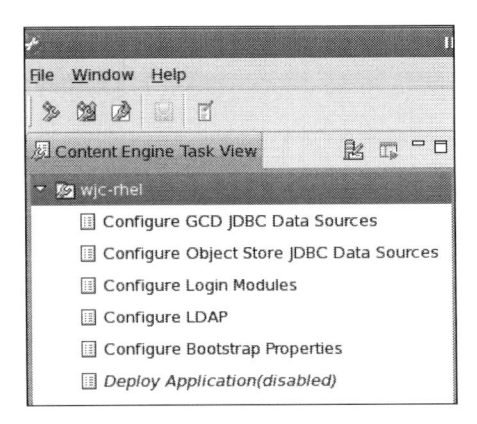

Although it's not required to do these tasks in the order listed, it's a reasonable order and we recommend following it. Most tasks in the list require some information from you. Right-click each one and select **Edit Selected Task** from the context menu. You can perform each task after supplying the information for it (right-click and select **Run Task** from the context menu), or you can run them all at once (via the toolbar button with the green triangle) after you have provided information for all of them. Our personal preference is to edit and run each task individually, but you can do it either way. As each task is completed successfully, its icon receives a small green checkmark decoration (a white checkmark inside a green circle).

You can accept the defaults offered for each task except where you are asked to provide required information and where we note below for LDAP configuration. You might like to change some things for reasons of style or memorability. For example, the default datasource name for the first Object Store is FNOSDS, but it's more memorable to change that to FNOSTORE1DS to remind yourself of the associated database name. If you have used the installation worksheet to gather information as you went along, providing the necessary information in these panels will be a piece of cake.

If you are doing what we did and creating additional Object Store databases, you can copy the **Configure Object Store JDBC Data Sources** task, give the copy a meaningful name (for that matter, you can give the original a suggestive name, like Configure OStore1 JDBC Data Sources), edit the associated information to point to the other database, and then execute the task.

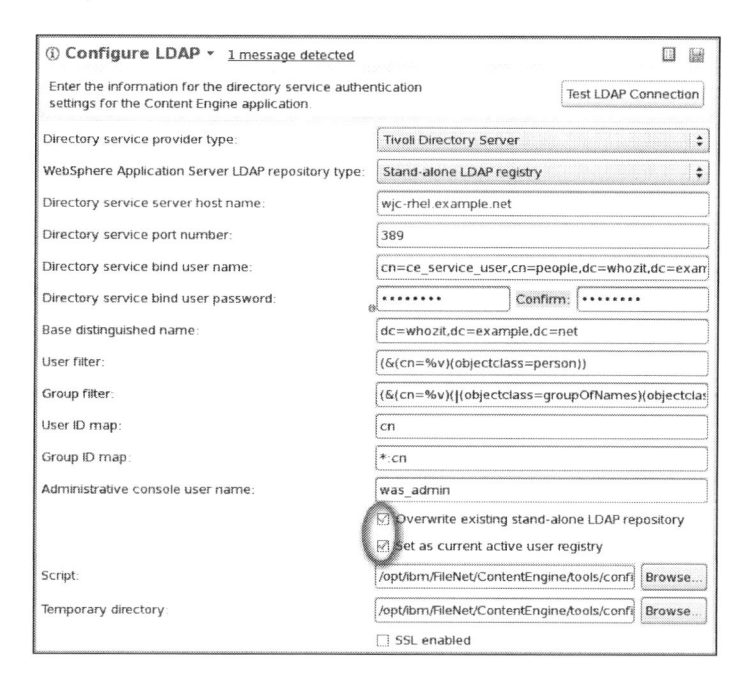

*Installing the Content Engine*

You will probably end up with your own favorite area, but, for us, the trickiest part is supplying values for the LDAP directory. This task is marrying the TDS data to WAS. In WAS jargon, the TDS instance will represent a Realm.

Consider the following points as you provide information for the **Configure LDAP** task:

- For the LDAP repository type, you want **Stand-alone LDAP registry**, if only because it's simpler to get it working. The **Federated repositories** choice is also supported, of course, but it has one or two more moving parts that can lead to unexpected complications. When you are more familiar with the environment, you might like to switch.

- For the **Directory service bind user name**, you must provide the full distinguished name. From our example above, that would be `cn=ce_service_user,cn=people,dc=whozit,dc=example,dc=net` (in contrast, use only the short name for the bootstrap user in the **Configure Bootstrap Properties** task coming up later; in our case, that's `ce_bootstrap_admin`).

- From our example directory, the **Base distinguished name** is `dc=whozit,dc=example,dc=net`. That's the most specific point in our directory hierarchy that includes both users and groups.

- Your directory service probably runs on port 389. If you select the use of TLS/SSL for directory lookups (common in production environments, but not really necessary for our all-in-one environment), be sure to change the port value to your directory's TLS/SSL port (probably port 636).

- For the **Administrative console user name**, use the short name `was_admin`. The Configuration Manager will be changing the repository used by our WAS profile. From this point forward, any WAS interactions will be done using identities and credentials from our TDS instance. After doing the **Configure LDAP** task, if you repeat any of the earlier steps that involve configuring WAS, be sure to switch the WAS console user from `admin` to `was_admin` and supply the appropriate password.

- Be sure that you do check the boxes for **Overwrite existing stand-alone LDAP repository** and **Set as current active user registry**.

> When manipulating authentication plumbing, be sure to double check all of your entries for typographical errors. It's very easy to mistype a combination of things that will leave you locked out of the WAS console. If it happens to you, you might feel a little frustrated, but all is not lost. Describing how to fix that is beyond our scope here, but you can find advice readily enough by doing an Internet search for `websphere admin console lockout`. You'll find you're not the first one. There is a good chance you will end up manually editing a configuration file called `security.xml` in the CE WAS profile directory tree.

After you have provided information and run all other tasks, your final task in the Configuration Manager will be **Deploy Application**. You will probably find this task marked as disabled, so after you have provided the necessary information, click the button in the upper-right corner to enable the task. For our environment, change the **Deployment type** to **Standard** (as opposed to **Cluster** or **Network Deployment**).

Assuming all went well, you can exit the Configuration Manager. Remaining steps for configuring a new Domain will be done via FEM after a quick stop in the WAS console of the CE WAS profile.

## WAS console tweaks

Although the Configuration Manager deploys the CE application into the application server, it is not started automatically (except for an upgrade case). Log into the WAS console.

- Navigate to **Security | Global Security**. Ensure that **Administrative security** and **Application security** are selected, and ensure that **Java 2 security** is *not* selected. Click **Apply** and save the changes.
- We sometimes find that the LDAP configuration changes we have done in the Configuration Manager did not take effect in WAS. We're not sure why that happens sometimes, but the cure is to go through similar steps directly in WAS. If you can restart your CE WAS profile and then log in with `was_admin` instead of `admin`, then the Configuration Manager changes were probably made properly. Conversely, if the opposite is true, you probably need to do the following manual steps:
    - We start by clicking on the **Security Configuration Report** button on the **Global Security** page. We look at the entries in the **User Registry** section to make sure they match the values we supplied earlier.

*Installing the Content Engine*

- We then click the **Security Configuration Wizard** button on that same page. If all the values agree with expectations, then we just cancel out of the **Summary** screen.

    **Summary**

    Displays the list of values that are selected during the wiza security.

    | Options | Values |
    |---|---|
    | Enable administrative security | true |
    | Enable application security | true |
    | Use Java 2 security to restrict application access to local resources | false |
    | User repository | Standalone LDAP registry |
    | Primary administrative user name | was_admin |
    | Type of LDAP server | IBM Tivoli Directory Server |
    | Host | localhost |
    | Port | 389 |
    | Base distinguished name (DN) | dc=whozit,dc=example,dc=net |
    | Bind distinguished name (DN) | cn=ce_service_user,cn=people |
    | Bind password | ******* |

- Again, from the **Global Security** page, go to the **User account repository** section. You should see the **Current realm definition** with a value of **Standalone LDAP registry**. If it is not, use the nearby drop-down menu to select that value, click the **Set as current** button, and then click **Apply**.

- Click the **Configure** button in the **User account repository** section and again check that the information presented there matches expectations (yes, we know, this is approximately our 73rd double check, but you can't be too careful). Under **Additional Properties**, select **Advanced Lightweight Directory Access Protocol (LDAP) user registry settings**. If you are not already familiar with LDAP filters and queries, the information on this page may seem a bit cryptic.

- If necessary, change the **User filter** value to (&(cn=%v)(objectclass=person)). Recall that our users in TDS had a structural object class of person and that we used the cn attribute to uniquely identify them.

[ 82 ]

- If necessary, change the **Group Filter** value to
  `(&(cn=%v)(|(objectclass=groupOfNames)
  (objectclass=groupOfUniqueNames)
  (objectclass=groupOfURLs)))`. Recall that our groups in
  TDS had a structural object class of `groupOfNames` and that
  we used the `cn` attribute to uniquely identify them. The group filter
  string here will recognize groups in that class and a couple of other
  commonly-used classes.
- If necessary, change the **User ID Map** value to `*:cn` as we are not
  using the `uid` attribute.
- Navigate to **Applications | Application Types | WebSphere
  enterprise applications**. You will see the CE application,
  named **FileNetEngine**, but it's status will show a red "x". Select
  **FileNetEngine** and click the **Start** button. The application will start
  and its status icon will change to a green arrow.

Stop and restart the CE WAS profile, and verify that you can log on to the WAS admin console with the `was_admin` user ID.

## Installing FEM

**FileNet Enterprise Manager (FEM)** is the main administrative tool for CM. It is intended for people concerned with installing, maintaining, troubleshooting, and upgrading CM. It is not a tool for the everyday user, and it assumes a certain familiarity with CM concepts and architecture that goes beyond mere familiarity with CM applications. In fact, FEM will generally refuse to do anything useful if you don't have privileges ordinarily considered the provenance of administrators. As the owner of this all-in-one installation, you will probably find yourself frequently using FEM to check out some detail of your system or to tweak some setting.

> Before we get started with the installation, we'd like to clear up one question that often comes up. Does FEM use some secret, internal "admin API"? No, it does not. FEM's communications with the CE ultimately use the same APIs that are available to every application writer. We won't go into the various layers that make up the FEM technology stack, but it definitely is using the CE .NET API underneath. Of course, as an application, FEM has in it a lot of logic for wizards, consistency checks, and user helpers that are not part of any CE API, but it does not have a secret back-channel to the server. In principle, any suitably motivated and skilled person or team could write an application just like FEM.

*Installing the Content Engine*

You must install FEM in order to complete the setup of the Domain. Unlike most of CM, FEM is a thick client that can only run on supported versions of Microsoft Windows. It is implemented as a snap-in to a framework called **Microsoft Management Console (MMC)**. Because it is Windows-only, we can't install it directly on our Linux server. If you were using a non-Windows server as a physical machine, you could run a Windows virtual machine if you didn't happen to have another suitable Windows machine handy. FEM is relatively decoupled from other CE software, so installing FEM on a typical desktop machine does not drag in an enormous pile of other pieces.

> CM 5.0 introduces a new tool called Administrative Console for CE (ACCE, pronounced like "ace"). It is a web-based client that is installed as part of the basic CE server installation. ACCE has limited initial features that will be expanded over several releases. Until ACCE reaches a suitable point of feature wealth, FEM will remain the primary administrative tool for CE.

The FEM installer is part of a combined CE server installation disk (or download). In CM 4.5.1, the CE Windows server installer is called `P8CE-4.5.1-WIN.EXE`. Run it like any typical Windows program. After installer start-up and splash-screen activity, you will be presented with the welcome screen for a step-by-step installation wizard. There are a few Windows-versus-Linux detail differences, but this installer is otherwise a lot like the installer we ran earlier to install the CE server. One big difference is that it has a functional **Choose Components** panel, as seen in the following screenshot. Select **FileNet Enterprise Manager** as a subcomponent of **.NET Clients**.

> For our installation, we will not be installing the **Content Engine Server** or **Tools** on Windows. Those things were already installed on Linux. It's easy to get carried away and just install everything without paying too much attention. So pay attention.

> If you don't already have Microsoft Windows **Web Services Extensions** (**WSE**) 3.0 installed, you'll get a warning about it. WSE 3.0 is not needed for the CE server. Along with Microsoft .NET Framework 2.0, it's only needed for applications using the CE .NET API, and that includes FEM. You should have no trouble finding WSE 3.0 on Microsoft's web site as a free download. Be sure to get version 3.0 and not an earlier version. You can install WSE before or after FEM, but you will not be able to do anything useful in FEM until WSE is installed.

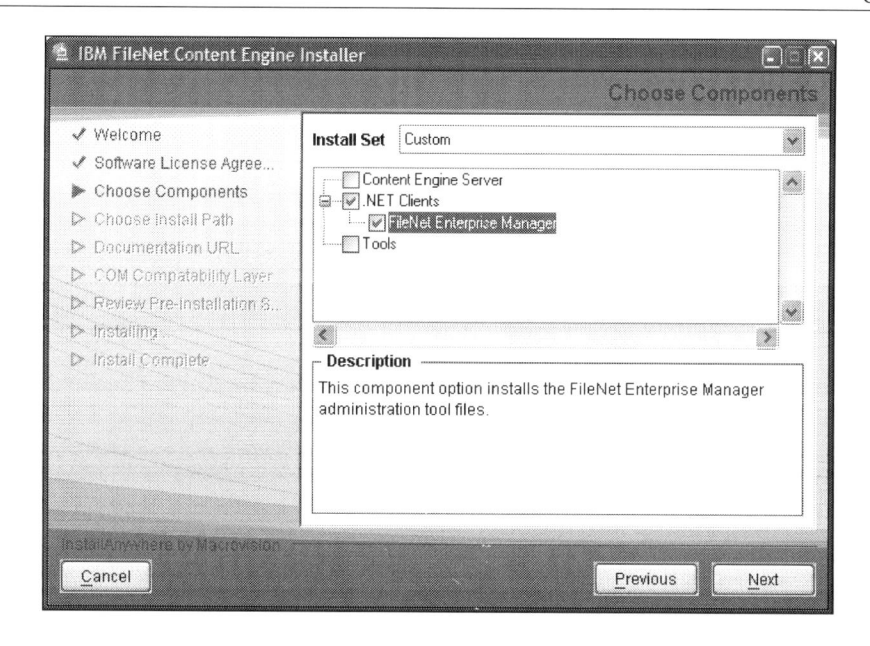

You'll eventually reach the prompt to **Specify Documentation URL**. If you have locally installed and deployed the downloadable documentation, you can supply that local URL. The documentation URL comes into play when you select a help link or button while running FEM, and it is also used for creating a Windows menu item and desktop shortcut for quick access to the documentation. Complete documentation for all of the CM components is available online from IBM's website `http://publib.boulder.ibm.com/infocenter/p8docs/v4r5m1/index.jsp`, so many sites forego installing the documentation locally. You can use the just-mentioned URL in the installation panel, or you can create your own bookmark or shortcut to it later.

Unless you have a legacy application which uses the CE COM API, which would be unusual, you can click past the panel that asks for the **COM Compatibility Layer** (**CCL**) server URL.

*Installing the Content Engine*

Once the installer has completed, you'll find an entry for FEM on the Windows **Start** menu and a shortcut for it on the desktop. Be sure that you have installed WSE 3.0, as noted above, before launching FEM. Without it, FEM will run, but it will be unable to connect to the CE.

FEM can connect to any number of CE servers in any number of Domains. You have to tell it where the CE is (the server URL) and, of course, supply login credentials. On your very first run of FEM, it won't know any of those things, and so you cannot get past the logon screen without adding at least one set of connectivity information.

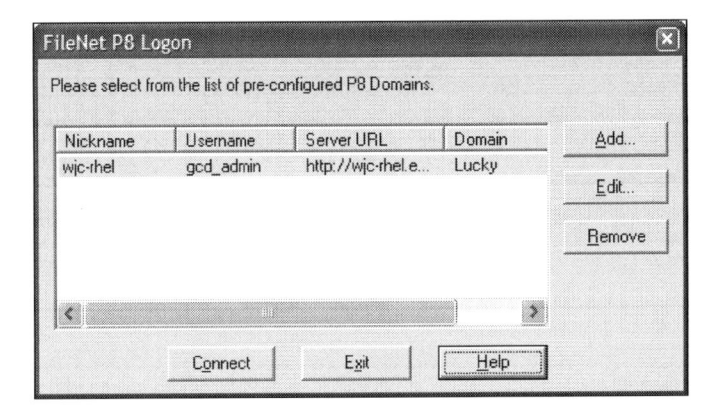

When you click the **Add** button, you'll see a configuration panel like the following, where you can enter connectivity details. Several fields are pre-populated. You are likely to only need to supply the **Nickname** and modify the **Server** and **Port** values for your local environment. Recall that our CE is running in a second profile in our WAS server, and all of the port numbers are shifted up by one from the default values. So, rather than take the WAS default of 9080 or 9443, change it to 9081 or 9444 for HTTP or HTTPS, respectively. Notice that you can change it either in the **Port** field or the **URL** field, and the other field is automatically adjusted.

[ 86 ]

> The **Connection** field offers choices of **http** and **https**. Even if your local security policy doesn't require it, it's a good idea to get in the habit of using **https** (in other words, a connection protected by TLS/SSL). Your CM data might not be particularly sensitive, but your administrator credentials are sent over that connection (except for the case of integrated login).

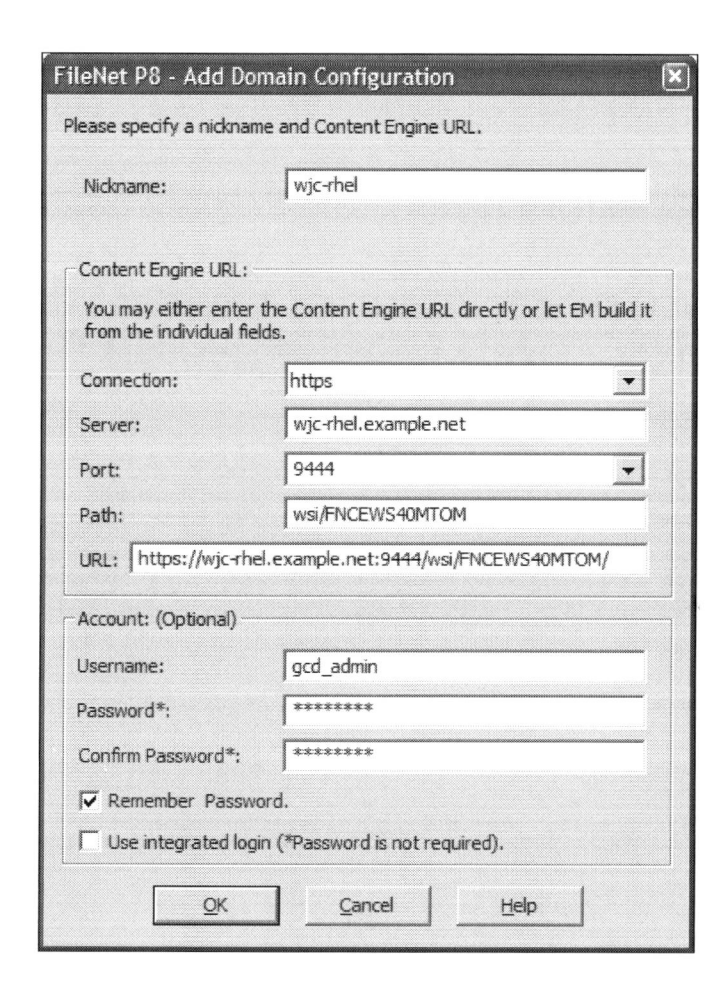

*Installing the Content Engine*

# Bringing up the P8 Domain

On your first FEM connection to the new CE installation, you will be guided through a series of steps that we informally call *Domain bring-up*. It's the final phase of configuration that leads to a functional Domain. The very first step in that is the choice of a name for the Domain. The Domain name doesn't show up in many places because the use of a given CE connection URL implies a particular Domain. So, you can call it pretty much anything you want. For our examples, we'll call our Domain `Lucky`.

The next step is the wizard for creating a directory configuration. Based on how much time we spent with directory data in the Configuration Manager and the WAS admin console, you could probably type this information in your sleep. The earlier steps were done so that WAS could do authentication. The CE steps are done so that the CE can resolve group memberships for authorization and also so it can service user and group searches done via CE APIs. We won't belabor the attribute values again, but the main configuration panel looks as follows:

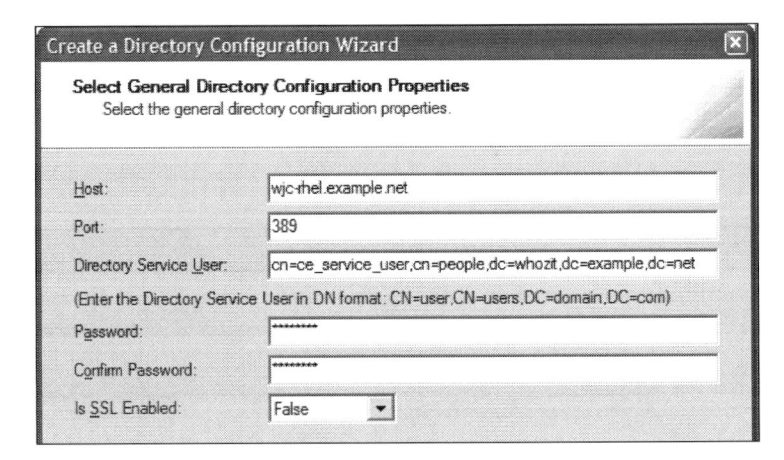

The user directory configuration properties look like this:

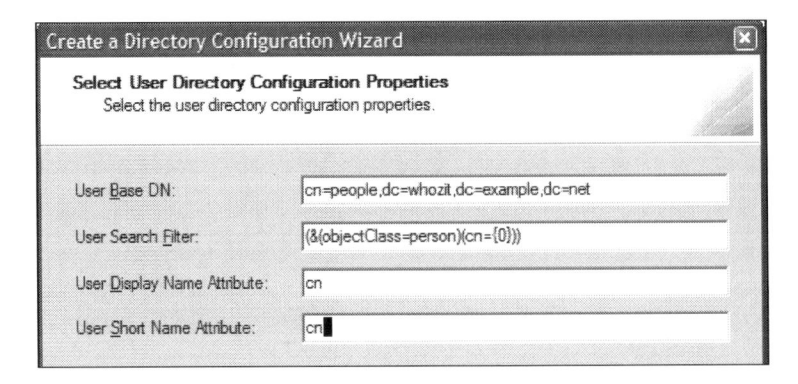

The group directory configuration properties look like this (the fields that can't be read because they are too long are just the defaults provided by the wizard).

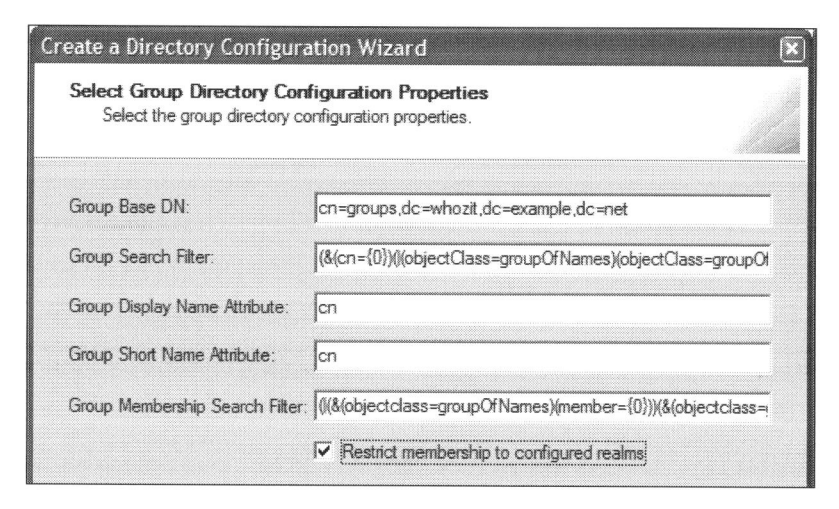

Notice that for the user and group base distinguished names, we were able to be more specific than we were earlier. That's because the CE makes a distinction between the configuration for a user search and for a group search, and we did not have to use a hierarchy level that was high enough to include them both.

The next wizard helps you set up the list of Domain administrators and the Domain permissions. The list of Domain administrators should be pre-populated with the information for the `gcd_admin` user ID. You can add other users or groups now, or you can add them later via FEM.

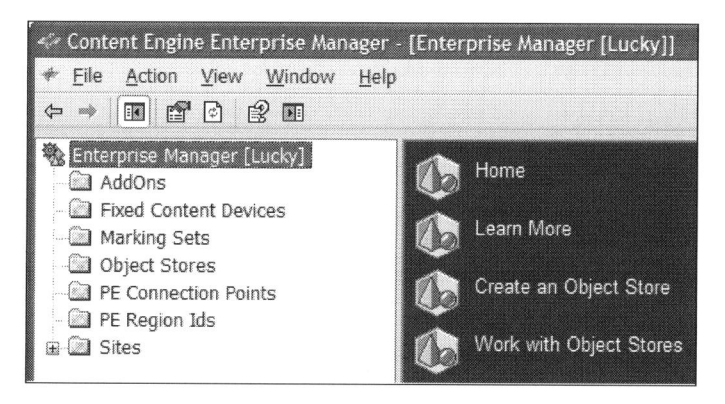

*Installing the Content Engine*

> Some people follow the questionable practice of using the `ce_bootstrap_admin` user for other purposes, including using it as the first user for connecting to the CE server and running the Domain bring-up steps. The P8 documentation warns against this, and we second that. The `ce_bootstrap_admin` user should not be used for anything other than the bootstrap configuration steps in the Configuration Manager.
>
> If you do use `ce_bootstrap_admin` for the Domain bring-up steps, that user will be the default Domain administrator account. You should definitely not allow that situation to persist. You will be using an account intended to have very low privileges for perhaps the most powerful role in the CM installation.
>
> `ce_bootstrap_admin` does need read access to the GCD (that is, the Domain object). FEM automatically creates an entry giving the pseudo-group `#AUTHENTICATED-USERS` read access to the GCD, and that should be sufficient as all users (including `ce_bootstrap_admin`) are automatically members of that pseudo-group. If you manually manipulate Domain permissions, be sure that `ce_bootstrap_admin` continues to have read access to the Domain, directly or via a group, and that it has no additional Domain privileges.

Finally, when that wizard is complete, you'll be greeted by the fully-opened FEM application. We still have some steps to do, but when you've gotten this far, you deserve to celebrate a little bit. Take a five minute break and we'll see you in the next section.

## Create an Object Store

Now that you are back from your long holiday break, let's create an Object Store. We already have a fully-functional Domain, but there isn't much in it. At this point, it's just a few tables in the `GCD` database we created earlier. We also created the `OSTORE1` database earlier, but it's still empty at this point. The wizard for creating an Object Store will guide us through the steps to flesh it out.

To launch the wizard, you can either click on the **Create an Object Store** link pictured above, or you can select the **Object Stores** node, right-click, and select **New Object Store** from the context menu. An Object Store has both a display name and a symbolic name, with the symbolic name having a restricted character set. They need not be the same, and they need not have any relationship to the name of the database nor the WAS datasources, though it is customary to align those names for bookkeeping convenience. We'll use the display name Object Store One and the symbolic name OStore1.

You'll recall that we created two datasources via the Configuration Manager—FNOSTORE1DS and FNOSTORE1DSXA. Supply those values when asked. The **Advanced** button on that wizard panel leads to some specialty database settings that are not of interest here.

For the default content store, you could select **Database Storage Area**. That would be fine for a small demo system like the one that we're creating, but it's not realistic for most production sites. Most (but not all) real-world content is stored in either a **File Storage Area** or a **Fixed Storage Area** (a reference to a specialized hardware device). Select **File Storage Area**. In the panel that follows, either type or browse to /p8filestores/fs1. Recall that we created that directory in *Chapter 2*. (Actually, as we didn't create an actual fileshare for that directory, you won't be able to browse to it. You will have to enter the name directly. It's a directory on the CE server machine, not the client machine where FEM is running.) You can take the defaults for the next panel that gives File Storage Area parameters.

The next few panels are concerned with establishing the initial security for the Object Store. The list of Object Store administrators should already be pre-populated with the gcd_admin user. Use the **Add** button and the search box to add the object_store_admin_group group. Recall that group includes the object_store_admin user, so it's not necessary to add that user individually.

For the initial users and groups who are allowed to connect to this Object Store, we want to be fairly lax for our demo system. Use the **Add** button and the search box to add the #AUTHENTICATED-USERS group. This is not a real group from the directory. It's a pseudo-group representing any authenticated user. In other words, anyone who can successfully log in via the TDS directory can connect to this Object Store. Finer-grained security can be used to restrict access to business objects. We'll cover that in *Chapter 8* when we talk at length about security.

*Installing the Content Engine*

The final step is the selection of AddOns to install into the Object Store. An AddOn is a collection of classes and properties, typically in support of some specific application. We would ordinarily caution you to select **Minimal Configuration** because it's easy to install additional AddOns later. For our all-in-one system, it's nice to have lots of things to look at, so click **Workplace/Workplace XT**, which selects almost all of the available AddOns.

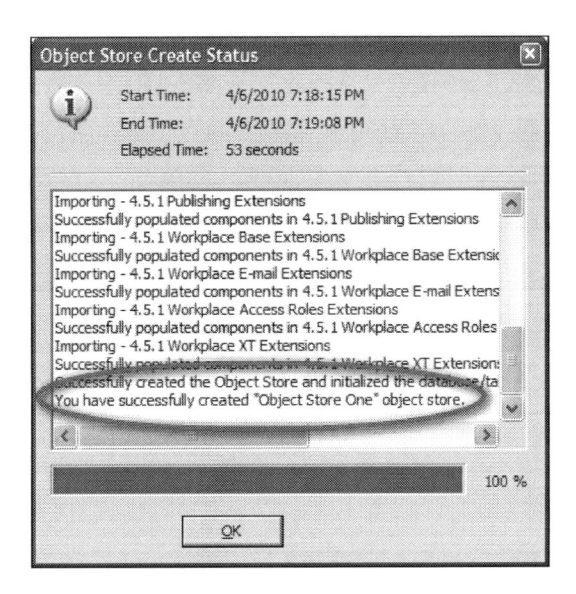

When you see the upbeat message in the figure above, your Object Store will be ready for use, and you will have reached the end of the journey for installing the CE. We'd suggest another five minute break to celebrate, but let's not get all crazy.

# Summary

In this chapter, we successfully installed the CE into an all-in-one environment. That built on top steps we did in *Chapter 2*; configuring the operating system, and installing and configuring a database system, a directory server, and a J2EE application server. Once the CE was installed and running, we installed the administrative tool, FEM, and used it to initialize our Domain and create our first Object Store.

Now that you've done all that once with most of the choices made for you, you can feel comfortable using the PPG and installation worksheet to try it with different software components or with different choices for things.

In the next chapter, we'll use FEM to explore some basic aspects of this CE system that is still bare bones at this point.

# 4
# Administrative Tools and Tasks

In *Chapters* 2 and 3, we spent quite a bit of effort to set up the environment and install the **Content Engine** (**CE**). In *Chapter 5*, we'll spend time installing additional components and tools to round out the **Content Manager** (**CM**) environment. Let's take a little break in this chapter and see some features of CM in action.

Although we will be using **FileNet Enterprise Manager** (**FEM**) to illustrate most of these features, remember that these are really features of the CE itself. As such, they are sometimes available in other tools and always available via the CE APIs. The point is not to show how to operate FEM itself, but to illustrate CM features. Because FEM is an administrator's tool, we'll concentrate mostly on administrative concepts and tasks.

Recall that FEM must run on a Microsoft Windows machine. Even if you are using virtual machine images or other isolated servers for your CM environment, you might wish to install FEM on a normal Windows desktop machine for your own convenience.

In this chapter, we'll cover:

- A discussion of the P8 Domain and what's in it
- How to use topology levels to configure your environment
- A discussion of the objects that reside directly within a Domain
- A discussion of an Object Store and what's in it
- A example of creating a custom class and adding custom properties to it

*Administrative Tools and Tasks*

# Domain and GCD

Here's a simple question: what is a P8 Domain? It's easy to give a simple answer—it's the top-level container of all P8 things in a given installation. That needs a little clarification, though, because it seems a little circular; things are in a Domain because a Domain knows about them.

In a straightforward technical sense, things are in the same Domain if they share the same **Global Configuration Database (GCD)**. The GCD is, literally, a database. We created and configured a GCD as part of the installation steps in *Chapters 2 and 3*. There, we were only concerned about a single CE server. If we were installing additional CE servers, they would share that GCD if we wanted them to be part of the same Domain.

When you first open FEM and look at the tree view in the left-hand panel, most of the things you are looking at are things at the Domain level. We'll be referring to the FEM tree view often, and we're talking about the left-hand part of the user interface, as seen in the following screenshot:

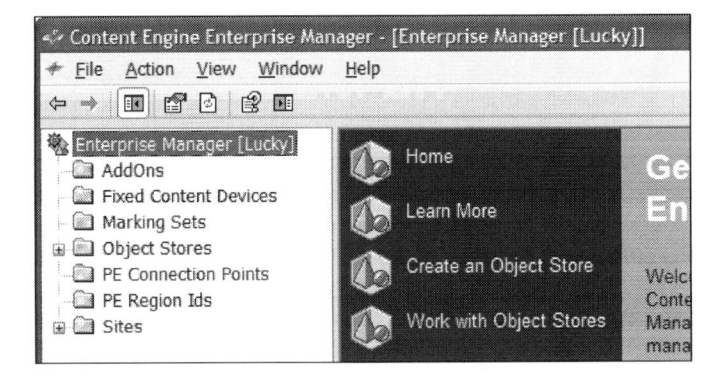

> FEM remembers the state of the tree view from session to session. When you start FEM the next time, it will try to open the nodes you had open when you exited. That will often mean something of a delay as it reads extensive data for each open Object Store node. You might find it a useful habit to close up all of the nodes before you exit FEM.

Most things within a Domain know about and can connect directly to each other, and nothing in a given Domain knows about any other Domain.

The GCD, and thus the Domain, contains:

- Simple properties of the Domain object itself
- Domain-level objects
- Configuration objects for more complex aspects of the Domain environment
- Pointers to other components, both as part of the CE environment and external to it

It's a little bit subjective as to which things are objects and which are pointers to other components. It's also a little bit subjective as to what a configuration object is for something and what a set of properties is of that something. Let's not dwell on those philosophical subtleties. Let's instead look at a more specific list:

- **Properties**: These simple properties control the behavior of or describe characteristics of the Domain itself.
    - **Name and ID**: Like most P8 objects, a Domain has both a Name and an ID. It's counterintuitive, but you will rarely need to know these, and you might even sometimes forget the name of your own Domain. The reason is that you will always be connecting to some particular CE server, and that CE server is a member of exactly one Domain. Therefore, all of the APIs related to a Domain object are able to use a defaulting mechanism that means "the current Domain".
    - **Database schemas**: There are properties containing the database schemas for an Object Store for each type of database supported by P8. CM uses this schema, which is an actual script of SQL statements, by default when first fleshing out a new Object Store to create tables and columns. Interestingly, you can customize the schema when you perform the Object Store creation task (either via FEM or via the API), but you should not do so on a whim.
    - **Permissions**: The Domain object itself is subject to access controls, and so it has a Permissions property. The actual set of access rights available is specific to Domain operations, but it is conceptually similar to access control on other objects.
- **Domain-level objects**: A few types of objects are contained directly within the Domain itself. We'll talk about configuration objects in a minute, but there are a couple of non-configuration objects in the Domain.
    - **AddOns**: An AddOn is a bundle of metadata representing the needs of a discrete piece of functionality that is not built into the CE server. Some are provided with the product, and others are provided by third parties. An AddOn must first be created, and it is then available in the GCD for possible installation in one or more Object Stores.

- ○ **Marking Sets**. Marking Sets are a Mandatory Access Control mechanism, which we'll discuss in *Chapter 8, Security Features and Planning*. Individual markings can be applied to objects in an Object Store, but the overall definition resides directly under Domain so that they may be applied uniformly across all Object Stores.

- **Configuration objects**:
  - ○ **Directories**: All CM authentication and authorization ultimately comes down to data obtained from an LDAP directory. Some of those lookups are done by the application server, and some are done directly by the CE server. The directory configuration objects tell the CE server how to communicate with that directory or directories.
  - ○ **Subsystem configurations**: There are several logical subsystems within the CE that are controlled by their own flavors of subsystem configuration objects. Examples include trace logging configuration and CSE configuration. These are typically configured at the domain level and inherited by lower level topology nodes. A description of topology nodes is coming up in the next section of this chapter.

- **Pointers to components**:
  - ○ **Content Cache Areas**: The Domain contains configuration information for content caches, which are handy for distributed deployments.
  - ○ **Rendition Engines**: The Domain contains configuration and connectivity information for separately installed Rendition Engines (sometimes called publishing engines).
  - ○ **Fixed Content Devices**: The domain contains configuration and connectivity information for external devices and federation sources for content.
  - ○ **PE Connection Points and Isolated Regions**: The domain contains configuration and connectivity information for the Process Engine.
  - ○ **Object Stores**: The heart of the CE ecosystem is the collection of ObjectStores.
  - ○ **Text Search Engine**: The Domain contains configuration and connectivity information for a separately-installed Content Search Engine.

In addition to the items directly available in the tree view shown above, most of the remainder of the items contained directly within the Domain are available one way or another in the pop-up panel you get when you right-click on the Domain node in FEM and select **Properties**.

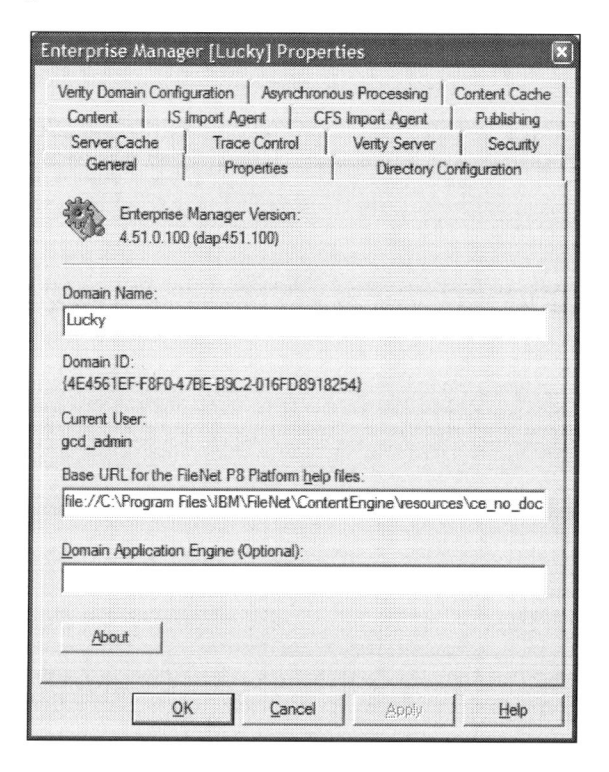

![Enterprise Manager [Lucky] Properties dialog showing the General tab with Enterprise Manager Version 4.51.0.100 (dap451.100), Domain Name "Lucky", Domain ID {4E4561EF-F8F0-47BE-B9C2-016FD8918254}, Current User gcd_admin, and Base URL file://C:\Program Files\IBM\FileNet\ContentEngine\resources\ce_no_doc]

> The pop-up panel **General** tab contains FEM version information. The formatting may look a little strange because the CM release number, including any fix packs, and build number are mapped into the Microsoft scheme for putting version info into DLL properties. In the previous figures, **4.51.0.100** represents CM 4.5.1.0, build 100. That's reinforced by the internal designation of the build number, **dap451.100**, in parentheses. Luckily, you don't really have to understand this scheme. You may occasionally be asked to report the numbers to IBM support, but a faithful copying is all that is required.

## Topology levels

There is an explicit hierarchical topology for a Domain. It shows up most frequently when configuring subsystems. For example, CE server trace logging can be configured at any of the topology levels, with the most specific configuration settings being used. What we mean by that should be clearer once we've explained how the topology levels are used. You can see these topology levels in the expanded tree view in the left-hand side of FEM in the following screenshot:

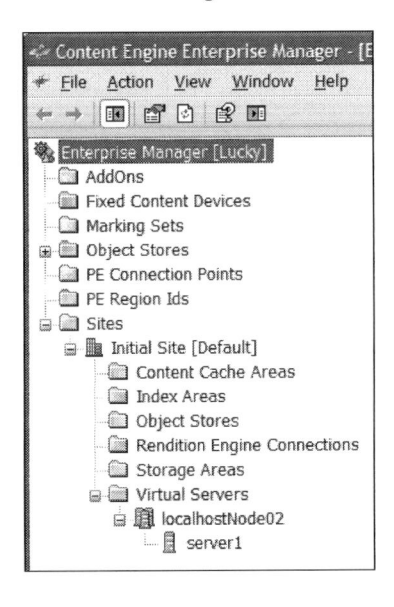

At the highest level of the hierarchy is the **Domain**, discussed in the previous section. It corresponds to all of the components in the CE part of the CM installation.

Within a domain are one or more **sites**. The best way to think of a site is as a portion of a Domain located in a particular geographic area. That matters because networked communications differ in character between geographically separate areas when compared to communications within an area. The difference in character is primarily due to two factors—latency and bandwidth. Latency is a characterization of the amount of time it takes a packet to travel from one end of a connection to another. It takes longer for a network packet to travel a long distance, both because of the laws of physics and because there will usually be more network switching and routing components in the path. Bandwidth is a characterization of how much information can be carried over a connection in some fixed period of time. Bandwidth is almost always more constrained over long distances due to budgetary or capacity limits. Managing network traffic traveling between geographic areas is an important planning factor for distributed deployments.

A site contains one or more **virtual servers**. A virtual server is a collection of CE servers that act functionally as if they were a single server (from the point of view of the applications). Most often, this situation comes about through the use of clustering or farming for high availability or load balancing reasons. A site might contain multiple virtual servers for any reason that makes sense to the enterprise. Perhaps, for example, the virtual servers are used to segment different application mixes or user populations.

A virtual server contains one or more **servers**. A server is a single, addressable CE server instance running in a J2EE application server. These are sometimes referred to as physical servers, but in the 21st century that is often not literally true. The CE that we installed into a WAS profile in *Chapter 3, Installing the Content Engine* corresponds to a server in this sense. In terms of running software, the only things that tangibly exist are individual CE servers. There is no independently-running piece of software that is the Domain or GCD. There is no separate piece of software that is an Object Store (except in the sense that it's a database mediated by the RDBMS software). All CE activity happens in a CE server.

There may be other servers running software in CM—Process Engine, Content Search Engine, Rendition Engine, and Application Engine. The previous paragraph is just trying to clarify that there is no piece of running software representing the topology levels other than the server. You don't have to worry about runtime requests being handed off to another level up or down the topological hierarchy.

Not every installation will have the need to distinguish all of those topology levels. In our all-in-one installation, the Domain contains a single site. That site was created automatically during installation and is conventionally called `Initial Site`, though we could change that if we wanted to. The site contains a single virtual server, and that virtual server contains a single server.

This is typical for a development or demo installation, but you should be able to see how it could be expanded with the defined topology levels to any size deployment, even to a deployment that is global in scope. You could use these different topology levels for a scheme other than the one just described; the only downside would be that nobody else would understand your deployment terms.

## Using topology levels

We mentioned previously that many subsystems can be configured at any of the levels. Although it's most common to do domain-wide configuration, you might, for example, want to enable trace logging on a single CE server for some troubleshooting purpose. When interpreting subsystem configuration data, the CE server first looks for configuration data for the local CE server (that is, itself). If any is found, it is used. Otherwise, the CE server looks for configuration data for the containing virtual server, then the containing site, and then the Domain. Where present, the most specific configuration data is used.

> A set of configuration data, if used, is used as the complete configuration. That is, the configuration objects at different topology levels are not blended to create an "effective configuration".

CE has a feature called request forwarding. Because the conversation between the CE server and the database holding an Object Store is chattier than the conversation between CE clients and the CE server, there can be a performance benefit to having requests handled by a CE server that is closer, in networking terms, to that database. When a CE server forwards a request internally to another CE server, it uses a URL configured on a virtual server. The site object holds the configuration options for whether CE servers can forward requests and whether they can accept forwarded requests.

Sites are the containers for content cache areas, text index areas, Rendition Engine connections, storage areas, and Object Stores. That is, each of those things is associated with a specific site.

## Exploring Domain-level items

Let's spend a little time looking in more detail at some of the Domain objects. In the APIs and some documentation, these are sometimes called non-repository objects to distinguish them from objects that reside within a repository, that is, an Object Store. These objects are primarily of interest to an administrator and are seldom manipulated by end-user applications. We saw several of these during the initial Domain bring-up in *Chapter 3*. We'll look at some others here.

There are two common ways to access these objects and dialog boxes in FEM. Some are accessed directly from the tree view in the left-hand side, sometimes by right-clicking and selecting from the context menu. Others are available via the multi-tabbed pop-up dialog when you select **Properties** from the context menu of the Domain node in the tree-view.

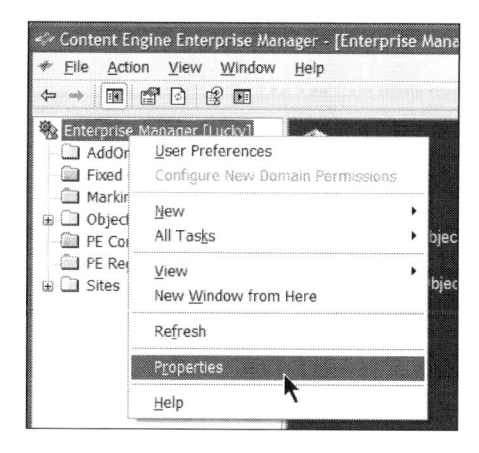

As is generally the pattern in FEM, everything in the Domain is available, though in more of a self-guided form, if you select the **Properties** tab on that pop-up panel. This property sheet, available for most objects, lets you view or edit individual properties of the object. It is always the case that the CE server is the enforcer of things like allowable property values, security access, and referential integrity. FEM is sophisticated, but it's still just a client application. FEM cannot allow you to violate CE rules, although it cannot always prevent you from doing unwise things. The following screenshot is the dialog box that opens after you select **Properties** as shown in the previous screenshot:

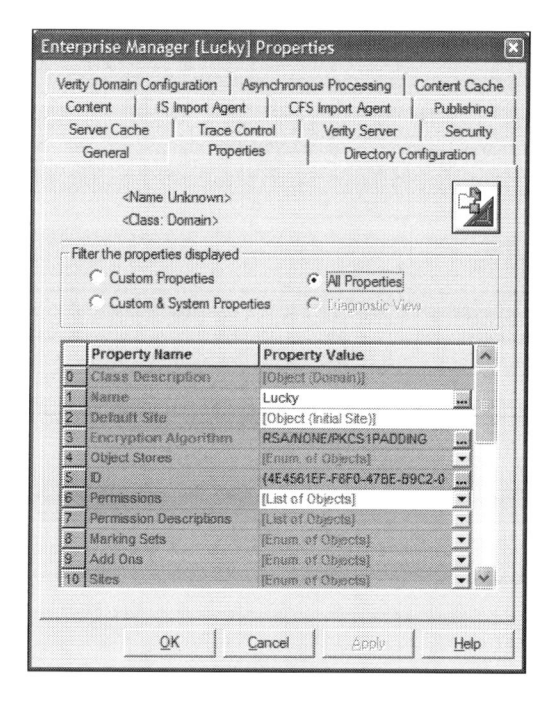

# AddOns

An AddOn is a CE packaging mechanism containing metadata (and possibly instance data) for an Object Store. An AddOn is expected to represent things needed for some discrete application or piece of functionality, but that's not enforced. AddOns are *created* in the GCD but are *installed* into individual Object Stores.

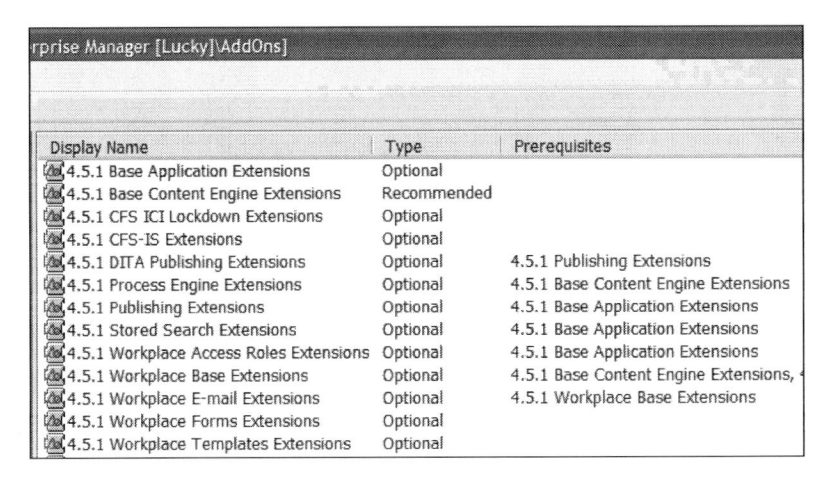

| Display Name | Type | Prerequisites |
| --- | --- | --- |
| 4.5.1 Base Application Extensions | Optional | |
| 4.5.1 Base Content Engine Extensions | Recommended | |
| 4.5.1 CFS ICI Lockdown Extensions | Optional | |
| 4.5.1 CFS-IS Extensions | Optional | |
| 4.5.1 DITA Publishing Extensions | Optional | 4.5.1 Publishing Extensions |
| 4.5.1 Process Engine Extensions | Optional | 4.5.1 Base Content Engine Extensions |
| 4.5.1 Publishing Extensions | Optional | 4.5.1 Base Application Extensions |
| 4.5.1 Stored Search Extensions | Optional | 4.5.1 Base Application Extensions |
| 4.5.1 Workplace Access Roles Extensions | Optional | 4.5.1 Base Application Extensions |
| 4.5.1 Workplace Base Extensions | Optional | 4.5.1 Base Content Engine Extensions, |
| 4.5.1 Workplace E-mail Extensions | Optional | 4.5.1 Workplace Base Extensions |
| 4.5.1 Workplace Forms Extensions | Optional | |
| 4.5.1 Workplace Templates Extensions | Optional | |

If you click the **AddOns** node in the tree, you will see a list of AddOns available in the GCD. All of the AddOns you see in the screenshot are provided with CM, but additional AddOns may be present in any installation because AddOns can be created via the CE APIs.

In addition to being **Recommended** or **Optional**, an AddOn may have **Pre-requisites**. The CE server will not let you install an AddOn into an Object Store unless its prerequisites are installed, either beforehand or concurrently.

There is a mechanism for superseding an AddOn with an updated version, but AddOns cannot be uninstalled from an Object Store once installed. You will therefore want to consider carefully before installing an AddOn into an Object Store. A step near the end of the wizard for creating an Object Store offers to install AddOns for you, but you can also install them at any later time (by right-clicking an individual Object Store node and navigating to **All Tasks | Install AddOn**). The `Base Content Engine Extensions` AddOn should always be installed into a new Object Store as most applications depend on the few things it provides (for example, the custom property `DocumentTitle`). For any other AddOn, we suggest you avoid installing it at Object Store creation time unless you are sure you will actually need it.

# Fixed Content Devices

Document content can be stored in the Object Store database, a traditional filesystem, or in what CM calls a Fixed Content Device (FCD). The term FCD includes vendor-provided devices that do not allow changes to content once it is written, but the name is arguably a slight misnomer because it also includes federated content sources. From the point of view of the CE server, none of these devices allow updates to content files.

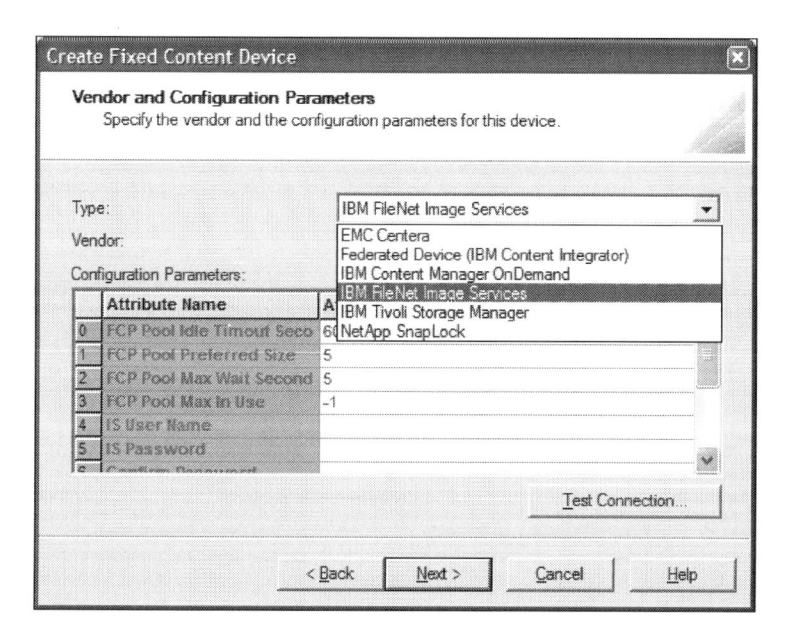

Before you can use any FCD from an Object Store, you must first register it in the GCD so that the CE server will know how to communicate with it. If you right-click on the **Fixed Content Devices** node in the FEM tree view and select **New Fixed Content Device**, a wizard will walk you through the steps of configuring connectivity to the FCD. The configuration parameters that are needed vary with the device type.

# Server Cache configuration

The **Server Cache** tab gives you control over the characteristics of several caches maintained internally by the CE server. As you can probably tell from the names of the items and the general subject of caching, the values set here can have a dramatic impact on performance. The purpose of each of these items is described in the P8 product documentation.

## Administrative Tools and Tasks

> You shouldn't change these values recklessly. The default values are chosen to be reasonable for most use cases, though circumstances do vary. The same advice applies for other performance tuning settings described in this chapter.
>
> Specific changes will sometimes be recommended by IBM support in response to specific situations. There is also some guidance for appropriate values in the *FileNet P8 Performance Tuning Guide*.

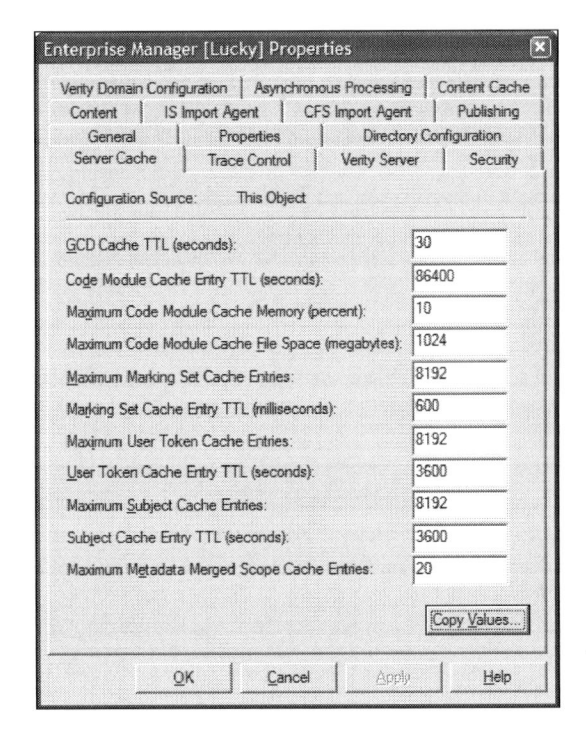

| Enterprise Manager [Lucky] Properties | |
|---|---|
| Verity Domain Configuration / Asynchronous Processing / Content Cache | |
| Content / IS Import Agent / CFS Import Agent / Publishing | |
| General / Properties / Directory Configuration | |
| Server Cache / Trace Control / Verity Server / Security | |
| Configuration Source: This Object | |
| GCD Cache TTL (seconds): | 30 |
| Code Module Cache Entry TTL (seconds): | 86400 |
| Maximum Code Module Cache Memory (percent): | 10 |
| Maximum Code Module Cache File Space (megabytes): | 1024 |
| Maximum Marking Set Cache Entries: | 8192 |
| Marking Set Cache Entry TTL (milliseconds): | 600 |
| Maximum User Token Cache Entries: | 8192 |
| User Token Cache Entry TTL (seconds): | 3600 |
| Maximum Subject Cache Entries: | 8192 |
| Subject Cache Entry TTL (seconds): | 3600 |
| Maximum Metadata Merged Scope Cache Entries: | 20 |

Near the bottom right corner is a button labeled **Copy Values**. This is a general mechanism that you will see in several of the configuration panels. We mentioned earlier that many subsystem configurations could be set at the domain, site, virtual server, or server levels, with the more specific entries being used. The **Copy Values** button gives a convenient way to copy a set of configuration values from one of those other topology nodes to this node. If you click the button, you will see a pop-up panel that lets you navigate to any node from which you wish to copy values.

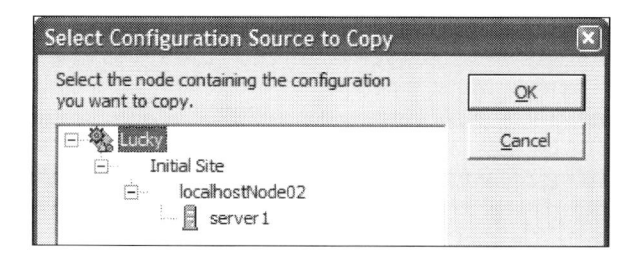

## Content configuration

The **Content** tab contains settings for tuning the behavior of background operations for content uploads, downloads, and related movements. Compared to other kinds of updates, content uploads (from the client to the CE server) can take a long time to complete. The CE server and APIs avoid transaction timeout issues by arranging to upload the content outside of the transaction that actually commits the content to the repository. Under some circumstances, content is uploaded in chunks that must be reassembled for final storage.

Both of these things lead to a certain amount of behind-the-scenes bookkeeping, background processing, and clean-up. The settings on this tab tune the performance and behavior of that background activity.

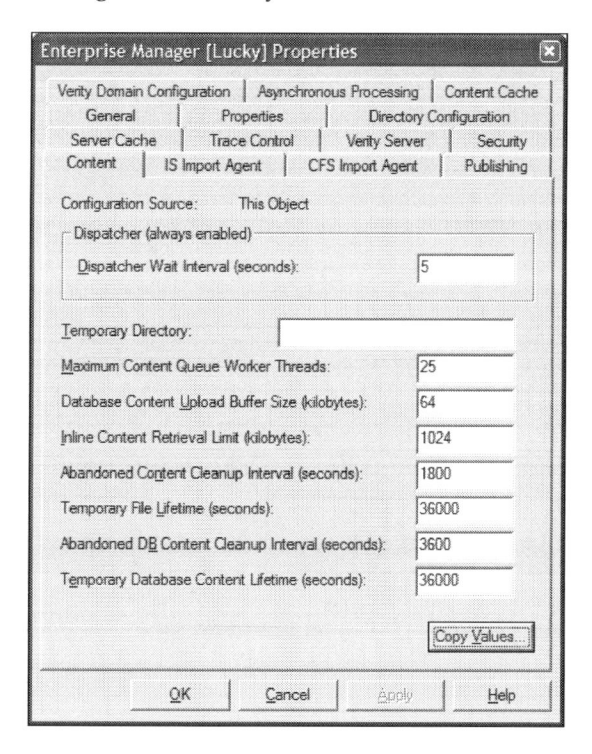

Administrative Tools and Tasks

This panel has the **Copy Values** button that we noted earlier. Another thing to notice, directly under the tabs, is the information **Configuration Source: This Object**. If you looked at the same tab on the site, virtual server, or server topology node, you would see similar text indicating that the configuration came from the Domain level, and all of the input boxes would be disabled. That's a handy way of seeing where the configuration actually lives and whether or not you have overridden the higher-level configuration at a particular topology node. In contrast, the figure below shows the Content tab for server server1.

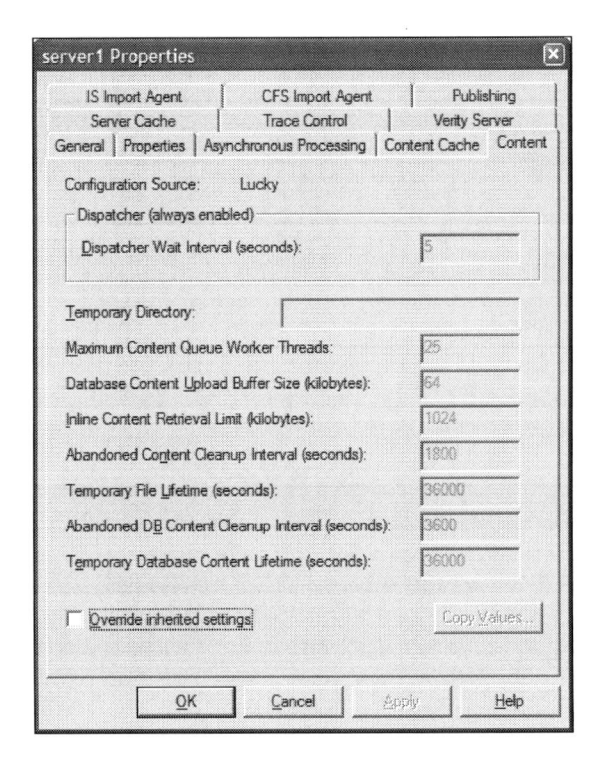

## Trace logging

The CE server writes two kinds of log files. The error log file is for important exceptions and is always enabled. The trace log file is for troubleshooting and has to be specifically enabled. The **Trace Control** tab is for configuring tracing inside the CE server.

> Although similar technologies are used to provide trace logging in the client APIs, the configuration mechanisms are completely separate. The panels in FEM control only tracing within the CE server and do not apply to any client tracing.

The trace log files themselves are intended for use by IBM support personnel. The formats and meanings of the trace log files, therefore, are not precisely documented and often change from release to release. Also, the contents of trace log files are not localized in the way that other IBM components are. You will generally be enabling trace logging under the direction of IBM support, in which case they will tell you specific things to enable.

You may become familiar with some of the contents of trace log files in the natural course of events, and you may decide to gather trace log files for your own purposes. There's nothing wrong with that, but there are a few important things to remember:

- Trace logging can be very verbose in the output it produces. It's generally a good strategy to start with a minimal amount of trace logging and add to it to widen your diagnostic search. Even the most obvious diagnostic clues can be missed when buried amidst tons of irrelevant material.
- Trace logging can have a significant performance impact on the CE server. This is not just because of the volume of logged output that has to be written. When trace logging is enabled, conditional code in the CE server will sometimes do additional lookups, calculations, and other expensive operations to create the logged entries.

Let's look at the **Trace Control** tab for configuring trace logging:

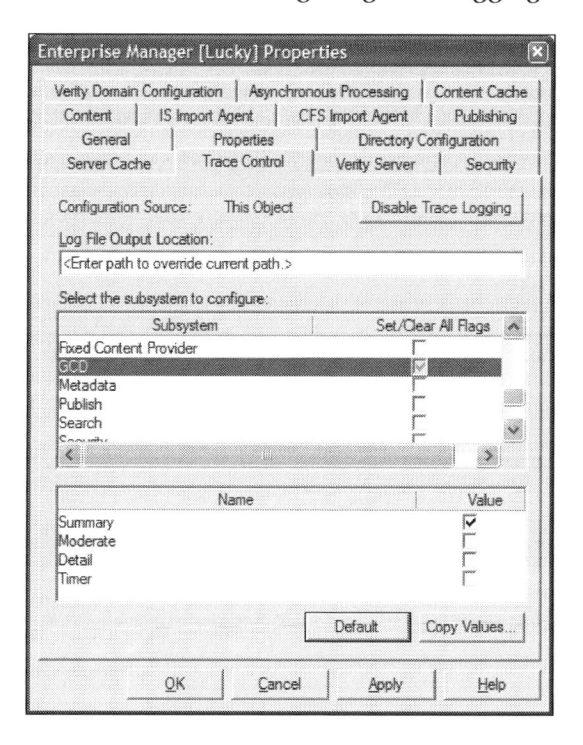

Trace logging is organized in two ways:

- There are functional subsystems that can be individually enabled or disabled. The names of these subsystems are suggestive (and documented in the P8 product documentation). When troubleshooting a particular situation, it is very rare to need to select more than a handful of subsystems. IBM support will often request logging for only one or two subsystems.
- There are different levels of verbosity: **Summary**, **Moderate**, **Detail**, and **Timer**. Although the user interface makes it look like these verbosity levels are strictly hierarchical (if you select **Detail**, the user interface will automatically select **Moderate** and **Summary**), they are actually independent. Nevertheless, you will always want to select a verbosity level and all of the less verbose levels.

The figure above shows an example where trace logging has been enabled for the **GCD** subsystem at the **Summary** level. It's common to have to do trace logging in multiple sessions when diagnosing elusive problems. For more elaborate trace logging configurations, it can be an annoyance to re-create the configuration each time. The trace logging subsystem has a feature that allows you to have trace logging configured but completely disabled. That's what the **Disable Trace Logging** button is for.

> If you find that performance still drags or that the trace log file continues to grow even after you have disabled trace logging in the Domain configuration, it could be that trace logging is still configured at a more specific level. That's very easy to overlook, especially in more complex deployments or where CM administration duties are shared.

By default, CE server trace log files are written to an application server-specific directory. Unfortunately, the FEM configuration panel won't tell you what the default location is, so you'll have to consult the product documentation. For example, on our WAS setup, the trace log files are written to `/opt/ibm/WebSphere/AppServer/profiles/AppSrv02/FileNet/server1/p8_server_trace.log`. You can specify a different location for the trace log files by supplying a value for that field. Remember, the location is from the CE server's point of view, not the local filesystem of the machine where FEM is running.

## Content cache

The final domain level feature we'll look at is content caching. Content caching is a CE feature useful in geographically distributed deployments. It enables you to have a transient local copy of document content while the true master copy is stored at a distant site. Although the content is a cached copy, the CE server always performs the normal security access checks and also guarantees that an application will not be seeing a stale copy of the content from the cache. A content cache is affiliated with a specific site, but the configuration of cache tuning parameters can be done for a site or on a domain-wide basis.

# Exploring Object Store-level Items

Let's turn our attention now to the Object Store and things inside it. Since an Object Store is a repository, things that reside inside an Object Store are called **repository objects**. It's a slightly technical point, but the Object Store itself is not a repository object.

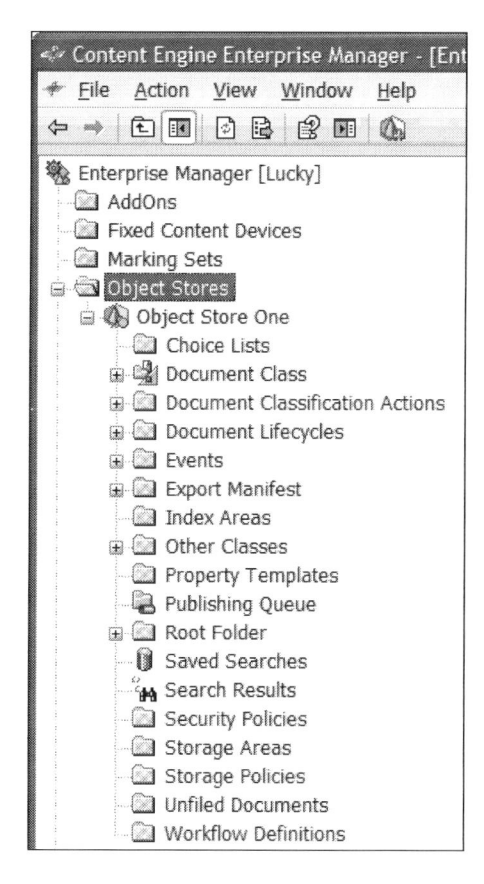

*Administrative Tools and Tasks*

As with the Domain, there are two basic paths in FEM to accessing things in an Object Store. The tree-view in the left-hand panel can be expanded to show Object Stores and many repository objects within them, as illustrated in the screenshot above. Each individual Object Store has a right-click context menu. Selecting **Properties** from that menu will bring up a multi-tabbed pop-up panel. We'll look first at the **General** tab of that panel.

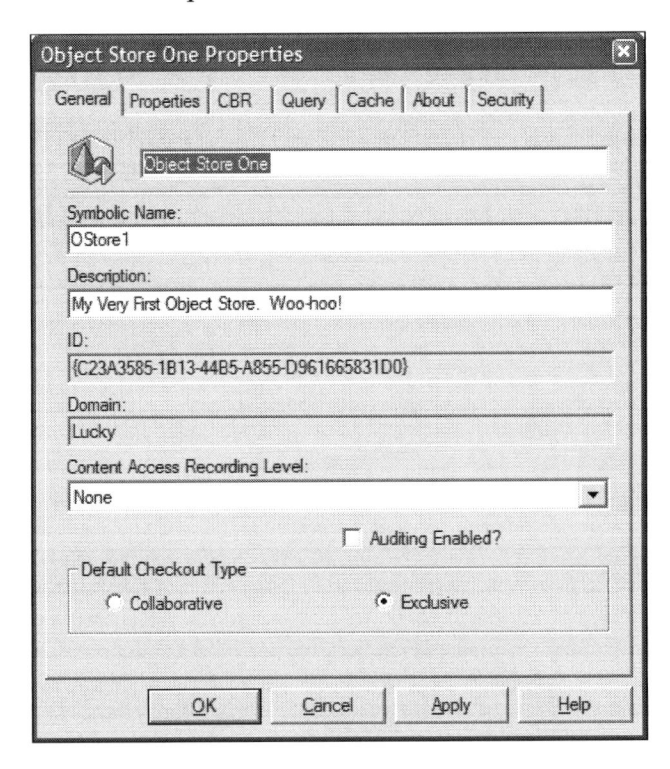

## Content Access Recording Level

Ordinarily, the CE server does not keep track of when a particular document's content was last retrieved because it requires an expensive database update that is often uninteresting. The ContentAccessRecordingLevel property on the Object Store can be used to enable the recording of this optional information in a document or annotation's DateContentLastAccessed property. It is off by default.

It is sometimes interesting to know, for example, that document content was accessed within the last week as opposed to three years ago. Once a particular document has had its content read, there is a good chance that there will be a few additional accesses in the same neighborhood of time (not for a technical reason; rather, it's just statistically likely). Rather than record the last access time for each access, an installation can choose, via this property's value, to have access times recorded only with a granularity of hourly or daily. This can greatly reduce the number of database updates while still giving a suitable approximation of the last access time. There is also an option to update the `DateContentLastAccessed` property on every access.

## Auditing

The CE server can record when clients retrieve or update selected objects. Enabling that involves setting up subscriptions to object instances or classes. This is quite similar to the event subsystem in the CE server that we'll describe in *Chapter 7, Major CM Features*. Because it can be quite elaborate to set up the necessary auditing configuration, it can also be enabled or disabled completely at the Object Store level.

## Checkout type

The CE server offers two document checkout types, **Collaborative** and **Exclusive**. The difference lies in who is allowed to perform the subsequent checkin. An exclusive checkout will only allow the same user to do the checkin. Via an API, an application can make the explicit choice for one type or the other, or it can use the Object Store default value. Using the default value is often handy since a given application may not have any context for deciding one form over another.

> Even with a collaborative checkout, the subsequent checkin is still subject to access checks, so you can still have fine-grained control over that. In fact, because you can use fine-grained security to limit who can do a checkin, you might as well make the Object Store default be Collaborative unless you have some specific use case that demands Exclusive.

*Administrative Tools and Tasks*

# Text Index Date Partitioning

Most of the values on the **CBR** tab, as shown in the figure next, are read-only because they are established when the **Content Search Engine** (CSE) is first set up.

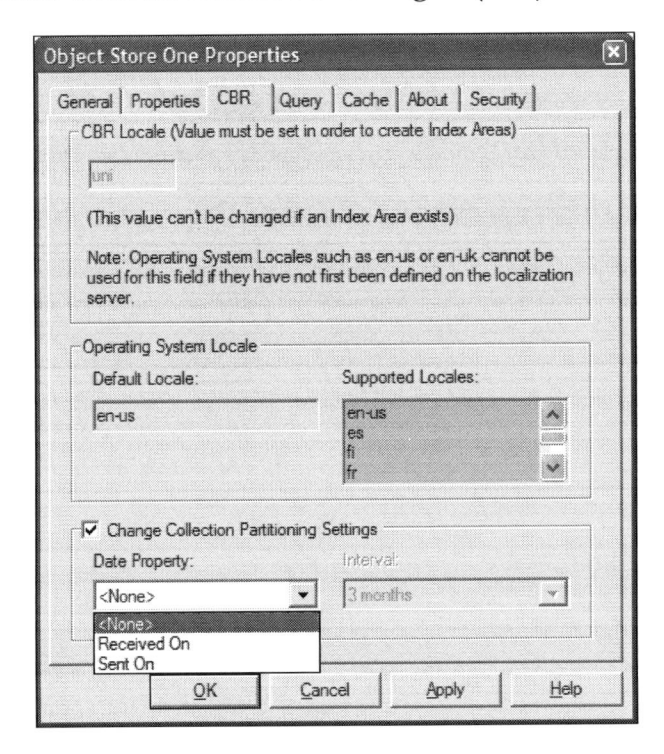

One item that can be changed on a per-Object Store basis is the date-based partitioning of text index collections. Partitioning of the text index collections allows for more efficient searching of large collections because the CE can narrow its search to a specific partition or partitions rather than searching the entirety of the text index.

By default, there is no partitioning. If you check the box to change the partition settings, the **Date Property** drop-down presents a list of date-valued custom properties. In the screenshot above, you see the custom properties **Received On** and **Sent On**, which are from email-related documents. Once you select one of those properties, you're offered a choice of partitioning granularity, ranging from one month up to one year.

Additional text index configuration properties are available if you select the **Index Areas** node in the FEM tree-view, then right-click an index area entry and select **Properties**. Although we are showing the screenshot here for reference, your environment will not yet have a CSE or any index areas if you are following our installation procedures. We'll get to the CSE in *Chapter 5, Installing Other Components*.

*Chapter 4*

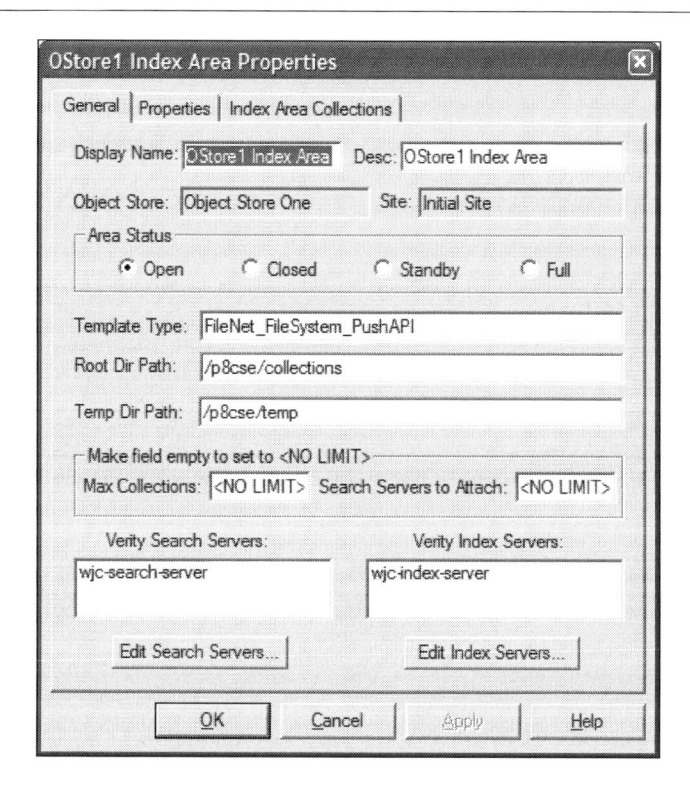

## Cache configuration

Just as we saw at the Domain level, the **Cache** tab allows the configuration of various cache tuning parameters for each Object Store. As we've said before, you don't want to change these values without a good reason. The default values are suitable for most situations.

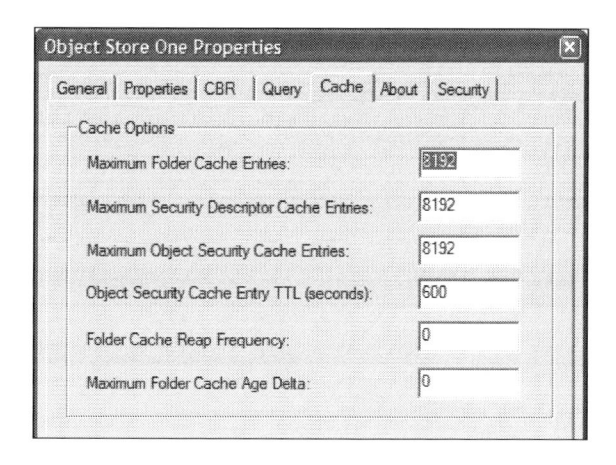

## Metadata

One of the key features of CM is that it has an extensible metadata structure. You don't have to work within a fixed framework of pre-defined document properties. You can add additional properties to the Document class, and you can even make subclasses of Document for specific purposes. For example, you might have a subclass called CustomerProfile, another subclass called DesignDocument, yet another subclass called ProductDescription, and so on. Creating subclasses lets you define just the properties you need to specialize the class to your particular business purpose. There is no need to have informal rules about where properties should be ignored because they're not applicable. There is also generally no need to have a property that marks a document as a CustomerProfile versus something else. The class provides that distinction.

CM comes with a set of pre-defined system classes, and each class has a number of pre-defined system properties (many of which are shared across most system classes). There are pre-defined system classes for Document, Folder, Annotation, CustomObject, and many others. The classes just mentioned are often described as the business object classes because they are used to directly implement common business application concepts. We'll be discussing them in more detail in later chapters, especially in *Chapter 7*.

System properties are properties for which the CE server has some specifically-coded behavior. Some system properties are used to control server behavior, and others provide reports of some kind of system state. We've seen several examples already in the Domain and Object Store objects.

It's common for applications to create their own subclasses and custom properties as part of their installation procedures, but it is equally common to do similar things manually via FEM. FEM contains several wizards to make the process simpler for the administrator, but, behind the scenes, various pieces are always in play.

## Property templates

The foundation for any custom property is a property template. If you select the **Property Templates** node in the tree view, you will see a long list of existing property templates. Double-clicking on any item in the list will reveal that property template's properties. A property template is an independently persistable object, so it has its own identity and security.

> Most system properties do not have explicit property templates. Their characteristics come about from a different mechanism internal to the CE server.

| Display Name | Description | Data Type | Created By | Create Date |
|---|---|---|---|---|
| Animation Enabled | Animation Enabled | Boolean | gcd_admin | 4/6/2010 7:18:52 PM |
| Application Name | Application Name | String | gcd_admin | 4/6/2010 7:18:43 PM |
| AssociatedPropertyID | AssociatedPropertyID | ID | gcd_admin | 4/6/2010 7:18:38 PM |
| Cc | Cc | String | gcd_admin | 4/6/2010 7:19:07 PM |
| Component Binding Label | Component Binding La... | String | gcd_admin | 4/6/2010 7:18:38 PM |
| Container Type | Container Type | String | gcd_admin | 4/6/2010 7:19:01 PM |
| Custom Object Type | Custom Object Type | String | gcd_admin | 4/6/2010 7:19:01 PM |
| Dependent Documents | | Object | gcd_admin | 4/6/2010 7:18:55 PM |
| Description | | String | gcd_admin | 4/6/2010 7:18:43 PM |
| Description | Entry Template Descri... | String | gcd_admin | 4/6/2010 7:18:44 PM |
| Document Title | Document Title | String | gcd_admin | 4/6/2010 7:18:37 PM |
| Email Dependent Reference | Email Dependent Refe... | Object | gcd_admin | 4/6/2010 7:19:07 PM |

Property templates have that name because the characteristics they define act as a pattern for properties added to classes, where the property is embodied in a property definition for a particular class. Some of the property template properties can be overridden in a property definition, but some cannot. For example, the basic data type and cardinality cannot be changed once a property template is created. On the other hand, things like settability and a value being required can be modified in the property definition.

When creating a new property with no existing property template, you can either create the property template independently, ahead of time, or you can follow the FEM wizard steps for adding a property to a class. FEM will prompt you with additional panels if you need to create a property template for the property being added.

# Choice lists

Most property types allow for a few simple validity checks to be enforced by the CE server. For example, an integer-valued property has an optional minimum and maximum value based on its intended use (in addition to the expected absolute constraints imposed by the integer data type). For some use cases, it is desirable to limit the allowed values to a specific list of items. The mechanism for that in the CE server is the choice list, and it's available for string-valued and integer-valued properties.

If you select the **Choice Lists** node in the FEM tree view, you will see a list of existing top-level choice lists. The example choice lists in the screenshot below all happen to come from AddOns installed in the Object Store. Double-clicking on any item in the list will reveal that choice list's properties. A choice list is an independently persistable object, so it has its own identity and security.

*Administrative Tools and Tasks*

> We've mentioned independent objects a couple of times, and more mentions are coming. We'll describe them more fully in *Chapter 7*. For now, it is enough to think of them as objects that can be stored or retrieved in their own right. Most independent objects have their own access security. Contrast independent objects with dependent objects that only exist within the context of some independent object. If that still sounds like gibberish, just ignore words like "independent" and "persistable" until you get the full explanation in *Chapter 7*.

| Display Name | Description | Data Type | Created By | Create Date |
|---|---|---|---|---|
| Entry Choices | Entry Choices | String | gcd_admin | 4/6/2010 7:18:44 PM |
| Form Types | Form Types | String | gcd_admin | 4/6/2010 7:18:48 PM |
| Preference Type | Preference Type | String | gcd_admin | 4/6/2010 7:19:01 PM |

A choice list is a collection of choice objects, although a choice list may be nested hierachically. That is, at any position in a choice list there can be another choice list rather than a simple choice. A choice object consists of a localizable display name and a choice value (a string or an integer, depending on the type of choice list). Nested choice lists can only be referenced within some top-level choice list.

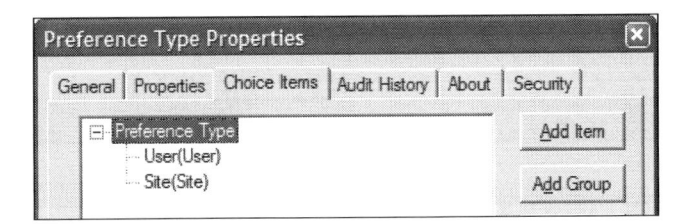

## Classes

Within the FEM tree view are two nodes describing classes: **Document Class** and **Other Classes**. Documents are listed separately only for user convenience (since `Document` subclasses occur most frequently). You can think of these two nodes as one big list. In any case, expanding the node in the tree reveals hierarchically nested subclasses. Selecting a class from the tree reveals any subclasses and any custom properties. The screenshot shows the custom class `EntryTemplate`, which comes from a Workplace AddOn. You can see that it has two subclasses, `RecordsTemplate` and `WebContentTemplate`, and four custom properties.

> When we mention a specific class or property name, like `EntryTemplate`, we try to use the symbolic name, which has a restricted character set and never contains spaces. The FEM screenshots tend to show display names. Display names are localizable and can contain any Unicode character.

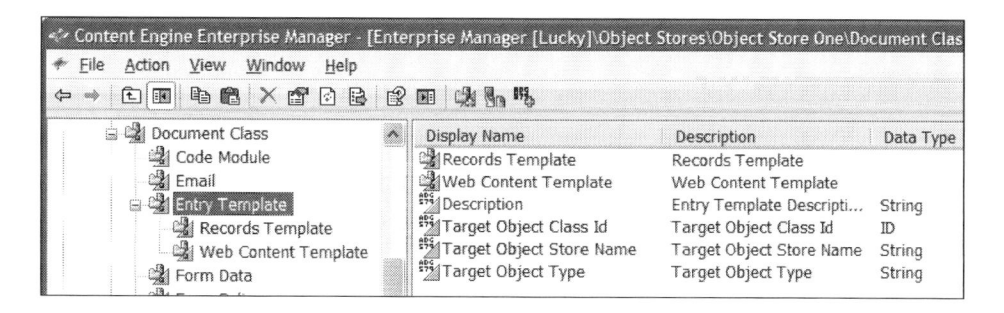

Although the subclassing mechanism in CM generally mimics the subclassing concept in modern object-oriented programming languages, it does have some differences.

- You can add custom properties to an existing class, including many system classes.
- Although you can change some characteristics of properties on a subclass, there are restrictions on what you can do. For example, a particular string property on a subclass must have a maximum length equal to or less than that property's maximum length on the superclass.

## Subclassing example

The right-click context menu for individual classes in the tree-view has selections to launch wizards for creating a new subclass (**New Class**) and for adding properties to the given class (**Add Properties to Class**). We'll finish up this section with a quick example of creating a new `Document` subclass called `WjcWorkOfLiterature` with a small number of custom properties. This class is used in some examples in *Chapter 6, End User Tools and Tasks* and we will also refer you back to this section for creating the classes and properties used by the sample application in *Chapter 12, The DUCk Sample Application*.

Right-click the **Document Class** node in the FEM tree view and select **New Class**. The **Create a Class Wizard** is launched.

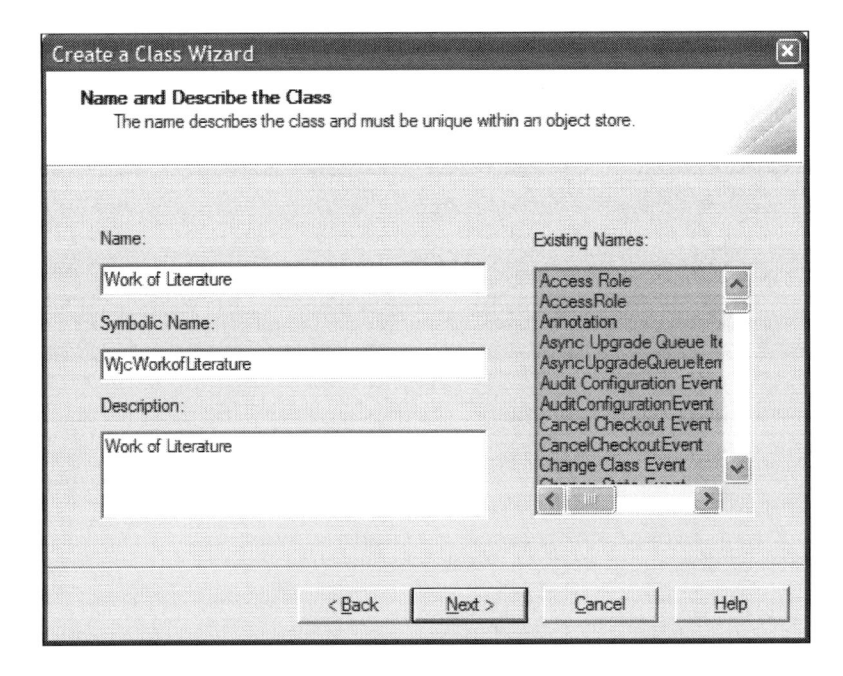

The first panel asks for the **Name** (which actually means the display name) and the **Symbolic Name**. As you type the display name, FEM automatically constructs a default symbolic name by removing spaces and other unacceptable characters. You can modify the symbolic name to something else; we added the prefix **Wjc** because symbolic names must be unique, and using a short prefix reduces the chances of collision with something else. The description is optional, but you can supply whatever descriptive text you'd like.

The next panel shows the inherited properties on the class and invites you to add more. Since we have not previously created the property templates, click the **New** button to launch the **Create a Property Template** wizard.

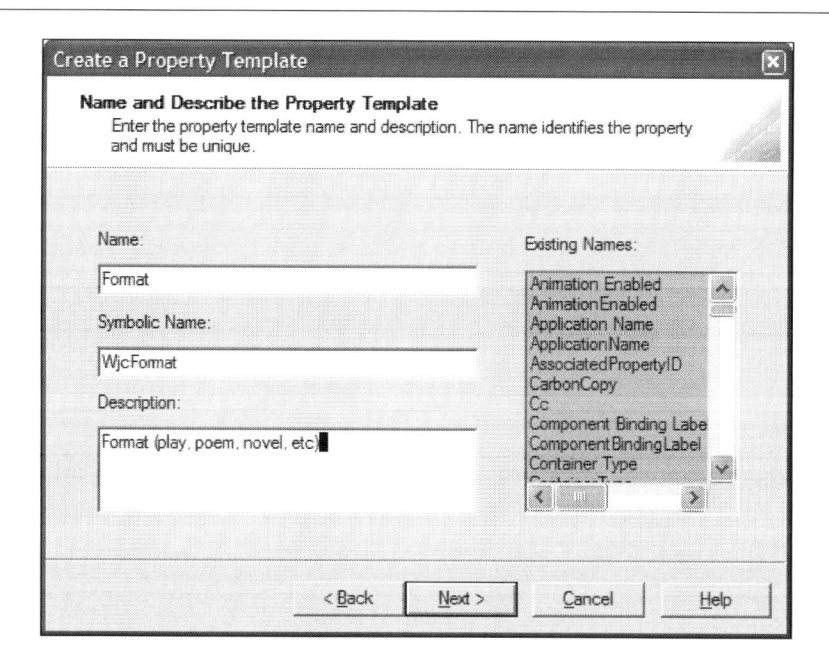

*Chapter 4*

As in the class wizard, the first panel asks for names and a description. Enter the same values shown in the screenshot for the `WjcFormat` property and click the **Next** button. We'll use a choice list for this property, so select that option and click the New button to launch the **Create a Choice List** wizard.

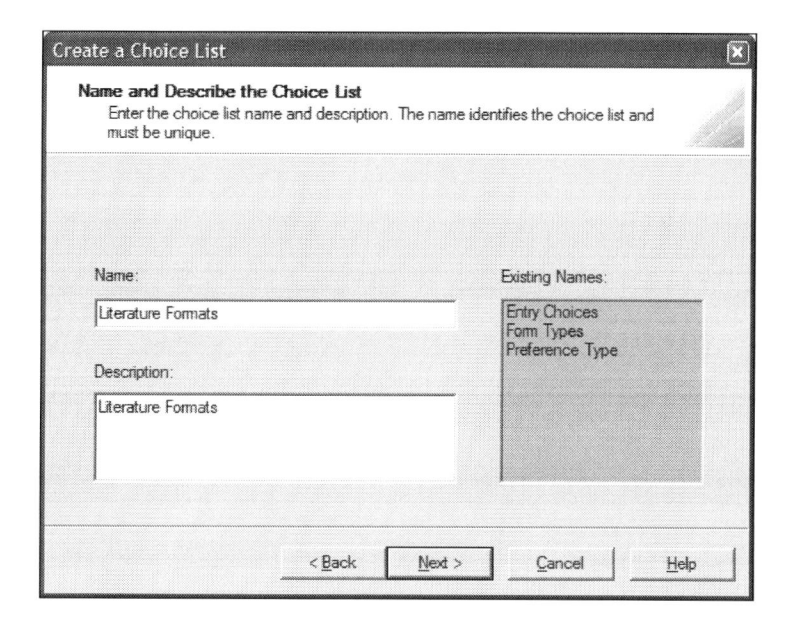

*Administrative Tools and Tasks*

Choice lists don't have a symbolic name, but the display name is required to be unique. We called the choice list **Literature Formats**. What really matters here for referential integrity is the Id of the choice list, but FEM is automatically creating the necessary linkages and doesn't bother us with it. Click the **Next** button and select **String** as the **Choice List Data Type**. Click Next again to be brought to the **Add Choice List Elements** panel.

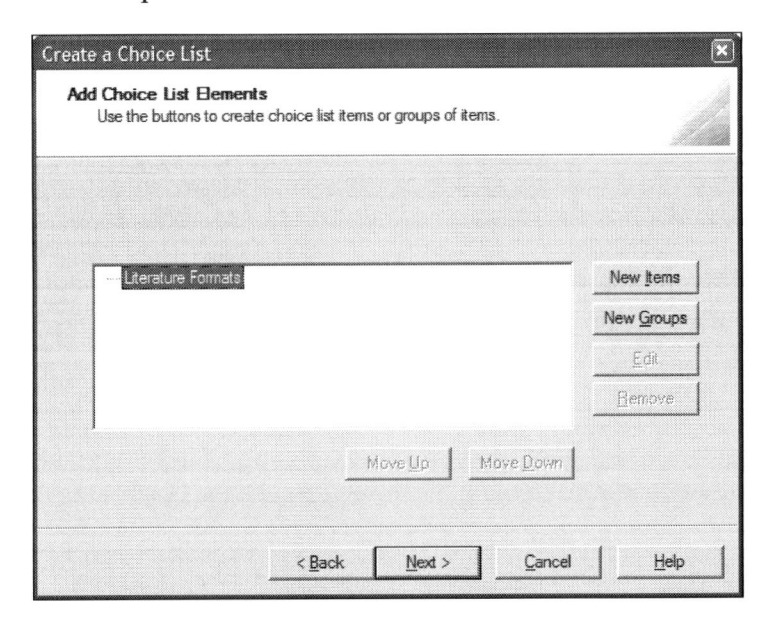

If we were making a hierarchical choice list, we'd use the **New Groups** button. We're making only a simple list, so click the **New Items** button.

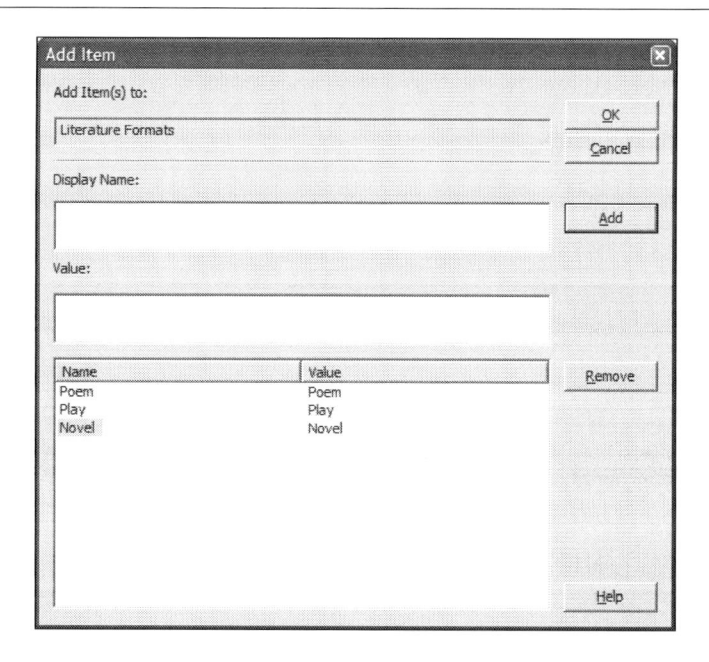

Use the **Add Item** panel to add the three values shown. An application using a choice list will usually show the **Name** to the user, but the **Value** will actually be used as the property value. When you have completed the **Create a Choice List** wizard, you will be returned to the **Create a Property** wizard already in progress.

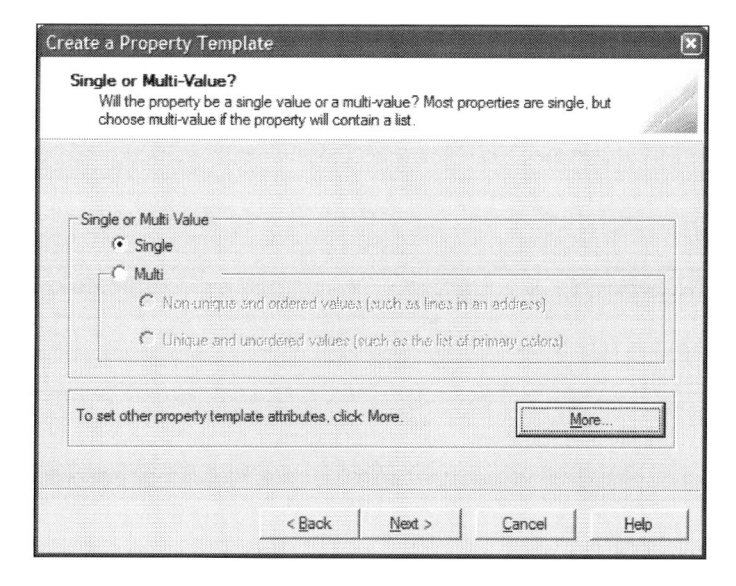

Select **Single** (this is the property cardinality) and click the **More** button to define additional characteristics of the `WjcFormat` property.

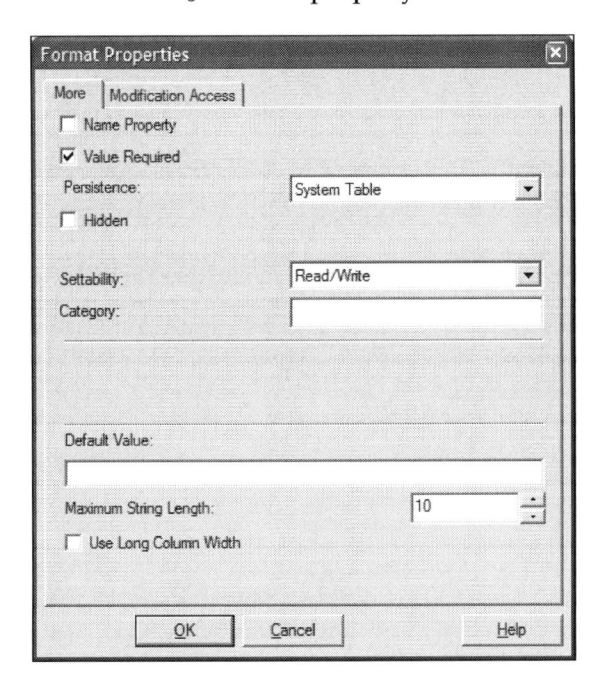

The most important things to notice in this panel are that we have selected the **Value Required** checkbox, that we have made the property **Read/Write**, and that we have specified a **Maximum String Length** of 10 characters.

When you have completed the **Create a Property** wizard, you will be returned to the **Create a Class Wizard** already in progress at the **Select Properties** panel. Before moving on, let's create three more new properties which will show up in some examples in *Chapter 6*.

- `Genre` (`WjcGenre`), a multi-valued string property (unique and unordered). It should have **Value Required**, be **Read/Write**, and have a **Maximum String Length** of 25. Use a choice list called `Literature Genre` with values `Drama, Comedy, Farce, Science Fiction, Western, Romance, Sonnet, Epic, Unknown,` and `History`.
- `AuthorLastName` (`WjcAuthorLastName`), a simple string property. It should have **Value Required**, be **Read/Write**, and have a **Maximum String Length** of 64. It does not have a choice list.
- `AuthorFullName` (`WjcAuthorFullName`), a simple string property. It should not have **Value Required**, be **Read/Write**, and have a **Maximum String Length** of 64. It does not have a choice list.

Your **Create a Class Wizard** should look like this:

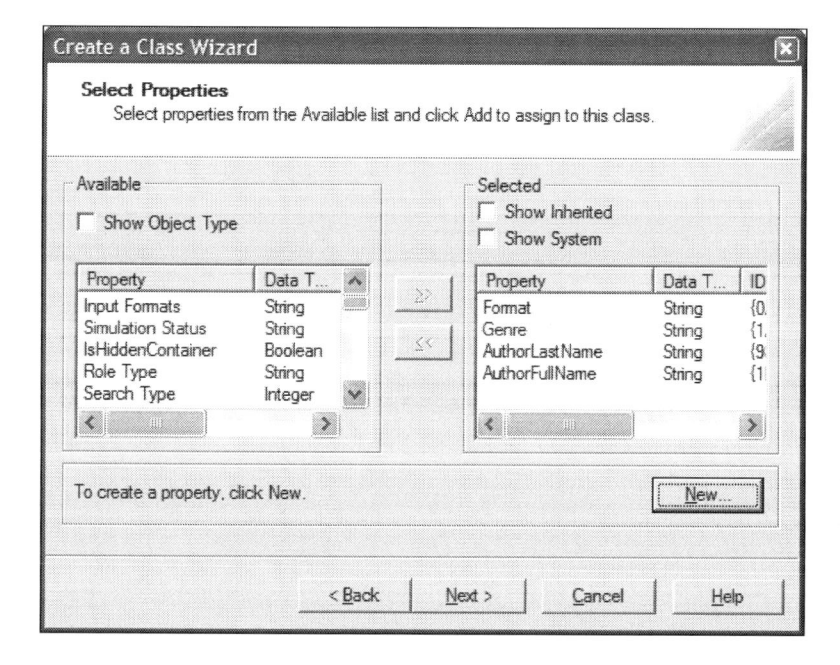

Finally, the last panel of the **Create a Class Wizard** will show a summary of the things you defined along the way. Click the **Finish** button to create the class.

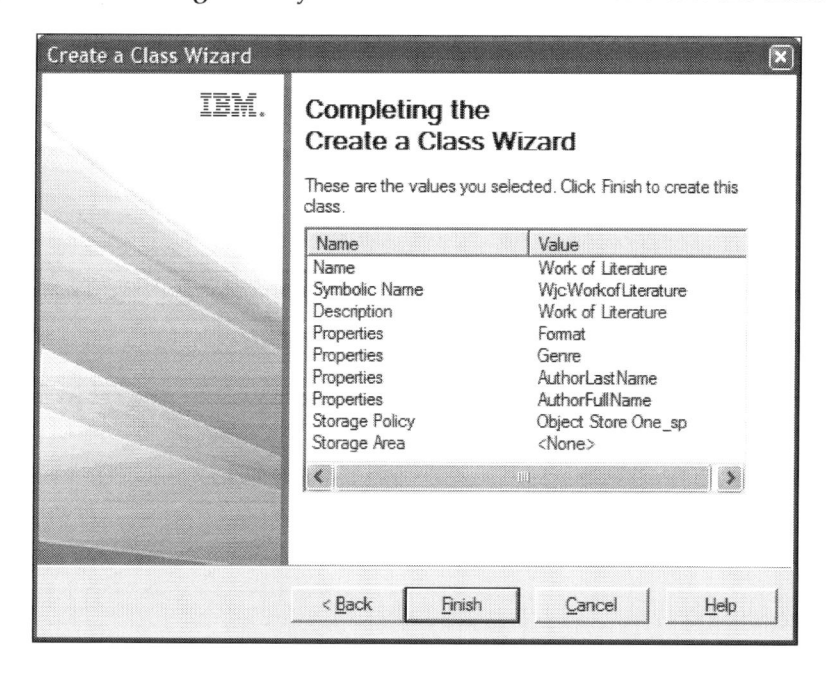

*Administrative Tools and Tasks*

> Although the final step in the Create a Class Wizard will still let you cancel the creation of the class, any property templates and choice lists you created along the way will already have been created in the Object Store. If you wish to completely undo your work, you will have to delete them manually.

## Object Browse and Query

The highest level folder in an Object Store is called the root folder, and its path name is simply /. It is represented by the **Root Folder** node in the FEM tree view. Every folder and every contained document or custom object appears somewhere hierarchically under the root folder.

> FEM contains another node called **Unfiled Documents**. FEM goes to a lot of trouble to make this look like a folder in the user interface. It is not, although it is common to hear people experienced with CM call it "the unfiled documents folder". If you select that "folder", FEM issues a query to find documents which do not appear in any actual folder.

We'll have more to say about browsing and navigating in *Chapter 6* where we'll illustrate it using XT.

For now, we'll just point out the query interface in FEM. If you right-click on an Object Store and select **Search** from the context menu, you'll see a dialog box that lets you define a query step by step.

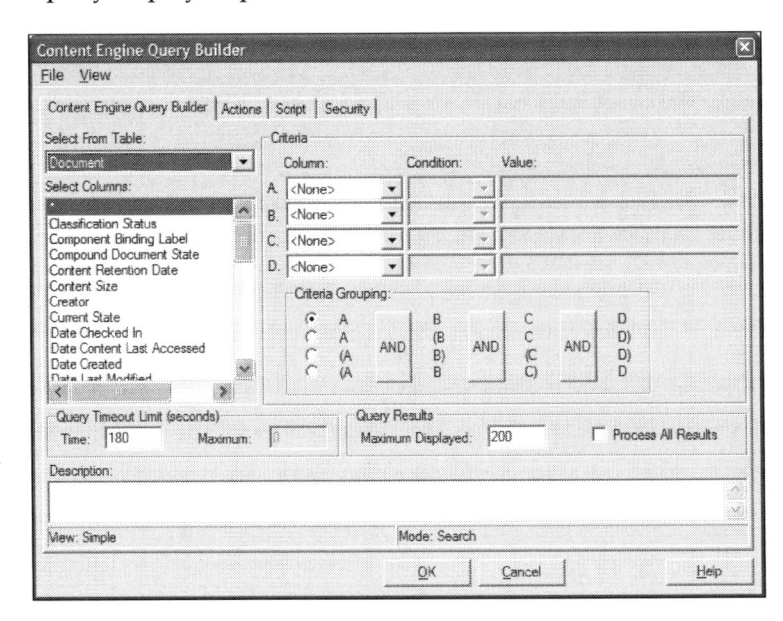

We won't go through the details of this dialog box because it's more about FEM user interface than about CM. It is worth noting that you can do queries against the CE server using a SQL-like query language. In fact, we call it **CE SQL**; it is a SQL-92 variant. Using these queries is very common in applications, and you can do it manually from this dialog box in FEM. Behind the scenes, FEM is composing a CE SQL query.

Another mode for that dialog will let you simply paste in a query that you have constructed on your own. From the **Content Engine Query Builder**, select View > SQL View.

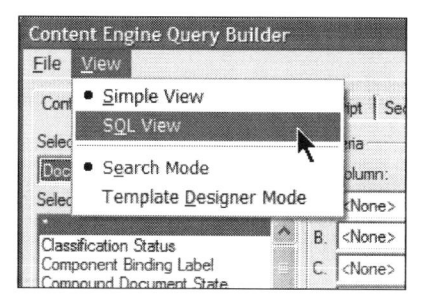

The resulting view is prepopulated with a rather elaborate CE SQL query string. You can delete that and type or paste in your own query string.

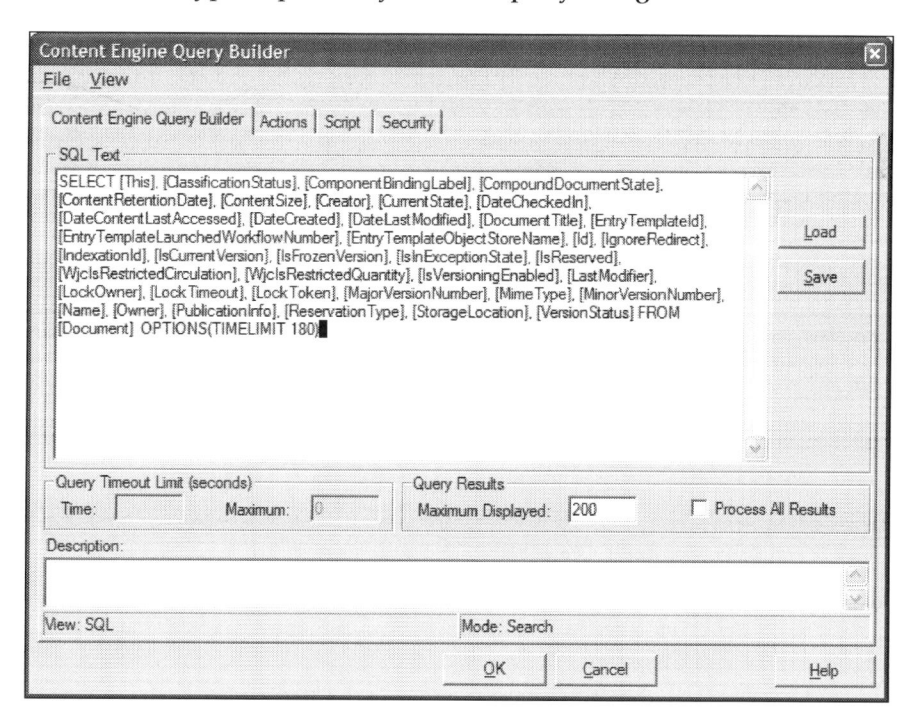

When you click OK, the query will be executed and FEM will display the results. There is also an option to save a local copy of a query so that you can load and re-execute it later. (This feature is unrelated to the Workplace and XT feature called Stored Search.)

> A historical quirk of the FEM query interface is that the SELECT list must begin with the `This` property. That is not a general requirement of CE SQL.

## Summary

In this chapter, we took a brief tour of some common administrative features of CM. Most people experience these through the FEM tool. However, everything FEM does is done through the CE APIs, so it is also possible to write custom applications which do some or all of these things.

There is a lot more to CM than these things, but we first have to install a few more components before we can look at them. We'll resume our CM installation adventures in *Chapter 5, Installing Other Components*.

# 5
# Installing Other Components

In *Chapter 2*, we installed basic infrastructure components such as a database engine (DB2), an LDAP directory server (Tivoli), and an J2EE application server (WebSphere), and in *Chapter 3*, we installed the Content Engine itself. We also installed the FileNet Enterprise Manager (FEM), the principal administrative application for the CE. In this chapter, we'll resume our installation adventures by installing a few additional components that are part of the CE environment. In particular, we'll be installing the Content Search Engine.

In this chapter, we'll install the Workplace XT (XT). The XT and the Application Engine (AE) are application tiers that can be used for running out-of-the-box applications. In the case of AE, the out-of-the-box application is Workplace. It is now sometimes referred to as "Workplace classic" to distinguish it from the newer application, Workplace XT.

You'll recall that we had to install FEM on Microsoft Windows because it is a Windows-only application. It turns out that a few other components are not supported on Linux, though they are supported on various other flavors of Unix. We're installing everything on Linux except where we are forced to install elsewhere, in which case we are installing on Windows.

Perhaps we should recap where things are or will be installed. The following table below describes where various components can be installed; the **bold** entries are the places we actually have installed or will install those components. This table is greatly simplified for the sake of giving an at-a-glance understanding of where we are installing things. To see where something can be installed in your environment, you should definitely check the *IBM FileNet P8 4.5 Hardware and Software Requirements* document since there are some combinations of things and specific releases of supporting software and operating systems that are not supported.

*Installing Other Components*

| Component | Linux | Other Unix | Windows |
|---|---|---|---|
| CE server | Yes | Yes | Yes |
| CE client | Yes | Yes | Yes |
| FEM | No | No | Yes |
| CSE | Yes | Yes | Yes |
| SD | Yes | Yes | Yes |
| PE server | No | Yes | Yes |
| PE client | Yes | Yes | Yes |
| AE | Yes | Yes | Yes |
| XT | Yes | Yes | Yes |
| RE | No | No | Yes |

For now, don't worry too much about the abbreviations in the first column of the table, though they are the same as we used in the overview diagram in *Chapter 3*. We'll explain each one in its own section next.

> We're now going to spread our all-in-one installation over two different machines. (We hope you're looking the other way when you think about that statement.) The smart way to set up these machines would be with static IP addresses, and if it's easy for you to do that, that's the right way to do it. If you are doing what we often do — getting by with dynamically assigned IP addresses for virtual machine images — then you will probably want to add entries to your local hosts file.
>
> On Linux, it's /etc/hosts, and on Windows it's C:\WINDOWS\system32\drivers\etc\hosts. (We have trouble remembering the Windows path, so we have a shortcut to it on our Windows desktop.) In either case, the format is the same, and the entries will look something like this:
>
> 10.0.129.12 wjc-w2k3 wjc-w2k3.example.net
> 10.0.129.29 wjc-rhel wjc-rhel.example.net
>
> If your DHCP server suddenly assigns either host a new address, you need simply update those two files and you'll be back in business with them referring to each other by name.

# Content Search Engine (CSE)

The CSE is a full-text search engine. You can selectively enable full-text indexing for document body content as well as selected string properties. In CM jargon, you will sometimes see the notion of a text index referred to as **content-based retrieval** (**CBR**). That's just another name for the same thing. The internals of the CSE are Verity's K2 engine, but Verity was acquired by Autonomy a few years ago, so you will see it mentioned all three ways—Verity, K2, and Autonomy—in documentation.

The CSE is not a J2EE application, and it runs separately from the CE. In production environments, it is run on separate servers from the CE so that loads can be better managed. In our lightly-loaded all-in-one environment, we'll be installing it on the same Linux server that holds our CE installation. When you look at the CSE topics in the PPG, you will find quite an assortment of different logical server types that make up a CSE environment. You will certainly want to consider that information carefully for your production environment, but our single Linux system will hold all of those server roles in our installation.

> There is a general requirement that if the CE is on Windows, then the CSE must also be on Windows. If the CE is on Linux or Unix, then the CSE must be on Linux or Unix. The important distinction is Windows versus non-Windows; for example, you could run the CE on Linux and the CSE on Unix.

Getting to a working CSE involves these steps:

1. Run the CSE installation program
2. Manually configure some things from the command line
3. Configure the CSE via the K2 Dashboard
4. Configure the CE (via FEM) to know about the CSE configuration

These steps can seem a bit tedious or even mysterious the first time through, but you can mostly just blindly follow the documented steps and things will work as expected. For us, there is no doubt that the CSE installation is the most complicated piece of a normal CM setup, but we urge you to not skip it. Text-based searching has become increasingly popular with users in recent years.

*Installing Other Components*

## The CSE user

Create an operating system user under which the CSE software will run. We use the userid k2_os_user, the same as the figurative account name from the PPG and installation worksheet terminology. Also create an operating system group, k2_sec_group, and make that the primary group for k2_os_user. Give k2_os_user membership in ecmgroup as a secondary group. We'll say more about these group memberships in the section *Command Line Configuration Steps* later.

Log onto the Linux system as k2_os_user. We will perform all CSE installation tasks as that user.

CSE needs Java and is particular about the versions of Java that can be used. It can use Java 1.4.2 or Java 5, but it cannot use Java 6. On Windows, it cannot use a 64-bit Java.

Locate Java on your machine and set the JAVA_HOME environment variable generally or just for k2_os_user. Since we just installed several IBM Java-based programs on this system, there is no shortage of Java versions from which to choose. JAVA_HOME must point to a full Java Development Kit (JDK), not just a Java Runtime Environment (JRE). We located a Java 5 JDK on our server, though the path will surely be different on yours. We added the following line to ~k2_os_user/.bashrc (depending on the shell used by k2_os_user, you might need to put it in some other shell initialization file; for example, .profile):
export JAVA_HOME=/usr/lib/jvm/java-1.5.0-ibm-1.5.0.11.2.x86_64

You'll need that environment variable to be in force *before* you run the CSE installer in the next section. If you're not sure how to do that, simply log out and log in again as k2_os_user.

## Running the CSE installer

> The CSE installer will offer a default path for installing the CSE software (/opt/ibm/FileNet/ContentEngine/verity on Linux). Since you are running the installer as k2_os_user but have run other installers as other users, you might like to make sure (outside of the installer) that user k2_os_user will have sufficient access rights to create or update the folder.

Locate and run the CSE installation program, P8CSE-4.5.1.0-LINUX.BIN. After the usual welcomes and license panels, you'll be asked to decide between installing as a **Master Administration Server** or a simple **Administration Server**. We're only installing CSE on one server, so choose **Master Administration Server**. Administration Servers are in addition to the required Master Administration Server.

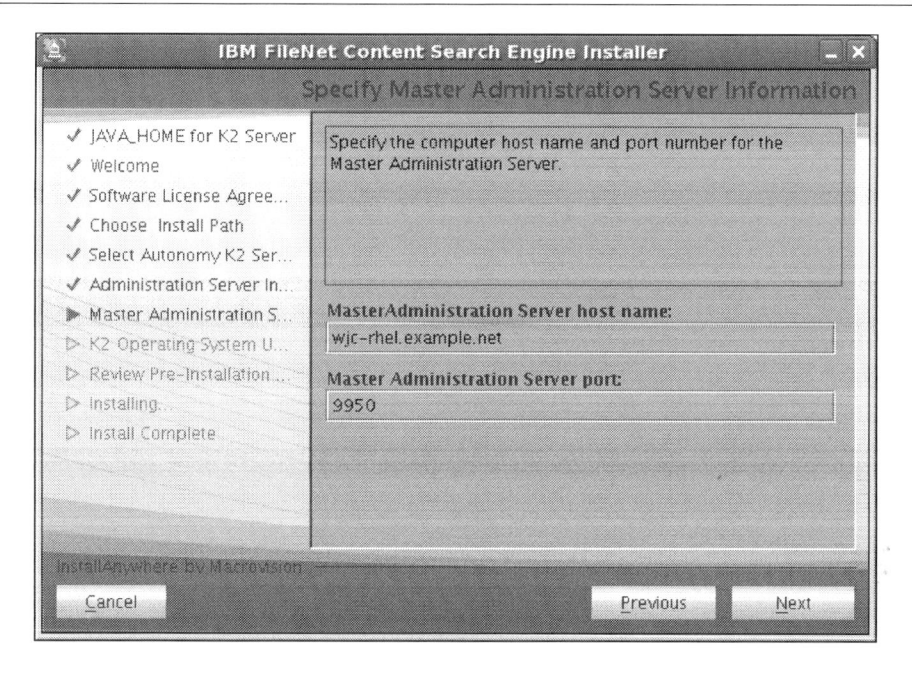

When prompted in a later panel for the host and port number for the **Master Administration Server**, specify the server name, `wjc-rhel.example.net`, and any convenient port number. What's a convenient port number? In this case, it can be any port number that will not otherwise be used on the server. If you don't have a preference, we suggest you use port 9950 so that your selection will agree with the default port listing in the P8 platform documentation. The installer may fill in that port number by default.

> Since you are running the CSE installer and eventually the CSE itself on the same machine as the CE, you might be tempted to use `localhost` as the CSE server host. From the CE point of view, that would be technically correct. However, exploiting little tricks like that is a bad habit to get into. It certainly won't work in any environment where you install the CSE separately from the CE or have multiple CSE servers installed. We suggest you use a proper host name.
>
> For example, in our case, we used `wjc-rhel.example.net`. Be sure to get the server name correct since the installer and the Verity software will sprinkle it liberally throughout several configuration files. If it is not correct by default (which is one of the hazards of using dynamic IP addresses), correct it now.

*Installing Other Components*

When asked for the K2 user account, give the user ID and password of the `k2_os_user`. You can name the Verity domain whatever you want. We used the name `VerityLucky` so it would be suggestive of the associated P8 Domain name.

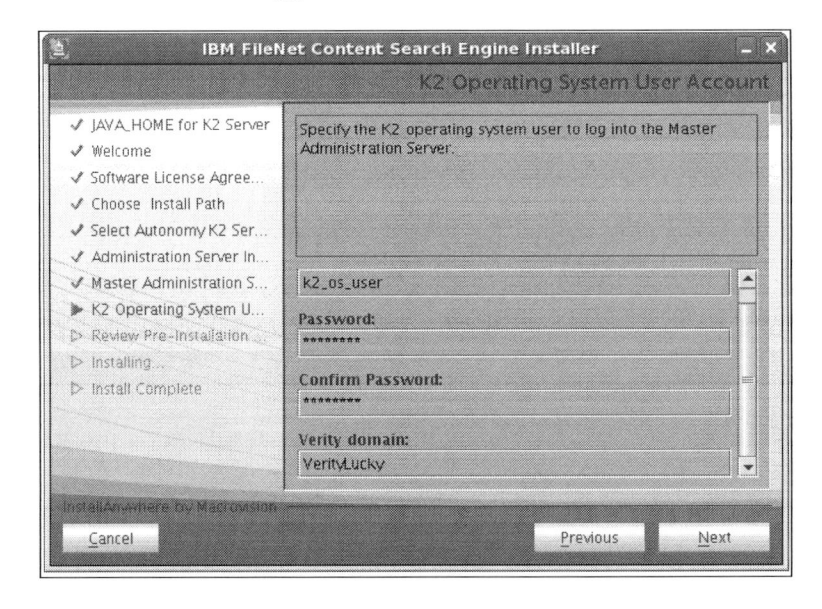

After you have finished running the CSE installer, the CSE will be running. You can assure yourself of this by using `telnet` to connect to port 9950 (or whatever port you selected). You should be greeted by a strange-looking string of gibberish from the K2 server. Once you see that (as opposed to **connection refused**), you will know your CSE is running and you can exit `telnet`. On Microsoft Windows, CSE runs as a couple of Windows services (look for services with **Verity K2** in the name), but on Linux it runs as a few standalone daemon processes.

By default, those daemon processes are not automatically started on Linux and Unix systems at system startup time. You can start and stop them by running the `k2adminstart` and `k2adminstop` commands, which you will find under the installation destination directory (for example, `/opt/ibm/FileNet/ContentEngine/verity/k2/_ilnx21/bin/k2adminstart`). You'll want to run them as user `k2_os_user`, of course.

For a production system, we would suggest making an appropriate entry in `/etc/init.d/` or a similar mechanism. For our demo system, it's sufficient to run them manually, and we added the K2 commands to the `up.sh` and `down.sh` scripts we showed in *Chapter 2*. Some documentation advises running the startup script in the background and with output redirected via `nohup`, but we have found that the `k2adminstart` command disconnects itself from the terminal where it's started; the `nohup` is not necessary.

# Command line configuration steps

Once you have run the CSE installer, and before you move on to the configuration tasks in the next section, you must change the security on one of the K2 executables, vspget, to make it "setuid root". That means that it will run as if the root user executed it regardless of who the actual user was. From a Linux command prompt, while logged in as root, do the following commands:

```
# cd /opt/ibm/FileNet/ContentEngine/verity/k2/_ilnx21/bin
# chown root vspget
# chmod u+s vspget
```

You will need to create a couple of directories for use by both the CE and the CSE. As usual, these would be fileshares in a production distributed environment. These will need full permissions for access by k2_os_user. Again, from the Linux command line, while logged in as root, do the following commands:

```
# cd /
# mkdir p8cse
# mkdir p8cse/collections
# mkdir p8cse/temp
# chown -R k2_os_user p8cse
# chgrp -R ecmgroup p8cse
# chmod -R 770 p8cse
```

Some corresponding adjustments are also needed for the CE filestore directories:

```
# cd /
# chgrp -R ecmgroup p8filestores
# chmod -R 770 p8filestores
```

Finally, using operating system tools, give user k2_os_user a secondary group of ecmgroup (of course, we did that latter step earlier in this chapter).

By setting up the group memberships as we did, and by creating directories with those owners and groups and using 770 permissions, we've made an arrangement where the CE and the CSE can share files through the filesystem. The K2 servers are running as user k2_os_user and the CE is running as user ecmuser. The two servers must be able to create and read files from each others' directories in order to communicate. There are other ways to enable this sharing, and you should find a mechanism that works according to your local security policies when you use fileshares.

*Installing Other Components*

The K2 configuration file must be manually edited to be aware of the location of the `/p8cse/collections/` directory you just created. Open the file `/opt/ibm/FileNet/ContentEngine/verity/k2/common/verity.cfg` with a text editor and set the "6" series of tags to the following values:

```
alias6=path1
mapping6=/p8cse/collections
dirmode6=rw
```

## Configuring CSE via the K2 Dashboard

The next step uses the native Autonomy K2 Dashboard web application to configure various subcomponents of K2 itself. There is a lot of flexibility in how you deploy K2 subcomponents, and you'll want to consider the possibilities when planning your production environment. We'll be the first to admit that the steps described in this section seem random because we haven't explained what each of the various kinds of K2 components are. In addition to the CM documentation resources, complete "native" Verity documentation is included with the CSE installation. Look in directory `/opt/ibm/FileNet/ContentEngine/verity/data/docs/pdf/`.

For now, we'll just go through the steps of setting up the necessary infrastructure for using CSE in the all-in-one environment. If you follow these steps (which we distilled from the CSE installation guide), it definitely will work. In these instructions, we'll use simple naming and default port numbers. If you make different choices, writing them down will simplify the steps in the *Configuring CE for CSE via FEM* section below.

Connect to the K2 Dashboard with your web browser on port 9990, for example: `http://wjc-rhel.example.net:9990`, and select **Dashboard**. You will not be prompted for credentials at this time; they'll be added at a later step in this section. Various kinds of K2 subcomponents will be listed in the **System View** on the left-hand portion of the screen.

> CM has incorporated several CSE releases and updates over the years. The screens for the K2 Dashboard still bear a 2005 copyright date. The specific list of browsers supported by the K2 Dashboard is rather limited, and you are likely to be redirected to a warning screen about that. We have found only minor formatting and layout glitches when using an unsupported browser. If you notice large functional gaps in the K2 Dashboard, a more likely cause of the problem is that the value of `JAVA_HOME` that you set earlier may not be right. Check that it points to a Java 1.4.2 or Java 5 JDK.

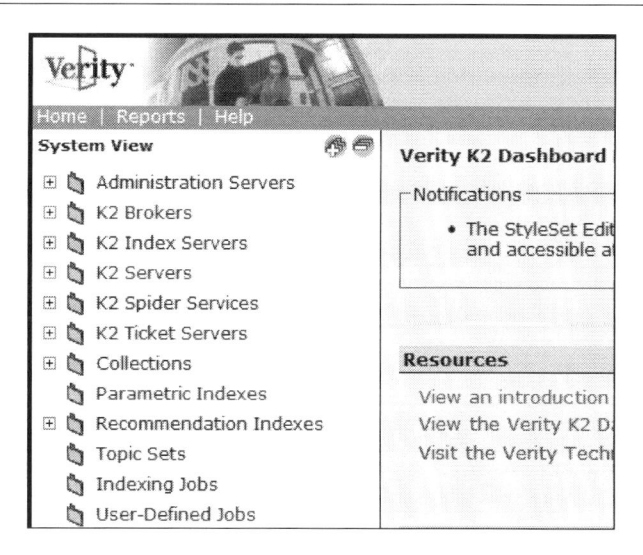

1. From **System View**, select **K2 Index Servers | Add a K2 Index Server**. Type **wjc-index-server** as the **Service Alias** and use **Port 9960**. Click **Next** and change the access type to **Authorized Administrator**. Click **Finish**.

2. From **System View**, select **K2 Brokers | Add a K2 Broker**. Type **wjc-broker** as the **Service Alias** and use **Port 9900**. Click **Finish**.

3. From **System View**, select **K2 Servers | Add a K2 Server**. Type **wjc-search-server** as the **Service Alias** and use **Port 9920**. Click **Next** twice, which will bring you to the screen for K2 brokers. From the drop-down, select **wjc-broker** that we just created above. Accept the defaults for various types of worker threads, and click **Finish**.

4. From **System View**, select **Collections | Manage Style Sets**. If you see a notice about the style sheet editor, you can ignore it (we don't use that feature). Click **Import**. Type **FileNet_FileSystem_PushAPI** as the **Style Set Alias** and type **/opt/ibm/FileNet/ContentEngine/verity/data/stylesets/FileNet_FileSystem_PushAPI** as the **Source Path**. The style sheet subdirectory will be found in that directory relative to the CSE software installation location. Click **Import**.

5. From **System View**, select **K2 Ticket Servers | Add a K2 Ticket Server**. Type **wjc-ticket-server** as the **Service Alias** and use **Port 9910**. Click **Next** and make sure that **UNIX** is selected as the **Login Module type**. Click **Next** and make sure that **File and Memory** is selected as the **Persistent Store Module type**. Click **Finish**.

*Installing Other Components*

6. Now it's time to set up authentication for administering the K2 subcomponents. From the previous step, the **wjc-ticket-server** configuration screen should be visible. If it is not, select **wjc-ticket-server** from the **System View**. Click **Manage Administration Security**, and, from the drop-down, select **wjc-ticket-server**. In the credentials fields, enter k2_os_user and the password you created for that operating system user. Click the **Modify** button. Success here will mean that the K2 Dashboard will close and require you to login again as k2_os_user.

> If you find you cannot log in with the k2_os_user credentials, you may have overlooked the step of changing the security on vspget described earlier in this chapter.

7. After you log in, you will see some notices about services needing a restart. This is because of the changes we just made. You can either make a note of the services mentioned, or you can just go down through all the servers you created in the **System View** and restart the ones that say they need it. Although a **Quick Restart** may be sufficient, a **Full Restart** may prove more reliable. If you're unsure if you've successfully restarted everything you need to restart, click **Home** to go to the main K2 Dashboard screen. Services still needing a restart will be mentioned there.

8. From **System View**, select **K2 Ticket Servers** and select **wjc-ticket-server**. Select **Manage K2 Broker/K2 Server Security**. For both **K2 Servers** and **K2 Brokers** (these are modified as separate steps), highlight the server, **wjc-search-server** and **wjc-broker**, respectively, that we created in the steps above and click **Modify**.

9. The services **wjc-broker** and **wjc-search-server** will require full restarts, as described just above.

If any of the above steps did not go as expected, you can find a link to the applicable K2 log file in the K2 Dashboard. The log file is likely to provide a clue about what went wrong.

## Configuring CE for CSE via FEM

In the previous section, we configured the CSE from the CSE's point of view. Now we must inform the CE of some of the choices we made. The CE communicates with the CSE for two reasons: it informs the CSE of new content to be indexed, and it queries the CSE as part of content-based retrieval (CBR). Therefore, the CE must know some things about the CSE configuration so that the communications can happen as expected. We also must tell CE what content and properties we, the site administrators, would like to have indexed.

Correspondingly, there are two parts to the CE configuration for the CSE: configuration for the entire Domain (mainly communication parameters) and configuration per Object Store (Document classes and properties to be indexed).

## Configuring the P8 Domain

Let's begin with the Domain configuration:

1. Start up the FileNet Enterprise Manager (FEM) application on your Microsoft Windows machine, and log in as the `gcd_admin` user. Select the top-level (Domain) node in the tree, right-click, and select **Properties**.

2. From the pop-up panel, select the tab **Verity Domain Configuration**. Enter the host name and port number for the Verity Master Administration Server that we created in the previous section. We used host **wjc-rhel.example.net** and port **9950**. The credentials are the same `k2_os_user` credentials that we used to log in to the K2 Dashboard earlier. Click **Create Configuration**. The additional K2 server names that appear will look familiar from the previous section.

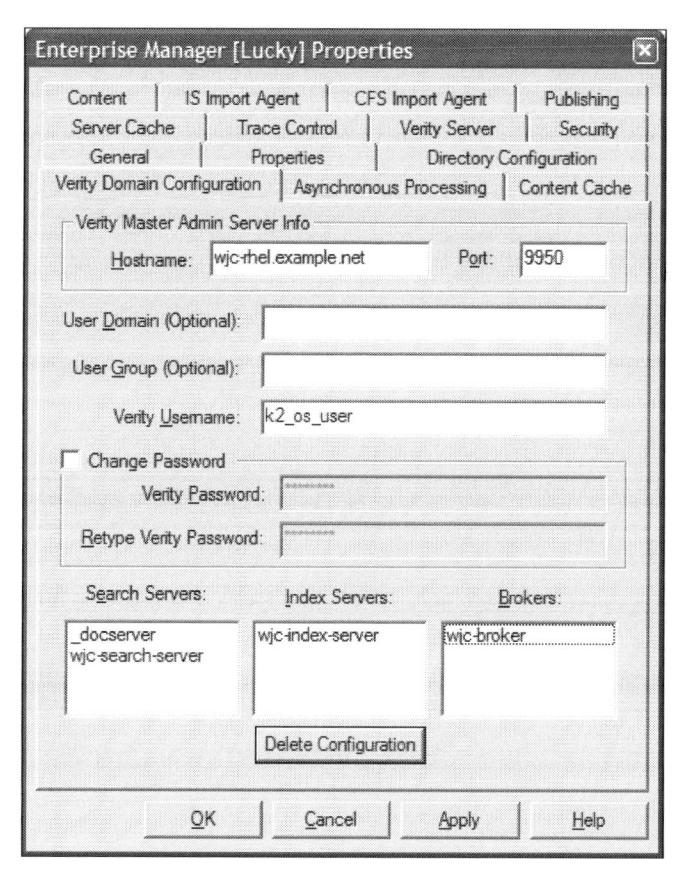

*Installing Other Components*

3. From the same pop-up panel, select the **Verity Server** tab. Move **wjc-broker** from **Brokers AVAILABLE** to **Brokers SELECTED**. Click **OK** to apply the setting and close the pop-up panel.

This concludes configuring the Domain for CSE, and we'll move on to configuring our single Object Store, Object Store One, `OStore1`.

## Configuring an Object Store

Select the **Object Store One** node in the tree, right-click, and select **Properties**. From the pop-up panel, select the **CBR** tab. There is only one field that you can edit on this panel. Set the **CBR Locale** field to **uni**. Click **OK** to apply the setting and close the pop-up panel.

> `uni` stands for Unicode and is generally the best choice for mixed-languages support. If you think you don't need mixed-languages support, there's a pretty good chance you are mistaken, even if all of your users have the same locale settings in their environments. In any case, if you are tempted to use a different CBR locale, you should first read the K2 locale customization guide, since it's a reasonably complicated topic.

An Index Area is the CE's way of referring to CSE locations. Create a Verity Index Area for this Object Store by right-clicking Object Store One and selecting **New | Index Area**. The wizard for creating an index area will appear.

1. Click next past the first few panels, and, when prompted, type the name `OStore1 Index Area` as the name of the Index Area.

2. On the panel **Enter Verity Directories**, enter values chosen in the earlier section while configuring the CSE via the K2 Dashboard. See the figure below. Notice that it looks like we entered the simple directory name `FileNet_FileSystem_PushAPI` for **Template Type** rather than the full path. Actually, we entered the alias name that we assigned earlier, and it just happens to be the same as the simple directory name.

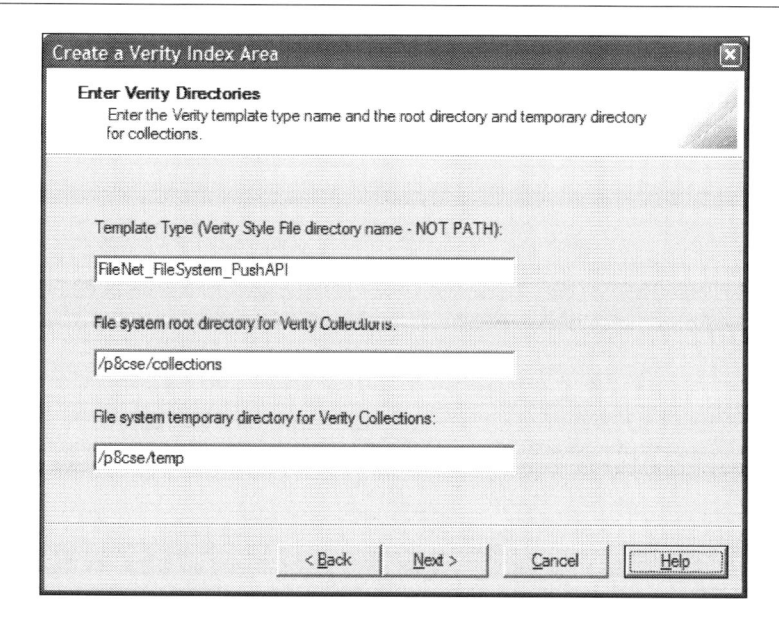

[Screenshot: Create a Verity Index Area — Enter Verity Directories panel, with Template Type "FileNet_FileSystem_PushAPI", File system root directory "/p8cse/collections", and File system temporary directory "/p8cse/temp".]

3. On the next two panels, select the K2 search server (**wjc-search-server**) and index server (**wjc-index-server**) defined earlier.

4. Other than these explicit choices, take defaults on all panels and click through to the end to create the index area configuration and close the wizard.

The final panel of the wizard summarizes the configuration choices we made:

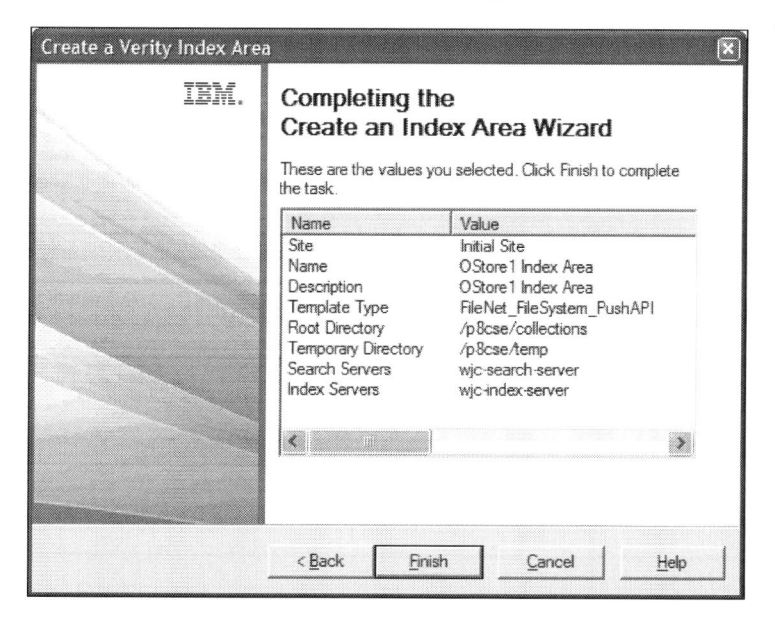

[Screenshot: Completing the Create an Index Area Wizard, summarizing values — Site: Initial Site; Name: OStore1 Index Area; Description: OStore1 Index Area; Template Type: FileNet_FileSystem_PushAPI; Root Directory: /p8cse/collections; Temporary Directory: /p8cse/temp; Search Servers: wjc-search-server; Index Servers: wjc-index-server.]

*Installing Other Components*

> To review this configuration later, you can navigate to it via the **Index Areas** node for an Object Store within FEM.

The final step in configuring CBR is to specify the Document and/or Annotation subclasses that you would like to have indexed in the CSE. For simplicity in this description, we'll just index all Document classes, including the `Document` base class. If you have a sizable volume of content and can rule out text indexing for functional reasons on a significant fraction of those documents by class, it could be a good performance win. In addition to indexing the content of documents, you can optionally index one or more string-valued properties. (String-valued property indexing can also be done for Folder and Custom Object classes, but, of course, they do not have content.) As an example, we'll enable text indexing of the `DocumentTitle` property.

1. In the tree on the left side in FEM, select **Document Class** within **Object Store One**. Right-click and select **Properties**. On the **General** tab, you will see a checkbox for **CBR Enabled**. Select it to enable CBR indexing and click **Apply**. You will be prompted for whether you want to also apply that choice to all subclasses. You do, so click **Yes**. (It may take some time for FEM to complete this step after you click **Yes**.)

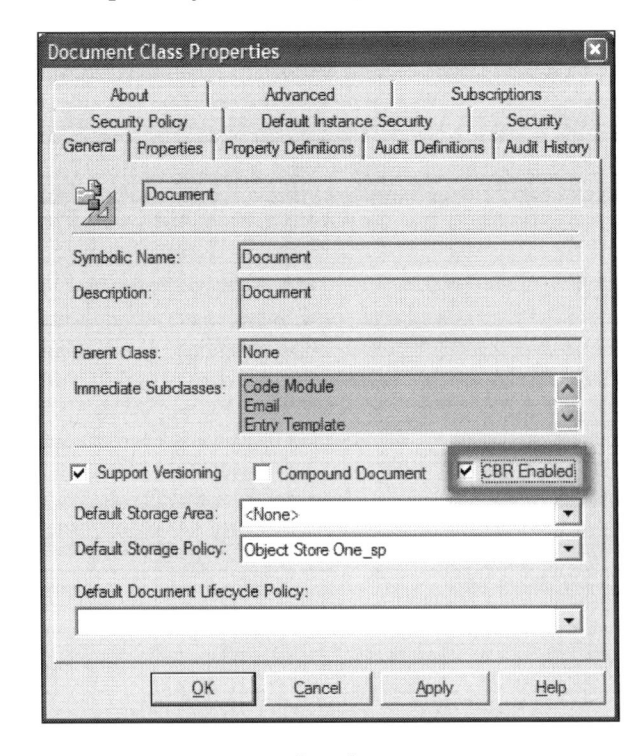

**[ 140 ]**

2. Again, from that same **Document Class Properties** dialogue, select the **Property Definitions** tab. Highlight the row for **Document Title** and click **Edit**. On the **General** tab, you will see a similar checkbox for **CBR Enabled**, this time applying only to this specific property. Select the checkbox to enable CBR indexing, and click **OK** to apply the settings and close the panels. (Again, this step may take some time after you click **OK**.)

This completes the CSE installation and configuration. The CE and the CSE are loosely coupled and some indexing is done in batches for performance reasons, so it can take a few minutes for new content to show up in the text index. By default, the CE dispatcher background thread runs every three minutes. Some additional time may be needed for indexing if the CSE has to first extract the text from a word processing document or similar file.

You can test that your CE and CSE servers are configured correctly by adding some documents to Object Store One (for test purposes, plain text documents are the simplest), waiting at least three minutes, and then doing a simple keyword search for those documents from the K2 Dashboard. To do that, open the K2 Dashboard with your web browser and navigate to **System View | K2 Servers | wjc-search-server**. On the page that opens, click the **Test Search** link. Type a search term that you know is present in the document in the **Search for** field and click **Search** button. Your test document should be found.

Now let's turn to another major component, the Process Engine.

# Process Engine server (PE server)

IBM FileNet Business Process Manager (BPM) is a world-class process management suite available from IBM. Like CM, it consists of many tools and other software components. The centerpiece of BPM is the Process Engine, and CM includes a limited-use license for PE. We'll see later that AE and XT include two pre-defined workflow definitions that you can use out-of-the-box with PE.

*Installing Other Components*

The PE is not currently supported on Linux (though it is supported on various other flavors of Unix, and it will be supported on Linux in the P8 5.0.0 release), so we will be installing it on a Microsoft Windows server. We can, however, still use the Linux-based DB2 instance that we already installed on `wjc-rhel.example.net`. In a production environment, the databases would likely be installed on their own set of servers, and we would want the PE database close—in geography and network topology—to the PE servers. For our all-in-one environment, we're simply reusing the already-installed DB2 instance for our own convenience.

At a high level, the following are the steps in installing the PE server:

1. Configure operating system accounts on both Linux and Microsoft Windows. There is also an LDAP directory user and group.
2. Configure database for PE use.
3. Install database client software on Microsoft Windows.
4. Install and configure PE server software on Microsoft Windows.
5. Configure PE items in CE.

## Users and groups

As we have done in other examples, the user and group accounts we're using here are the same as the figurative names used in the PPG and the installation worksheet. You can choose different names if you'd like. If you use different names, then watch for the note about aliases when we get to the PE installation program.

On the Microsoft Windows server (where the PE will be installed), create the following. Our environment is not part of a Windows domain, so all of our users and groups are local.

- Group `fnop`: Members of this group are PE operators.
- Group `fnusr`: Members of this group are PE users but not operators.
- Group `fnadmin`: Members of this group are PE administrators.
- User `fnsw`: Add this user to groups `fnop`, `fnadmin`, and `fnusr`. If there is a Microsoft Windows group `Administrators`, also add this user to that group. This user account is used to start and stop PE software. We will also use it for installing the PE server software.

On the Linux server (where DB2 is installed), create the following local operating system accounts:

- User `f_sw`: This is the PE's primary runtime user ID for database activity
- User `f_maint`: Used by the PE for database maintenance

In the Tivoli (TDS) directory, create the following. If you need help with creating TDS users and groups, refer to the section for adding CE users and groups in *Chapter 2*.

- Group pe_admin_group: Members of this group automatically get certain administrator privileges in PE.
- User pe_service_user: The PE uses this account when contacting the CE. This user must be a member of the LDAP group pe_admin_group.

# Database configuration

The database steps consist of creating tablespaces (Linux), configuring user account permissions (Linux), and installing the DB2 client software (Windows).

## DB2 database and tablespaces

Although we could create the PE-related tablespaces within one of the CE databases, it's easier to see what's going on if we keep things completely distinct. We'll use the same DB2 instance, but we'll create a database for PE use. We'll use the conventional name for this (VWDB), but you could use a different name.

Using the DB2 Command Center for instance db2inst1 (see *Chapter 2* if you need a refresher on how to launch it), perform the following actions:

1. Create the new database, VWDB, with automatic maintenance.
2. All PE-related tablespaces need a minimum page size of 8 KB. The default buffer pool probably has a page size of 4 KB. Within database VWDB, create a new buffer pool with a page size of 8 KB. As a mnemonic, we'll call it VWDB8K. We'll use that buffer pool with all the tablespaces we create in this database.
3. Create a new system temporary tablespace.
4. Create a new user temporary tablespace.
5. Create three large tablespaces with automatic storage and a minimum size of 200 MB. Use these names: VWDATA_TS, VWINDEX_TS, and VWBLOB_TS.
6. You can delete the default tablespace that was created with the database.

## DB2 user permissions

In a previous step, we created a couple of Linux operating system user accounts, f_sw and f_maint, that PE will use for its database interactions with DB2. Now it's time to give database permissions to those accounts. Because we are using Linux user accounts for a PE server running elsewhere, we will use DB2 server authentication. We'll just summarize the necessary permissions here. If you need a refresher on how to do this in DB2, see the DB2 configuration steps for CE in *Chapter 2*.

For user f_sw:

1. Connect to database.
2. Create tables.
3. Use privilege for each of the "VW" tablespaces that we just created.

For user f_maint:

1. Determine the Linux operating system group that has SYSADM rights. You can do that by running the command db2 get dbm cfg and examining the output. In our configuration, it's the group db2iadm1 that was automatically created during DB2 installation.
2. Determine the primary group of the DB2 instance owner db2inst1. It's most likely the same group db2iadm1 just mentioned.
3. Make the f_maint user a member of the groups in the previous two bullets.

## DB2 client software

The PE running on the Windows server needs DB2 client software to be able to talk to the DB2 server running on the Linux server. Installation of the DB2 client software is straightforward, and we don't cover it in detail here. We'll just mention a few specific points:

- From the DB2 installation program, you need only install the IBM Data Server Client package. Unless you are really tight on disk space, we suggest you do the "typical" installation option.
- For simplicity, we uncheck the box labeled **Enable operating system security**.
- The default installation location is C:\Program Files\IBM\SQLLIB\.

Launch the *DB2 Configuration Assistant* from the Windows Start menu by navigating **Start | All Programs | IBM DB2 | DB2COPY1 (Default) | Set-up Tools | Configuration Assistant**. (Your DB2 instance name might be different from **DB2COPY1**.) The *DB2 Configuration Assistant* provides a convenient graphical interface for configuring DB2 client software connectivity to a remote database. Locate and configure a connection for database `VWDB` in DB2 instance `db2inst1` on host `wjc-rhel.example.net`. The tool provides many helpers for browsing or discovering these components. Give the database an alias that is the same as the database name (`VWDB`).

If you find yourself manually configuring the DB2 connectivity, you can find or confirm the port number by running the *DB2 Control Center* for instance `db2inst1` on the DB2 server (our Linux server). Right-click the node for instance **db2inst1** and select **Setup Communications**. From the panel that appears, click the **Properties** button for **TCP/IP**. The connectivity parameters will be displayed, including the port number. In our case, it was port 3801. Also make sure that the port is not blocked by a firewall so that `wjc-w2k3.example.net` can connect to it.

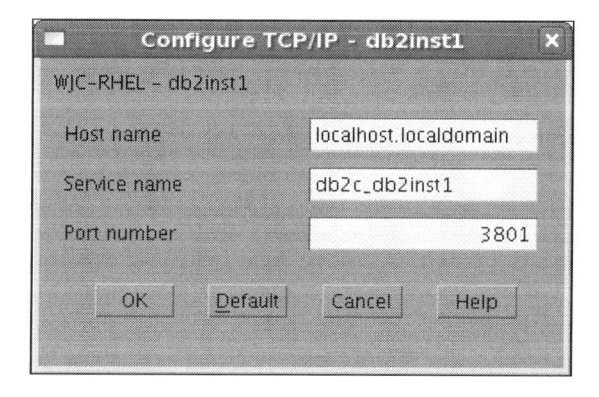

After you have configured the local connectivity to the remote database, the **DB2 Configuration Assistant** gives you the opportunity to test the connection. You should do so, testing with both the `f_sw` and the `f_maint` userids. Assuming that all went as expected, you can close the **DB2 Configuration Assistant**.

# PE server installation and configuration

Now that DB2 client software and its connectivity to the DB2 server have been taken care of, it's time to install and configure FileNet software on the Windows server.

*Installing Other Components*

## PE server installation

It's time to run the PE server's installation program. It will have a name like `P8PE-4.5.1-WIN.EXE`, possibly with a different version number in your installation. We won't detail each step of the installation, but here are a few key points:

- You want to run the installer as the operating system user `fnsw`, so either log in as that user or use Microsoft Windows "run as" feature (right-click on the installation program name in Windows Explorer and select **Run As**; select the user `fnsw` from the drop-down menu and enter `fnsw`'s password).

- Tell the installation program that your database is DB2 and that it is not on zOS (unless your DB2 *is* on zOS, in which case, you know what to do).

- If you set up your DB2 database with the names we used above, then the defaults in the installation program's **Specify DB2 Configuration Parameters** panel will already be correct for you. If they are not, make any necessary adjustments.

- If you used the default user and group account names, as we did above, then you can say "no" on the panel **Determine Administrator User and Group Aliasing Method**. Otherwise, you must say "yes" and enter the names you used on the next panel.

At the conclusion of the installation, the **Process Engine Services Manager** Windows service should be automatically started.

## CE client installation

Install the CE client software on the PE server. This software gives the PE the ability to initiate a connection to the CE server for various purposes. The installation program will have a name like `P8CE-CLIENT-4.5.1-WIN.EXE`.

- As above, run this installer as the user `fnsw`, either by logging on as that user or by using the Windows "run as" feature.

- In the panel **Select FileNet P8 Applications**, the entry for **Process Engine** will probably already be checked. If not, select it.

- A default value will be provided for the CE server URL, but it will not be correct. Change it to this value: **cemp:http://wjc-rhel.example.net:9081/wsi/FNCEWS40MTOM/**. (Except for the **cemp:** prefix, this is the same URL that you configured for connecting to the CE server with FEM in *Chapter 3*.)
    - The **cemp:** prefix is there for legacy reasons and may be gone in the version of the installer that you run.
    - As usual, the CE server host name is **wjc-rhel.example.net**.

- ○ We used a second WAS profile for the CE server, so the HTTP port is 9081 instead of the default value of 9080.
- ○ The scheme **http:** and the path element **wsi/** indicate that we will be using the CE API's CEWS transport (which used to be called WSI transport).
- ○ The path element **FNCEWS40MTOM** indicates that we will be using MTOM format (a web services standard) for attachments in our SOAP requests. The alternative that you may sometimes see is **FNCEWS40DIME**. Choosing MTOM instead of DIME (an older, obsolete web services standard) makes very little difference to you, but the DIME format is deprecated and and will not be supported as of CE 5.0.0.

- Complete the rest of the CE client installer program.

## PE server configuration

Most PE server configuration will be done by using the Process Task Manager.

1. Run it by navigating from the Windows Start menu: **Start | All Programs | IBM FileNet P8 Platform | Process Engine | Process Task Manager**. You will probably see a PE server with the same name as the Windows host name, and it will not be running. Right-click on it and select **Start** to start the Process Service. Once it is started, the red "x" on the icon will disappear.

> If the Process Service does not start, check to make sure that the Windows service named **Process Engine Services Manager** is started. If not, start it manually and make sure it is marked it for automatic startup.

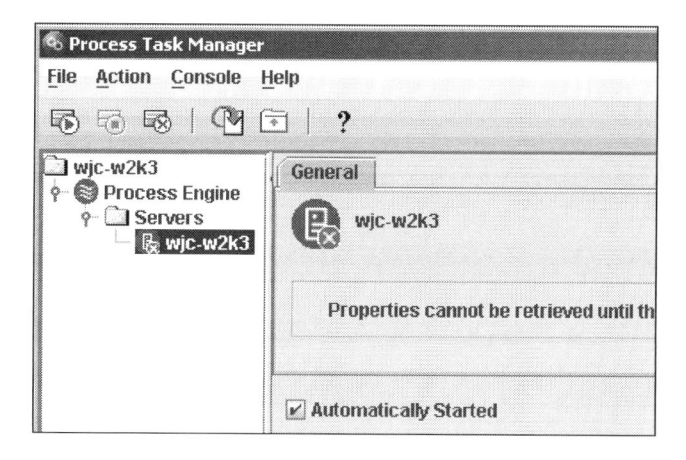

*Installing Other Components*

2. When the Process Server is running, you will be brought to the **Process Engine** multi-tabbed properties panel. If that doesn't happen automatically, select **Process Engine** from the tree and select the **Security** tab from the displayed panel.

3. The **Security** tab will already be showing the CE connection URL that you provided during the CE client software installation. Enter the **pe_service_user** userid (and password) and the **pe_admin_group** group. Leave the **Configuration Group** field empty (we did not create one).

4. Click **Apply** and click **Yes** when prompted to restart the Process Service.

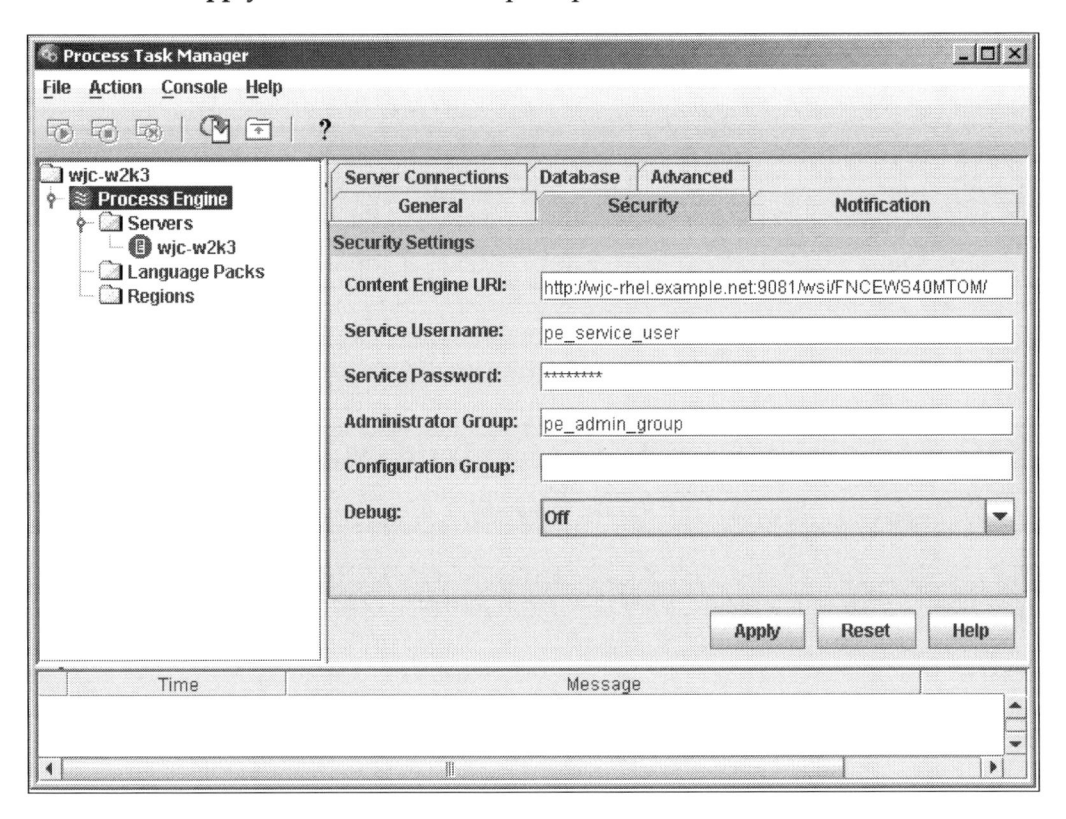

5. Select the **Regions** node in the tree. Right-click and select **New** to create a new PE isolated region.

[ 148 ]

6. On the **General** tab, we'll choose a number for the isolated region. The PE uses isolated regions to identify essentially distinct partitions of PE operations and data within a physical PE server. The isolated region number is an arbitrary value as long as you don't choose one that is already in use for something else in this Domain. It probably won't surprise you to learn that the most popular choice is 1; the highest allowed value is 999. For variety, let's use **398**. Whatever you choose, remember that value for later. Use the default tablespace.

7. One the **Security Settings** tab, enter a password for the isolated region. Obviously, you must also make a note of that value for later.

8. Click **OK** and click **Yes** when prompted to restart the Process Service. Exit the Process Task Manager application.

# Shared memory

The PE server uses shared memory extensively in its internal architecture, so it's rather important to give it access to as much contiguous shared memory as you can. The PE provides a utility for figuring that out and creating a Windows registry update file to configure the base address of that large shared memory segment.

From a command line on the Windows server, opened as user `fnsw`, run these commands:

```
C:\> c:\fnsw\bin\set_shm_address.exe -r shm.reg
C:\> type shm.reg
C:\> shm.reg
C:\> del shm.reg
```

The first line runs a PE utility which computes the shared memory segment information and creates the registry update file, `shm.reg`. The third line applies those registry settings. You will probably be prompted for a confirmation.

After doing this step, you should restart the PE software. In fact, for good measure, it might be a good idea to completely reboot the Windows server at this point. The necessary PE services should restart automatically.

*Installing Other Components*

## Test the connections

After all of those configuration steps spread across two servers and several components, the time has now come for a small moment of truth. We will test the PE server's connectivity to the database using the configured information. From a command line on the Windows server, opened as user `fnsw`, run the command `c:\fnsw\bin\vwcemp -l`. If successful, `vwcemp` will report some cryptic facts about the connection and configuration. The important part is that it doesn't report an error. If there are errors, you'll have to recheck the configuration steps in the sections above.

In the event you have problems connecting from the PE to the CE, the PE team in IBM has published this *Troubleshooting the PE to CE Security Configuration* tech note: `http://www-01.ibm.com/support/docview.wss?uid=swg21328045`.

## CE configuration for PE

The PE server is installed and has been configured for connectivity initiated from the PE server to the CE server. We must now configure the opposite direction to enable communications to be initiated from the CE to the PE. This happens, for example, when a CE event handler launches a PE workflow. The CE uses the notion of PE connection points to identify PE connectivity and security information for a PE isolated region. You will be creating and configuring those kinds of objects via FEM.

1. Run FEM and connect to `wjc-rhel.example.net` as user `gcd_admin`.
2. In the tree on the left, select **PE Region Ids**, right-click and select **New PE Region Id**.
3. Follow the wizard steps, and supply the PE isolated region information from earlier sections in this chapter (PE server **wjc-w2k3.example.net**, region number **398**).
4. The region password is the same as the one we entered a previously when we created isolated region `398` on the PE server.
5. In the tree on the left, select **PE Connection Points**, right-click and select **New PE Connection Point**.
6. You can give the connection point any name you want as long as it's unique among connection points within the Domain. We used **wjc-w2k3-398**.
7. Select the just-created isolated region.

> Before you can use the workflow-related features of XT, you must configure a **Process Engine Connection Point** on the **General** tab of XT site preferences. You will be offered a list in a drop-down menu and should select the connection point that we just created.

[ 150 ]

## PE client software

A bit later, we'll install the PE client software into the XT environment. Because the CE server is on the same physical machine, the PE client installer will notice them both and perform the update in one pass. If, for some reason, you are not installing either AE or XT, then you must install the PE client software for the CE server's use. Follow the steps described below for installing the PE client software for XT.

## Application Engine (AE)

AE terminology can be slightly confusing. On the one hand, you install the AE in order to deploy the Workplace application. Workplace is the primary out-of-the-box application aimed at an end user audience. On the other hand, the AE is also a platform upon which custom applications can be built. Many of the features of Workplace can be directly exploited through integration points in a custom **Model-View-Controller** (**MVC**) framework. The AE includes a toolkit for building such applications: the **Web Application Toolkit (WAT)**.

If you plan to use all custom applications in your environment, do you need to install and deploy the AE (or XT)? No, you do not; that is, unless your applications are built on top of WAT. If your applications are built directly on top of the CE and PE APIs, then you can skip installing the AE. However, even if that is the case, we would suggest you install the AE or XT, at least in your development environments. It is quite handy to have an out-of-the-box tool for verifying this or that little detail, or to compare against your own custom coded efforts.

Because the AE and XT have similar places in the CM ecosystem, we'll skip the installation of the AE and go directly to installing XT in the next section. If you would like to install the AE in your environment, you will find the installation quite similar to the XT installation. In particular, the LDAP directory preparation steps are exactly the same and need only be done once if you are installing the AE and XT into the same WAS profile. The feature discussions in other chapters will focus on XT instead of AE, although in many cases the features are functionally equivalent.

## Workplace XT (XT)

Workplace XT is an out-of-the-box web application for accessing many CM features. You can browse, search, and directly manipulate many types of objects in the CE, and you can also participate in workflows running in the PE. XT runs in a J2EE web container. Because it communicates with the CE via EJB transport, XT must run on the same brand and version of application server as the CE server.

*Installing Other Components*

The Workplace application in the AE (now informally called "Workplace classic") originally had the constraint of working in an HTML 3.2 environment. XT, on the other hand, uses a more modern UI paradigm, with more of a so-called Web 2.0 look and feel. XT developers started with the Workplace classic code base and, subsystem by subsystem, have modernized the UI. Although there are still a few pieces of the Workplace classic code within XT, most of it has been rewritten. XT does not include the full WAT for custom application integration, but there are still several hooks where custom menu items and actions can be added. XT uses an industry standard MVC framework, so augmenting it is less of a specialist task than doing the same for Workplace.

We'll install XT inside its own WAS profile on the same physical server as the CE. It is not supported to install them into the same profile (due to both performance and functional reasons). In a production environment, except for environments with light loads, you probably would not install XT and CE on the same physical server. Splitting them gives you better control over load balancing and their individual scaling behaviors.

The installation process for XT consists of:

- Preparation steps (LDAP directory and trust relationships)
- Installing the software
- Configuring and deploying the software

## Configure LDAP

Recall that in *Chapter 3* we installed the CE server into profile `AppSrv02`. We'll now install XT into profile `AppSrv01`. It's a requirement that XT uses the same LDAP directory setup as the CE server, so our first step will be to make sure `AppSrv01` matches the LDAP setup we already did in `AppSrv02`. There are a couple of approaches to that. If you are something of a WAS expert, you can just copy relevant sections of the WAS configuration files from `AppSrv02` to `AppSrv01`. You could also use the Configuration Manager (as we did for the CE install in *Chapter 3*), retargetting it to `AppSrv01`, and applying the LDAP configuration. We will instead manually configure things via the WAS administrative console.

> Because these are two separate profiles, we could theoretically have the consoles open simultaneously in separate browser windows, which would facilitate side-by-side comparisons. In practice, this is likely to confuse the browser cookies holding the session information and drive you slightly crazy. If you have two different browsers installed, for example Firefox and Internet Explorer, you can open one console in each.

1. Log on to the WAS console for `AppSrv01`. Navigate to **Security | Global Security**.
2. In the section for **User account repository**, select **Standalone LDAP registry** from the drop-down list, and click **Configure**.
3. Click **Advanced Lightweight Directory Access Protocol (LDAP) user registry settings**.
4. Enter these values in the configuration panel:
    - **User filter**: `(&(cn=%v)(objectclass=person))`
    - **Group filter**: `(&(cn=%v)(|(objectclass=groupOfNames)(objectclass=groupOfUniqueNames)(objectclass=groupOfURLs)))`
    - **User ID map**: `*:uid`
    - **Group ID map**: `*:cn`
5. Click **OK** to return to the previous panel.
6. Enter these values in the configuration panel:
    - **Primary administrative user name**: `was_admin`
    - **Type of LDAP server**: `IBM Tivoli Directory Server`
    - **Host**: `wjc-rhel.example.net`
    - **Port**: `389`
    - **Base distinguished name**: `dc=whozit,dc=example,dc=net`
    - **Bind distinguished name**: `cn=ce_service_user,cn=people,dc=whozit,dc=example,dc=net`
7. Click the **Test connection** button. If for any reason the connection to the directory is not successful, you must correct it at this point. If you proceed without correcting any problems, you might lock yourself out of the WAS console for this profile. (Don't ask us how we know this.)
8. Click **OK** to return to Global security.
9. Click **Set as current** to make this configuration the current realm definition.
10. Select the checkboxes for **Enable administrative security** and **Enable application security**. Uncheck all boxes in the section for **Java 2 security**.
11. Click **Apply**.
12. Near the top of the screen, you will see links to **Save** or **Review** your changes. Click **Save**.

*Installing Other Components*

If you log out of the WAS console and then log back in, you'll notice that you are still using the old credentials. You must restart WAS profile **AppSrv01** to bring the LDAP changes into effect; do so. From this point, you must use userid `was_admin` to log on to the WAS console for `AppSrv01`, just as you have been doing for `AppSrv02`.

## Trust relationships and LTPA

During user authentication, an object called a JAAS Subject will be created on the XT application server. That Subject must be trusted by the CE application server. Different vendors use different techniques to enable this so-called trust relationship.

The technique used by WebSphere involves a mechanism called Lightweight Third Party Authentication (LTPA). The usual practice is to export WAS LTPA keys from the CE server and import them into the XT server.

To export LTPA keys, use the WAS console for `AppSrv02`. Navigate to **Security | Global Security**. In the **Authentication** box, make sure that **LTPA** is selected, and click the **LTPA** link.

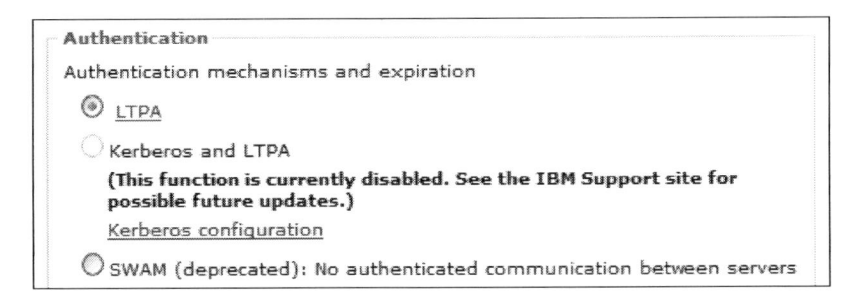

Supply the password and filename requested in the **Cross-cell single sign-on** box and click **Export keys**.

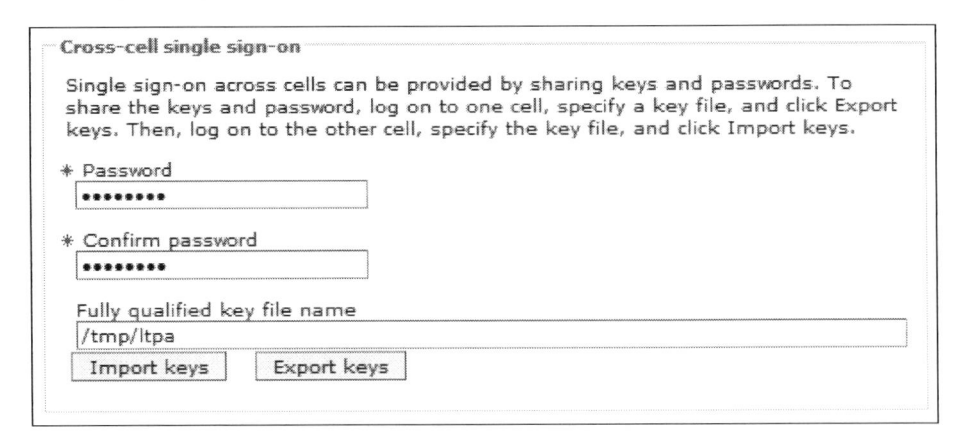

Log off the WAS `AppSrv02` console, log in to the WAS `AppSrv01` console, navigate to the same area, and click **Import keys**. We suggest you restart `AppSrv01` after importing the LTPA keys.

## Run the installer

Locate and run the XT installer image appropriate to the server operating system, in our case `WorkplaceXT-1.1.4.0-LINUX.bin`. For most questions that the installer will ask, the answer will be obvious or you can just take the supplied default.

> Disk space used by XT may exceed your expectations. We recommend having at least 2 gigabytes of disk space available when doing an XT installation. A lot of that can be recovered after XT is deployed into the application server.

When prompted for the CE API configuration, use the value **cemp:iiop://wjc-rhel.example.net:2810/FileNet/Engine** in all three fields, as shown in the following screenshot. Notice, in particular, the port number is **2810** instead of the usual WAS default of 2809.

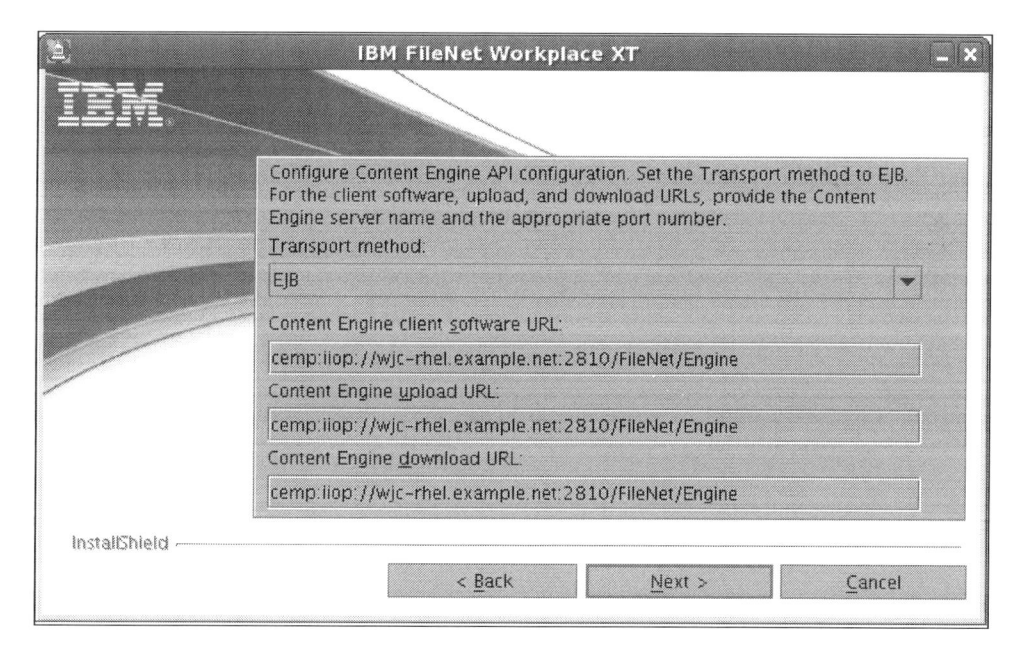

[ 155 ]

*Installing Other Components*

> On the panel for configuring user token security settings, leave the box unchecked for **Create maximum strength keys**. That will be fine for this demonstration system. For production, maximum strength keys are a good idea, but you may have to configure the WAS Java environment with a policy file download. We're avoiding that complication for now, but you can read about user tokens and related cryptography settings in the XT documentation.

Choose EAR file deployment (not WAR file deployment). Work through the remaining installer panels and complete the XT software installation. When you have finished, the XT software will have been installed, but the XT EAR file is not yet deployed to the J2EE application server.

XT writes log files to a directory within the installation tree. So that the running WAS process can create files in the directory, perform the following command, which changes the ownership of the XT logging directory to `ecmuser` and the group to `ecmgroup`:

```
# chown ecmuser:ecmgroup /opt/ibm/FileNet/WebClient/LogFiles
```

## CE and PE client software

XT communicates with both the CE server and the PE server. Like any other application, XT needs access to the client-side software provided by those servers.

> If you are installing both AE and XT, you can do these steps after you have run the installers for both AE and XT, in which case the client updates will be done for both. It's no different from doing them separately for AE and XT; it just saves you a little trouble.

### CE client

The CE client software and configuration files must be installed into the XT environment. This is similar to the step we did earlier for the PE server. In this case, the CE client installer name is `P8CE-CLIENT-4.5.1-LINUX.BIN`. The presence of the XT installation should be automatically detected if you used the default path in the XT installer. The rest of the installation should be uneventful.

Since you are going to be installing the PE client software immediately after this, you can save a little time by skipping the creation of the EAR file right now. On the **Create Deployment File** panel, select **Create the file later**.

## PE client

The PE client software and configuration files must also be installed into the XT environment. In this case, the PE client installer name is `P8PE-CLIENT-4.5.1-LINUX.BIN`. The presence of the XT installation should be automatically detected if you used the default path in the XT installer. It will also detect the presence of the CE server, so leave both boxes checked.

The PE client needs to connect to the CE server, and it wants to use the CE Java API's CEWS transport. For the CE connection URL, use the value `http://wjc-rhel.example.net:9081/wsi/FNCEWS40MTOM/`. As we've noted elsewhere, this is the same URL used to configure FEM. It is possible to configure the PE client to use EJB transport, but it requires some complicated manual configuration steps, and there is no good motivation for doing it.

Do select the installation of the PE REST service when asked. It's needed by the ECM Widgets. If you don't install it here, you can add it later by re-running the PE client installer.

We're done updating the XT environment, so select **Create the WAR or EAR deployment file now**. It was probably already selected by default.

## XT pre-deployment configuration

There are a few optional configuration steps that can be done to XT before it is deployed to the application server:

- **SSO**: You can configure XT to participate in various standardized single sign-on (SSO) schemes
- **User Tokens**: You can configure XT's user token cross-authentication mechanism to allow for third-party integration with XT

We won't be describing the SSO setup here, but several CM components do exploit user tokens (for example, the XT Image Viewer applet), so let's enable them:

1. Copy the following JAR files to `/opt/ibm/WebSphere/AppServer/lib/ext/`. Of course, we show the default paths for the JAR files and the destination directory:
    - `/opt/ibm/FileNet/WebClient/WorkplaceXT/authenticationFiles/authentication-websphere.jar`
    - `/opt/ibm/FileNet/WebClient/WorkplaceXT/WEB-INF/lib/log4j.jar`

*Installing Other Components*

2. Specify a JAAS configuration file for WAS profile `AppSrv01`. In the WAS console, navigate to **Servers | Server Types | WebSphere application servers | server1**. On the **Configuration** tab, select **Java and Process Management | Process definition**, and from there select **Java Virtual Machine**. In the field **Generic JVM arguments**, add this Java command line argument (keep any other arguments that might already be there): **-Djava.security.auth.login.config=/opt/ibm/FileNet/WebClient/CE_API/config/jaas.conf.WebSphere**.

3. Enable trust association:
   - Still in the WAS console for profile `AppSrv01`, navigate to **Security | Global security | Web and SIP security | Trust association**. Select the checkbox to enable trust associations, and click **Apply** and then **Save**.
   - Return to the **Trust association** page, click **Interceptors**, and add a new interceptor with class name **com.filenet.ae.authentication.tai.UserTokenInterceptor**. Click **OK** to return to the list of interceptors. Click **Save** to update the WAS configuration.

4. Log out of the WAS console, and restart the WAS profile `AppSrv01`.

## Deploying XT

> All of the changes we just made were to WAS itself and not to files under the XT install directory. If you make any such changes to the XT files, or if you asked the CE or PE client installers to not automatically rebuild the deployment files, then you must rebuild the deployment files (EAR or WAR) manually. You'll find scripts for that purpose in the directory `/opt/ibm/FileNet/WebClient/deploy/`.

Actual deployment of XT is mostly a standard WAS EAR deployment done via the WAS console:

- Log on to the WAS console for profile AppSrv01 and navigate to **Applications | Application Types | WebSphere enterprise applications**. Click **Install** to add a new application.
- On the panel that opens, you're prompted for the location of the XT EAR file, on either the local or remote filesystem. "Local" means the machine where you are running the browser, and "remote" means the machine where WAS is running. In whichever case is appropriate for you, enter the filename **/opt/ibm/FileNet/WebClient/deploy/web_client.ear**, and click **Next**.
- Work through the remaining WAS panels for installing a new EAR. We suggest you take the WAS **Fast Path** and accept the defaults offered. Some of the steps may take a bit of time because the files being manipulated are quite large. Be sure to **Save** your changes on the final panel.

You'll be brought back to the **Enterprise Applications** list. You'll see WorkplaceXT in that list, but it will not yet be started. Before starting it, we have to make a few important configuration changes, described in the following subsections.

## Classloader configuration

Click on **WorkplaceXT**, and then click **Class loading and update detection**. Select the radio button to choose **Classes loaded with local class loader first (parent last)**. Click **OK**. (This classloader policy was called "application first" in earlier versions of WAS.)

That should bring you back to the WorkplaceXT configuration page. Click **Manage Modules**, and select **WorkplaceXT**. (The seeming redundancy is because this is the WAR file within the EAR file.) From the drop-down list, choose **Classes loaded with local class loader first (parent last)**. Click **OK**.

**Save** the changes.

*Installing Other Components*

## Map special subjects

Mapping special subjects enables the Container-Managed Authentication (CMA) aspects of XT.

Again, navigate to **Enterprise Applications | Workplace XT**. Click the link **Security role to user/group mapping**. Select the **All Authenticated** row, and from the **Map Special Subjects** drop-down menu, choose **All Authenticated in Application's Realm**.

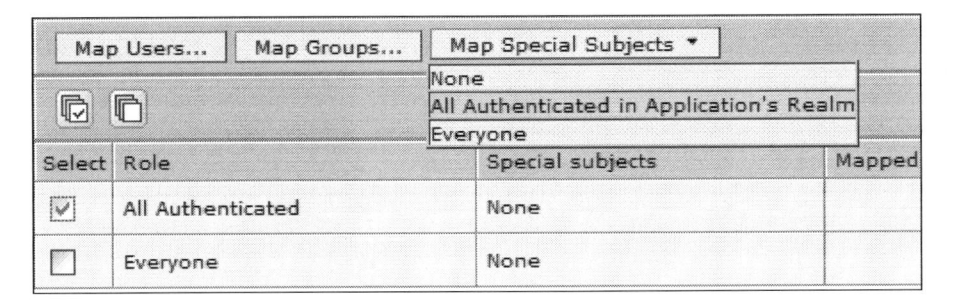

Select the row **Everyone**, and map it to the **Everyone** entry from the drop-down.

**Save** these changes.

## ORB uniqueness

This item is required because of the special circumstance of installing XT (or any CE application using EJB transport) on the same server host as the CE server. Without this configuration, JNDI lookups can become confused. You must make this change in both `AppSrv01` and `AppSrv02`.

Navigate to **Servers | Server Types | WebSphere application servers | server1**. From there, select **Java and Process Management | Process definition**. Click the link for **Java Virtual Machine** and select **Custom properties**. Create a new property, **com.ibm.websphere.orb.uniqueServerName**, and give it the value **true**.

**Save** these changes. Don't forget to do the same configuration for the other WAS profile.

## Running XT the first time

After all of the configuration items in the previous sections, it's a good idea to restart both of the WAS profiles. Restarting `AppSrv01` will have the side-effect of starting XT if it was not started earlier.

Connect to XT by entering this address into your web browser: `http://wjc-rhel.example.net:9080/WorkplaceXT`.

The very first login to XT should be done from an administrator userid. That userid will automatically be added to a list of **Application Engine Administrators**. That's a list of users who are allowed to make changes to XT site preferences. The first XT screen seen on the first login will be the **Bootstrap** preferences page. You can read the information available via the **Instructions** link or consult XT documentation for guidance, but it's reasonable to take the defaults for our demo system.

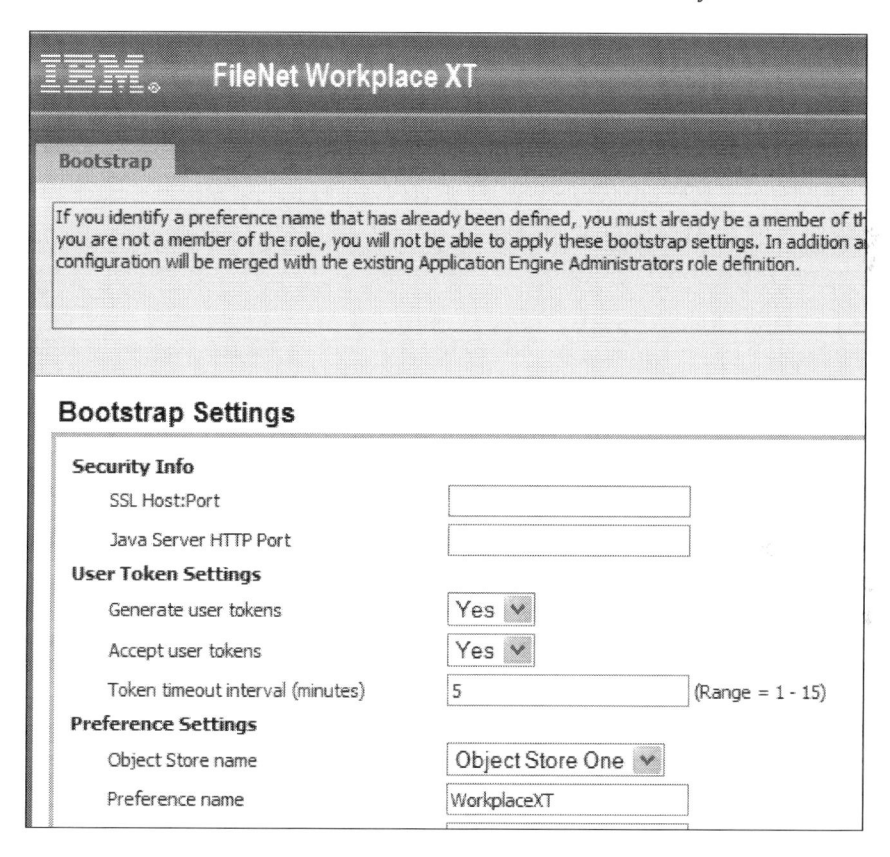

> Before you can use the workflow-related features of XT, you must configure a connection point in XT site preferences. **Navigate to Tools | Administration | Site Preferences**. In the **General** tab, locate the entry for **General Settings | Tasks | Process Engine Connection Point**. You will be offered a list in a drop-down menu and should select the connection point that we created earlier in this chapter, **wjc-w2k3-398**.

*Installing Other Components*

# IBM System Dashboard for ECM (SD)

Once you have your CM system up and running, its ongoing operational health will become interesting, especially for your production environment. Almost all P8 technical components constantly gather statistics on many aspects of ongoing activity. Statistics are gathered on throughput rates, average transaction times, and so on. When something seems to be operating incorrectly, it can be invaluable to look at the trends of internal counters for various components. The meaning of "normal values" will vary from site to site, but the administrator of a given site will often be able to tell at a glance which component is unusual.

> System Dashboard is included with CM. It should not be confused with an add-on product called IBM FileNet System Monitor. Although they are built on much of the same infrastructure, counters, and statistics, System Monitor is a more proactive tool, able to continuously monitor target systems and provide alerting, automated routine responses, restarts, and so on.

SD is an included component that gives a view into the counters and other statistics maintained by various components. You can use SD to drill down into specific areas for problem solving and troubleshooting. Also, routine use of SD can help an administrator detect potential problem areas before they impact end users.

The single SD installation file contains installation programs for all supported platforms as well as complete product documentation in PDF format. Using the root account on the Linux server, run the command `Linux_ECMDashboard.bin` to launch the graphical installation process.

> It may be necessary to make the installation program executable (`chmod +x Linux_ECMDashboard.bin`). If you are installing from a physical disk or image, you will probably have to copy things to a temporary location where you can make that kind of change.

Accept the defaults to get a "typical" installation into the `/opt/ibm/FileNet/Dashboard/` directory. Run the Dashboard by executing the `Dashboard` executable in that directory.

Configuration of System Dashboard is simple for our two machine setup.

1. Navigate to directory `/opt/ibm/FileNet/Dashboard/`, and run the `Dashboard` command. From the opening screen, select the **Clusters** tab.

2. Click **New** to add a new cluster, giving it whatever name you would like. We suggest you give it the same name as your Domain, **Lucky**.

3. Highlight the cluster name just added to the list and click **Edit**.
4. Use the **Add** button to add both of our server hosts, **wjc-rhel.example.net** and **wjc-w2k3.example.net**.
5. Click **OK** to close the edit panel.
6. Use menu **File | Save Clusters As** to save your cluster definition to a file in a convenient location. In future runs of the Dashboard, you'll be able to load cluster file definitions instead of recreating them each time.

[ It is normal to get an error for any host in the cluster that does not happen to be running any P8 software components. If P8 components are running on a given host, they will normally be discovered automatically even if the Dashboard is running remotely. ]

# Rendition Engine (RE)

RE, also known as the Publishing engine or service, can transform commonly-used business document formats into HTML or PDF. The content of the documents is not changed, and the format is rendered as faithful to the originals as possible. The CE maintains links between the original version (called the **source** document) and the rendered version (called the **target** document).

[ RE is separately licensed and is not included in a basic CM license. ]

There are two typical use cases for RE:

- A site might want to make content available on a web site in a format that is either vendor-neutral or usable by the widest possible audience (or both). Both HTML and PDF fit this scenario.

- A site might want to permanently capture, for compliance or other reasons, the exact state of a document at some instant in time. Although CM reliably keeps track of all content changes and prevents any content change once a document version is checked in, there are sometimes external reasons for wanting an official snapshot of the content. For many scenarios, PDF is the format of choice for this sort of snapshot.

Installation of RE is straightforward, but, for the sake of brevity, we won't show it here. In a production environment, RE would be installed on a separate server from CE so that you can better manage the two different kinds of loads. In an all-in-one environment, RE and CE can be installed together, though RE is limited to running under Microsoft Windows.

## Summary

Although we said the centerpiece of CM is the CE, you can see from this chapter that there are many more components that make up the entire CM picture. We installed several of those components and described a few more. This ends our installation and configuration for the time being, and we'll use these tools to look at more CM features in *Chapter 6*.

# 6
# End User Tools and Tasks

In *Chapter 4, Administrative Tools and Tasks* we saw how to do a number of administrative activities, mostly in **FileNet Enterprise Manager (FEM)**. We'll see a few more of those type of topics scattered throughout the later chapters, but in this chapter, we'll turn mostly to something else—things that end users would be likely to do. Our primary tool for that will be Workplace XT (XT), though many of the same features are also available in Workplace "classic". As in Chapter 4, our primary motivation is to show concepts more than it is to present a tutorial for particular applications.

This chapter covers the following topics:

- An overview of the XT application
- Browsing and related operations
- XT entry templates
- Workflow interactions
- Document versioning
- Properties and security manipulation
- XT search interfaces

Parts of some of these topics will cover things that are features of the XT application rather than general features of CM and the P8 platform. We'll point those out so there is no confusion.

# What is Workplace XT?

IBM provides complete, comprehensive APIs for writing applications to work with the CM product and the P8 platform. They also provide several pre-built, ready to use environments for working with CM. These range from connectors and other integrations, to IBM and third-party applications, to standalone applications provided with CM. Business needs will dictate which of these will be used. It is common for a given enterprise to use a mix of custom coding, product integrations, and standalone CM applications. Even in cases where the standalone CM applications are not widely deployed throughout the enterprise, they can still be used for *ad hoc* exploration or troubleshooting by administrators or power users.

XT is a complete, standalone application included with CM. It's a good application for human-centered document management, where users in various roles actively participate in the creation and management of individual items. XT exposes most CM features, including the marriage of content management and process management (workflow).

> XT is a thin client web application built with modern user interface technologies so that it has something of a Web 2.0 look and feel. To run XT, open its start page with your web browser. The URL is the server name where XT is installed, the appropriate port number, and the default context of WorkplaceXT. In our installation, that's http://wjc-rhel.example.net:9080/WorkplaceXT. We don't show it here, but for cases where XT is in wider use than our all-in-one development system, it's common to configure things so that it shows up on port 80, the default HTTP port. This can be done by reconfiguring the application server to use those ports directly or by interposing a web server (for example, IBM HTTP Server, IHS) as a relay between the browser clients and the application server. It's also common to configure things such that at least the login page is protected by TLS/SSL. Details for both of these configuration items are covered in depth in the product documentation (they vary by application server type).

For some of the examples in this chapter, we'll log on as the high-privileged user poweruser, and, for others, we'll log on as the low-privileged user unpriv. We mentioned both of those directory users in *Chapter 2, Installing Environmental Components*. If you didn't create them, you can create them now or substitute any pair of non-administrator accounts from your own directory.

*Chapter 6*

# Browsing folders and documents

Let's have a look at XT's opening screen. Log onto XT as user `poweruser`. With the folder icon selected from the top-left group of four icons, as in the figure below, XT shows a tree view that allows browsing through folders for content.

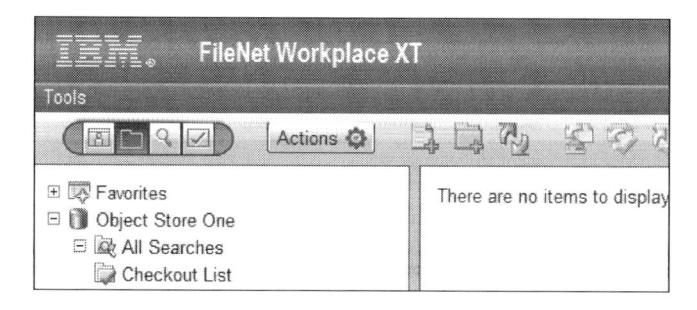

Of course, we don't actually have any content in the Object Store yet, so all we see when we expand the **Object Store One** node are pseudo-folders (that is, things XT puts into the tree but which are not really folders in the Object Store).

Let's add some content right now. We'll have a lot more to say about the technical features of foldering and containment in *Chapter 7, Major CM Features*. For now, we'll concentrate on the user view of things.

# Adding folders

In the icon bar are two icons with small, green "+" signs on them (you can see them in the screenshot above). The left icon, which looks like a piece of paper, is for adding documents to the currently expanded folder. The icon to the right of that, which looks like an office supply folder, is for adding a subfolder to the currently expanded folder.

Select **Object Store One** in the tree view, and click the icon for adding a folder.

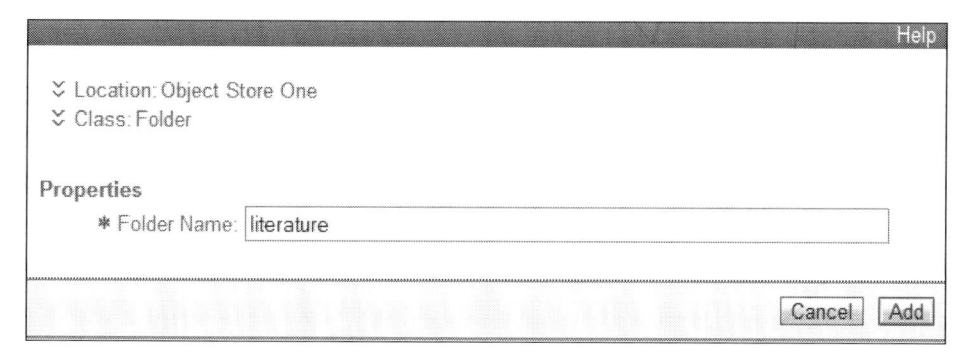

[ 167 ]

*End User Tools and Tasks*

The first panel of a pop-up wizard appears, as shown above, prompting you for a folder name. We have chosen the name `literature` to continue the example that we started in *Chapter 4, Administrative Tools and Tasks*. Click the **Add** button, and the folder will be created and will appear in the tree view. Follow the same procedure to add a subfolder to that called `shakespeare`. That is, create a folder whose path is `/literature/shakespeare`.

You can modify the security of most objects by right-clicking and selecting **More Information | Security**. A pop-up panel shows the object's **Access Control List (ACL)**. We'll discuss ACLs in more detail in *Chapter 8, Security Features and Planning*. For now, we just want to allow other users to add items to the `shakespeare` folder (we'll need that for the illustration of entry templates when we get to that section below). Open that folder's security panel. Click the link for **#AUTHENTICATED-USERS**, and check the **File In Folder** box in the **Allow** column, highlighted in the following screenshot:

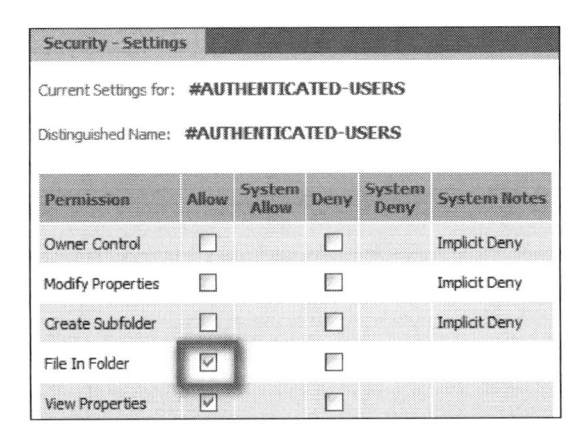

| Permission | Allow | System Allow | Deny | System Deny | System Notes |
|---|---|---|---|---|---|
| Owner Control | ☐ | | ☐ | | Implicit Deny |
| Modify Properties | ☐ | | ☐ | | Implicit Deny |
| Create Subfolder | ☐ | | ☐ | | Implicit Deny |
| File In Folder | ☑ | | ☐ | | |
| View Properties | ☑ | | ☐ | | |

Current Settings for: **#AUTHENTICATED-USERS**
Distinguished Name: **#AUTHENTICATED-USERS**

## Adding documents

Now let's add some actual documents to our repository. We'll add a few of Shakespeare's famous works as sample documents.

> There are many sources for electronic copies of Shakespeare's works readily available on the Internet. One of our favorites for exercises like this is at the Massachusetts Institute of Technology: http://shakespeare.mit.edu. It's handy because it's really just the text without a lot of notes, criticisms, and so on. The first thing you see is a list of all the works categorized by type of work, and you're only a click or two away from the full HTML text of the work. It doesn't hurt that they explicitly state that they have placed the HTML versions in the public domain.

*Chapter 6*

We'll use the full versions in a single HTML page for our sample documents. In some convenient place on your desktop machine, download a few of the full text files. We chose *As You Like It* (`asyoulikeit_full.html`), *Henry V* (`henryv_full.html`), *Othello* (`othello_full.html`), and *Venus and Adonis* (`VenusAndAdonis.html`).

Select the `/literature/shakespeare` folder in the tree view, and click the icon for adding a document. The document add wizard pops up, as shown next:

Browse to the location of the first document file, `asyoulikeit_full.html`, and click the **Next** button. Don't click **Add Now** or you won't get the correct document class for our example.

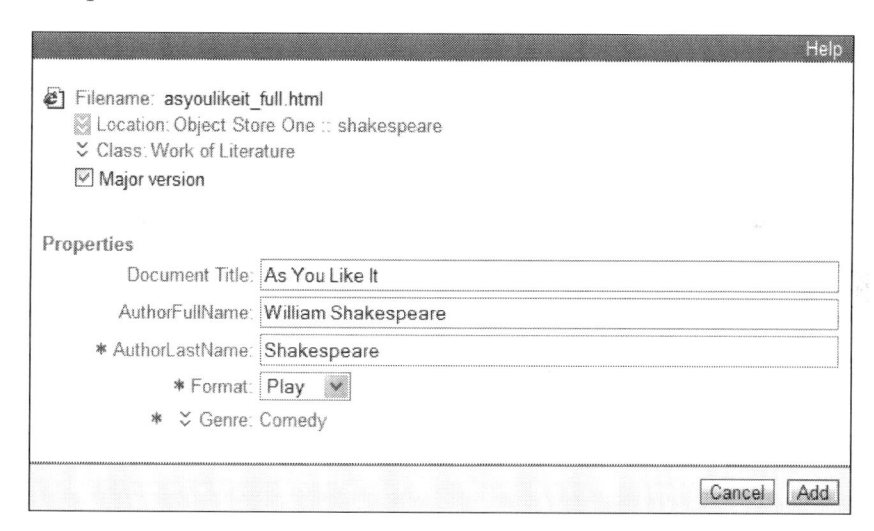

Initially, the class **Document** is indicated. Click on **Class** and select **Work of Literature**. The list of properties automatically adjusts to reflect the custom properties defined for our custom class. Supply the values indicated (note in particular that you have to adjust the **Document Title** property because it defaults to the file name). XT uses the usual convention of marking required properties with an asterisk. Click **Add**.

[ 169 ]

End User Tools and Tasks

Repeat the above steps for the other three documents. You'll now have a short list in the `shakespeare` folder.

| Name | Size | Modified By | Modified On | Major Version |
|---|---|---|---|---|
| As You Like It | 226 KB | poweruser | 10/16/10 1:10 PM | 1 |
| Henry V | 263 KB | poweruser | 10/16/10 1:13 PM | 1 |
| Othello | 298 KB | poweruser | 10/16/10 1:21 PM | 1 |
| Venus and Adonis | 63 KB | poweruser | 10/16/10 1:22 PM | 1 |

XT also provides a "landing zone" for the drag-and-drop of documents. It's located in the upper right-hand corner of the browser window, as shown next. This can save you the trouble of browsing for documents in your filesystem. Even though it can accept multiple documents in a single drag-and-drop, it prompts only for a single set of property values that are applied to all of the documents.

> Logged in as: poweruser
> Preferences | Help | Log out
>
> Drag files here to add

## Viewing documents

Clicking on a document link in XT will lead to the download of the content and the launching of a suitable application. For most documents, the web browser is used to find and launch an application based on the document content type, although XT does have some configurability in its site preferences for customizing that behavior. The behavior you can normally expect is the same as if you clicked on a link for a document on any typical website.

For graphical image content (JPEG, PNG, and similar formats), XT launches the Image Viewer applet. The Image Viewer applet is especially handy for dealing with **Tagged Image Format Files (TIFF)** graphics because most browsers do not handle TIFF natively. It is common for fax and scanning applications to generate TIFF images of pages. However, even for common graphics formats that can be rendered by the browser, the Image Viewer applet has more functionality. The most interesting extra features are for adding textual or graphical annotations to the image. Rather than directly manipulating the original image, the annotations are created in an overlay layer and saved as Annotation objects in the repository. For example, in the image below, being displayed in the Image Viewer applet, the stamp tool has been used to mark it as a **DRAFT**. That annotation can easily be repositioned or even removed without affecting the original image.

> The **included Image Viewer applet is licensed only** for use within the **FileNet components** where it's already integrated. It is an OEM version of **ViewONE from Daeja Image Systems**. The ViewONE Pro application, which has additional functionality, is available for license directly from Daeja and can be integrated into FileNet applications as a supported configuration. However, in such cases, support for the viewer itself comes directly from Daeja.

# Entry templates

Although each step of document and folder creation is individually straightforward, taken together they can become bewildering to non-technical users, especially if coupled with naming, security, and other conventions. Even when the process is completely understood, there are several details which are purely clerical in nature but which still might suffer from mis-typing and so on.

From these motivations comes an XT feature called Entry Templates. Someone, usually an administrator, creates an entry template as an aid for other users who are creating folders or documents. A great many details can be specified in advance, but the user can still be given choices at appropriate points.

To create an entry template, navigate to **Tools | Advanced Tools | Entry Templates | Add**. A wizard is launched from which you can define a **Document Entry Template** or a **Folder Entry Template**. We won't go through all of the steps here since the user interface is easy to understand. Both types of entry templates are Document subclasses, and XT files created entry templates into folders. When you double-click on an entry template, XT presents a user interface that adheres to the entry template design. For example, in this screen shot which uses an entry template called **Shakespearean Document**, the document class and target folder are already selected and cannot be changed by the user. Likewise, the author last and full names are pre-populated. Other properties, which genuinely need user input, can be edited as usual.

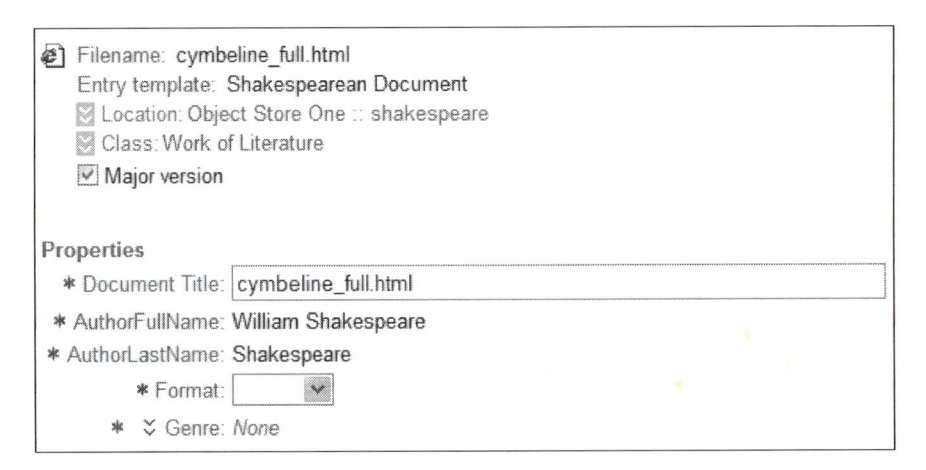

```
Filename: cymbeline_full.html
Entry template: Shakespearean Document
☑ Location: Object Store One :: shakespeare
☑ Class: Work of Literature
☑ Major version

Properties
  * Document Title: cymbeline_full.html
  * AuthorFullName: William Shakespeare
  * AuthorLastName: Shakespeare
  * Format: [   ▼]
  * ⌄ Genre: None
```

# Workflow interactions

XT not only communicates with the CE for content management, but it can also communicate with the **Process Engine (PE)** to manage workflows. Among the choices offered when you are creating an entry template is the launching of an associated workflow. Like many other features discussed in this chapter, there are multiple ways to launch workflows from XT, but using them in entry templates is a common one.

# One-time isolated region setup

You will recall that we configured a PE isolated region in *Chapter 3, Installing the Content Engine* and we selected that isolated region in the XT site preferences in *Chapter 5, Installing Other Components*. Before using that isolated region, it must be initialized.

As user `gcd_admin` or any other user who you have made an Application Engine Administrator, navigate to **Tools | Administration | Process Configuration Console**. The Process Configuration Console is implemented as a Java applet. In the tree view, locate the **wjc-w2k3-398** isolated region. Right-click and **Connect** to it. Right-click again and **Initialize Isolated Region**. The PE database for the isolated region will be populated with various structures, as seen here:

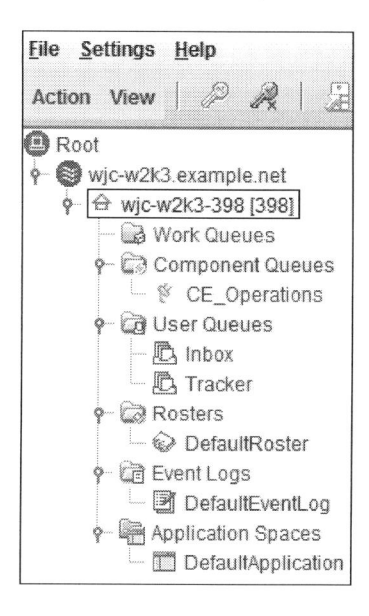

Running workflows can make calls back into the CE to modify documents and other objects. You might, for example, have an approval workflow that updates a document's lifecycle state to reflect approval or rejection. The PE mechanism for allowing running workflows to call out to other systems is called **Component Integrator**, and the specific implementation for calls to CE is called **Content Extended Operations**. It is reflected in the **CE_Operations** component queue seen in the above image.

> The Component Integrator is an extremely powerful feature of PE, and you are not limited to the specific things implemented in CE_Operations. You can implement your own components, including making additional types of CE calls.

*End User Tools and Tasks*

There are many configuration parameters for tuning Content Extended Operations, but our immediate interest is in the credentials that it will use when calling back into the CE. Right-click the **CE_Operations** node and select **Properties**. On the **Adaptor** tab, as seen here, are fields for the **User Name** and **Password** to be used. This user must have sufficient CE access rights to perform the operations that will come through Content Extended Operations. In general, this means the ability to make a very flexible set of changes to many or most objects in the CE. Obviously, that is a very powerful account. Our advice is to make a dedicated directory account for just that purpose, as we have shown here, and take precautions to protect it from compromise.

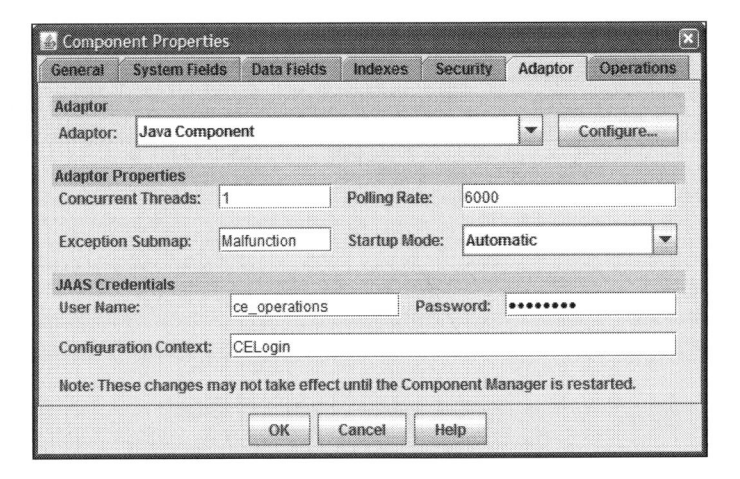

# Approval workflows

If you have a full BPM license, you will have a variety of tools for creating and managing workflows. With a CM license, you have a PE server and two workflow definitions provided with XT. Both are offered during the **Select Workflow** step of entry template creation.

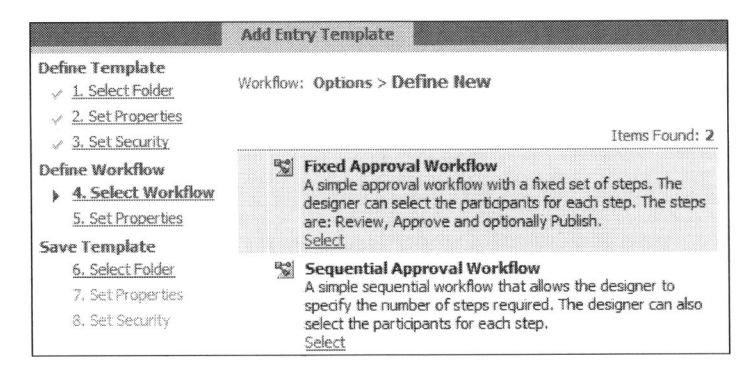

As you can see from the captions in the previous screenshot, the **Fixed Approval Workflow** consists of a pre-defined two or three step workflow. This satisfies many common use cases for simple document approval. For more complex cases, the **Sequential Approval Workflow** allows you to create additional steps. The names of the specific steps are merely suggestions and can be renamed to anything you want. Participants in each workflow step can be specified when the workflow is associated with the entry template or can be left to the user to assign at run time.

## Tasks in XT

Participants in workflows can see pending items in XT inboxes. In this screenshot, you can see that the user, poweruser, is looking at the **Tasks** area of XT. Because poweruser is listed as a participant in the **Reviewers** step of the **Fixed Approval Workflow** that was launched when someone added the Cymbeline document, that approval step appears in the inbox, ready to be approved or rejected.

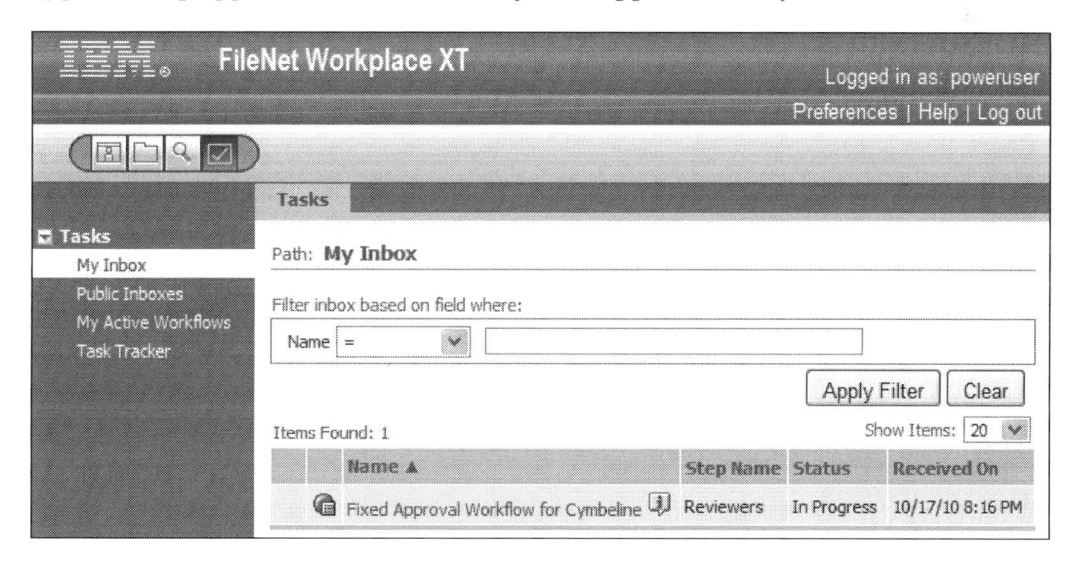

If the user clicks on the link, XT's HTML step processor will open. The reviewing user will have a pointer to the document as the primary workflow attachment and can see that the workflow was launched by the user **unpriv**. For this scenario, that means that **unpriv** added the document. If **poweruser** approves the workflow step, the work item will be moved from his/her inbox to the inbox of the participants listed in the **Approvers** step. On the other hand, while the workflow is in progress, **unpriv** can check its progress by looking at the **My Active Workflows** menu item.

*End User Tools and Tasks*

# Versioning

Adding and browsing documents is one thing, but documents must often be manipulated in various ways. The most fundamental manipulation is **versioning**. In an ECM context, versioning means the controlled ability to modify the content of a document. In CM, you can't literally modify the content of a document, but you can create a new version of the document and modify the content of that new version in the process. We'll cover versioning in more technical detail in *Chapter 7, Major CM Features*. For now, let's just see how it works.

While logged onto XT as `poweruser`, select the `/literature/shakespeare` folder in the tree view. Let's imagine we've noticed a typographical error in one of the texts. We'll simulate correcting it by making an inconsequential change. Select **Venus and Adonis**, and perform a checkout operation. You can do that in a couple of different ways in XT. For our purposes, right-click and select **Check Out and Download** from the context menu. You'll be prompted for a location to save the contents of the file downloaded from the repository. Select any convenient location, but don't overwrite your original. You'll see that a small red check mark appears next to the document in XT to indicate that it's checked out. Nobody else can check out the same document until we check it back in or cancel our checkout.

> While we have a document checked out, you might be interested in clicking the **Checkout List** pseudo-folder in the tree view to see that our document is, indeed, on the list.

Open the downloaded file `VenusAndAdonis.html` with an editor (not with a web browser). If you happen to have an HTML editor or a word processor that understands HTML, that's fine. Otherwise, just use any text editor. The files we got from MIT have Unix-style line endings, so editors such as Windows Notepad may show them as a hard-to-read jumble, but never mind that for now. Make some small change to the file. For example, you might change the spelling of Shakespeare's name. Anything that you will recognize later is fine. Save the changed file and exit your editor.

Return to XT, select the document again, and this time select **Check In** from the context menu. You'll be prompted to browse for the modified file on your local machine. Once you've done that, click the **Options** button (do not click the **Check In** button yet). You'll see a property sheet like the next figure, which is very similar to the one we originally used to enter the documents into the repository:

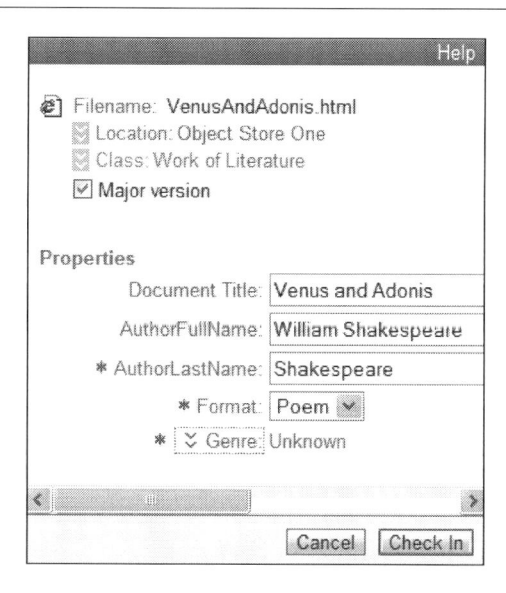

Notice that most or all property values are already populated with values from the previous version. We could change some of those property values here if we were so inclined.

Click the **Check In** button to complete the operation. Notice that the **Major Version** column is bumped from **1** to **2** in XT to indicate that this is the second version of the document. The modification date is also updated to the current date and time.

What happened to the previous version of the document? It's still in the repository and available. From the context menu, navigate to **More Information | Versions**.

You'll notice a pop-up window displaying a complete list of the available versions of the document. It's typical to express the major and minor version information in decimal notation, or, in our case, **2.0** and **1.0**. You can probably guess that you can create minor versions of documents and that there are other **Version Status** labels beyond the **Released** and **Superseded** values that you see in the screenshot. Those details are part of the wider discussion of versioning in Chapter 7.

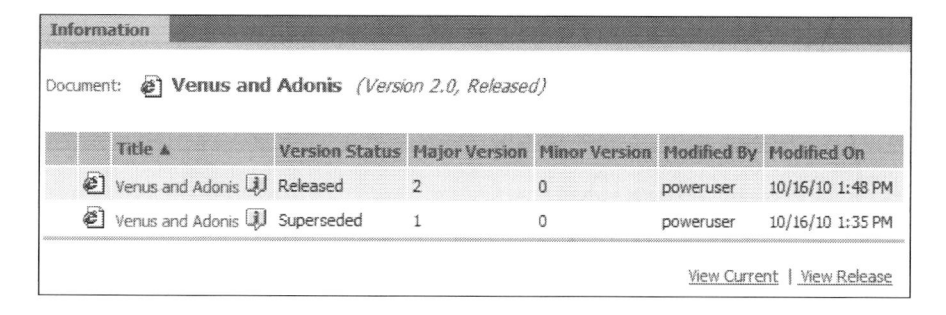

*End User Tools and Tasks*

From that same pop-up screen, you can directly examine the content or property sheet for any version still available in the repository. If you click the hyperlinked value in the **Title** column, that version should open in a web browser. For the Released version, you should be able to spot the change you made. Close the pop-up to return to the main XT screen.

Suppose you've come to regret your decision to modify the document. (Who do you think you are, anyway? Shakespeare?) One option would be to do another checkout/checkin cycle and attempt to restore the file's original contents. Of course, you'd still be leaving around a record of your impudent editing, and you may or may not be able to get back to the original contents for a complex document (unless you realize that you can download the content from an earlier version in the repository). What we really want, in this case, is more of an "undo" for the checkout/checkin cycle that is already completed.

Within the CE, each document version is a separate object that can be manipulated individually. The delete action in XT (and most other tools) acts behind the scenes to delete all of the versions of a document because that is the most common use case. XT also offers the option to delete individual versions. Right-click the document again, and from the context menu navigate to **More Actions | Delete Versions**. You'll see a pop-up listing all available document versions, similar to the previous pop-up. This time, the individual versions have checkboxes next to them, and you can decide which versions you want to delete. Beware that once you delete them, they really will be gone from the repository.

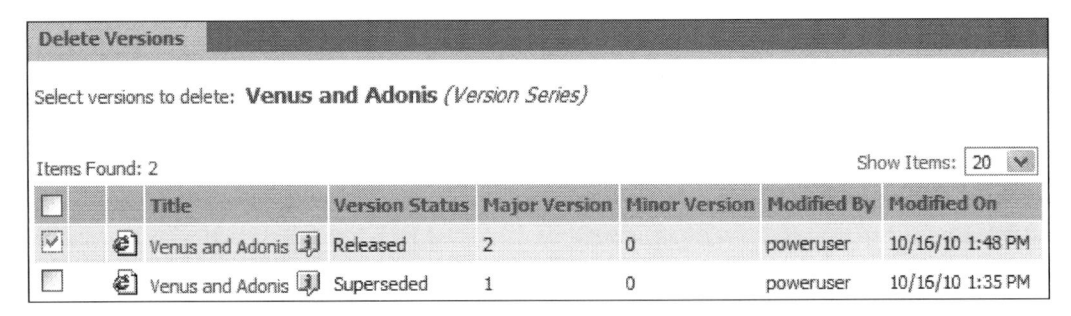

**Delete Versions**

Select versions to delete: **Venus and Adonis** *(Version Series)*

Items Found: 2                                                                 Show Items: 20

| | Title | Version Status | Major Version | Minor Version | Modified By | Modified On |
|---|---|---|---|---|---|---|
| ✓ | Venus and Adonis | Released | 2 | 0 | poweruser | 10/16/10 1:48 PM |
| ☐ | Venus and Adonis | Superseded | 1 | 0 | poweruser | 10/16/10 1:35 PM |

Interestingly enough, it's not just the older versions that you can delete. Notice that you can delete any version, including the current version. Go ahead and do that: check the box for the **Released** version and click **Accept** (do not check the box for the older version). When you get back to the main XT window, you'll see that the major version is once again **1**. If you look at that document's content, you'll see the original, unmodified text, as expected.

Hey presto! It's content management.

> Deleted objects are really, permanently deleted. There is no undo or recycle bin or similar mechanism unless an application implements one.

## Properties and security

While we're here in the browsing portion of the XT user interface, let's briefly look at a few items that can be viewed and updated for a document. Although we'll be examining a document, it illustrates a pattern that is also applicable to folders and other objects in the repository, including the Object Store itself.

Click on a document, for example, **Venus and Adonis**, and select **Properties** from the context menu. A very familiar-looking property sheet will pop up, as shown next. One difference from the property sheets we saw earlier is that this one has a section at the bottom for **System properties**. Every object in the repository has system properties, though the actual properties vary by object type. There are some custom and system properties that XT doesn't show, but all properties are visible to administrators in FEM. Many or all custom properties can be updated from this property sheet, depending on security and how the property was defined. XT will not let you change any values that it can't save to the repository.

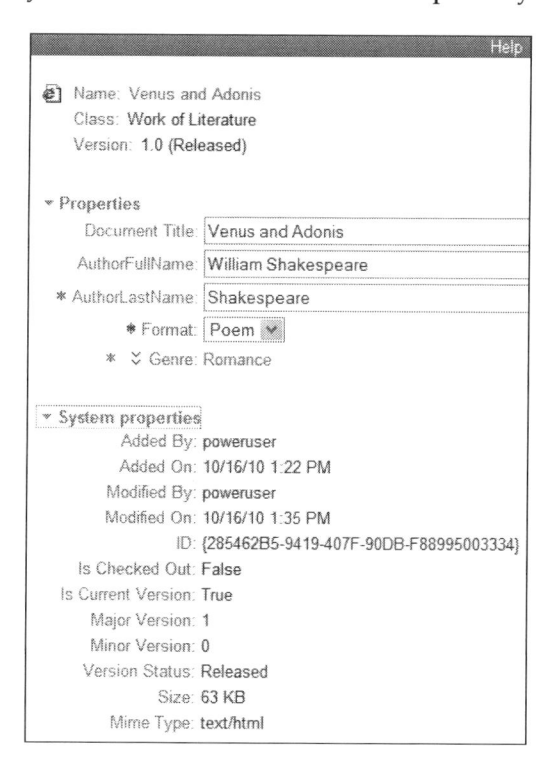

```
                                                                    Help
  Name: Venus and Adonis
  Class: Work of Literature
  Version: 1.0 (Released)

▼ Properties
       Document Title: Venus and Adonis
       AuthorFullName: William Shakespeare
     * AuthorLastName: Shakespeare
             * Format: Poem
           * ⌄ Genre: Romance

▼ System properties
          Added By: poweruser
          Added On: 10/16/10 1:22 PM
       Modified By: poweruser
       Modified On: 10/16/10 1:35 PM
                ID: {285462B5-9419-407F-90DB-F88995003334}
    Is Checked Out: False
  Is Current Version: True
     Major Version: 1
     Minor Version: 0
    Version Status: Released
              Size: 63 KB
         Mime Type: text/html
```

End User Tools and Tasks

If you click on a document and navigate to **More Information | Security** from the context menu, you'll see a pop-up window giving details of the document's access control list (ACL). What we see below is a typical arrangement. The owner, `poweruser`, and the administrators have many rights to do things with the document. Everyone else, members of the pseudo-group `#AUTHENTICATED-USERS`, have only limited rights. The fine-grained security in CM is one of its strongest features, and we'll cover it in detail in *Chapter 8, Security Features and Planning*.

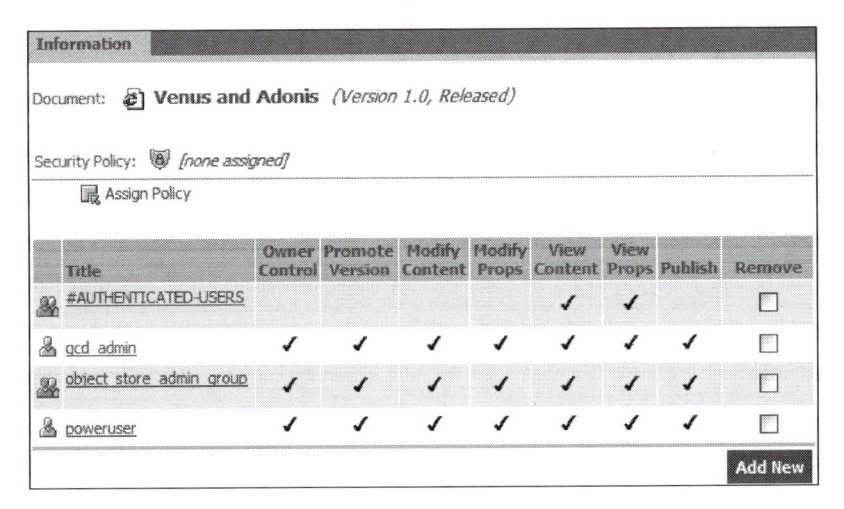

# Searches

Browsing through folders for documents is nice in many respects. It feels natural to most computer users. Once you get to a large number of documents, it can be tedious or impossible to use this technique to find things you want. If you've ever clicked around fruitlessly among the folders on your computer looking for a recipe that someone gave you or for your resume from five years ago, you probably know that you sometimes need a better way.

CM offers two major kinds of searches, and it's even possible to combine the two types into a single search.

- The first type of search has a long history in the ECM and database worlds. It is structured searching based on property values. This is also sometimes called metadata searching.
- The second type of search is of more recent vintage but is available on most ECM platforms today. It is full-text searching based on the content of documents and annotations. CM also offers full text searching for string-valued properties on documents, folders, custom objects, and annotations.

These days, most non-technical users are more familiar with full-text searching because it is quite similar to the type of searching offered by Internet search engines. Non-technical users are less familiar with metadata search.

XT attempts to present both types of searches to users in a way that is rational and easy to use. If you click on the magnifying glass icon, you will see XT's three search types: **Simple**, **Keyword**, and **Advanced**. We'll look at each in turn.

> XT exposes a large percentage of CM search features, but some things are not available. The complete set of search features is available via a Structured Query Language (SQL) dialect specific to the CE. CE SQL can be used directly via the APIs, via FEM, and via a few other tools. We'll have more to say about that in *Chapter 7*.

## Simple Search

The aim of Simple Search is to provide a straightforward interface that serves the most common searching needs. The options pretty much speak for themselves. A user doesn't have to be too concerned with the names of properties and other technical factors. He or she merely clicks the applicable checkboxes, enters a term or two, and XT does the rest. This image shows the results of a search for documents whose name starts with the word "Venus".

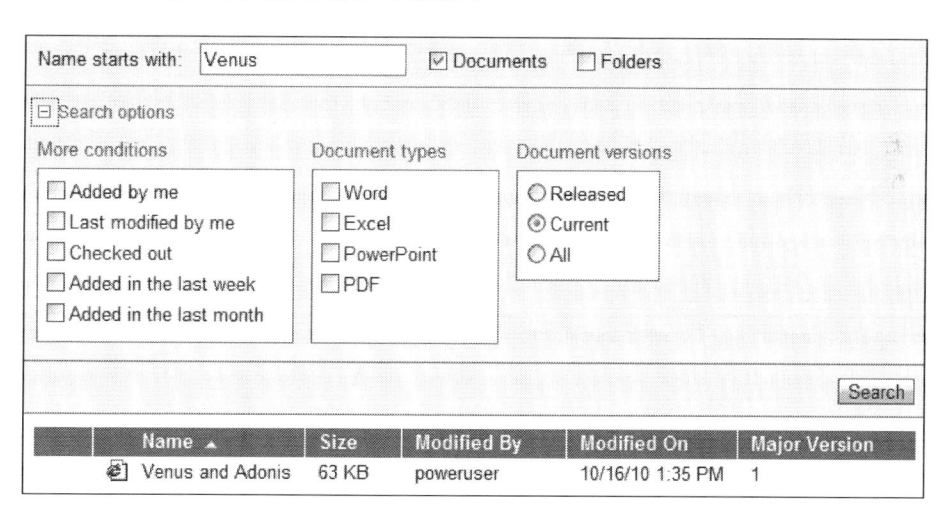

To parody a modern cliché, however: with limited responsibility comes limited power. The simple search does not provide many options for customization or more sophisticated searching capability.

*End User Tools and Tasks*

## Keyword Search

Keyword Search is XT's terminology for full-text searching. You will recall that we configured all Document classes for content-based retrieval (CBR) in *Chapter 5*. CBR is just another term for full-text searching. The XT keyword search can only find things that someone has chosen to index via the CE administrative tools.

In this screenshot, we show a simple keyword search for the word "dispatch", which happens to occur in three of the four documents we added. Keyword search results contain a **Score** column, which is a judgment of the text search engine on how well a document matches the search keywords. If you go and browse around in the text, you will find that *Othello* contains the word "dispatch" four times, *Henry V* has it three times, and *As You Like It* has it only twice. The relative scores reflect that more occurrences of a keyword equates to a better match, at least for simple lists of keywords.

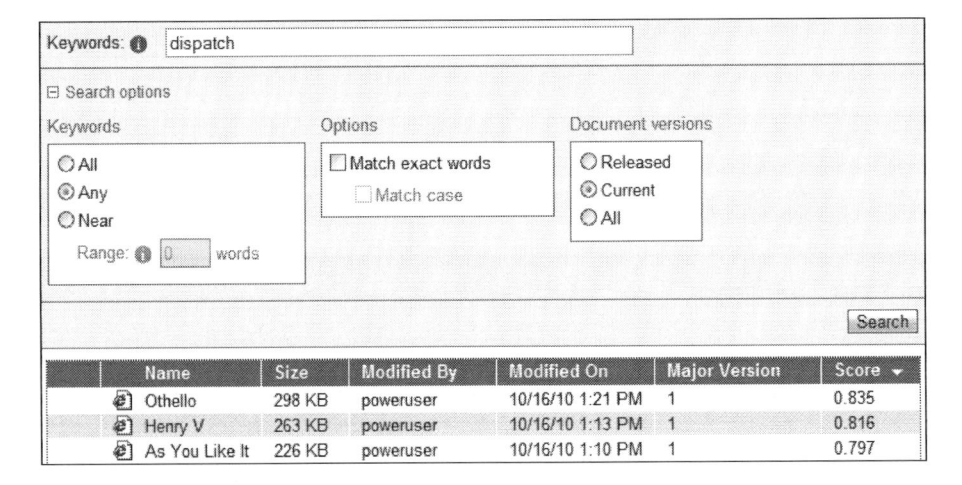

| Name | Size | Modified By | Modified On | Major Version | Score |
|---|---|---|---|---|---|
| Othello | 298 KB | poweruser | 10/16/10 1:21 PM | 1 | 0.835 |
| Henry V | 263 KB | poweruser | 10/16/10 1:13 PM | 1 | 0.816 |
| As You Like It | 226 KB | poweruser | 10/16/10 1:10 PM | 1 | 0.797 |

## Advanced Search

The Advanced Search not only combines the metadata search of Simple Search with the full-text search of Keyword Search, but it also provides powerful features for adding sophisticated custom property conditions to the search. In the screenshot, we've shown just a couple of properties and operations, but rather elaborate conditional expressions can be constructed.

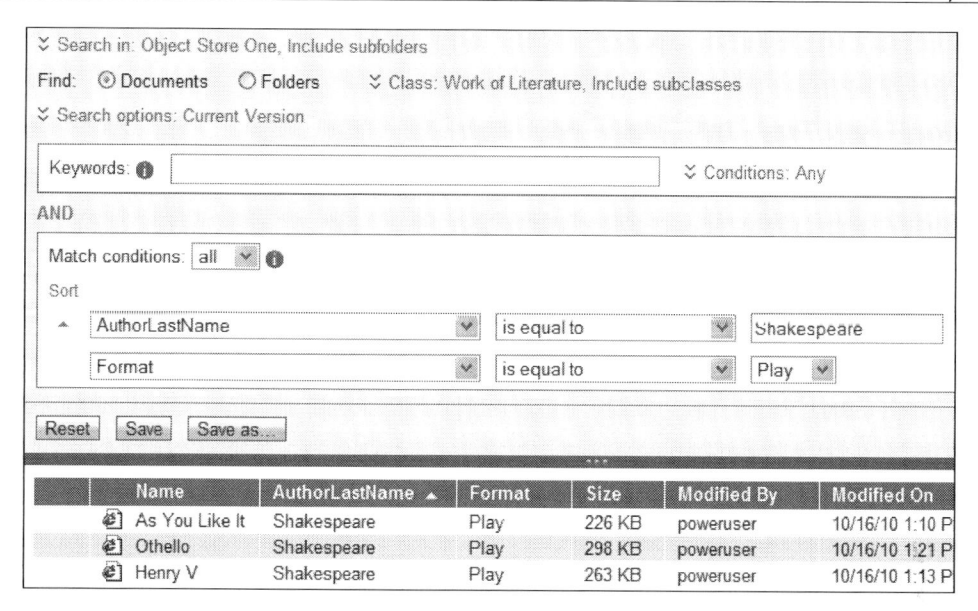

Once you have tuned your search to find just what you are looking for, you can click the **Save as** button to name and save your search. When you come back to XT's search interface, your saved searches are listed on the left-hand side as **My searches**.

## Stored Searches and Search Templates

XT has a feature for pre-defining searches. The usual use case is that an administrator or someone who is technically adept creates the search definition. A more general population can then run the searches with less technical knowledge about the CE and application data models.

The difference between a **Stored Search** (SS) and a **Search Template** (ST) is that the template allows some input from the user at run time. The user who designs an SS or an ST has a great deal of flexibility in predefining restrictive conditions which the running user cannot evade, but there is equal flexibility in the input collected from a user. An SS or an ST is created using a Java applet called **Search Designer** (SD). You launch SD from XT by navigating to **Tools | Advanced Tools | Search Designer**. The SD interface is relatively straightforward, so we'll instead show what the user interface for a Search Template looks like when a user executes it in XT. (We'll show an SD screenshot in our discussion of searching in *Chapter 7*.)

*End User Tools and Tasks*

Stored Searches and Search Templates are Document subclasses, and SD files them in folders of the designing user's choice. When browsing in XT, searches are part of folder contents, just like other documents, though they do have a distinctive icon in the user interface. If you double-click on a Stored Search, XT immediately runs the search and displays the results. If you double-click on a Search Template, XT displays an interface for supplying values according to the ST definition. The search is actually performed when the user clicks the **Search** button.

The following image shows both the search parameters and the search results for an ST that searches for document of class "Work of Literature" and which either have a Document Title that starts with the word "Venus" or have the word "dispatch" within the content. If you have been following the earlier examples, you will not be surprised to see that it returns all four of our sample documents.

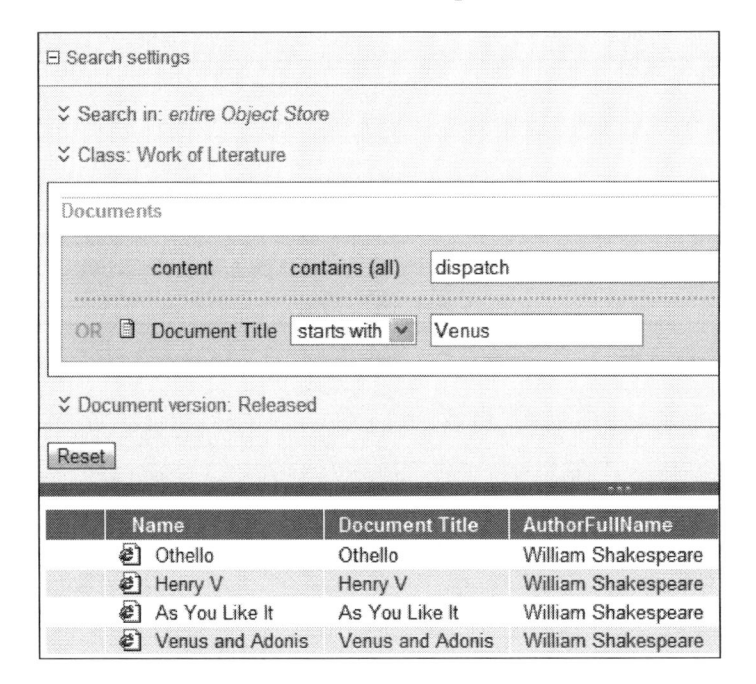

⌐ Search settings

⌵ Search in: *entire Object Store*
⌵ Class: Work of Literature

Documents

| content | contains (all) | dispatch |

OR  Document Title | starts with ▾ | Venus

⌵ Document version: Released

[Reset]

| Name | Document Title | AuthorFullName |
|---|---|---|
| Othello | Othello | William Shakespeare |
| Henry V | Henry V | William Shakespeare |
| As You Like It | As You Like It | William Shakespeare |
| Venus and Adonis | Venus and Adonis | William Shakespeare |

> This example contains a case of simple pattern matching on a string-valued property. The same thing is available several other ways in XT searches, and all use the CE SQL `LIKE` function. You should be aware that matching the beginning of a property ("starts with") is generally reasonably efficient, but matching the middle ("contains") or the end ("ends with") is an inefficient operation at the database level. Unless other conditions are used in the search to refine the potential results set, "contains" or "ends with" can result in database table scans that can gravely impact performance.

# Summary

XT has many more features than we've shown here. The point of this chapter was to give a look at a few typical end user features and operations. You can read more about XT, including customization and site and user preferences, in the CM product documentation.

Now that we've seen things from the end user's point of view, you are probably eager to get to a more in-depth discussion of CM features as they are actually implemented. That is exactly what we will cover in *Chapter 7*, with security topics getting their own treatment in *Chapter 8*.

# 7
# Major CM Features

This chapter is an exploration of most of the features of Content Manager (CM) and a discussion of the major component architecture. Although most of these features show up in one way or another in the out of the box tools included with CM, all CE features can be used in custom code via exposed APIs. It is quite possible to exploit these features to create entirely different conceptual models (from those used by out of the box tools) to be presented to end users. These features, then, should be considered the building blocks and raw materials from which an overall system can be built.

Most of these features are features of the Content Engine (CE), but a few are features of other components. If a feature is part of a component other than the CE, we'll indicate it specifically. As a reminder, CM is a product suite, whereas CE is one of several server platform components.

In *Chapter 1, What is ECM?* we broadly described several must-have features for any ECM system. It is no coincidence and will come as no surprise that most of those are core strengths of CM. In this section, we'll cover many CM features of various sizes and importance. It's quite a long list, but, even so, it doesn't cover everything. Like any set of building blocks, there is some magic in those pre-built pieces, but the greater magic is in the things you can build from them.

We'll cover the following topics in this chapter:

- Documents and document management-related features
- Search-related features
- Features related to folders and containment
- Metadata features and concepts
- Custom Objects, Annotations, and Link objects
- The event subsystem
- Feature AddOns

Because it is a rich topic, we are saving most of the discussion of security for *Chapter 8, Security Features and Planning* which is entirely devoted to security concepts.

# Documents

No questions asked, the single most fundamental feature of any content management system is to be able to, well, manage content. Like many other areas of modern software practice, we use the acronym **CRUD—create, retrieve, update, delete—**to describe interactions with documents. It turns out that many of the features we describe for documents are also features of other object types in the CE, but we'll get to that a bit later in this chapter.

A document in the CE is an independently addressable object that has properties and optional content. Although it's not usually very interesting to create documents without content, it can be done and is sometimes used for things like content that will arrive later.

You may already be familiar with the notion of documents with associated internal properties. Most office productivity applications apply internal properties to the documents they create. These can include things like the author's identity, the time spent editing the document, a copyright notice, or any number of other things. The CE's properties are not directly associated with those internal properties, but it's not unusual for an application adding a document to a CM repository to extract those internal properties from the document and use them to populate similar CE properties. Although the roles for the properties are analogous, you will see that the CE's model for properties is quite a bit richer.

# Content

A document can contain any number of **content elements**. It's easy to understand a content element as being "the actual bits" of a document. If you have a text file, a PDF, a word processor document, or an HTML page on disk, that entire file is the thing we are talking about. The CE stores the file verbatim. No transformation or interpretation is done on the file's contents. When someone later retrieves that document, the content will be 100%, bit-for-bit identical to the content that was uploaded.

One of the key features of the CE is that document content is immutable once it's uploaded to the repository. While a document is checked out (see the *Versioning* section later), you can replace the content as often as you would like, but there is still no such thing as modifying a particular content element. Once a document is checked in, the list of content elements is frozen, and none can be added, deleted, or replaced.

# Multiple content elements

Hold on a minute. What's this about multiple content elements? Why would anyone need that? If you had multiple chunks of content, why wouldn't you just make multiple documents?

There are often cases where a single document falls logically into chunks that are really part of one big document. The most common example is that of documents comprised of fax images. These systems often store the fax image as one page image per content element. These aren't really separate logical documents. They just happen to be broken up into page-sized chunks. It's quite reasonable to use multiple content elements (in a single document object) for this with the content element position in the list representing the fax page number.

There are other kinds of content that consist of multiple logical chunks, and using multiple content elements within a single document may or may not be appropriate. We'll cover compound documents and renditions later in this section to show a couple of examples where there are specific enabling features that suit those use cases. There are also application-specific use cases where it is the application that decides what to put into the multiple content elements. For example, a photo album application might store an image in one content element and the corresponding thumbnail image in another content element. The disadvantage is that other applications would be unlikely to understand that particular convention or many others like it.

The key concept behind using multiple content elements within the same document is that the document as a whole is the thing that is addressable, and all of the document properties, including security, apply to the collection of content elements as a whole. If some content elements will need different security or other properties, then separate documents may be appropriate.

There is substantial infrastructure in the CE to handle multiple content elements, but most use cases use a single content element per document.

# Content transfer and content reference

So far, we have talked only about content that will be stored explicitly within the CM repository in one way or another. Within the CE data model, these are referred to as **Content Transfer** elements (because the content is transferred directly to or from the repository.) There is another kind of content element, the **Content Reference**. As its name suggests, this kind of content is stored elsewhere, and a reference to it is stored in the CM repository. The reference is simply a string representing a URL, and the URL is not transformed or interpreted by the CE. It is common for applications to understand content references and resolve the referenced content, either directly or by passing it off to an operating system utility.

The list of content elements for a given document may consist of any combination of Content Transfer and Content Reference elements.

A Content Transfer element has some interesting properties in addition to the actual content bits. The `RetrievalName` property is not used by the CE but instead serves as a hint for a simple filename for a downloading application to use (for example, `VenusAndAdonis.html`). It's usually set to the original filename (if known) by the uploading application. The `ContentType` property, which is a property of both kinds of content element and, again, typically set by the uploading application, identifies the type of content and can be used as an operating system hint for finding an appropriate application to open the content after download. If the uploading application does not provide a value for `ContentType`, the CE has a fairly simple guessing algorithm based on the `RetrievalName` file extension. It is always better for the uploading application to set both of these properties explicitly, but not all applications do so.

Contrast the content element property `ContentType` with the Document property `MimeType`. These properties are similar in nature but not exactly the same thing. If a value is not provided by the application before checkin, `MimeType` is computed based on the `ContentType` values of the content elements. For documents with a single content element, the two properties will have the same values, but for documents with multiple content elements, the `MimeType` property will indicate a composite type. For convenience, the list of all of the `ContentType` values is available in the multi-valued property `Document.ContentElementsPresent`.

## Content element numbering

Because the list of content elements is, in fact, a list, each element has an implicit position number within the list. Whether the numbering starts at 0 or 1 depends upon the programming language being used, but to users it's just a list of items, so the actual position number seldom matters for user interface purposes. Each content element has an explicit number associated with it in a property called `ElementSequenceNumber`. That number is associated with a specific physical content element; it is not a position number. It never changes and is never re-used (within that document), no matter how many times the list of content elements is changed before the document is checked in.

| Position | ESN |
| --- | --- |
| 0 | 114 |
| 1 | 376 |
| 2 | 248 |

For example, refer to the table above. If you start with a list of three content elements, they will be implicitly positioned at locations 0, 1, and 2 (or 1, 2, and 3) in the content elements list. Let us suppose, for the sake of example, they have `ElementSequenceNumber` values 114, 376, and 248, respectively. If you delete the middle content element, you will still have elements at positions 0 and 1 (or 1 and 2), but the `ElementSequenceNumber` values will be 114 and 248. If you insert a new element between those two elements, you'll be back to the original list of position numbers, but the `ElementSequenceNumber` value for that content element will not be 376. It will be a new number that has never been used before for that document.

## Versioning

After getting content into and out of a repository, perhaps the next most important feature of content management is **versioning**. Versioning, in its most basic definition, refers to being able to update content while keeping track of prior versions. There are many details worth exploring in the CE's versioning.

> What's a revision? Although **version** is a term with a clear and distinct technical meaning in CM, the term **revision** is used less formally and with often overlapping semantics. It is sometimes used to refer to any update of content, including the multiple updates that an author might make to a document in a single checkout/checkin cycle. It is also sometimes used to refer to the notion of an editorially sanctioned set of changes to a document that might have undergone several checkout/checkin cycles during the revision process. Our advice is to always look for context to clarify the particular meaning of revision being used. In any case, do not assume that revision and version are synonymous.

In the CE, as a document is repeatedly versioned, each new version is a Document object in its own right. It has an independent identity, security, property values, and content. In other words, if someone has the ID of a particular document, that ID will always refer to exactly the same document version. (The same is not usually true when referring to a document by path, but we'll get to that in a bit.)

It's not especially handy if each edit of a document is a separate object floating around in the repository, and that's not how it works in the CE. All of the separate versions of that one logical document are united in a collection object called a **Version Series**. The Version Series has its own ID. The property `VersionSeries.Versions` is an ordered collection of the documents related through versioning. In fact, it turns out that the Version Series object doesn't really have any properties of its own. All of its properties come directly from or are synthesized from properties on the documents in it. The access control for the Version Series object is taken from the current document.

*Major CM Features*

As an illustration, here is an XT depiction of the documents in a version series that has had several checkout/checkin cycles. You may wish to refer to this figure as you read about versioning concepts in the rest of this section.

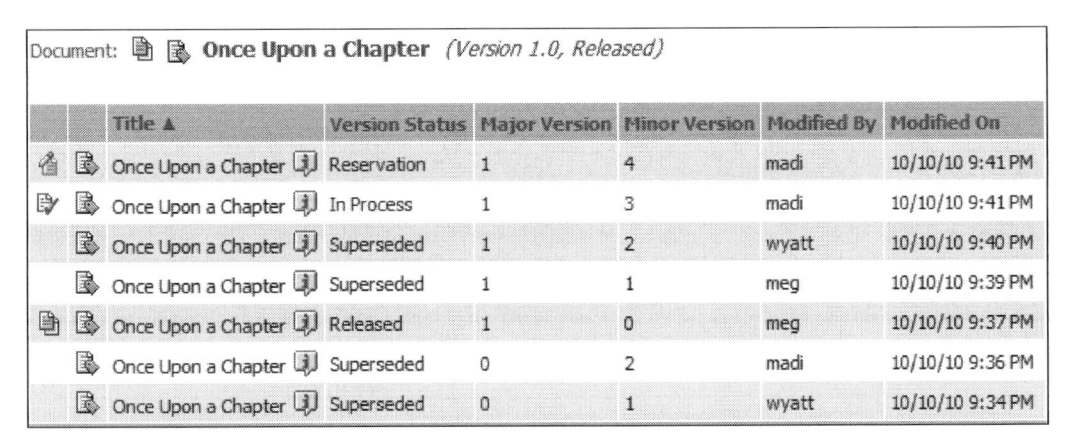

| | | Title ▲ | Version Status | Major Version | Minor Version | Modified By | Modified On |
|---|---|---|---|---|---|---|---|
| | | Once Upon a Chapter | Reservation | 1 | 4 | madi | 10/10/10 9:41 PM |
| | | Once Upon a Chapter | In Process | 1 | 3 | madi | 10/10/10 9:41 PM |
| | | Once Upon a Chapter | Superseded | 1 | 2 | wyatt | 10/10/10 9:40 PM |
| | | Once Upon a Chapter | Superseded | 1 | 1 | meg | 10/10/10 9:39 PM |
| | | Once Upon a Chapter | Released | 1 | 0 | meg | 10/10/10 9:37 PM |
| | | Once Upon a Chapter | Superseded | 0 | 2 | madi | 10/10/10 9:36 PM |
| | | Once Upon a Chapter | Superseded | 0 | 1 | wyatt | 10/10/10 9:34 PM |

Document: Once Upon a Chapter *(Version 1.0, Released)*

Let's recap: All Document objects are also part of a Version Series object. As the documents undergo versioning, the new versions are automatically made part of the same Version Series object. Each document version and the Version Series itself have individual identities. From any Document object, you can navigate to the Version Series object, and from the Version Series object you can navigate to any Document object in that Version Series. (There are short cuts so that you can navigate directly from one Document object to another in the same Version Series.)

## Checkout and checkin

The versioning process in the CE uses a **checkout/checkin** model. That is, someone wishing to make a new version of a document first checks that document out. That action creates a new document version (remember, it's a completely distinct object) which is marked as being a **reservation**. It is the reservation version that actually gets updated and is then eventually checked in. In contrast, the document version that was checked out is said to be **reserved**.

There can be only one checkout operation at a time for a Version Series, and the checkout is always done on the most recently created document version. As you can see, the checkout acts as a sort of lock on the Version Series to prevent another caller from also performing a checkout. The first checkout must be resolved, either by a subsequent checkin of the reservation or by canceling the checkout. (Canceling a checkout is an API artifact that is also carried into many applications. In fact, there is no such operation in the CE server. You cancel a checkout by doing an ordinary delete of the reservation document version. The CE automatically updates the checkout bookkeeping if you delete the reservation.)

> Don't confuse the notional locking that comes via checkout with the unrelated feature of cooperative locking. Cooperative locking is an explicit mechanism for applications to mark a Document, Folder, or Custom Object as being locked. As the name implies, this only matters for applications which check for and honor cooperative locks. The CE will not prevent any update operation—other than locking operations themselves—just because there is a cooperative lock on the object.

Content updates can only be done on a document when it is a reservation (which includes a newly created document before it has had its first checkin). While a document is a reservation, callers can freely update the list of content elements in arbitrary ways arbitrarily many times. The actual content previously uploaded is not changed; it is simply replaced, as we described earlier. Once a reservation is checked in, it is no longer a reservation and the list of content elements (and the individual content elements themselves) can no longer be updated.

The CE provides two kinds of checkout which together serve several use cases. A checkout can be **collaborative**, in which case anyone with appropriate permissions can do the corresponding checkin. A checkout can be **exclusive**, in which case only the owner of the reservation can do the checkin.

## Freeze

We said earlier that content for a particular document version could not be changed once that version was checked in. What about other properties of document versions? Some properties are marked as being settable only at creation time or settable only before a checkin, but the general case for custom properties is that they can be updated at any time, even on older document versions. It is sometimes desirable to also prevent property updates, and the CE has a feature for that. You can **freeze** a document version. Once a document version is frozen, attempts to update properties will fail. (This does not apply to system properties, which are updated behind the scenes.)

There is no "unfreeze" operation. Once frozen, a document version stays frozen until it is deleted.

## Major and minor versions

Document versions in the CE have a two-part version number reflected in the automatically maintained system properties `MajorVersionNumber` and `MinorVersionNumber`. These are both integers, but it is common to refer to the combination using decimal notation (for example, 3.2 or 3,2, depending on locale conventions). Although a version series can contain a variety of patterns of major and minor version numbers, the combinations—when taken together—are always in a naturally increasing order. For example, version 3.2 always comes after version 3.1, and version 4.0 always comes after all versions with a major version of 3. Informally, we refer to document versions with a minor version of 0 as a major version (for example, 4.0) and all others as minor versions. The decision to make a version a major version or a minor version is made at checkin time (a reservation document is always created as a minor version). Because of the semantics often ascribed to major and minor version numbers, there are separate permissions available for each type of checkin.

The split of version numbers into major and minor parts is intended to satisfy a very common use case. It is typical in a document revision cycle to go through any number of draft revisions before settling on an approved, official next revision of the content. The usual model is to use major versions (document versions with minor version 0) as the official revisions, and minor versions as draft revisions. There is nothing in the CE itself that enforces that model, so you can do whatever suits your use case. In fact, it's not unusual for some applications to completely forego minor versions and exclusively use major versions.

A document version has a system-maintained integer property `VersionStatus` related to the major/minor use case. It reflects the four possible states for a document version in that model. You can see these version status values in the earlier figure illustrating a version series.

- **Reservation** (value 3) indicates a new document version that is still in the reservation state. Content can be updated by authors.
- **InProcess** (value 2) indicates a checked-in minor document version with no higher major version number in the version series. This status only applies to the highest minor version for that major version.
- **Released** (value 1) indicates the document version with the highest major version and a minor version of 0.
- **Superseded** (value 4) indicates a document version which is no longer in one of the previous statuses. It can be either a major version or a minor version.

> By the way, *superseded* is the most frequently misspelled word in the CM lexicon.

As you perform checkout/checkin cycles, the CE automatically keeps track of and updates the version status of each document version in the version series. There are cases where you might want to change the version status of one or more document versions. For example, you might make a mistake in the type of checkin you do for a particular reservation, or it might be the case that you'd like to say that the last draft revision is the one that was approved, and you don't want to bother making a new version. The CE allows this in limited ways:

- You can promote a minor version into a major version. This has the effect of superseding any earlier major version that was a released version.
- You can demote a major version into a minor version.

There are restrictions on when promotion and demotion can be done. Most significantly, there cannot be a reservation and the affected document must be the current version. The calling user must have the appropriate access rights (creating a major version for promotion, creating a minor version for demotion). These restrictions are reasonable when you consider that the primary motivation is for correcting the designation of a checkin as the wrong kind of major/minor version.

## Document lifecycles

If you have fairly straightforward use cases for how documents progress from creation to deletion, the combination of the checkout/checkin model and the two-level versioning may be completely adequate for your needs. If you have more elaborate bookkeeping needs for documents undergoing revision (or any other complex change), you might create a custom property to keep track of which of various states the document is in. You would then have to arrange to update the state property at appropriate times, make sure state values were valid and consistently applied, and so on.

The CE has a built-in feature to simplify that for you. The feature is called **document lifecycle**. To use it, you create a Document Lifecycle Policy object and assign it the Document property of the same name.

*Major CM Features*

The policy object defines an ordered list of lifecycle states. You can think of them as simple string values even though they are slightly more complicated. You can move a document forward or backward through those states. That's called document lifecycle promotion and demotion (but it's unrelated to the promotion and demotion of document version status). You can set the lifecycle into an exception state (meaning it needs some kind of application-defined attention) or clear that exception state. You can't promote or demote a document while it's in the exception state, and you obviously can't demote beyond the first state or promote beyond the last state in the list. Additionally, each state has a property that says whether demotion from it is allowed.

So far, it seems like document lifecycle policies are just some convenient bookkeeping for a system property, `CurrentState`, that keeps track of a position in a list that you define. You still have to change the state yourself and manage the exception state yourself. The interesting part comes from the Document Lifecycle Action associated with the Document Lifecycle Policy. The lifecycle action has associated with it a piece of custom code (that is, code that you provide) that runs in the server whenever the lifecycle state changes. This handler code knows the document involved and the before and after lifecycle states, so it can take an appropriate action. Document Lifecycle Policy has sometimes been called "a poor man's workflow", but it turns out that one of the most popular actions to perform in the handler is the launching of a workflow via the P8 Process Engine.

There is one final piece to Document Lifecycle Policy, and that is the automatic modification of the document's security via template permissions associated with each state. We'll describe that in more detail in *Chapter 8, Security Features and Planning* along with other security topics.

## Autoclassification

One scenario for adding documents to an Object Store is to have a general purpose bulk loading application which gathers content from somewhere and adds it to CM. A typical bulk loading application is optimized for performance and may consciously avoid the entanglements of use case business logic. As a result, some facts interesting for document ingestion may be deferred to a later point in processing.

The CE provides a feature called **autoclassification** to help with this scenario. The ingesting application indicates that it would like to trigger the autoclassification feature and then creates the document as an instance of the Document base class or some other generic placeholder class. The autoclassification mechanism inside the CE looks at the content type of the added document and asynchronously calls a registered classifier (custom code that you provide) for that content type. The classifier can do a fairly flexible range of changes to the document. The most popular choices are changing the document's class to something more specific, populating interesting properties on the document, or filing the document into a folder based on a scheme known to the classifier.

The CE includes an example of a classifier called the XML Classifier. It uses site-provided XML Property Mapping Scripts for examining and/or transforming an incoming XML document using the autoclassification feature.

# Compound documents

There are documents which naturally decompose into logically independent pieces. Perhaps they are chapters of a larger work. Perhaps they are a mesh of document parts that refer to each other, like a collection of HTML pages. Or perhaps they are something as simple as boilerplate graphics and text used by many documents.

In the CE, these linked parts are referred to collectively as **compound documents**. The pieces are managed independently as separate documents in the CE data model, but they are explicitly linked to one another. Once a document's CompoundDocumentState property is set to Compound Document (instead of Standard Document), that document can have links to any number of parent documents and child documents. The CE provides a structure for creating the linkages, but the meanings of the links depend on the use case.

We have described it in a way that makes a particular document seem to be a natural starting point, but that is not always the case. The chain of parent or child links may lead in a circle or any other graphical topology. The most frequent use case is to define some number of independently reusable pieces and then link them together to create various aggregate documents.

## DITA publishing

The CE has specific support for a particular compound document use case. The **Darwin Information Typing Architecture (DITA)** is an industry standard for organizing technical documentation. Fundamental pieces of content are created as DITA **topics**, often consisting of no more than a paragraph—just enough to describe a self-contained item. Other DITA constructs are used to knit together the topics into larger documents. It is frequently the case that a given DITA topic can be reused in many different composite documents. Of course, things like logos and boilerplate text are authored separately and also reused many times, both within a single composite document and across multiple documents.

Besides the compound document linkage, the CE has support for the asynchronous combining of the DITA topics into composite documents in various formats. This process is called **DITA publishing**.

Several popular technical documentation authoring tools understand DITA constructs and mechanisms, and some understand overlaying a DITA data model onto the CE compound document feature. Those same tools that understand CE compound documents are likely to also know how to use the DITA publishing feature to create finished documents.

## Rendition Engine

CM contains another feature that is sometimes called publishing, but it is not directly related to DITA publishing. Formally, the feature is called **rendition** support. There is a separately licensed and separately installed **Rendition Engine (RE)** available for the CM product. The purpose of the RE is to asynchronously convert individual documents into some other format. For example, an office productivity document might be rendered into PDF or HTML.

It's referred to as rendition because the conceptual content of the document is not changed. It is merely the format that is altered. You are probably familiar with PDF and know that creating a PDF of a document is usually of very high fidelity. HTML results vary. In RE jargon, the original document is called the **source** document and the rendered document is called the **target**. The CM support for renditions includes automatically creating a link between the source and target documents.

*Chapter 7*

# Search

> When the topic of searching comes up, it is often followed by an interest in querying the underlying database tables directly, bypassing the CE server. The CM team discourages that idea because there are many useful abstractions and additional capabilities in the CE layer. Not the least of these abstractions is security access checks; those are completely bypassed if the CE is bypassed. Still, the feeling is that it's your data so you should be able to read it. You should not do it unless you have a strong reason. On the other hand, the CM team does not support any updates done directly to rows and columns of the underlying database. Only updates done by the CE are supported.

The CE provides a flexible API for searching for documents and other objects. This is exposed in partial or full form in various applications. Whether composed from information collected from users or hard-coded according to application logic, queries can be submitted to the CE.

The center of the feature is a Structured Query Language (SQL) dialect for search expressions. For clarity, we refer to that dialect as **CE SQL** to distinguish it from the native DB SQL that the CE uses to talk to the databases. The data model presented by the CE is mapped in various ways onto tables and columns in the underlying Object Store database. Applications issue queries to the CE using CE SQL. The CE interprets the CE SQL and issues the appropriate native DB SQL statements. Conceptually, documents and other object classes act in the role of tables in CE SQL and their properties act as columns.

Here is an example of a type of CE SQL query:

```
SELECT TOP 50 Id, DocumentTitle, WjcFormat
FROM WjcWorkOfLiterature
WHERE 'Unknown' IN WjcGenre AND IsCurrentVersion = true
ORDER BY DocumentTitle ASC
```

You can imagine using this sort of query in an administrative or clean-up application. It looks for items with an unknown genre value in our Work of Literature subclass. The search results will be limited to 50 items and ordered by the Document Title values. In CE SQL, symbolic names are always used when referring to classes and properties (thus, "WjcFormat" instead of "Format"). Case is not significant in class and property names.

It is often helpful to run queries manually while you are trying to refine them to give precisely the sort of results you are looking for. One of the easiest ways to do that is via FEM. Select **Search Results** from the left-hand tree, right-click and select **New Search**. The pop-up panel can guide you through selecting properties, structuring conditions, and so on. Once you gain some experience with CE SQL, you will probably find it more efficient to compose your CE SQL by hand. From the pop-up panel, navigate to **View | SQL View**, as seen here.

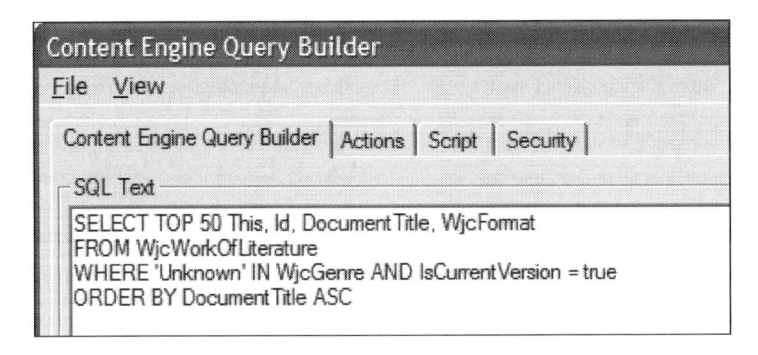

```
Content Engine Query Builder
File  View
Content Engine Query Builder | Actions | Script | Security
SQL Text
SELECT TOP 50 This, Id, DocumentTitle, WjcFormat
FROM WjcWorkOfLiterature
WHERE 'Unknown' IN WjcGenre AND IsCurrentVersion = true
ORDER BY DocumentTitle ASC
```

# Merge mode

The discussion so far has concerned only searches within a single Object Store. You may have been thinking that you could combine search results from multiple Object Stores by running the queries individually and combining the results within your application. You certainly could do that, and, for simple scenarios, it's straightforward. For more complex scenarios, the bookkeeping can become quite daunting. For example, you might have Object Stores with classes and properties of interest that are functionally equivalent but which have different ID values for their class or property definition objects.

The CE query API allows you to search over one or several Object Stores. Each Object Store is called a **scope**, and a search of multiple Object Stores is called a **merged scope query**. A merged scope query can be done in one of two modes:

- **Intersection** mode means all classes and properties referenced in the query must be present in all of the Object Stores in the merged scope
- **Union** mode means all classes and properties referenced in the query must be present in at least one of the Object Stores in the merged scope

If you happen to have functionally equivalent (or nearly so) classes or properties defined in multiple Object Stores and you would like to use them in a merged scope query, the CE has a facility for defining them as aliases of each other via Class Definition and Property Definition objects.

# Selectable and searchable properties

Properties have two characteristics specifically related to their appearance in a CE SQL query string.

A WHERE clause can only reference properties that are **searchable**. Most properties are searchable, but a few are not due to complexities of mapping the object model onto a series of relational database tables and columns. So, unfortunately, a few properties cannot be directly used as part of the matching conditions for the query. To find out if a particular property is selectable, check the Property Description property IsSelectable, or do what we do—just try it and see if it works.

A SELECT clause can only reference properties that are **selectable**. This is a bit of an anachronism these days. As of CM release 4.0.0, all properties are selectable.

# Property searches and full-text searches

The WHERE clause of a CE SQL query can contain two different kinds of conditions, and the two can be combined via a simple JOIN construct.

When using property names in traditional SQL expression constructs, it's called a property search or a metadata search. There's really no standardized term for it, and those two terms are the most commonly used for the same thing. The CE SQL conditions are translated to native DB SQL and evaluated against data in the Object Store database. If you are somewhat familiar with relational database queries, this should sound very familiar to you. Most of what you know about indexes, query optimization, query plans, and related concepts applies pretty well to these kinds of CE queries.

String-valued properties and content of documents and annotations can be designated as being **CBR enabled**. CBR stands for **content-based retrieval** and is just another name for full-text searching. When content or a property value is CBR enabled, it is indexed by a text search engine that is independent of the database that holds most Object Store data. It is the Content Search Engine (CSE) component that we installed in *Chapter 5, Installing Other Components*.

*Major CM Features*

You undoubtedly have an intuitive feeling for full-text searching since it is very similar to the type of searching done via Internet search engines. What you may not be familiar with is the range of powerful operators typically available via a modern text search engine. To use a text search in a CE SQL WHERE clause, you use the CONTAINS() function. The full-text search conditions supplied as a string argument to CONTAINS() are passed directly to the text search engine for evaluation. Results returned by the text search engine are combined with results of metadata searches so that only objects satisfying all conditions are returned to the caller. For CM release 4.5.1, the CSE is based on Autonomy K2. The expression language for that is called Verity Query Language (VQL). The CSE installation includes VQL documentation; we described where to find that documentation in *Chapter 5*.

CE SQL allows both metadata search conditions and text-based search conditions to be combined into a single query, but you have to use a JOIN operator to do it. Although we can reason through the mechanics of this particular JOIN, some weak neurons in our brains prevent us from being able to remember it when we need it, and we just look it up every time (or copy it from some other query). Rather than send you off to the CE SQL reference material, we'll repeat it for you here, which at least gives you another place to look it up.

```
SELECT ...
FROM Document DOC INNER JOIN ContentSearch CBR on DOC.This = CBR.QueriedObject
WHERE CONTAINS(...) AND ...
```

Just as a reminder, you can do full-text searching on Folder, Annotation, and Custom Object classes as well as Document classes.

## JDBC provider

If you are a software developer working with CE searches, you definitely want to use the CE API features for doing queries. They are extremely powerful and flexible, and the data returned is in the same form as other object and property items fetched from the CE.

You might sometimes be faced with the need to perform queries using an off-the-shelf reporting package or other software framework that demands an industry standard interface for searches. The most popular standardized interface in the Java world is **Java Database Connectivity (JDBC)**. The CE Java API provides a read-only JDBC driver that can be used to do queries using CE SQL.

The driver for this JDBC interface is located in the Java class `com.filenet.api.jdbc.Driver`. It accepts any legal CE SQL statement, but typical JDBC-based application software will only use simple expressions based on property data types. Property values returned are converted into standard JDBC datatypes. For example, a CE 64 bit floating point property value will be converted to the JDBC type `java.sql.Types.FLOAT`.

> Do not confuse the CE Java API JDBC provider with the JDBC providers configured in the application servers. These are two entirely different things, though they both use the JDBC interface and paradigms.

## Search Templates and Stored Searches

Workplace and Workplace XT provide two related features called **Search Templates (ST)** and **Stored Searches (SS)**. Both provide for someone to pre-create a CE search that can later be run by the same person or by an entirely different set of people. An applet called Search Designer (SD) is used to create either a SS or ST. The primary difference between the two is that an ST provides more opportunities for the person executing the search to supply values or other parts of the search criteria at the time the search is run. The author of the SS or ST decides what aspects of the search are pre-determined and which can be modified by the user.

Here is a screenshot of SD in the midst of defining a stored search that is approximately the same as the query we showed earlier in this section:

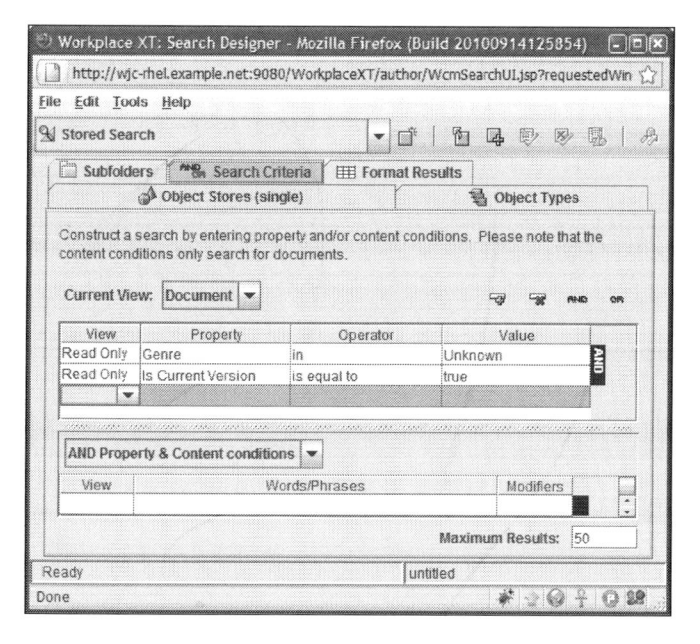

# Folders and containment

Within an Object Store, a lot of things present themselves as part of something that looks like a traditional filesystem. There is a tree of folders, with the topmost folder having the special name of **root folder**. A folder can contain subfolders, which can then contain further subfolders, to any arbitrary depth. Any of those folders at any level can contain documents and custom objects. Each folder has a name, and you can give the full path to a folder by starting at the root folder and listing each folder's name in order until you get to the one you are looking for. In CE notation, you start with a forward slash character and use another forward slash between each pair of folder names. That sounds complicated, but it really just means something familiar: folder paths of the form `/once/upon/a/time/machine`. (There's an intense computer science discussion topic about whether the root folder is called / or the forward slash is just a separator between an empty name and the first subfolder name. Maybe it's best to avoid discussions like that.)

Folders in the CE are always rooted. That is, they are always in a chain starting at the root folder. Said another way, every folder (except the root folder) must have a parent folder, pointed to by the folder's `Parent` property.

# Referential containment

All of this will seem fairly intuitive to even non-technical users. There are some aspects of CE foldering that are useful as powerful features but which may seem less familiar to non-technical users. Specifically, the CE uses something called **referential containment**. A folder contains a reference to the documents rather than the actual documents themselves. That sounds a bit technical and complicated because we're used to thinking in terms of our keys being contained in our coat pocket or a book being contained on a shelf. The desktop paradigm of modern computer user interfaces has reinforced this notion, but for objects in a computer it's completely artificial.

In literal terms, a folder does not contain anything other than a list (and even that is a little white lie for the sake of keeping the explanation simple). Suppose that we lived near each other and jointly owned a DVD collection. We could each make a list of DVDs we had already watched, DVDs we would like to watch, and so on. We might have some overlaps in our lists, but we would still only be talking about a single actual DVD in each overlapped case. It's the same with documents in the repository. Each one is stored somewhere, and folders can point to it. We don't need multiple copies of a document to do that.

Referential containment is accomplished by using a third object to link the folder and the contained object together. The CE has two different types of objects for that, and they are almost exclusively referred to by their acronyms because their names are quite impressive: **Referential Containment Relationship (RCR)** and **Dynamic Referential Containment Relationship (DRCR)**. Both have properties pointing to the folder (the `Tail` property) and the contained object (the `Head` property).

> The idea of the `Head` and `Tail` property names is that you can imagine an arrow drawn from the Folder to the contained object. The tail of the arrow is at the Folder, and the head of the arrow is at the contained object. Our own unscientific data suggests that that analogy is completely intuitive and easy to remember for about half of the people who come across `Head` and `Tail`. It's completely counter-intuitive and impossible to remember for the other half. If you're in that latter half, sorry about that!

You will almost always want to use a DRCR when filing documents, and most applications will make that assumption. An RCR's `Head` property can point to a Folder, Custom Object, or a specific Document version. Even if the document is versioned, the RCR will still point to that same specific Document version. The dynamic part of DRCR is that its `Head` property is automatically adjusted to always point to the current Document version in the Version Series.

Both RCR and DRCR are subclassable, so you can add additional properties relevant to application-defined relationship behaviors.

# Filing

Some specific facts about foldering:

- When a document is filed into a folder, it gets a **containment name**. Although the containment name typically means something useful for people about the document, it is technically just an arbitrary string label. You can reference a document by path by taking the folder's path and appending a forward slash and the document's containment name. That usually feels pretty natural, even to non-technical users.

- No two documents in the same folder can have the same containment name. We say that there is a **uniqueness constraint** on the containment names within a folder. That's pretty easy to understand when you consider referencing documents by path. How could you tell two of them apart if they had the same containment name?

*Major CM Features*

> Some applications show something other than the containment names when they display the list of objects contained in a folder. For example, they might display `DocumentTitle` or some other property for contained documents. That can give the appearance of violating the uniqueness constraint, but it's only because they are not showing the containment names themselves.

- A document may be filed in multiple folders. Each such folder counts it among its containees. The document may have different containment names in different folders. Remember, the folder just has a list of things.
- A document might be filed in no folders at all. This can be a little unsettling for non-technical users the first time they come across it because the desktop paradigm has taught them that they can't have a document without putting it somewhere. Of course, in the repository, the document definitely is somewhere, and it can be referenced by its unique identifier instead of, or in addition to, any of its paths.

> You may have noticed in FEM something that looked like a folder and called **Unfiled Documents**. What's that? FEM simulates a folder when you click on that by running a query and listing the results. The query it runs is "find a list of documents that are not filed in any folders".

- A document can be filed multiple times into a single folder. Since a folder just contains a list of documents, we can list a given document more than once (as long as we give each filing a different containment name). Why would you do such a seemingly useless thing? Typically it's because you want to identify a document in a folder by path because that document is for a certain purpose. If you have more than one such case, it could happen that a single document fulfills multiple purposes.

Everything we've just said about documents and filing in folders is equally true for Custom Objects. We'll come back to Custom Objects in a later section in this chapter. For now, just think of them as objects that don't have content. They do have properties.

> OK, we're going to tell you something, but you have to promise to forget about it. Ready? Promise? A folder can also referentially contain other folders. This is a bit like Unix/Linux symbolic links to a directory or Microsoft Windows shortcuts to a folder. Before you get all excited and start dreaming up fun uses for this feature, you should know a few things: First, you won't find any tools that will let you create referentially contained folders. Second, you won't find any tools that understand a referentially contained folder. Third, the INFOLDER and INSUBFOLDER CE SQL operators don't include referentially contained folders in their ruminations. Are you getting the idea that you shouldn't use referentially contained folders? Good! Now do as you promised and forget about them.

## Containment names

When you file a document or custom object into a folder, it has to have a containment name, and that containment name must be unique for all objects filed into that folder. The filing application can specify an explicit containment name, and that is usually the best way to do things.

If you attempt to file an object using a containment name that is already being used, you'll get an exception from the CE. However, if you are writing the application, you can choose to make use of the CE **autouniqueness** feature. If the name you are using is already in use and you ask for autouniqueness, the CE server will automatically append a numeric suffix to the containment name. It does this in such a way that it finds a unique containment name, and it then uses that.

The containment name may not contain any of the following characters:

- forward or reverse slash (/ \)
- colon (:)
- asterisk (*)
- question mark (?)
- double quotation mark (")
- left or right angle bracket (< >)
- vertical bar (|)

If you don't specify any containment name, the CE server will provide a default containment name. The default is obtained by looking at the object being filed and using the value of its `Name` property. If there is no `Name` property, the string form of the object's `Id` property is used. In either case, any illegal characters are silently discarded, a filename extension (based on the `MimeType` property) is added for documents, and the whole thing is silently shortened if necessary so that it will fit into 255 characters.

## The decision to file documents

Here is a question that we would like you to think about when creating or configuring applications: Why should you file a document? Here's the answer: You should file it if you have a reason for filing it. We're not just talking in circles. Sometimes people think they should file everything, but in a world where it costs something in performance or other resources to do just about anything, you should weigh whether or not you need to file all your objects.

If your use case is primarily that of people manually adding documents to the repository in an *ad hoc* way and also retrieving them pretty much the same way (in other words, if they are using the repository just like they use filesystems on their workstations), then you have a built-in good reason for filing them. People file things so they can find them later, and keeping track of a path to a document is easier than remembering ungainly document ID values.

On the other hand, if you have a use case where one or more applications is adding many documents to the repository, then whether you file them or not depends on some other things. How will the documents be retrieved? Will some query be run to select them based on well-defined selection criteria? Is there a natural hierarchical folder structure that people might use to navigate to subsets of the documents? A good first test for whether there is some natural reason to file things is to consider whether there is going to be a good scattering of the containment names. If you are going to end up with thousands of containment names that are all based on the `Name` property value "Invoice", then that containment name is not going to do you much good for navigation.

There are two common performance hot points that you might experience with poor filing strategies:

- The act of filing things into a folder takes longer than expected because the algorithm for generating unique containment names has to work harder if there are more collisions.

- The database index that keeps track of containment names develops what DB administrators call index skew. That means that the DB software decides there is so little variety in the values being indexed that the index is useless. The net result is the dreaded DB table scan. IBM discusses this situation in the *FileNet P8 Performance Tuning Guide*, but the usual resolution is finding out that the filing isn't logical in the first place.

We're not trying to scare you away from filing things into folders. Far from it. It's an extremely useful feature and is very helpful for users in many cases. We're just suggesting that you avoid filing things if there isn't any particular reason to do it.

# Custom properties and classes

The metadata class structure in the CE is hierarchical and has much in common with classes used in the field of object-oriented programming. It's not an exact match with the programming concept, and by no means do you need to be a programmer to understand and use custom classes and properties.

A custom subclass represents a specialization of a CE base class or another custom subclass. For example, we used the custom Document subclass Work of Literature to illustrate some thing in earlier chapters (we created it at the end of *Chapter 4, Administrative Tools and Tasks*). Although being a custom subclass alone serves to identify a more specific type of object, the usual case is that there are some additional properties relevant to that type of object. For example, we added a few custom properties to the Work of Literature custom class. It is also possible to define additional custom properties on an existing class, including most system classes that are of interest to application business logic.

It is possible to add some pieces of custom business logic via mechanisms described later in this chapter, but most object behavior is customized through and determined by properties of custom class definitions and custom property definitions. We have already seen some of these on the way to creating the Work of Literature custom class and its custom properties. We'll briefly catalog some of the more interesting properties of class definitions and property definitions. We're concentrating here mostly on the properties that directly influence feature behaviors. All metadata in the CE data model is discoverable, which means that an application can find out the details of any class or property (including custom classes and properties) and need not rely on externally obtained information.

## Properties of Class Definitions

We've already mentioned a few times that CE classes are arranged in a hierarchy. We won't say much more about that here, except we'll note that a Class Definition contains the information you see how it fits in the hierarchy. The `SuperclassDefinition` and `ImmediateSubclassDefinitions` properties allow navigation up and down the hierarchy. Collectively, those properties allow reconstruction of the entire hierarchy.

There are also properties that control whether instances of a class may be created (`AllowsInstances`), whether custom properties may be added to a class (`AllowsPropertyAdditions`), and whether a class may be subclassed (`AllowsSubclasses`). Most of the classes you are likely to be interested in for business logic allow all of these.

When an object of a class is created, the calling application may specify an owner and a set of permissions for the created object. If the application does not specify those things explicitly, the Class Definition provides defaults (`DefaultInstanceOwner` and `DefaultInstancePermissions`, respectively). The default owner is usually the special value #CREATOR-OWNER. At object creation time, it is dynamically changed to the identity of the calling user.

Perhaps the most important property of a Class Definition for the purposes of the current discussion is `PropertyDefinitions`. It is a list of Property Definition objects, each one describing a property that an instance of the class will have. We'll consider those next.

## Properties of Property Definitions

Although there is a `PropertyDefinition` base class, the Property Definitions that you will see are all instances of a subclass tuned to a particular data type. Here are the data types available in the CE data model: Binary, Boolean, DateTime, Float64, Id, Integer32, String, and Object. The subclasses are mainly used to provide specialization in the allowed and default values for a particular property.

The data type of a property is fundamental. Equally as fundamental is a property's `Cardinality`, which describes whether it is a single-valued or multi-valued property. Although that's only a relatively small semantic distinction, it has major implementation considerations for the CE's storage and manipulation of property values.

When a document is versioned, it is often desirable to carry forward most of the properties of the previous version. As a convenience, so that calling applications don't have to do it, a property's default behavior in this respect is controlled by the `CopyToReservation` property. If true, the property is automatically copied to the reservation.

A system property will have a true value for the `IsSystemOwned` property, whereas a custom property will have a false value.

The `Settability` property controls when and if a property's value can be changed by any caller (this is not a security feature because it doesn't depend on the identity of the caller). The `READ_ONLY` and `READ_WRITE` values are easy to understand. There are two other values which are more specialized: `SETTABLE_ONLY_ON_CREATE` means that the property can be set only at creation time of the object. `SETTABLE_ONLY_BEFORE_CHECKIN` is similar, but applies only to reservation documents and allows property updates until the document is checked in.

A property may have a default value that is used if the calling application does not explicitly provide one. The properties holding the default values vary by Property Definition subclass and have names like `PropertyDefaultString`, `PropertyDefaultBoolean`, and so on.

The `PersistenceType` property has three possible values and is mainly used to control whether a multi-valued property of a primitive data type gets its own database table (sometimes an important performance trade-off). However, the most interesting value is `NOT_PERSISTENT`, meaning that the property value is not stored anywhere. These are also known as *transient* properties. You're probably wondering why anyone would create a property that doesn't get stored. There are two practical uses for it:

- Although any update to a transient property value eventually gets discarded, it survives long enough to be seen by event handlers. It can thus be used by applications as a signaling device to event handlers for whatever is privately arranged between the event handler and the applications. Typically, it is used to somehow identify the calling application. You should not think of this as some kind of security mechanism or a way of signaling that a trusted application of some kind is calling since an attacker could trivially exploit it.
- If a property is transient but has a default value, it acts as a class constant. Any fetch of that property will see the default value. This can be another way of distinguishing subclasses or efficiently providing information about the entire class to applications.

There are a few interesting properties that apply only to `PropertyDefinitionObject`, and we'll consider those next.

`RequiredClassId` imposes a restriction on the classes of the objects that may be pointed to by this property. As you would expect, if this property indicates the Work of Literature class, then the object property may only point to a Work of Literature object (or an object from a subclass of Work of Literature).

`ReflectivePropertyId` indicates a specific property of the class indicated by `RequiredClassId`. It's used to create a reflective property arrangement. When you ask for the value of the property for this object, the CE server performs a query to find all of the objects of the required class (and subclasses) whose reflective property points to this object. That's why you never set the multi-valued end of a reflective property arrangement. The CE dynamically resolves it when you ask for the value, and these two properties are the particulars that control that resolution.

`DeletionAction`, as you would expect, controls some of the CE's behavior when a caller attempts to delete an object. If the deletion action value is NONE, then there's no particularly special behavior. The object is simply deleted, subject to the usual security access checks and so on. If the deletion action value is PREVENT, then the object cannot be deleted as long as this property has a non-null value. If the deletion action is CASCADE (usually called by the shorthand term *cascade delete*), then deletion of this object will also cause deletion of any pointed-to object or objects (which may in turn be controlled by their own `DeletionAction` properties). All of the accumulated deletions must be successful or the entire transaction rolls back and no objects are deleted.

## Custom objects

A Custom Object is an object that can be used for any application-specific purpose that does not need content. If content is not needed, custom objects are much lighter weight than documents, primarily because there is no versioning bookkeeping or content bookkeeping.

The Custom Object base class has very few properties. It has only the sorts of properties that are common to most object types: an owner, permissions, creation and modification bookkeeping properties, and so on. The point of custom objects is to allow you to add your own properties for keeping track of application-specific data. In DB terms, this would be like adding your own tables and columns, but—like all CE objects—there is an object model on top of it. For example, you can create a property on a document that references a custom object of some kind (and *vice versa*, of course).

Custom Object instances can rightly be thought of as "a bag of properties". There are very few restrictions on how Custom Objects can be used. They have access control like other business objects. They can be filed into folders. They can have their string properties indexed for full-text searching. They can have annotations. They can be attachments to workflows. They are subscribable and can trigger event firing (described a bit later in this chapter).

Here's a small example of how you could use custom objects. Suppose you were keeping records of your DVD collection in the repository. You might create a custom object subclass representing a single DVD. Custom properties might include things like the DVD title, content rating, year of production, date you acquired it, and so on. If you had a graphics file of DVD disk or cover art, you might create documents with those graphics files as content, and then create **object-valued properties** (**OVPs**) pointing from the DVD custom object to the artwork documents. As we mentioned earlier, you might use folders to create lists of DVDs for various reasons by filing the DVD custom objects into those folders.

# Annotations

The implementation of CE annotations is one of those features that was created with more or less a single use case in mind, but which is an interesting and flexible feature in its own right.

The canonical use case for annotations is for documents whose content is some kind of graphical image. In the ECM world, this often means a **Tagged Image Format File (TIFF)** image obtained via fax or scanner input. During the lifecycle of the document, particularly in the early period during and just after ingestion, many business processes require marking up the image, perhaps to highlight certain areas, perhaps to clarify unclear text, or perhaps just to add different graphical or textual boilerplate items. There is frequently a business or regulatory reason for keeping the original image unmodified, so the annotations are done as separate objects that are graphically combined on-screen by a rendering program.

Modern office productivity applications usually have their own built-in mechanisms for adding annotation-like items to document content, but there is still sometimes a use case for annotations that are not tied to a particular application.

The `Annotation` base class is very simple and does not assume any particular format for annotations. Instead, `Annotation` subclasses are made for particular annotation purposes. Just like any other custom class, application-defined properties can be added. An `Annotation` object already has a Content Elements collection, just like documents, but annotations are not versionable. Although the CE does not pre-define any specific annotation subclasses, many out of the box applications understand the particular annotation format federated from IBM FileNet Image Services and rendered by the Image Viewer applet included with XT.

Annotations can be applied to Documents, Folders, and Custom Objects, all of which have an `Annotations` property giving an enumeration of their annotations. Although an `Annotation` is an independent object with its own identity and security, it cannot exist on its own. The `Annotation` property `AnnotatedObject` is required to have a value. That property also forms a reflective property arrangement with the `Annotations` property of Document, Folder, or Custom Object classes. The deletion action of the `Annotations` property is cascade, which means the annotations are automatically deleted when the annotated object is deleted.

An annotation for a document is an annotation for a specific document version. Annotations are not automatically carried forward to new versions during a checkout/checkin cycle. That's usually the desired behavior, but if a use case demands copying the annotations forward, it is an application responsibility.

Because an annotation typically applies to a particular content element, there is an additional optional integer property, `AnnotatedContentElement`. The usual practice, when annotating a document, is to populate that with the `ElementSequenceNumber` of the applicable content element. The property has no standard meaning if annotating a Folder or Custom Object, so it may be used for an application-specific purpose or left unset.

There is no rule that says `Annotation` subclasses have to be used in the way just described. Another popular use is to store optional extra information about some other object to take advantage of the cascaded deletion. For example, if a document contained some kind of graphics, an annotation could be used to store a thumbnail image for it. An application that uses annotations should select and use only the annotation subclasses that it understands. Other annotations should be preserved unless there is an obvious use case for doing something else.

Annotations have access security, and they inherit security through the `AnnotatedObject` property. We'll discuss security inheritance in *Chapter 8*.

# Links

When we described containment, we described the RCR and DRCR classes for establishing containment relationships between a Folder and a Document or Custom Object. Using a third object to create a relationship allows you to create **many-to-many** relationships. Folder containment is a good example of a many-to-many relationship. A folder may contain many documents, and a document may be contained in many folders.

Sometimes it is useful to create many-to-many relationships for application-defined purposes. Using containment may not be appropriate, either because it doesn't meet the technical requirements for containment or because you don't want to have the connotation of containment. The Link exists to fill this need. It is a generic relationship object, with `Head` and `Tail` properties, for creating arbitrary many-to-many relationships.

To use it, create a subclass of the `Link` base class and narrow down the required types for the `Head` and `Tail` properties to the particular classes of objects that you will use in your relationships. Although the `Head` and `Tail` properties are pre-defined and must have values, you don't have to use them as-is if they don't make sense for your use case. It is common to define completely new properties with names that are meaningful for some particular type of relationship.

The Link is not as well known as some other object types, and it is not unusual to see another CE class pressed into service as the third object in a many-to-many relationship. For example, it's easy to do this with a Custom Object. Is that a good idea or a bad idea? We couldn't really call it a bad idea, but you might want to use a Link object instead for these reasons:

- Merely by being a kind of Link, there is a connotation for what your `Link` subclass is doing.
- Links are stored in a different database table from Custom Objects, and that can make a performance difference if you have a large number of relationships or Custom Objects used for other purposes. (Don't worry about competing with RCR and DRCR. They have their own table, too.)

## Subscriptions, events, and auditing

The usual place for business logic is in applications. In CM terms, the applications are clients to the CM server components. This arrangement is certainly the easiest to understand and coordinate. However, there are well-known disadvantages to this in certain scenarios (and not just for CM):

- If you have multiple applications—a fairly common scenario—you have to coordinate the business logic across all those applications. For example, if a certain property can only have a certain range of values, all applications must enforce that constraint. It obviously makes sense to exploit a server-side feature for this even if you want to put client validation logic in place for user experience purposes.

- Even if your business requirements are limited to a single application, a malicious attacker might be able to get access to or even create an alternative application to bypass your business logic. Applications lie outside the trust boundary. By that we mean that the CM server components do not trust any clients to have done anything correctly. Client logic is always assumed to be potentially faulty, whether by accident or by design. For example, if a particular range of values is specified in the CE metadata for a property, the CE server will always check incoming property updates against that constraint and will never assume the client has already done so.
- If there is server logic to accomplish a particular business objective, then it is typically more expensive in development, test, and support time to redundantly implement similar logic in applications.

We're obviously making the case for exploiting server-side mechanisms wherever possible. CM server components have rich palettes of server-side mechanisms already available. For some examples, look at the section on defining custom properties earlier in this chapter.

There are cases where you would like to extend the server-side functionality so that you can use your own custom business logic but still get the advantages of a server-side implementation. The CE event subsystem fulfills this role, and it is also one of the central features in what CM product documentation calls *active content*. In this section, we describe event handling via subscriptions. Because the mechanism for audit logging is so closely related, conceptually and mechanically, we also describe that in this section.

## What is an event?

An event is simply something that happens to an object in a CE repository. Examples include creation of an object, checkout of a Document, and filing an object into a Folder. Most events are update events, while the only non-updates event are the retrieval of an object or the retrieval of Document or Annotation content. An event has a triggering object (the object which caused the event to fire), and various types of actions may be triggered when the event is fired.

- For update events, event handlers may be executed to perform site-defined activities
- For update events and object and content retrievals, audit logging records may be written
- For document lifecycle promotion or demotion, a lifecycle event handler may be executed

In addition to the system-defined events, it is also possible to define custom events. A custom event is created by making a subclass of the Custom Event base class. As usual, the subclass can have custom properties defined on it. A custom event is fired by an application calling the `Subscribable.raiseEvent(CustomEvent)` method. Once triggered, event handlers are called as for a system event. At first glance, it may seem pointless to have applications firing custom events just to call event handlers with custom logic. The advantages are the same as mentioned at the beginning of this section: moving business logic out of the application and into the server tier. We'll show an example of using custom events in this way in the sample application in *Chapter 12, The DUCk Sample Application*.

## Subscriptions

Tying events to handlers is done via a subscription mechanism. On the one hand, a subscription points to a class or an instance from which events can be triggered. On the other hand, the subscription points to an Event Action which identifies the event handler to be executed and other details. Finally, the subscription includes a list of event types of interest.

A subscription may be applied to a specific object, in which case it's called an **instance subscription**. A subscription may be applied to an entire class of objects, in which case it's called a **class subscription**. A class subscription is used whenever any instance of that class (including subclass instances) has an event. For performance purposes, a filter expression— similar to a CE SQL WHERE clause— may be supplied. A subscription is only used if the filter expression evaluates to true for the triggering object.

There can be any number of separate class or instance subscriptions for a particular object. Within the synchronous and asynchronous types, there is no defined order in which the event handlers are called. In fact, the order may change from one event firing to another.

A subscription is classified as either **synchronous** or **asynchronous**, depending on when the associated event handler is executed. There is more difference between these than the timing, however, and the difference is commonly misunderstood.

> As a terminology convenience, events or event handlers are sometimes referred to as being synchronous or asynchronous. This is not technically correct because the designation is always made on the subscription object. An event can have either kind of subscription, and an event handler can be invoked both ways.

*Major CM Features*

A synchronous subscription executes the event handler before any object update has actually been commited. Its purpose is to either allow or veto the update. The event handler may not modify the triggering object. It is executed within the same application server transaction as the triggering update. This has two consequences:

- The logic within the event handler is included within the transaction timeout of the overall update. This makes it fairly important that the event handler logic be executed efficiently and not include things like waiting for responses from distant servers.
- If the event handler code throws an exception, it causes the entire update transaction to roll back, and the calling application will receive that exception (though it will be wrapped in one or more other exceptions). This is the desired behavior and is exactly the mechanism for vetoing the update. If the event handler approves of the update, it merely exits normally without an exception.

> The CE does not throw an exception if the event handler for a synchronous subscription updates the triggering object. This has allowed many developers to ignore the rule, assuming it is merely a best practice. Nonetheless, it has always been the rule that synchronous subscription event handlers are not allowed to do that. Even if it works in a particular instance, it may fail at random times that escape detection in testing. Don't fall into this trap!

An asynchronous subscription executes the event handler after any object update has been committed. The time delay is typically small, but there is no timing guarantee. There is an ordering guarantee for multiple updates to the same triggering object (but not for multiple subscriptions on the same triggering object). Obviously, an asynchronous subscription event handler cannot veto a change that has already been committed. Its purpose is to react to a change. It might implement other CM changes or even updates to external systems. If an event handler for an asynchronous subscription throws an exception, the calling application will not be notified because the processing is being done in a background thread in the CE. In fact, the only notification is via the CE server logs. The event handler is called within its own transaction, so an exception will not affect any other event handlers or application threads.

Because event handlers are server-side code and are not controlled by the access rights of the user performing the action that triggered the event, security access checks are disabled for event handler code (though it is always possible for an event handler to find out who the triggering user was). Needless to say, only event handlers from trustworthy sources should be used.

# Audit logging

For compliance, governance, or other business reasons, it is sometimes necessary to record who performed various actions. The CE feature for this is called **audit logging**. Audit logging can record not only who performed an action but also who attempted to perform an action and failed for security access reasons. In addition to update events, audit log entries can be configured for object retrievals and document content retrievals (those activities are not available for normal subscriptions and event handlers).

Because the types of activities for which audit logging is desirable are very similar to the types of events for which event handlers might be used, there is quite a bit of synergy in the two subsystems. The counterpart to the event subscription object is the audit definition object. Audit definitions are configured as a list directly on a class definition and cannot be applied to an object instance.

Audit logging records are written to a database table within the Object Store, and those records are exposed as objects of the CE class `Event`. They can be directly queried like any other CE object via CE SQL. The audit definition controls some of the information that is recorded in the Event table for update events. You can choose to record a copy of the modified (post-change) object, the modified and original (pre-change) object, or neither.

> When the original or modified object is retrieved via an `Event` object, the objects come from the copies in the Event table. They often bear little resemblance to the object as it exists in the main part of the Object Store repository since it may have undergone many changes or even have been deleted since the audit record was written.

# Content Access Recording Level

Documents have a property called `DateContentLastAccessed`. As you can guess from the name, it records the timestamp of the last content retrieval for that document. Most sites do not really need this information, and there is a non-trivial performance cost for the CE to maintain it.

Therefore, frequency of update of that property can be controlled via the Object Store property `ContentAccessRecordingLevel`. The choices are not at all (the default), daily, hourly, or on every access. For example, if the configured value is daily, then the `DateContentLastAccessed` property on a given document will not be updated if the previous value is within 24 hours of a retrieval operation.

*Major CM Features*

# Event handlers

The event handler is the piece of site-supplied code that will be executed by the CE in response to a triggered event.

Event handlers are written in Java and implement the CE API `EventActionHandler` interface. The CE calls a method on that interface to inform the handler about the circumstances of the triggered event. The event handler is provided with the Id of the subscription object involved in the event firing and an event object which provides specific details. The class of event object and information available within it will be specific to the type of event fired, but it always includes a copy of the triggering object. There is always sufficient information for the handler to deduce the specifics of the changes that triggered the event.

The code for the event handler is stored in a CE object called a Code Module, and an event handler is linked indirectly to it. A code module is a `Document` subclass whose content is either a Java class or a **Java Archive (JAR)**. We prefer to use a JAR file because it makes it simple to divide the implementation into multiple classes, associate resources with the event handler, and just generally package things neatly.

[ Whether packaged as a Java class or as a JAR file, the code module is pointed to by the `Action.CodeModule` property. If you create a new version of the code module, that property will still point to the previous specific document version. This is generally not an issue in production, but it can cause some head-scratching during development. ]

It's also possible to put the code for an event handler onto the classpath of the application server. That can save some time during iterative development, but is not recommended for production deployment. Besides the added logistical inconvenience of deploying the event handler code to multiple application server instances, the presence of the event handler code on the most general classpath can have unexpected behavioral side-effects for other applications or for the application server itself.

# Workflow launch

One particular event handler is provided with the CM product. It is used to launch workflow processes in the configured **Process Engine (PE)** server. This event handler knows all the logic involved in contacting the PE server and actually launching the workflow. There is a pair of subscription subclasses called Instance Workflow Subscription and Class Workflow Subscription. Each has properties specific to workflow launch. For example, each has an `IsolatedRegionNumber` property which indirectly gives connectivity information for the PE server.

One of the properties on the workflow subscription object is a reference to a Workflow Definition object. `WorkflowDefinition` is a subclass of `Document` in which the content is an encoded workflow definition. A workflow definition is usually created via an application called **Process Designer (PD)**. PD is not included with the basic CM license, but two pre-defined workflow objects are included and can be easily accessed from XT.

The Fixed Approval Workflow consists of three pre-defined workflow steps for reviewing, approving, and optionally publishing a document. It's called "fixed approval" because the steps are pre-defined. The Sequential Approval Workflow lets you define a flexible number of steps for the approval process. In both cases, XT provides an interface for defining the participants for each step and other details for each use of the workflow.

# AddOns

We earlier described how to create custom classes and properties. That's a powerful feature for establishing an application-specific data model that follows object oriented principles. It's pretty straightforward to create those classes and properties manually using FEM, but that leaves you with the problem of how to re-create those classes and properties in the deployment environment.

Because everything you can do with FEM can also be done via CE APIs, one solution would be to write a custom application to programmatically create custom metadata in a target Object Store. That idea is appealing because it puts you in complete control of the process. There are some disadvantages, including:

- It's another custom application to write and maintain. Depending on your enterprise or other business requirements, this can mean an installation program, application documentation, and other consumability details.
- As needs change, the application must be updated. This is a nuisance, especially if the application has to keep track of multiple versions of the custom metadata.
- Although it's reasonably documented, the programmatic process of creating or updating metadata is among the lesser traveled roads in the CE APIs, and it's common to see application programming errors in this area.

## AddOn components

The CE has a feature specifically to deal with this need. An AddOn is a bundle of things that can define a custom feature from the CE's point of view. The AddOn bundle can contain any or all of the following items (all are optional):

- **Metadata definitions for custom classes and properties**: If a class or property already exists in the target Object Store, the data from the AddOn bundle is merged with it instead of replacing it. This is especially useful for the case of adding custom properties to an existing class.

- **Instance data**: You can include instances of Documents, Folders, Custom Object, or, in fact, almost any CE class, including things like subscriptions and event handlers. The classes and properties in the instance data must already be defined, but those definitions can be in the metadata part of the same AddOn. If the instance already exists in the target Object Store, an exception is thrown. Although there are no technical restrictions on instance data, it should be obvious that large document content can bulk up the AddOn bundle and be a bit cumbersome to manage.

- **Pre-installation and Post-installation Scripts**: There are occasional details of a custom feature that can be difficult to express purely with metadata and instances of CE objects. In case your AddOn falls under this fairly rare circumstance, you can include either of two optional scripts to do small amounts of CE API programming. One script, if provided, is run before any metadata and instance data is imported into the target Object Store. The other script, if provided, is run afterwards. The scripts must be written in JavaScript.

## Creating and installing AddOns

The management of AddOns can be slightly confusing on first encounter. An AddOn is *created* (in the sense of creating any other CE object) under the Domain object. After it is created, it is available to be *installed* into an Object Store.

When you first create a Domain, you will see that a dozen or so AddOns are already created in the Domain as shown in the figure below. One of these, Base Content Engine Extensions, contains a few items that are not system properties and classes but are so popularly assumed by applications that they are considered to be essential. For example, the property DocumentTitle is not a system property but is instead created by this AddOn. Other AddOns provide custom data used by one or more IBM-provided applications.

| Display Name | Type | Prerequisites |
|---|---|---|
| 4.5.1 Base Application Extensions | Optional | |
| 4.5.1 Base Content Engine Extensions | Recommended | |
| 4.5.1 CFS ICI Lockdown Extensions | Optional | |
| 4.5.1 CFS-IS Extensions | Optional | |
| 4.5.1 DITA Publishing Extensions | Optional | 4.5.1 Publishing Extensions |
| 4.5.1 Process Engine Extensions | Optional | 4.5.1 Base Content Engine Extensions |
| 4.5.1 Publishing Extensions | Optional | 4.5.1 Base Application Extensions |
| 4.5.1 Stored Search Extensions | Optional | 4.5.1 Base Application Extensions |
| 4.5.1 Workplace Access Roles Extensions | Optional | 4.5.1 Base Application Extensions |
| 4.5.1 Workplace Base Extensions | Optional | 4.5.1 Base Content Engine Extensions, 4.5.1 Ba |
| 4.5.1 Workplace E-mail Extensions | Optional | 4.5.1 Workplace Base Extensions |
| 4.5.1 Workplace Forms Extensions | Optional | |
| 4.5.1 Workplace Templates Extensions | Optional | |
| 4.5.1 Workplace XT Extensions | Optional | 4.5.1 Workplace Base Extensions |

AddOns can be installed into an Object Store at any time. The FEM Object Store creation wizard prompts for AddOns as one of its final steps. Because you can install AddOns at any later time, and because there is no uninstall for an AddOn, you should install the minimal set at Object Store creation time. Otherwise, you are likely to find a certain clutter of metadata that you might never use in that Object Store.

## Authoring an AddOn

Where do AddOns come from? How do you create a new one?

The first step is to define the custom classes, properties, and instance data you plan to bundle in your AddOn. You will find it more convenient if you do this in a development environment, which is typical anyhow, in an Object Store used just for that purpose. In other words, create a new Object Store, avoid installing any more than the P8 Essentials AddOn (unless there are prerequisite AddOns for yours), and then manually create your own objects in that Object Store.

FEM contains a feature called **export** which can be used to create an XML representation of most types of objects from an Object Store. Use FEM to export your objects to create such an XML representation. You will probably find that your exported XML contains several bits of system data. You can manually edit the XML to delete that system data. That will reduce the size of your AddOn and also lessen the chances of installation failure due to conflicts.

If necessary, write AddOn pre-installation and post-installation scripts.

Use FEM to create your AddOn in your development Domain.

Finally, using another new, empty Object Store, test the installation process for your AddOn.

> If you don't happen to be a perfect person, you might have to iterate a few times until you get things exactly the way you want them. For the sake of mere mechanical efficiency, we usually do this kind of work using a virtual machine image that includes a snapshot capability. We make a snapshot just before creating the AddOn in the P8 Domain. Then we do the testing. If we need to iterate, it's pretty fast to roll back to the snapshot point.

# Summary

In this chapter, we looked at most of the major features available in CM. Although we did not dive deeply into all of them, we hope to have at least laid out the landscape and given you a good grounding in the features available and an understanding of what they do.

One major set of features was barely mentioned: security. We've given security its own chapter, and that's coming up next.

# 8

# Security Features and Planning

This chapter addresses the many aspects of CM security. We've seen security in other chapters, in little pieces, here and there. It's now time to take a more comprehensive look at things.

In every discussion of security, someone always says security is a complicated topic. Well, it is! We will describe to you the individual security features and provide some guidance on how you might use those features to meet your particular needs. Each feature is, in isolation, pretty easy to understand. From these tiny parts, elaborate machinery can be built.

More specifically, we'll cover the following topics:

- CM authentication mechanics
- Enterprise directory interactions
- The many CM authorization mechanisms, including discretionary and mandatory access control
- A walk-through of a somewhat complicated authorization scenario

## Authentication or authorization?

We're going to discuss the two major topics of authentication and authorization. Let's take a wild guess here and claim that you don't know the difference between those two things. It's OK if you don't, but you will soon. We'll further guess that, for every 100 readers of this paragraph, 85 will immediately admit that we're right. Ten readers will think they know, but they will actually be wrong (probably by having the terms backwards in their minds). The other five readers will actually know the difference. Let's catch everybody up.

*Security Features and Planning*

There is a lot of confusion about these two topics, undoubtedly because the terminology used sounds almost like the same word to the casual listener. It's only after much experience and even a bit of late-night chanting that we are able to use them correctly without thinking about it. The separation of security into authentication and authorization is by far the most common way to organize computer security and many other security arenas.

**Authentication** is the process of proving an identity. It obviously comes from the same root word as *authentic*. When looking at an alleged van Gogh painting, you might wonder if it's authentic, but you wouldn't wonder if it were authoritative. Depending on your personal circumstances, you might carry an employee badge, a student identity card, or some other credential that proves who you are. For some of these credentials, it's easy to get the concept a bit confused and think "this card proves I'm allowed to go into that building". Actually, the point of the card is to prove who you are.

**Authorization** is the process of seeing what actions you are allowed to perform, which might include checking what items you are allowed to see. When you think of a typical sign with wording like "Authorized Personnel Only" and a security guard watching over an entrance, you might think of the security guard looking you up on a list to see if you're allowed in. Authorization checks do not kick in until you have proven who you are. Interestingly, the authorization process doesn't care at all how you proved your identity. The authorization process trusts that the authentication process did its job and concerns itself only with the privileges of a person (or thing) with that identity.

# Authentication in CM

You already know that authentication is the process of having a user prove his or her identity.

In the realm of computer security, a **security principal** claims an identity and proves it by presenting one or more **credentials**. That sounds a lot more technical, but it really just means that things other than users can be authenticated. For example, in some cases, a particular computer or application can be authenticated, and the use of the term security principal just lets computer security professionals talk about it without having to constantly qualify their statements.

You might be thinking of the credential as a password, and, in most cases today, it is. When you enter a userid and the correct password, the authentication system believes you are the owner of that userid. There are many other kinds of credentials, and some environments will require you to present more than one to prove your identity (this is called **multi-factor authentication**). If you are a fan of techno-thriller fiction, you will know that every government building uses an eyeball scanner to identify people by the unique patterns of their irises. The more realistic non-password credentials, at least these days, are fingerprint scanners for workstations, and handheld security tokens for remote system access. There are many more possibilities.

> Our favorite imaginary non-password authentication scheme is called the dog-sniff test. It imagines a dog standing watch and giving each passerby a sniff. It knows the good guys from the bad guys merely by smell. The most famous example of this was practiced by Argos, the dog who immediately recognized his master, Odysseus, after having not seen him for twenty years.

# Java Authentication and Authorization Service (JAAS)

It used to be the case, not so long ago, that any complex system would tend to have its own authentication mechanism. For quite a few reasons, that was too inflexible to thrive in an enterprise environment. The most common modern setup, and the only setup supported natively by CM, is to entrust the authentication mechanism to the application server on which the CE runs. The mechanism J2EE application servers use is the Java Authentication and Authorization Service, abbreviated as JAAS and pronounced the same as "jazz".

Although JAAS can be used for both authentication and authorization, CM uses it only for authentication.

What exactly does this mean to say that CM supports JAAS for authentication? Via JAAS, the CE always receives from the application server an object called a **Subject** to indicate both a successful authentication and the identity of the authenticated user. If authentication fails, an exception is thrown and the application server does not give a Subject to the CE. The mechanism used to pass the Subject into the CE is reliable and secure, so the CE knows that it will not be given a forged Subject by some other software component. As a terminology shorthand, we say that the CE delegates authentication to the application server via JAAS.

It's all very well to say that the CE delegates authentication to the application server, but how does the application server perform authentication? All J2EE application servers use JAAS for authentication, but there is considerable variation in the low-level implementation details. A complete description of JAAS is beyond our scope here (it's easy enough to find many detailed treatments via a web search), but here is an outline of it:

- A site decides what mechanisms it will trust for authentication purposes. For example, it may only trust the traditional userid/password mechanism, or it may insist on handheld hardware token schemes.

- Each mechanism needs a software implementation called a JAAS **login module**. Application servers come with an assortment of login modules for popular purposes, and third party authentication-related software typically provides one or more login modules for the purposes of integration with the application server. An enterprise with sufficiently skilled and motivated staff could even write its own login module (though application server-specific requirements take this out of the realm of being a beginner's task).

- Further, the site decides which mechanisms are sufficient on their own for authentication and which need to be combined with other mechanisms to be sufficient.

- The site configures the application server JAAS component to reflect the above policy decisions. This is usually done via a configuration file that may also have a GUI editing program. The configuration consists of listing JAAS login modules, along with a designation like required or sufficient, into named groups called stanzas. The site is saying via the configuration that if you pick any one of those stanzas, follow the JAAS authentication rules, and provide the information demanded by the login modules, then it will trust JAAS (and the login modules) to properly authenticate users. For example, here is a panel from the WAS console showing the default set of JAAS modules for a WAS installation. Each row represents a named stanza.

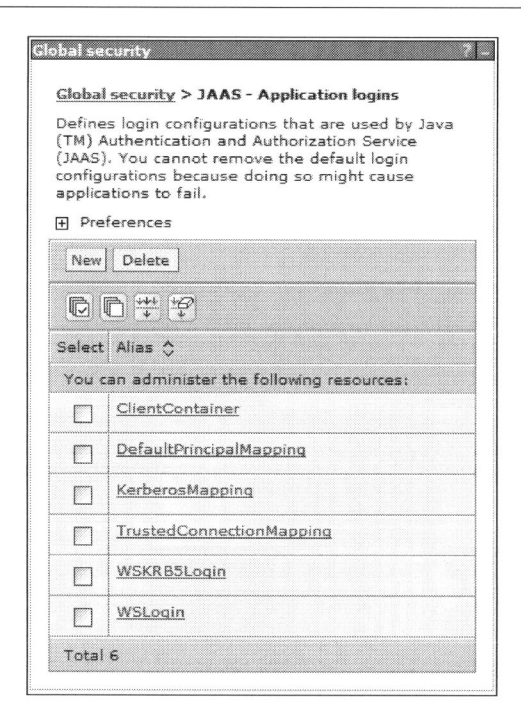

```
Global security > JAAS - Application logins
Defines login configurations that are used by Java
(TM) Authentication and Authorization Service
(JAAS). You cannot remove the default login
configurations because doing so might cause
applications to fail.

Preferences

[New] [Delete]

Select  Alias
You can administer the following resources:
   ☐   ClientContainer
   ☐   DefaultPrincipalMapping
   ☐   KerberosMapping
   ☐   TrustedConnectionMapping
   ☐   WSKRB5Login
   ☐   WSLogin
Total 6
```

- An application makes standard JAAS call to perform authentication. It may either explicitly select a named JAAS stanza, or it may let JAAS pick a default stanza. There is a programmatic way for the login modules to ask for information from the calling application (which, if the application so desires, can translate into a user interaction to ask for the information).

- If the application-provided information rings true to the login modules, then the application is given a Subject. If not, an exception is thrown.

- Given an authenticated Subject, there is a way for applications to associate that Subject with any calls they make. We refer to this as having an **ambient JAAS Subject** because, once established, it tends to be automatically available for the kinds of situations where we need to find it. Application programmers typically do not pass a Subject as a parameter to many different method calls. The CE Java API does provide some convenience methods for explicitly manipulating Subjects, but their use is strictly optional.

*Security Features and Planning*

If you haven't come across it before, that probably sounds like a lot of trouble when you usually just want to check a userid/password pair. In fact, the default JAAS configurations provided by application servers and the samples provided with CM arrange just that, and the CE APIs provide convenience mechanisms for dealing with userid/password authentication. The point of the more flexible, configurable authentication scheme is to accommodate other desires. Because JAAS is standardized and because you can provide your own login modules, you can implement your own completely unique credentials material. The applications and the application server are completely isolated from your scheme and do not need to change at all to use it. (We're still working on a login module that can somehow talk to that dog.)

# Where authentication actually happens

If an application runs in the web container or the EJB container of the same application server where the CE is running, it is probably intuitively obvious where authentication takes place. That's not typical and isn't even recommended (for performance and scaling reasons), so there must be some other places where authentication can happen. Let's look at those.

## Application Server trust relationships

A common J2EE architecture is to have at least two or three tiers of application servers communicating in an orderly way. Most commonly, a web application may use EJB calls to speak from the web container on a front-tier application server to the EJB container on a back-tier application server. When you use an application (such as Workplace XT) that makes CE API calls over EJB transport, the application is doing exactly that. It's just making ordinary Java calls, but the API internals are using EJBs as a remoting mechanism.

In that configuration, the JAAS authentication still happens on an application server, but it's a different application server instance than the one where the CE runs. J2EE application servers have mechanisms for establishing **trust relationships**. For our purposes, that simply means that the back-tier application server will trust a Subject created on a front-tier application server. The mechanisms for configuring trust relationships are vendor-specific, and so is the underlying mechanism that allows the trust to be, well, trustworthy. It's generally something involving digital signatures for the information inside the Subject.

When a remote call is made via an EJB, as happens inside the CE Java API when using EJB transport, the ambient JAAS Subject is automatically propagated to and made the ambient JAAS Subject for the receiving application server. This is done completely via the application server's EJB remoting implementation and does not involve any explicit code in the application or the CE Java API.

> When an application server sees a Subject that it doesn't trust (because there is no trust relationship with the sending application server), it will often simply discard the Subject or strip vital information out of it. That's why complaints from the CE that you are trying to do "anonymous access" often mean that there is something wrong with your trust relationship setup.

The EJB mechanism for passing the Subject automatically is reasonably standardized in J2EE. However, it is not normally possible to get the trust relationship or the exact details of the Subject internals to work properly across application server brands. There are a few isolated cases where a front-tier application server can do authentication in such a way that the back-tier application server will trust it, but those configurations tend to be fragile and easily broken by an otherwise innocuous vendor point release. This is one of the reasons that the CE Java API does not support EJB transport except among homogeneous application servers.

## Thick EJB clients

By **thick Java client**, we mean a client that does not run inside a J2EE application server. This can be a Java console application or a GUI application. Even though not running in an application server, it is still possible to use EJB transport for such applications with authentication support from the application server. The authentication takes place in a vendor-specific arrangement that involves cooperation between vendor-provided client-side support libraries and the application server.

The details of how these mechanisms work is not particularly important to this discussion. The end result is a Subject in the client that will be trusted by the application server when it arrives over an EJB call. In some cases, the credentials are passed to the application server at what the application believes is authentication time. In other cases, the credentials are sent more or less in their raw form at the time of EJB calls. You may even be given a configuration choice for which of the two ways will be used. To the application, this is transparent. As someone configuring thick clients, it's something that deserves your attention. One way or another, it is likely that raw credentials will be passing over the network. You will want to ensure that the path for that is protected by TLS/SSL, assuming it's your site policy or best practice to protect credentials that way.

# CEWS clients

There is another transport available to CE APIs. It's called **CE Web Services** (**CEWS**) transport, and it does not use EJB at all. Authentication details are somewhat different. CEWS transport is SOAP XML transported over HTTP or HTTPS (TLS/SSL) connections.

> You are undoubtedly familiar with XML files from many different situations. They are ubiquitous in software today. If you are not familiar with SOAP, all you need to know is that it's a standard for a particular way of expressing information in an XML file. It is usually used in request/response scenarios, such as the CE API calls to the CE server.

## Java clients with CEWS

With CEWS transport, we don't have the benefit of trust relationships and automatically propagated binary-compatible Subjects. Therefore, the application server never automatically trusts the client, and authentication always happens on the application server instance where the CE runs. The client sees an illusion of authentication or, indeed, an authentication that is trusted by components other than the J2EE application server.

To maintain a consistent application programming model, the CE Java API still uses JAAS for a simulated authentication when using CEWS transport. That simulated authentication, done via a CE-provided login module, merely collects the userid and password for later use. For each call from the CE API to the CE server, the raw credentials are passed explicitly in the SOAP XML.

> Because of the transmission of raw credentials, you will want to configure TLS/SSL connections when using CEWS transport.

CEWS requests are received by a web component called the CEWS listener. Although it is a component provided as part of the CE server installation (you don't have to do anything extra to install it; in fact, you can't avoid it), it is not automatically trusted by the main parts of the CE. We say it is outside of the trust boundary of the server. It's treated like any other web component, but it happens to be running inside the same application server instance as the rest of the CE. The CEWS listener extracts the raw credentials from the incoming SOAP XML and uses them to perform a JAAS authentication in the same way that any other web application would do it. The CEWS listener then makes CE Java API EJB calls. From that point, the CE doesn't know or care that the request originally came in via CEWS transport. The main part of the CE server sees all requests as coming in via EJB transport with Subjects trusted by the application server. That eliminates a lot of special handling code from the CE server.

## .NET clients and direct CEWS users

There are two other categories of clients that send requests to the CEWS listener: CE .NET API clients and clients directly using CEWS as a protocol. The CE .NET API can't use JAAS because of differences in technology stacks. Direct users of CEWS protocol may or may not be able to use JAAS for credentials collection, but their internals are in any case unknown to the CEWS listener.

The .NET API uses only the CEWS transport, and there is no JAAS illusion to maintain. Therefore, the .NET API has explicit mechanisms for applications to use in supplying supported credentials types. Credentials ultimately end up in the same or related places in the SOAP XML as those described for the CE Java API using CEWS transport, and those same places can be used by direct users of CEWS protocol.

We won't repeat the discussion of the CEWS listener here since it's exactly the same as described above for the CE Java API. The CEWS listener doesn't know the origin of an incoming request (at least in principle).

The CE .NET API has direct support for Kerberos-based Integrated Windows Authentication (IWA). Naturally, that's only available in a Windows environment. Because there is a place for Kerberos credentials in the SOAP XML, it can also be used by direct users of CEWS protocol. Using Kerberos does require that support for it be configured into the JAAS configuration used by the CEWS listener. CM only supports Kerberos in specific contexts.

> Integrated Windows Authentication (IWA) is a good example of client-side authentication for other purposes that is not trusted by the J2EE application server until it has had its own dog sniff at it. IWA has also been known, formally or informally, by several other names over the years. When you see discussions of Windows authentication and Kerberos, SPNEGO, or maybe even NTLM, it is almost certainly a discussion about IWA.

## Custom authentication and tunneling

If the standard mechanisms just described don't meet your needs, there are two customization techniques that are a bit like wild cards. They require sophisticated custom development, but they have virtually no limit in what they can do.

*Security Features and Planning*

The CEWS listener has explicit support for **Web Services Extensible Authentication Framework (WS-EAF)**. This is a feature—supported only for use by direct users of CEWS protocol—that provides a location in the SOAP XML where applications can place an arbitrary piece of well-formed custom XML. The CEWS listener extracts that piece of custom XML and makes it available to login modules during JAAS authentication. To use it, you would write a custom JAAS login module that understood your XML information, and you would deploy that login module into the JAAS configuration used by the CEWS listener.

Another mechanism, available to all clients, is called tunneling. The idea is simple. You use the existing userid/password slots to carry some custom information. You might, for example, use some unusual and distinctive fixed value for the userid to indicate that the password contains an encoded token of some kind. You would then write a custom login module that understood your convention and could validate the token. Your custom login module would then be deployed into the JAAS configuration used by the CEWS listener.

## Delegated authentication

This section isn't really about a different place for CM authentication, but a description of how applications do authentication for their own purposes.

A typical CM application will make calls to the CE, possibly the PE server, and possibly other third party servers or services. The application will usually only care about authentication to the extent that it is enforced by the servers and services the application uses. The application will not usually contain sensitive data or computations; those are left to the well-guarded back-end systems.

- An application making calls to the CE will use JAAS authentication or one of the other mechanisms discussed above because it knows the CE requires it.
- An application making calls to the PE will either do JAAS authentication or use one of the login methods provided by the PE API. Behind the scenes, the PE API makes calls to the CE to prove that the authentication is acceptable. The mechanism for this is a bit too complicated for our discussion here, but it is definitely true that the PE delegates authentication responsibilities to the CE (which in turn delegates to the application server).
- An application making calls to other servers or services will have to perform authentication acceptable to them. Often, this will be the same JAAS authentication or IWA being used for CE and PE authentication. If it's not, it's up to the application to work it out.

- Finally, as a special case, an application could, for its own purposes, exploit the CE for authentication by making some simple CE call and seeing if it failed for authentication reasons. In a J2EE environment, you could try to access any protected resource and see the result, but the CE happens to be a handy, well-defined example to use.

Because authentication needs and facilities are moving ever onward toward standardization, it is desirable to take it out of the hands of the applications entirely. IWA does this by having the user authenticate to the operating system, and the operating system reliably marks every application as being run by that user. J2EE has a similar mechanism called **container managed authentication** (**CMA**). The user can do authentication to the web or EJB container, and the resulting Subject becomes the ambient Subject for all application threads run on behalf of that user. Where they can be used, these higher-level authentication mechanisms can greatly reduce application dependencies on specific authentication techniques, and it also removes from applications the possibilities for most authentication-related security vulnerabilities.

# Single Sign-on

**Single Sign-on** (SSO) is the notion of having users log on once, typically on a workstation, and having their authentication automatically propagated to and trusted by all of the business applications they use throughout the day. Users love this idea for obvious reasons (although it might be more proper to say that most users have never heard of this idea and strongly dislike the lack of it when they encounter it). Given the realities of multiple, incompatible technology stacks in most enterprise environments, SSO is very challenging to implement completely.

We saw an example of an SSO technology earlier. IWA via Kerberos is widely used because of the simple fact of the prevalence of Windows-based workstations in most enterprises. Where the server infrastructure supports it, it can give good SSO integration between the workstation desktop, desktop applications, and web applications.

A common SSO compromise is for enterprises to settle for SSO across their web applications. This often provides a considerable simplification when workstations are Windows-based but the server infrastructure is not. We've seen already, though perhaps without full details, that JAAS Subjects along with trust relationships make a reasonable basis for SSO within tiers of J2EE application servers.

*Security Features and Planning*

There are many third-party SSO providers for J2EE environments. Almost all of them integrate via JAAS, though it is sometimes necessary to do some custom work of your own to get a completely smooth SSO environment for your users. For custom applications, CM supports any SSO solution supported by the SSO vendor and the application server vendor. For CM-provided clients, a specific list of qualified SSO solutions is given in the *IBM FileNet P8 Hardware and Software Requirements* document.

## Anonymous and guest access

We've made quite a fuss about knowing exactly who is doing what within a CM repository. That's the most common use case, but there are use cases where, for convenience or for some other reason, you don't want to make users go through authentication to access some part of your content.

For example, you might have a non-sensitive repository that backs a public-facing website. You don't want to put any artificial roadblocks in the way of members of the public getting your offered information. A variation of this occurs when you do want to make members of the public identify themselves, usually with low-grade credentials like an email address they control, but you want to keep track of them somewhere other than your enterprise directory. Without being in the enterprise directory, their authentication would fail for J2EE purposes in most environments.

The CE, by design, does not allow anonymous access. There is always an authenticated Subject accompanying a CE request, or the request will be rejected by the CE. This is really not any different from other software components. Except for ancient systems like DOS and CP/M, every process on a computer operating system runs as somebody. It may not be obvious who the somebody is in every case because the software components work together to make simulated anonymous access easy. Still, even a minimalist web server runs as some operating system user. (On many Unix/Linux systems, there is a designated low-privilege operating system user called `nobody` for just such purposes. Even `nobody` is somebody.)

The usual practice, for CM applications and for the other types of systems mentioned, is to simulate anonymous access by using something called **guest access**. Guest access means that a set of credentials is set aside specifically for use by these users (the guests). The guests themselves are not usually aware of this and do not know what the guest credentials are. The guest credentials are hard-coded into or configured for the application. Other names for this same idea include **system account** and **configured identity**.

Guest access is a trade-off between strict security and convenience. It may be a trade-off worth making for some use cases, but you should be aware of the risks:

- You may be controlling guest access with some application-level logic, but an attacker who discovers the actual guest credentials may be able to bypass your application logic and access back-end systems directly.
- Auditing and other logging systems will be unlikely to record anything other than the guest identity. You may be tracking more specific information at the application level, but matching up logging across multiple tiers can add considerable complexity and effort to any troubleshooting or forensics efforts. In other words, it may be pretty difficult to unravel the trail if someone does something malicious via a guest account.
- The CE, in particular, records several facts about access to and modification of objects in audit logs and system properties. That information can be no more accurate than the identity presented in the authenticated Subject.

# Impersonation and run-as

There is a special mechanism for guest access available in J2EE and a similar mechanism for IWA. In both cases, an application can be configured so that all or some part of it runs with an identity different from the actual user running the application. Windows calls this **impersonation**, and J2EE calls it **run-as**. The mechanisms differ in implementation, but both are administratively configured, and the net result is that the authenticated user identity seen by the CE is the impersonated or run-as identity.

> One of the first software patents — perhaps the very first — was granted to Bell Laboratories for the Unix *setuid* mechanism. That mechanism enabled impersonation on Unix and is still in use today in all Unix derivatives.

These mechanisms can obviously be used for guest access. You would simply arrange your software components so that the parts needing guest access were configured to run using either of these mechanisms with the guest account. Perhaps less obviously, the same mechanisms can be used to provide intentional access with elevated privileges.

Suppose you wanted to allow some set of users to perform an action for which they are not normally authorized. (We are jumping ahead to the authorization topic a bit, but please bear with us.) They are authorized to do it under some special circumstances, like only being allowed to do it on Wednesdays, when the moon is full, during leap years. In other words, it's under some conditions where no general purpose middleware system is going to provide the business logic needed for that special condition. You're going to have to write the business logic yourself.

You won't be able to just give those users that right in the middleware system without also empowering them do it outside of your special conditions. After all, they might write their own application or use some general purpose application to perform the operation without the benefit of your application logic. CM does not have a notion of privileges assigned to applications. It only has privileges assigned to users or groups of users.

To use the impersonation or run-as features for this use case, you would put the complex business decision logic into a separate software component and configure it to run as a user identity that did have the extra privilege. (The administrative configuration could not be done by unprivileged users to give their own software components the extra rights.) The business logic in that component would not exercise the extra privilege unless the special conditions were met; that's what the business logic is all about.

A couple of important points about this technique:

- You are explicitly trusting the configured component to do the right thing. So, you should obviously exercise due security diligence in inspecting the component before performing the configuration for impersonation or run-as.
- Remember that your configured component might be called in ways you are not expecting. Make sure that you are satisfied with the statement, "No matter how this component is called, I am willing to let it perform this operation as long as the business logic conditions are met."
- Complexity and good security are generally inversely correlated. You want only the barest minimum amount of logic that you can get away with inside the configured software component. The more you have in there, the more chance there is that an attacker can fool your component into doing something that it shouldn't.
- Finally, this is just a reminder that most systems will only log actions as having been taken by the configured identity and may not even be aware of the actual calling user identity. Be sure to analyze this and make sure it is acceptable.

# Enterprise directories

CM assumes the use of a directory containing user and group information. Technically, the CE does not care if the application server consults a directory for authentication, but there must at least be the illusion that the directory is used. The application server provides an authenticated Subject, and within that Subject is the identity of the authenticated user. The CE trusts the identity because it received it by trustworthy means from the application server.

The CE uses the directory explicitly for the following things:

- There are CE API calls for searching for directory users and groups in various ways. These are translated into directory service calls, and a handful of directory attributes are available to CE API callers.
- Access permissions can be assigned to directory groups. To see if a particular group access permission applies to the calling user, the CE uses directory service calls to discover group memberships. Depending on the directory in use, there may be groups nested within groups.
- The CE stores some user and group information using unique identifiers from the directory. This is different from the user and group names returned to callers. When necessary, the CE uses directory service calls to do the translation.

All CE directory calls are made using the **Lightweight Directory Access Protocol (LDAP)**. This is a standard, vendor-neutral protocol available for all modern enterprise directory servers. It would be nice if things were standard enough that you could provide a few configuration parameters and then use any LDAP-based directory access. Unfortunately, that amount of standardization is not currently available, and the CE has some amount of vendor-specific code for every supported enterprise directory. Each supported directory configuration undergoes a specific testing effort to ensure that it works properly with the CE. Details of specific directory brands and version numbers are given in the *IBM FileNet Hardware and Software Requirements* document.

Directory searches, especially for the resolution of group memberships, can cause a considerable amount of performance drag within the CE. The CE caches directory information to ease this burden. The sizes, refresh intervals, and other details of these caches can be tuned if a site has special requirements. The application server vendors also cache directory look-ups involved in authentication.

# Authorization in CM

We described JAAS in the section about authentication. Although the middle two letters of JAAS stand for authentication and authorization, CM does not use JAAS for authorization purposes.

Instead, CM provides its own fine-grained and richly-featured access control mechanisms. It is fine-grained because it can be applied with individual granularity to most objects within an Object Store. It includes both discretionary access control mechanisms and a mandatory access control mechanism. There are built-in features for setting and modifying the access control on objects to make it easy to implement a wide variety of popular use cases with minimal development or administrative effort.

The terms authorization, access control, and access check are similar enough that they can be used interchangeably for our discussion.

# Discretionary and Mandatory Access Control

Discretionary and Mandatory Access Control are industry standard terms for describing ways of establishing access control for objects in a computer system.

You are probably already familiar with the mechanics of **Discretionary Access Control**, even if you don't know that term, because it occurs in everyday computer systems. It refers to users being able to give someone else access to an object without system interference. It's discretionary in the sense that a user can just decide, based on his or her own discretion, to give (or deny) someone else access. The system does not evaluate the appropriateness of that action. **Mandatory Access Control**, on the other hand, is about using system enforcement to make sure that certain access can never be granted by one user to another, accidentally or intentionally.

If you're not used to these security concepts, they may seem like a lot of fuss over a minor difference. They are actually dramatically different, and that will probably be clearer once we've described the CM implementations individually. The first several mechanisms are discretionary, and we'll finish up with marking sets, the CE mandatory access control mechanism.

# Access Control Lists

An **Access Control List** (**ACL**, sometimes pronounced "ACK-el") is a list of access control specifications for a particular object. An individual item in the list is called an **Access Control Entry** (**ACE**). A single ACE always contains exactly the same types of conceptual information:

- The identity of the user or group to whom it applies. It's one or the other, never both a user and a group.
- An indication of whether the ACE is allowing some rights or denying some rights. Again, it's one or the other.
- The set of rights being allowed or denied by this ACE. It would be possible to specify a single right per ACE, but specifying a collection is both an efficient shortcut and a useful helper for thinking about how the rights confer access. In any case, the CE consolidates ACEs where it can.

An ACE also has an inheritable depth and a permission source, but we'll describe those later.

To view an object's ACL in FEM, select the object, right-click, and select **Properties**. Most objects have a **Security** tab in the pop-up panel.

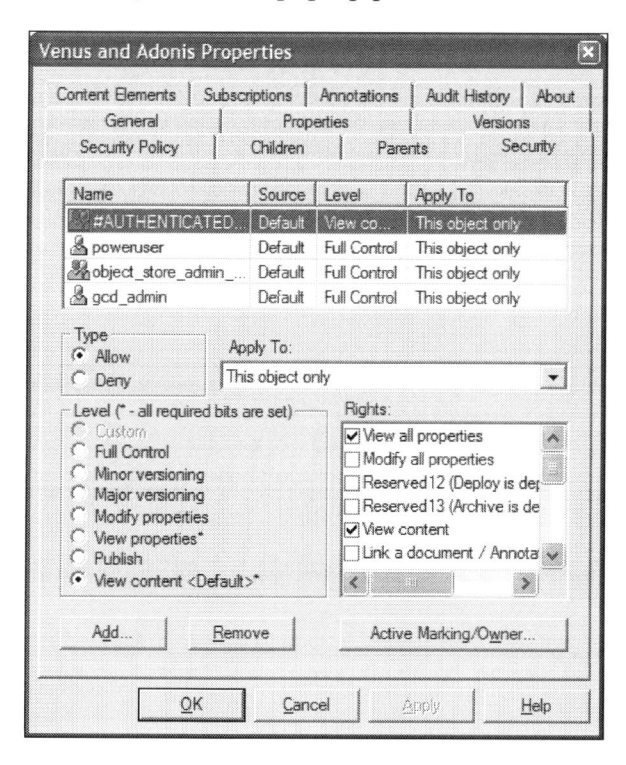

Security Features and Planning

The way to interpret an ACE is "for this (user or group), this ACE (grants or denies) this (set of rights)". When the authorization check in the CE is examining an ACE, it first decides if the calling user either matches the user mentioned in the ACE or is a member of the group mentioned in the ACE. If not, the ACE is completely ignored for access control purposes. When considering the entire ACL, after discarding the non-applicable ACEs, there are a few possibilities for any particular access right for the calling user:

- There are one or more "allow" ACEs applicable to that user, and there are no "deny" ACEs for that user. In that case, the given access right is granted.
- There are one or more "deny" ACEs applicable to that user. In that case, the user is denied the given access right. Because a "deny" overrules an "allow" for a given right, access is denied even if there are "allow" ACEs for the same right. A common mistake is to deny access to a group and then try to allow access to one or more individual members of the group. That doesn't work because the "allow" user ACE cannot overcome the "deny" group ACE.
- There are not any ACEs applicable to that user. In that case, the given access right is **implicitly denied** to that user. The implicit denial simply means that if a user or group is not mentioned at all in the ACL, then the ultimate default is to deny them access. It is common to avoid "deny" ACEs and allow implicit deny to limit access.

This evaluation scheme is actually slightly more complex because the ACEs in an ACL are organized by tiers according to the permission source for the ACE. There are four permission source possibilities organized into three tiers:

- **Direct/Default**: Includes ACEs which are directly applied to an individual object, explicitly or via the class Default Instance Permissions
- **Template**: Includes ACEs which are applied via a Security Template
- **Inherited**: Includes ACEs which are applied via security inheritance

The mechanisms behind the tiers will be described in other sections of this chapter. For now, all you need to know is that direct/default ACEs take precedence over template ACEs, and template ACEs take precedence over inherited ACEs. That is, an "allow" ACE in the direct tier can overcome a "deny" ACE in the template or inherited tier. Within a tier, the calculation is as described earlier, with "deny" taking precedence over "allow".

At the end of all these calculations (and a few other things to be described next), the CE will have a list of access rights that are granted to the calling user. That is referred to as the **effective access mask**. At the end of the calculation, it doesn't really matter how an access right got granted. It only matters that it was granted (or not) somehow.

## User and group access

An ACE may specify a particular user or it may specify a directory group. In the latter case, the ACE applies to all users who are directly or indirectly members of that group. (Indirect membership occurs because some directories allow groups to be nested within other groups.)

You could theoretically use only user ACEs and never use group ACEs, but that's usually a bad idea. In the first place, it would be pretty tedious and labor-intensive to list individual users when a group would do the job. In the second place, a group ACE is used dynamically in the sense that the group membership is evaluated at the time the ACE is examined (modulated slightly by the short-term caching in the CE). So, if a new user is added to a group, the ACE is automatically applicable to that user. If a user is removed from a group, the rights conferred by that group ACE are automatically withdrawn.

It's a best practice to use group ACEs wherever possible. The ACL is an attribute of an individual object, and it is generally impractical to update the security on thousands or even millions of objects as individual users come and go.

> There is another kind of ACE that is of interest only to application developers. It is an **unknown** ACE. It comes about because ACEs sometimes get orphaned. The user or group mentioned in the ACE gets deleted from the directory, but the ACE still exists in the repository. These ACEs will never match any calling user and so will never figure into any access control calculation.
>
> Application developers have to be aware of this kind of ACE when programmatically displaying or modifying the ACL. The unknown ACEs should be silently filtered out and not displayed to end users. (FEM displays unknown ACEs, but it is an administrator tool.) If updates are made to the ACL, the unknown ACEs definitely must be filtered out. Otherwise, the CE will throw an exception because it cannot resolve the user or group in the directory.

## Rights

Every action that a user can take that is controlled by an access check has an individually named access right in the CE. At the end of an ACL evaluation, a given access right is either allowed or denied (perhaps via implicit denial) to the calling user. There is never any shading or doubt: the user is allowed or denied for a given right. Likewise, mention of a right in an ACE is always an absolute "allow" or "deny" within the scope of that ACE. Rights are considered individually, and being granted or denied one right does not automatically grant or deny a user any other rights.

# Security Features and Planning

> The two-state nature of access rights makes it easy to compactly express them as a collection of bits in an integer field called a bitmask. Indeed, the CE does exactly that for efficiency. However, that is only interesting to application developers and students of the arcane. Most tools present the rights as individual checkboxes or similar UI items.

The set of possible rights varies by object type because the set of possible actions is different for different object types. A few access rights are available for all object types (for example, the right to read an object's property values), while others are more specialized (for example, the rights to create a major or minor version, which exist only for Document objects). As an illustration, there are eight individual rights defined for an Object Store, but there are fifteen individual rights defined for a Document object (plus two more that were used at one time but are not now obsolete).

## Levels

Although there is not a technical connection between individual access rights, it is certainly the case that some of them tend to travel together. For some use cases, you are likely to grant or deny a particular collection of rights to an object as a group to achieve some functional end. The CE APIs provide constants for many useful collections of rights, and many applications exploit this to display rights in various groupings. These groupings are called **access levels**. It is important to understand, however, that levels are not additional kinds of rights or a different mechanism. They are simply functionally interesting collections of existing access rights.

Earlier in this chapter, we showed a screenshot of the **Security** tab of a **Properties** panel from FEM. The access levels are used in FEM to create a series of radio buttons for quick selection. Here is a picture of the same sort of permissions as seen in XT:

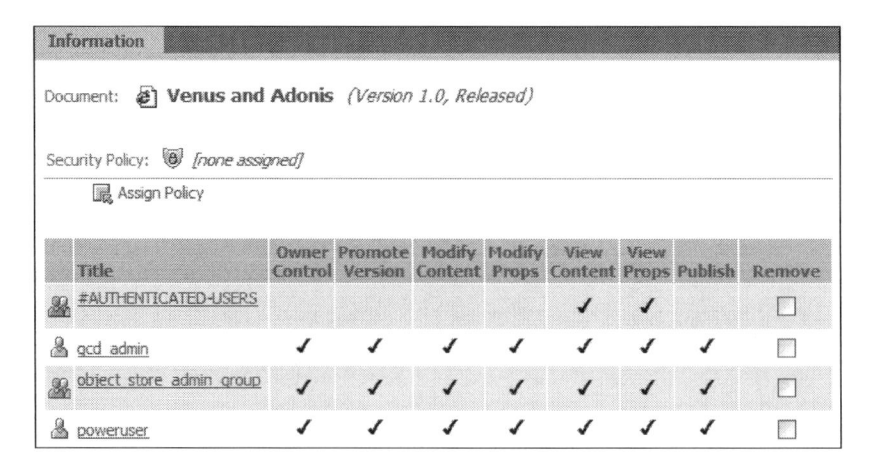

| Title | Owner Control | Promote Version | Modify Content | Modify Props | View Content | View Props | Publish | Remove |
|---|---|---|---|---|---|---|---|---|
| #AUTHENTICATED-USERS | | | | | ✓ | ✓ | | ☐ |
| gcd_admin | ✓ | ✓ | ✓ | ✓ | ✓ | ✓ | ✓ | ☐ |
| object_store_admin_group | ✓ | ✓ | ✓ | ✓ | ✓ | ✓ | ✓ | ☐ |
| poweruser | ✓ | ✓ | ✓ | ✓ | ✓ | ✓ | ✓ | ☐ |

Document: **Venus and Adonis** *(Version 1.0, Released)*

Security Policy: *[none assigned]*

FEM and XT use somewhat different terminology for combinations of rights. This is due mainly to the different audiences for the two tools.

If you are developing an application that displays or manipulates security details, you may or may not find the levels (defined in API class `AccessLevel`) to be interesting for your use case. If they're not helpful, don't use them.

## Unused bits

Now that you know that access rights are stored as a collection of bits and are manipulated programmatically as bits, you may find yourself looking more deeply into the defined access rights bits. The bits are stored as a 32-bit integer, but not all of the bit positions have defined meanings at this time. If you were to use some of those otherwise unallocated bits for your own purposes, that would not interfere with the CE's access check calculations. Of course, most tools won't even give you a way to set those bits, but you could do it programmatically. That is a bad idea, and here are some reasons why you shouldn't do it:

- Other applications shouldn't care about the bits you are using, but neither are they guaranteed to respect them. They might just clear them on the grounds that they know they are not defined for anything.

- Some applications have both simplified and detailed views of security. The simplified views are based on well-known combinations of access rights that the application thinks are meaningful. Setting unallocated bits is almost certainly going to cause those applications to abandon the simple view and always show the detailed view.

- Access rights bits don't change very often, but it's entirely possible that the next release of CM will define a meaning for the very bits that you are using. All unallocated bits should be considered reserved for future use by the system.

If it's such a bad idea, why would you want to do it in the first place? You might be thinking it's a handy place to do bookkeeping for your own private access rights. Maybe a synchronous event handler of yours would check those bits as part of its decision logic for whether to allow an operation. That's not a bad idea; it's just a bad idea to use unallocated access rights bits. You'll have to find some more traditional place for keeping track of such things.

## Implicit rights

In addition to the rights conferred via the ACL mechanism, there are two special cases where rights are implicitly given to calling users.

## Object Owner

An object has an `Owner` property. It is usually the case that the user who created the object is also the owner, but there are other possibilities. There is a particular access right called `WRITE_OWNER` (but often informally called "take ownership") that means someone (or some group) is authorized to assume ownership of the object.

The owner of an object is always allowed to update the object's ACL (even if not explicitly granted the `WRITE_ACL` right). Because of that, the owner of an object is indirectly given all other available rights for that object. We say it's indirect because the ACL must actually be modified to confer those other rights.

Suppose you wanted to eliminate this exception and limit actions to explicitly granted rights. (Records Management has this requirement, for example.) It's obvious how to make sure nobody has the `WRITE_OWNER` access right. What about the owner of the object? It's possible to set the value of the `Owner` property to null, in which case there is no owner, and there is nobody who has the implicitly-granted owner rights. A typical user with the `WRITE_OWNER` access right can only set the `Owner` property to his or her own identity. To set it to null requires an additional privilege discussed in the next section.

## Object Store administrator

There actually is no such thing in the eyes of the CE as an Object Store administrator. There are only authenticated users with or without various access rights. Tools like FEM have a working definition for an Object Store administrator, which is a user with full access rights to the Object Store object. That's mainly because routine matters in an administrator tool like FEM can become pretty sticky, pretty fast if the user doesn't have the rights to do various things.

However, there is one specific access right that, more than any other, feels like "the administrator bit". That access right is called `WRITE_ANY_OWNER` and is available only for Object Store objects. A user with this access right is allowed to update the `Owner` property of any object in the Object Store with any legal value, including null.

You can probably guess the next part: users with `WRITE_ANY_OWNER` rights on the Object Store are treated as if they also have `WRITE_OWNER` rights on each object, which means they have the right to modify each object's ACL; this means they can do pretty much whatever they want to those objects. It should be clear now why having the `WRITE_ANY_OWNER` right is often thought of as being the same as being an administrator.

Interestingly, the Object Store itself does not have a `WRITE_OWNER` access right. That's because it doesn't have an `Owner` property. It does have a `Creator` property, but that confers no special privileges.

## Special query right

To see an object, which really means to view an object's properties, users needs READ rights to that object. Otherwise, the very existence of the object is hidden from them. Users with WRITE_OWNER or WRITE_ANY_OWNER could update the object's ACL and grant themselves READ access. Before they could change the ACL, they would have to get a reference to the object. If they don't already have READ access, it can be difficult to get the object reference. The object will not show up in ordinary browsing.

The situation of owning an object but not having READ access is called the "lost object problem". It usually comes about by accident, and usually everyone has lost READ access to the object. The object is effectively invisible, but it still exists. That can be more than just an annoyance. For example, the lost object might still prevent deletion of other objects due to referential integrity checks in the CE.

To provide a solution to the lost object problem, there is a special case that happens only when query results are being returned. Objects for which the caller does not have READ access are normally silently excluded from the query results. However, they are not excluded if the calling user has WRITE_OWNER or WRITE_ANY_OWNER access. The idea is that lost objects could be located via such a query, thereby providing the needed reference so that the ACL could be updated (since those same calling users would also have implicit WRITE_ACL rights).

## Extra access requirements

Beyond ACEs and the various mechanisms for manipulating them, manually and automatically, there are a couple of common cases where you might want some additional control. CM has specific mechanisms for those cases. The mechanisms are both implementations of additional restrictions on setting specific properties on an object, and so they are configured in the property definition for the property in question.

### Modification Access Required

Sometimes you would like to put extra protection on a specific property so that even users with the right to update properties generally on an object still need a bit more access to be able to modify that particular property. The CE has ACLs on objects, not on properties of objects. A feature called **Modification Access Required (MAR)** lets you use the object ACL to protect a specific property.

The property `PropertyDefinition.ModificationAccessRequired` is an integer value that defines, in the usual bitmask representation, the access rights to the object that a user must have in order to be allowed to modify that property. In the usual case, the value is zero (in which case updates are governed by the object ACL), but you can define additional required access rights for your custom properties. For example, you might require that a calling user have right to delete the object before being allowed to update a particular property. That doesn't mean that they must be actually deleting the object; it merely means they must have the right to delete it. You can view or modify the MAR value in FEM by editing the Property Definition for the property. For example, here is the MAR for the inherited property `WjcWorkOfLiterature.Permissions`. Because it's a system property, you can't modify the MAR. It's not surprising to find out that that the **Modify permissions** right (`WRITE_ACL`) is required.

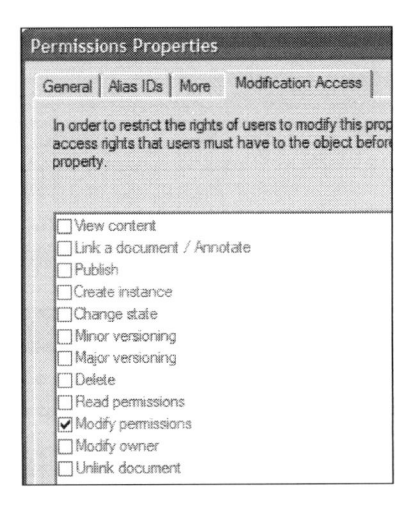

When an attempt is made to update property values on an object, the CE first computes the effective access that the calling user has for that object. Assuming all the object-level access checks pass, the CE looks at the modification access required for each property being updated. The calling user must also have all of those rights, or the update will fail.

## Target Access Required

There are many ways to form relationships between objects in CM. Most of them were described in *Chapter 7, Major CM Features*. We usually think of a relationship as updating a property on one object to point to another object, and we usually think about the right of the caller to update the property on the pointing object. It is sometimes useful to let the pointed-to object have some say in whether another object can point to it. A feature called **Target Access Required (TAR)** implements that.

The property `PropertyDefinitionObject.TargetAccessRequired` is an integer-valued property that defines, in the usual bitmask representation, the access rights to the pointed-to object that a user must have when setting the value of an OVP on the pointing object. In the usual case, there are no extra access rights required. As an example of using TAR, you may wish to require that the calling user has the right to delete the pointed-to object before setting up the pointer. You would add that right to the pointing object's target access required for that property. In other words, you would set it on the property definition of the pointing OVP.

## Default instance security

When an object is created, the creating application can explicitly set its access permissions. The `Permissions` property holds the ACL and can be set at creation time like many other properties. In that case, the ACL is applied as is, and each ACE becomes a direct ACE as we described above. It can be tedious and error-prone to have to correctly set the ACL explicitly for every new object, so there is a defaulting mechanism.

A Class Description has a property called `DefaultInstancePermissions`. This is just a pre-defined ACL. It doesn't apply to the Class Description itself. Rather, it applies to new object instances of that class if the ACL is not set explicitly by the caller. In that case, the ACEs are default ACEs. For access checking purposes, direct ACEs and default ACEs have the same effect. You will recall that they were in the same tier when we described the access control calculation earlier in this chapter. Here, for example, is the FEM view of the default instance permissions for the Work of Literature class:

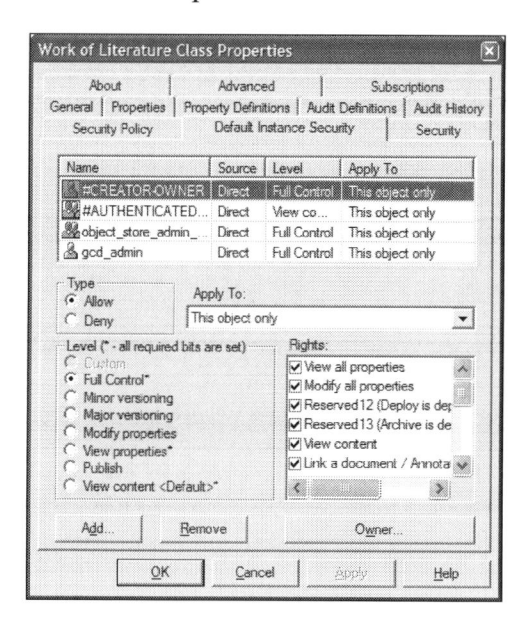

Many people misconstrue this defaulting mechanism as a kind of security inheritance. It definitely is not. If you modify a class's default instance permissions, it affects only object instances created after that point. It does not update the permissions of existing instances. If it really were inheritance, it would somehow be automatically reflected in those existing instances.

# #CREATOR-OWNER

If you are setting up default instance permissions for a class, you might like to allow or deny some access rights explicitly to the user who creates an instance. Obviously, you don't know who that user is until s/he actually creates an instance.

There is a special figurative user that solves this problem. When you create an ACE with a user identity of the literal string `#CREATOR-OWNER` (notice that it has a hyphen, not an underscore), that ACE is automatically transformed into the actual owner of the object. There is no user called `#CREATOR-OWNER` in the directory.

With a moment's reflection, you can see that it doesn't make much sense to do this substitution when you are directly updating an ACL (you know who the owner is and can just use that identity in an ACE). As it turns out, the CE will only accept this value in contexts where an ACL update is going to be done automatically. In other words, an ACL is being created or modified, but that ACL will only be applied at a later time. The class default instance permissions is one of those places, as are security policies and document lifecycle policies, both of which are described in the next section.

# Security policy and document lifecycle policy

An initial ACL is established for an object when the object is created. For many objects, the ACL is never changed for the entire life of the object. There are other use cases where the ACL is updated at planned times and in predictable ways. For example, as documents go through versioning cycles, you might like to systematically use different ACLs for obsolete versions, in-process versions, and so on.

CM provides a feature to facilitate this, and it's called **Security Policy**. A related mechanism is available as part of the document lifecycle policy feature (described in *Chapter 7*). Historically, the lifecycle-related feature existed first. The security policy feature is a bit more general. If you are already using document lifecycles for another reason, you may find it convenient to also use their security feature.

# Security Policy and Security Templates

Documents, folders, and custom objects have a `SecurityPolicy` property, which can be set to point at a **Security Policy** object. A security policy object has a list of **Security Template** objects. A security template is only a bit more than a collection of ACEs, and this is where ACEs from the template tier originate.

> `SecurityPolicy` is an ordinary object-valued property that can be updated at any time. Because the most common way to use it is to take the default value from the class definition at object creation time, security policies are usually thought of as applying to a class.

Each security template has a GUID-valued `ApplyStateId` property that is used as part of its behavior. You can set the `ApplyStateId` property to one of the four special values representing document versioning states (and defined in the CE APIs in the class `VersionStatusId`) or to a value determined by your application, depending on whether your security template is created as a `VersioningSecurityTemplate` or an `ApplicationSecurityTemplate`. Both types of templates can co-exist in the list of templates in a security policy object.

If this is your first exposure to CE security policies and security templates, you are probably scratching your head about the information we just described. Let's describe the behaviors:

- When a security template is applied to a target object, the list of ACEs is copied from the security template to that target object. Existing ACEs that came from any template are first removed. A boolean property on the security policy object determines whether any direct/default ACEs are also removed.

- Documents, folders, and custom objects in the CE APIs have a method called `applySecurityTemplate`. It applies a security template from that object's security policy to the object. The specific application security template is identified by its `ApplyStateId` value. This represents a way for applications to make a specific change to an object's security in a figurative way. The application does not need to have the specific ACEs coded into it.

- When a document undergoes a versioning state change (for example, when a reservation is checked in), the CE automatically finds and applies the versioning security template with an `ApplyStateId` corresponding to the target state of the document. This represents a way to configure document versions to automatically undergo specific security changes when they transition through versioning cycles. Calling applications do not have to take any action because the CE does this automatically based on the security policy object and its collection of versioning security templates.

The more popular of the two mechanisms just described is the versioning-related feature. You could achieve the effect of either type of security template by using a combination of other CM features, but it's typically more performance-efficient and simpler application logic to use the security policy features if they fit your use case.

## Document lifecycle policy

Document lifecycle policies have a feature quite similar to that of security policies, but the mechanics and terminology are slightly different. The lifecycle feature in general is described in *Chapter 7*. Here, we concern ourselves with just the feature for automatic security changes.

A document has a `DocumentLifecyclePolicy` property whose value is a Document Lifecycle Policy object. A document lifecycle policy object has a list of document state objects. Besides giving the lifecycle state details, the document state object also has an optional list of template permissions. The template permissions collection is just a list of ACEs.

Here's how this is used: When a document transitions to a particular lifecycle state, the list of template permissions for that state is copied to the document. Existing ACEs that came from a template are first removed. A boolean property on the document lifecycle policy object determines whether any direct/default ACEs are also removed.

You can see that this is quite similar in concept to the security template mechanism described above. In the lifecycle case, an application triggers the document lifecycle state transition, but the CE automatically updates the security based on the document lifecycle policy and document state objects.

## Dynamic security inheritance

Security inheritance is a powerful feature that can greatly simplify the administration of access control in your CM environment. We've mentioned security inheritance in passing before, but now we'll cover it in more detail.

> In CE, the feature is called *dynamic* security inheritance to emphasize the fact that it is evaluated dynamically (and instantaneously). Some earlier versions of CE used background copying of ACEs from parent to child to simulate inheritance. Although the functional effect is the same in terms of the security you would actually see on child objects, the mechanics had some occasional undesirable side-effects. Today's CE only uses true inheritance—and does not use background copying of ACEs wherever something is described as security inheritance.

# Inheritable depth

In our discussion of ACEs so far, we have talked about how they affect the object to which they are applied. They can be used to selectively allow or deny access rights on the target object. An ACE has an additional integer-valued property called `InheritableDepth` that is specifically related to security inheritance. The inheritable depth indicates how many generations of child objects will inherit that particular ACE.

- If the inheritable depth is `0`, no generations of children will inherit the ACE. In other words, the ACE applies only to the object on which it is originally defined.
- If the inheritable depth is `1`, a single generation of child objects will inherit the ACE.
- If the inheritable depth is the special value `-1`, then an unlimited number of child object generations will inherit the ACE. In practical terms, this is not much different from using a value of a million for inheritable depth, but having a special value may relieve a developer of a moment's hesitation over how big a number to use to be sure all the cases are covered.
- If the inheritable depth is any other positive value, then exactly that many generations of child objects will inherit the ACE. It's nice to have this flexibility, but the three previous bullets are the only likely cases to be interesting in practice.

An ACE that an object receives via inheritance is sometimes also called a **contributed ACE**. An ACE can only be modified on the object where it was originally defined (as a direct or default ACE). It is read-only for objects that receive it via inheritance.

# Parent and child security objects

What exactly are child objects when it comes to security inheritance? Although there are several predefined cases in system metadata, you can define your own security inheritance relationships via custom metadata. The predefined cases are evaluated in exactly the same ways.

The CE has a type of property whose value is a reference to another CE object. They are called **object-valued properties** (**OVPs**). In *Chapter 4* and *Chapter 7*, we described how to define your own custom properties, including OVPs. For example, an invoice line item object might have an OVP pointing to the containing invoice object. The property template for an OVP has a property called `SecurityProxyType`, and it is through that property that you establish a security inheritance relationship. The pointed-to object will be the parent object for security inheritance, and the object with the pointing property defined on it will be the child object for security inheritance. If the OVP has a null value, then there is no security inheritance through it since there is no parent object.

## Security Features and Planning

This screenshot shows the panel for setting **Security Proxy Type** on a Property Template object:

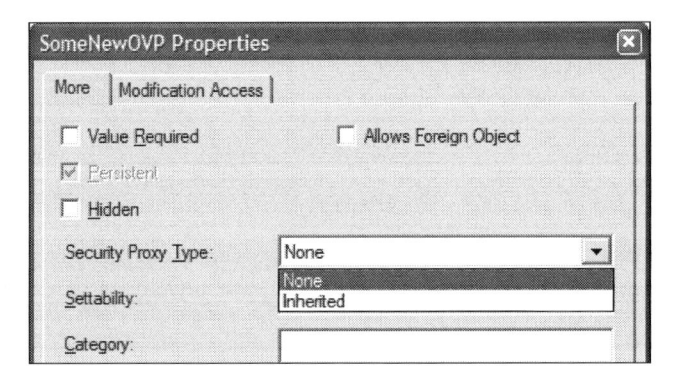

Possible values for the `SecurityProxyType` property are as follows. These values don't appear in FEM for property templates for a multi-valued (reflective) OVPs because security inheritance only works with single-valued OVPs.

- `NONE` (0): This is the typical case. The OVP does not create any security inheritance relationship.
- `INHERITED` (2): This property creates a new security inheritance relationship.
- `FULL` (1): You shouldn't use this value (and so FEM doesn't offer it as a choice). It causes the security for the parent object to completely replace the security of the child object (which is how the property came to be called `SecurityProxyType`). It's used by records management software for locking down the security of managed objects. Although the mechanism is well-defined for a single full proxy, the behavior in the presence of multiple full proxies is undocumented and likely to change in future releases.

What happens if a particular child object has multiple parents? In other words, what if the object has multiple OVPs with a security proxy type of `INHERITED`? All of the parent objects contribute ACEs with equal force (assuming the contributed ACEs have a deep enough inheritable depth to reach the child object). All contributed ACEs are lumped together into a single "inherited" tier when evaluating ACEs for security access calculations. The inheritable depth is used only for deciding how many generations to go in the inheritance chain and is not any kind of relative strength indicator among the contributed ACEs.

You have probably already figured out that a child object inheriting ACEs may also be a parent to yet another object for security inheritance. In addition to possibly contributing its own direct/default ACEs to children, an object will also pass along (unchanged) any inherited ACEs, assuming those inherited ACEs have sufficient inheritable depth.

> Providing a value for a property with a Security Proxy Type of INHERITED modifies the security of the receiving object. You probably want to control who can set values on those properties. A convenient way to do that is to use Modification Access Required (MAR) feature described earlier in this chapter. Assign a MAR value that includes at least the WRITE_ACL right.

## System-defined inheritance

There are several pre-defined security inheritance relationships in the CE system metadata. A few of those have special-purpose implementation code in the CE, but most of them use exactly the same mechanism that is used for custom properties:

- A folder inherits from its parent folder. Because a folder (other than the root folder) always has a value in its Parent property, there is another mechanism for preventing unintended security inheritance: the boolean property Folder.InheritParentPermissions.

- A ReferentialContainmentRelationship object does not have its own security. It always assumes the security of the Tail object, in other words, the folder that contains something.

- Documents and custom objects have a property SecurityFolder that can optionally point to a folder and thereby inherit security from that folder. There is no requirement that the object be filed in that pointed-to folder, although that is the usual use case. This replaces an earlier mechanism via a property called SecurityParent that pointed to a ReferentialContainmentRelationship object. The SecurityParent property still exists, but the CE emulates the old behavior via the SecurityFolder property.

- Documents, folders, and custom objects can have annotations. An annotation object inherits security from the annotated object. An annotation always has a value in its AnnotatedObject property.

- A Class Definition object can inherit security from its superclasses. The property creating the inheritance relationship is SuperclassDefinition. This is the security for the Class Definition object itself and does not affect Default Instance Security.

*Security Features and Planning*

# Roles and adapters

The usual cases for security inheritance are along the lines of "I want the security for this folder to apply to anything I file into this folder" or "I want this document's annotations to have the same security as the document". In other words, the first inclination to use security inheritance is for a rather static set of cases with the inheritance along functional lines. The dynamic aspect is also available, even in those use cases. If you update the security of the folder or the document, in the first and second examples, respectively, the inheriting objects automatically and instantly pick up the inheritable part of the change.

More complicated arrangements are possible, as we will illustrate with the following example.

# Project team example

What if you had a collection of objects that had a relationship in business logic but no obvious low-level technical relationship? It might be some folders that don't have a common parent folder, or it might be some documents or custom objects that are filed in different folders or perhaps no folders at all.

There are very few restrictions on OVPs, including those that cause security inheritance. You can make pointed-to objects whose whole purpose is to define inheritable ACEs. Many unrelated objects could point to a single instance of that object. Because of the way they are used, and which we are about to describe, they are commonly called **role** objects.

Suppose, for example, that you had a repository of documents and folders that belonged to various project teams, and your security requirement is that project team members should only have access to their own artifacts. You could create a series of role objects with one role object for each project team. ACEs on each role object would grant rights to members of the project team and would be inheritable to unlimited depth. By simply assigning a role object to an inheritance-defining property on each document, all project team members would have access due to inherited security. If the document had no ACEs of its own, the implicit deny would prevent access by anyone not on the project team.

This example could certainly be accomplished by other means. For example, if your project teams all happened to be in just the right directory groups, you could just use group-based ACEs on the documents. That does require a certain lucky alignment of circumstances in the directory. If you don't quite have that, then you're back to using some combination of user and group ACEs with allow or deny access on the documents to achieve just what you want. How is that different from using the role objects? The difference comes when the project team membership changes. If you have the access defined on individual documents, then you will have to update all of those documents somehow. Instead, you can just update the single role object and all inheriting objects are instantly updated. There is an obvious operational convenience to using security inheritance in the form of role objects.

## Project team adapters

The project team example is easy to understand, but things are often a little more complicated. Not every member of every team is created equal. It could be that different team members get different access rights. For example, it may be that all team members can contribute to drafts of new documents, but only some designated subset can actually approve them by promoting them to being released versions. It might even be that the approvers are not in the set of people who can make the changes. Still, it's not beyond the capability of the role object to define that sort of access. If people tend to work on multiple project teams, the number of combinations of things can get out of hand and become a burden to maintain.

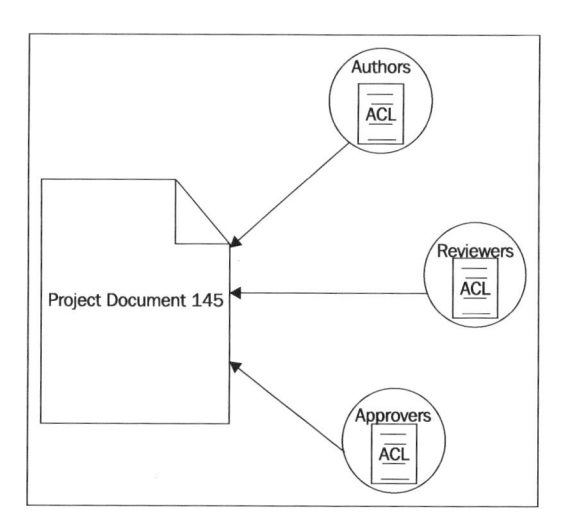

*Security Features and Planning*

Now, in many organizations, it could be good enough to approximate this sort of setup by giving everybody more rights than they need and dealing with policy violations in some offline manner. For a variety of other use cases, typically in highly regulated industries, that informality is not sufficient. It soon occurs to security architects to use multiple OVPs for the different functional roles. There might be one OVP pointing to a group of general project team members, another OVP for document approvers, perhaps another for "upper management", and so on. That's still pretty manageable because you have relatively few role objects that can be used in different combinations for documents. There are some disadvantages to this scheme, however:

- You are still defining the combinations on the document instances. If a project has a thousand documents, that's a thousand objects to get the appropriate set of multiple OVP settings.
- A year down the road, you might develop the need for an additional type of OVP and role object. It's easy enough to define the new OVP on your document classes, but you will have thousands of existing documents that do not have a value in that property. You'll have to populate them somehow.

A popular way to deal with this complexity is by using a convention called an **adapter object**. You create a new kind of role object that represents the entire project team and other groups of people who need access to project documents. You define your three or four OVPs (or however many you need) on the adapter object class. Just as you imagined them for the individual documents, those OVPs point to role objects defining the general members, approvers, and so on. Now, finally, you scale back the OVPs on your document class to just one. You have that OVP point to an adapter object.

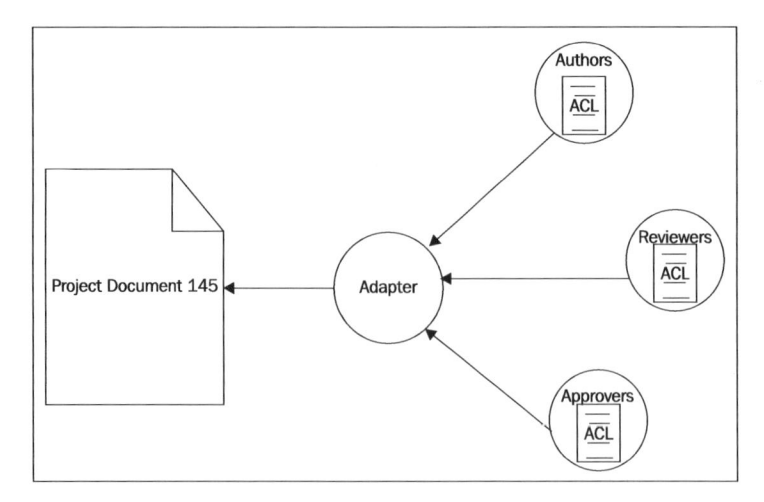

In effect, the adapter object now represents the uniform access you want applied to all project documents. You still get the decomposition into individual role objects for each functional role, but you don't have the update headache when you need to rearrange the security access requirements for a project. Finally, if there is a requirement for a new role, you only have to update some limited number of adapter objects (perhaps one per project). The layout of adapters maps nicely to the question of "who performs this role for this project?"

## Folders as adapters

Any folder, document, or custom object class can be used as a security inheritance source. Of those classes, the most lightweight for other reasons is the custom object. That makes custom objects the natural choice for role objects and adapter objects. It's just a question of defining the appropriate OVPs and perhaps a handful of other properties (for a description and so on), and you're done.

If you happen to be filing most or all of your documents into folders that are aligned with your security requirements (for example, all project documents go somewhere underneath a top-level project folder), then you can use those same folders as your security inheritance adapter objects. Folders are subclassable, so you can add the OVPs to point to the role objects, folder security can easily be inherited by subfolders, and documents and custom objects already have a `SecurityFolder` property that is a somewhat natural OVP to use to point to the folder acting as the adapter.

If you use folders as role objects or adapter objects, you can avoid a bit of clutter in your data model. However, before going down this path, you will want to carefully consider whether your needs might change with respect to either how you do your folder hierarchies or how you use the `SecurityFolder` property. If in doubt, our advice is to define it all via custom OVPs so you don't find yourself stuck in a corner later.

## Marking sets

Marking sets are the CM mechanism for mandatory access control. The idea behind marking sets is fairly intuitive. You put a particular marking on an object (by assigning its value to a specially configured string property, which is sometimes called a **marking-controlled property**), and only users who are authorized to see things with that marking can get access to that object. Users who are not authorized to see things with that marking are turned back. Think of the marking itself as a string value with magic powers. The thing that makes marking sets powerful (and inspires the adjective "mandatory") is that nothing can overcome the restrictions imposed by a marking set. It is the most powerful access control feature in CM, and it can only be used to remove rights that other mechanisms might grant.

*Security Features and Planning*

A marking set is defined at the P8 Domain level but is used to protect objects that are inside Object Stores. A marking set definition consists of a list of marking values and an overall indication of whether the marking set is hierarchical or flat:

- A flat marking set is a collection of marking values that can be applied independently of each other. There's no pre-defined relationship among the markings. The way you use a flat marking set determines whether the marking values are mutually exclusive or can be combined.
    - If the property receiving the marking value is single-valued, then it can only hold one marking. In that case, the markings are usually mutually exclusive.
    - If the property receiving the marking value is multi-valued, then it can hold multiple markings. In that case, the markings can be combined on a single object. Users must have rights on all applied markings to be able to access the object they protect.
- A hierarchical marking set is a collection of marking values with an implied precedence relationship. A user authorized to access objects marked with a particular marking is automatically authorized to access objects marked with hierarchically lower markings. It doesn't make sense to use hierarchical marking sets with a multi-valued property.

Let's discuss what gives a marking value its magic powers.

The property `Marking.MarkingValue` holds the actual string value for the marking. It is customary to make these something meaningful, but they can also be as cryptic as your security requirements demand.

A marking object also contains an ACL, but the possible rights are unusual if you are used to the discretionary access rights for folders, documents, and so on. There are three possible access rights for a particular marking object. Two of them are pretty easy to understand: **add** and **remove** rights mean that the user has the right to add or remove this specific marking value to or from an object. (It doesn't mean that the user can add or remove the marking from the marking set.)

The final marking right is **use**. It means that the user has the right to use an object protected by this specific marking value. In this sense, "use" means that the user can do the things specified by the marked object's ordinary discretionary access control rights. To say it another way, if a user has the "use" right for a marking, then that marking will not interfere with that user's ability to interact normally with objects that have that marking.

OK, so if marking sets are used to take away rights, how does that happen? If a user does not have the "use" right on a marking, then a set of rights is subtracted out of the effective access for the marked object. You define exactly what rights you want to remove by setting the `Marking.ConstraintMask` property. That's a set of access rights in the usual bitmask notation, but in this case the rights that are indicated will be subtracted from the marked object. If an object has more than one marking-controlled property, the calling user will have to pass the marking set check for each to get access to the object.

## A marking set example

You might find all the above facts a little confusing, so let's look at a concrete example. We assume you will do this as a thought experiment rather than actually going through the steps, so we don't describe them in detail:

- Define a flat marking set with three marking objects. The marking objects have the values `Siss`, `Boom`, and `Bah` or some values of your own choosing.
- Use the ACL on each marking object to define who has the "use" right for that particular marking. Give at least one user access (the "use" right) to a particular marking value and no access to the other marking values.
- For the constraint mask on each marking object, select all of the available rights. (There is no technical requirement to use the same constraint mask value for each marking object.) These are the things that will be denied to the calling user if they don't have "use" rights for that marking.
- On a document class, add a new string-valued property with a maximum length at least long enough to hold the longest marking value. In the FEM property template creation wizard, select the above marking set to use with that property.
- Make some document instances of that class and populate that string property on each one with one of the marking values. You can also make some document instances that leave that value unpopulated.

When a user tries to access a document, for retrieval or update, the CE goes through the following steps:

1. It uses the document's ACL to compute the effective access rights for that user for that document.
2. It then looks, in turn, at each string property controlled by a marking set. If the property has a value, the applicable marking object is consulted.

3. If the user does not have the use right for that marking value, then the rights mentioned in that marking value's constraint mask are removed from the effective access rights for that user for that document. In our example, the constraint mask has all rights, so all rights would be removed from the effective access.
4. After all marking set-controlled properties are considered, the effective access will have been updated to reflect mandatory access control on top of discretionary access control.
5. The CE then makes its decision whether to allow the attempted operation.

Of course, this is a simplified description since the CE also has to take all of the other access control mechanisms into account.

You may be asking yourself what is so special about marking sets and mandatory access control. If you didn't have marking sets, couldn't you accomplish the same thing with some elaborate ACL on the document itself, perhaps along with other access control mechanisms? Quite often you could do that, but there is a qualitative difference.

With the discretionary access control mechanisms, the user can often add access to a document for someone else on a case by case basis. That's what is meant by discretionary. If they decide to do it, they can, and they don't have to consider any technical factor, like the other user's authority to access certain types of documents.

With mandatory access control in general and marking sets in particular, someone with the right to modify domain level objects has to administratively set up the marking sets. It is that more privileged user who is, via the marking object ACL, effectively marking the *users* as having access to some things and not others. No matter what access someone else tries to grant to those users, the marking sets have the final say in letting the access proceed. It's extremely powerful, by design, although it can only be used to remove access rights.

## The final veto

It would be unusual, indeed, if you could not implement your access requirements using some or all of the bag of access control tricks described earlier in this section. If you do have that unusual situation, where your business logic for access control is elaborate, and the pre-defined mechanisms just aren't enough, then there is one more weapon you can use to deny access based on custom business logic.

In *Chapter 7*, we described the CE's event subsystem. As we said then, the main purpose for synchronous subscriptions is to provide an opportunity for the associated event handler to approve or veto a change to the triggering object. The event handler is custom code that you provide. It can implement whatever business logic you think is appropriate, including looking at other objects in CM. At the end of things, it simply decides, yes or no, whether it should allow the operation to proceed. If not, it throws an exception and the CE will roll back the transaction for that operation.

Synchronous event handlers can't be used to grant additional rights, but they can be used to deny rights that have been granted by all of the other CM authorization checks. The ability to use custom business logic is very powerful, but there are two important things to consider:

- There is a higher performance cost to doing this kind of thing via synchronous subscriptions compared to using the built-in access control mechanisms of the CE.
- There is no available event for retrieval operations, so you can't stop someone from reading property values or content via this mechanism.

# A hypothetical scenario

To illustrate most of the access control mechanisms described above, let's consider a somewhat complicated set of business requirements. This example is hypothetical, but it's not preposterous. It's actually a simplification of a CM security implementation question that came to our attention some time ago. We've changed the terminology and the motivations for the various things both to remove the specifics of the real scenario and to make the explanation clearer.

## The players

An enterprise has three major independently operating divisions: the Ninjas, the Pirates, and the Unicorns. There is also a corporate headquarters layer, HQ, that provides common services like human resources, finance, and so on.

## The business requirements

The divisions are very competitive with each other to the extent that it is necessary to have technical access control mechanisms in place to keep each division's nose out of other divisions' affairs. For routine matters, HQ is considered to be an honest broker and will not leak information from one division to another. That level of trust in HQ does not necessarily apply to more sensitive matters. (Hey, we said this was hypothetical. This kind of situation would surely never occur in any actual large enterprise. It certainly does not occur in your enterprise. We're thinking of something else entirely.)

## Security Features and Planning

Each division has a variety of projects of varying sensitivity. Here are the business rules we'll try to accommodate with our access control mechanisms. To simplify the description, we'll consider only read access to documents; other access rights, and other object types can be accommodated in straightforward extrapolations.

- An author of a document has access to his or her own documents unless another item in this list applies. For example, an author has access as long as the author stays in the same division, but it is not a requirement for the author to have continued access if the author changes divisions or moves to HQ. For convenience, we refer to this as *author access*.

- Typical access for run of the mill documents is that divisional personnel have access to documents within the same division. Personnel from other divisions do not have access to those documents. We refer to this requirement as *divisional restriction*.

- There are documents that deal with sensitive areas. Examples include human resources, finance, and medical information (about HQ or divisional personnel). Only specialists in those areas have access to those documents. We refer to this requirement as *functional restriction*.

- Each division has some especially sensitive projects. There is no overlap in special projects between divisions. Only personnel specifically authorized for each sensitive project can get access to related documents. Those personnel might be in the division or in HQ. We refer to this restriction as *special handling*.

- All HQ personnel generally have access to all divisional documents except functionally restricted and special handling documents.

- Functional area personnel, in HQ or in the same division, generally have access to functionally restricted documents of compatible types. For example, finance personnel from HQ have access to all finance documents. Finance personnel in the Unicorn division do not have access to HQ, Ninja division, or Pirate division finance documents.

- Likewise, there are HQ personnel who may have access to a divisional special handling project. The list of HQ personnel varies by project, and in some cases there are none at all.

Your first inclination after reading the above requirements might be to run screaming from the room or maybe just flip pages to the next chapter of this book. Stick with us, and we'll work through it.

## The strategy

We'll describe an implementation that meets all of the above requirements. You will probably be able to think of some special cases not quite covered by the above description and therefore maybe not quite covered by the implementation. We don't think of that as a weakness in not having detailed enough business requirements or a flexible enough implementation.

It is the case more often than not that an access control strategy is an informed balance between absolute access control and a liberal enough policy that people can get done the things they need to do. Our advice is to keep a list of any special cases you think of. Keep it right beside your list of ways you think someone might try to circumvent the controls for naughty reasons. Develop your access control strategy as a candidate, and then see if you have ways to accommodate the legitimate special cases and thwart the attacks. Refine your strategy until it does what you want.

For example, a strategy for special case access might be to contact someone and get a copy of a document outside the control of the repository. Software vendors don't really like to hear about that sort of workaround that bypasses carefully crafted system controls, but it happens all the time in real life. Blatant violations are typically dealt with via non-technical means.

Here's another piece of advice: use an access control strategy that is *fail safe*. That means that if something goes wrong, you will still get the safest result. For most scenarios, that means that you should err on the side of denying access, but there are certainly scenarios where the best course is to grant access if there is doubt. That's a business decision, and you should be guided by your enterprise's requirements for that.

## The implementation

We have to use several mechanisms together to implement all of these business policies. A few of them will seem obvious and straightforward:

- Our overall strategy is to use the implicit deny mechanism so that rights must be specifically granted somehow.
- Author access is obtained via divisional access. Explicit rights for #CREATOR-OWNER should not be granted. Should the author leave that division, he or she will lose those divisional access rights.
- Divisional access to divisional documents can be done using a group-based ACE granting general access to all members of the division. As division members came and went, they would automatically gain or lose access via that group-based ACE. The mechanism for applying the divisional group-based ACE to a document could be any of the mechanisms we described

above: direct application, class-based defaulting, or dynamic security inheritance through a folder or by using roles and adapters. The important part is that the divisional group-based ACE gets applied via some foolproof (and probably automated) mechanism.

- Functional restrictions can be handled via a marking set, where each marking value is `HR Use Only`, `Finance Use Only`, or something along those lines. Because functionally restricted documents might reasonably be so for more than one reason, we'll use a multi-valued property for the functional restrictions markings. Appropriate functional area personnel from all divisions and from HQ can be granted rights for each applicable marking value. This will not grant Ninja medical personnel the right to see Unicorn medical documents because a marking set can only remove rights. Other mechanisms keep the Ninjas and Unicorns apart.

- Special handling restrictions can be accomplished via a second marking set. Each marking value is some kind of code word or phrase that identifies a sensitive project. We're assuming there is no overlap in projects across divisions, and we'll make the simplifying assumption here that a given document is associated with no more than one sensitive project within a division. We can therefore use a single-valued string property to hold this marking. Division members with authorized access to a sensitive value are given "add", "remove", and "use" rights to the appropriate marking objects in the marking set. Likewise, specifically identified HQ personnel for each sensitive project can be given the "use" right for the associated marking.

- Assuming it is easy to identify HQ personnel via a single or small number of directory groups, a general ACE can be added to all documents granting access to those HQ personnel. This can be accomplished in the same way that the divisional group-based ACE is added.

- On an *ad hoc* basis, a user can deny specific users and groups access to a particular document. Because of the use of marking sets for critical mandatory access control areas, ordinary users can't grant access rights beyond those considered here.

Hmm, maybe that was simpler than we thought. Just kidding, of course. That's still a pretty complicated access control picture. There are two main criticisms of it:

- As we said, it's complicated. It's based on relatively complicated business requirements, and there might not be a simple way to meet those requirements. Still, security correctness and complexity tend to be inversely correlated. The greater the complexity, the more chance a problem might creep in without your seeing it.
- It is not defense in depth in some cases. It's a bit of putting together tightly matching puzzle pieces for some aspects of things. It would probably be a good idea to also have application or network level protections in place as redundant measures.

## The test

We want to reiterate something that we mentioned before. Once you have a strategy and a plan like this, brainstorm to get a list of all the special cases you can think of. Make another list of possible attacks on your system. There's a good chance the two lists will have some things in common. Make sure your plan accounts for everything you care about one way or another.

When your strategy and plan looks solid to you, you must prototype it and test it. Although we have tried to clearly explain each access control feature (and the CM product documentation does the same thing, in many cases with more explicit details), we cannot guarantee that you understood things precisely. A prototype will clarify your understanding of individual features and how they work together.

Keep all your lists and all your prototype test cases for when you do your final implementation. Test them all, plus anything new you think of. After you have deployed your implementation to the production system, test it again to make sure no configuration steps have gone astray. Periodically, audit your production system's configuration so that you will be more likely to catch configuration problems, whether they are accidental or deliberate. Perform penetration testing to see if you can get access to things inappropriately.

> Running tests against a production system is a dicey business. You will want to design your tests so that they don't have a significant performance impact on production operations.
>
> You will also want to make sure you have appropriate organizational approvals for any penetration testing. It can be difficult for upper management to distinguish between useful but unauthorized testing and devious acts by a person unworthy of trust.

## Summary

In this chapter, we covered the gamut of CM-specific security mechanism, both for authentication and for authorization. In the latter case, we finished with a brief analysis of a complicated access control use case. You should now have an understanding of individual security mechanisms available in CM and some thoughts about how to combine them into suites to accomplish your business goals for security.

We have now pretty much concluded our descriptions of basic CM features. In the next chapter, we will take up the pragmatic matter of how to go beyond the all-in-one system we set up in the first few chapters and plan for an enterprise-wide production deployment.

# 9
# Planning Your Deployment

In earlier chapters, we spent most of our time describing various individual features and uses for components that make up IBM FileNet Content Manager (CM). In this chapter, we'll move in a slightly different direction, considering some of the factors you will be looking at when you think about deploying ECM across your enterprise.

Our installation examples in *Chapters 2, 3*, and *5* used a so-called all-in-one system, where most of the components were installed onto a single server. We used a second server only for components that could not be installed onto our primary server. In those cases, it wasn't due to lack of resources or a case of things not fitting. It was instead done that way because our primary server was Linux, and a few components are not supported on Linux. An all-in-one system, especially a virtual machine image, is extremely handy for a lot of reasons, from random noodling around and experimenting to full-fledged development. For a variety of reasons (most of them explored in this chapter), you would be unlikely to use such a configuration in your enterprise deployment.

The following major topics are covered in this chapter:

- Functional tiers for typical deployments
- Considerations for custom applications
- Parallel environments for different purposes
- Factors for deciding how many Domains and Object Stores you should use
- Content storage
- Clustering, high availability, and disaster recovery

# Distributed deployments in functional tiers

Let's start with a look at how things might be logically arranged into functional tiers. Because web-based applications tend to dominate the landscape, we'll use them as an example. That might be Workplace XT, or it might be some custom application. This diagram shows an overview of the functional breakdown:

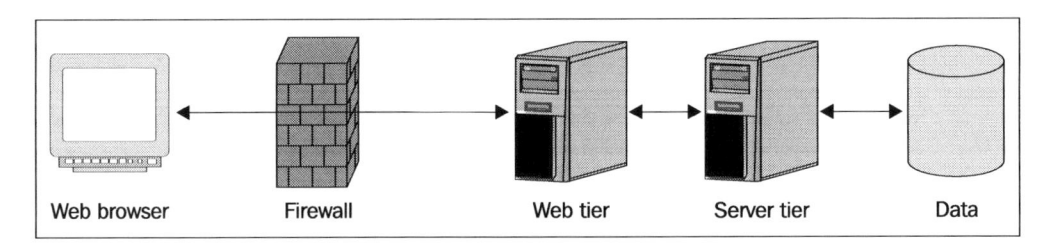

| Web browser | Firewall | Web tier | Server tier | Data |

> There can be strong feelings about the terminology used in describing multi-tiered architectures. We're going to try to avoid most of that by describing what things are done in various places. Whether something meets any particular person's strict definition of presentation tier or data tier or whatever is less important than deciding what things you will put in your data centers and how you will connect them.

No matter what your application mix, you will have to develop a plan for processing equipment and networking connections. It's customary to do this planning by grouping things into tiers. That doesn't mean you need some number of physical boxes for each tier. It means instead that you have a logical model for how processing happens. That might mean anything from multiple functions on a single physical box to groups of physical boxes arranged in clusters or farms to perform a single function.

## Web browsers

By definition, the presentation technology for a web application is the web browser. We probably don't need to say too much about web browsers in general (we're sure you've come across one somewhere), but the list of technologies for use with applications is growing.

The traditional web application used the web browser quite literally for presentation. It was seen as a more colorful and graphically rich version of alphanumeric terminals used for decades. A web browser was, as the saying goes, easy on the eyes.

There has been a high-velocity emergence over the past few years of application logic running in the browser. The primary constituents of this are JavaScript for actual application logic and a combination of asynchronous server calls and partial page rendering for a more pleasing and useful presentation experience. These things taken together are sometimes described as *AJAX* or *Web 2.0*.

> It's more technically correct to use the term ECMAScript (after ECMA-262 and related standards) instead of JavaScript. We just can't resist calling it JavaScript for two reasons. First, everyone else does, and it still sounds overly pedantic to call it ECMAScript. Second, dealing with browser idiosyncrasies in their scripting implementations is still big business. It seems hardly fair, even as of this writing, to imply that things are all settled.

There are other in-browser technologies for doing application logic. Since this isn't a book about developing web applications, we'll just note what they all share in common: sooner or later, they need to talk to some server layer to get productive work done. That might be via traditional HTTP page refreshes or via more granular calls.

## Web servers

Web browsers talk to web servers. That's simple enough. What happens on the web server?

Traditionally, the web tier is where **session state** is maintained. Session state is the information that answers such questions as: are you already authenticated, are you on panel two of a five-panel wizard, how long since your last call to the web tier, and so on. (With the emergence of in-browser application logic, this role for the web tier is often diminished or missing completely in some applications.)

The web tier can maintain session state because of a more general role that it plays. It represents the boundary between the uncontrolled world of browsers and client desktops and the world of the highly-controlled data center server landscape. Certainly, there are enterprises which lock down desktop configurations to varying degrees, but it's rare indeed to trust completely to client desktops even such simple things as maintaining the correct system time. It is often in the web tier that enterprises first enforce strong authentication.

*Planning Your Deployment*

The web tier is also the place where **services** are visible. We're going to be intentionally vague on the definition of services, because it can mean a lot of different things to different audiences. Here, we just mean "a thing that can be done as the result of a call from some other application". You might structure your browser interaction to lead to requests for business operations at some degree of granularity (for example, reserve this car, find documents matching these conditions, change these properties of this description of an extra-solar planet, and so on). Your web tier translates those business operations into the appropriate calls to CM servers.

CM and related products provide APIs that can be called directly from web browsers. These are not JavaScript bindings of the Java and .NET bindings. They are either web services definitions or **Representational State Transfer (REST)** APIs. In each of those cases, however, the target of those APIs is a servlet running in a web tier. Those servlets translate those incoming calls into native API calls. You could choose to develop the same sort of servlet for a custom application or re-use the components provided by IBM.

## CE, PE, and friends

We finally come to the CM server tier: the **Content Engine (CE)**, the **Process Engine (PE)**, and a few others associated with them. In ECM terms, this is the most trusted part of the system. CE and PE will determine your authority to perform various operations. Once you have passed authorization checks, those operations will be translated into appropriate low-level database operations.

Because the CE runs in an application server, its access to databases is not directly configured. Instead, it uses application server datasources. It is those datasources that contain database connectivity and credential information. The CE's configuration is limited to the association of datasources with Object Stores.

## Databases and filesystems

The CM servers don't have much innate information. What they know about your particular information is stored in back-end databases, filesystems, or other storage devices. You already know that metadata (properties) for documents and other objects are stored in relational databases. That is also true for most configuration data. In the case of the CE, much of that is stored in the aptly-named **Global Configuration Database (GCD)**.

Content for documents can be stored in the same Object Store database or in filesystems. We'll talk about content storage later in this chapter.

# Custom applications

You are undoubtedly going to make your decision about the use of custom applications based on many factors, and some of those factors will result in compromises or optimizations of competing requirements. It's usually more expensive to create and support your own custom applications, but the payoff is that they are more likely to do exactly what you want.

CM provides some out-of-the-box applications, such as Workplace and Workplace XT, but they are necessarily generic in nature. It is certainly the case that many customers use them as primary end-user applications. It's also the case that some customers don't install either of the applications at all for end-users (or only install them in development environments for comparison purposes).

There is a middle ground between developing your own fully custom applications and using the CM-provided applications. There is a rich ecosystem of consultants (both inside and outside of IBM) and IBM business partners who specialize in building custom or customized applications based on CM. They can perform services ranging from simple time-and-materials implementation tasks all the way up to complete system design. Because of their experience in helping many clients with diverse requirements, they can bring a wealth of practical experience to the table. Even if you do your own development work, it is worth considering engaging these consultants for a design review.

How does the possible presence of custom applications figure into your deployment decisions? It only means that you will have to consider their resource needs and special requirements when planning your environment. For example, if you will be using thick applications, whether based on Java or Microsoft technologies, that will probably have a bearing on how you do authentication.

# Parallel environments

Once you figure out how you want to deploy your ECM infrastructure, you'll have a good idea about how much server equipment you will need, what the redundancies are to provide the availability you need, and so on. Many enterprises find it useful to also build out some additional parallel environments.

*Planning Your Deployment*

# Pre-production

The purpose of the pre-production environment is to serve as a test bed for any proposed changes to the production environment. It should match, as nearly as possible, the server and network topologies of your production environment. At the very least, all operating system components, CM software, and third party components should be exactly the same as those in the production environment (except, of course, when you are actually using it to test changes that will later go to production).

We can guarantee that your production environment will need to change over time. Even if you have no plans to ever change the configuration of your running applications, you will certainly want to install patches and upgrades for your CM software, your operating systems, and various third party components.

Do you need a pre-production environment? It depends; if your CM environment can tolerate periodic downtime, then you might be able to get by with directly modifying your production environment. What that would mean, though, is that you would have to perform a complete backup of the production system (which might mean being offline during that time), then apply changes, and test the changed environment. Your scheduling has to account for the time to roll back to the previous configuration if things don't go well.

If you can reasonably afford it, our advice is to have a pre-production environment. Besides shortening the downtime possibilities, you avoid the risk that your testing phase will modify the live data in ways you didn't intend or cannot tolerate. If you happen to be using virtual machine images, you may be able to use snapshot and cloning features of your virtual machine environment to create pre-production images on an as-needed basis. If you are not using virtual machine images, you can still schedule the use of pre-production environment equipment for your planned change windows (rather than having dedicated equipment that is often idle).

# Development and testing

You may only need to consider these environments if you do custom development work.

A development environment is established so that developers can share expensive resources while working on custom tasks. We've seen developer groups work both ways. They can use shared installations of the tiers that they don't work on directly or they can use their own installations on servers that they control exclusively. The efficiency trade-off depends on what type of work they are doing. For most cases, shared CE, PE, and database servers will work fine. Shared web tiers may or may not work out, depending on how much one developer's work interferes with another's.

Development environments are usually considered "dirty" in the sense that developers tend to make all sorts of non-standard environmental changes as temporary workarounds. It's the responsibility of the developers to keep track of such things and undo them at appropriate times.

A test environment, on the other hand, should be tightly controlled and use configuration settings and procedures that are identical or very similar to those of the production environment. The reasoning is pretty obvious: the purpose of the test environment is to prove that things work according to officially documented procedures and change-controlled software and data. Any use of *ad hoc* configuration or other workarounds should give the testers an uncomfortable feeling until things are returned to normal.

In any of these cases, virtual machine images are very handy. They can be cloned, snapshotted, and rolled back in a fraction of the time it takes to reconfigure the physical servers.

> We've mentioned virtual machine images several times. We don't advocate any particular virtual machine technology or product (we use more than one ourselves). If you find one that meets your needs, use it like you would use any other productive software component. It can save you enormous amounts of time, effort, and energy when you need to reconfigure or clone environments.
>
> Several years ago, CM product documentation said that virtual machine technology was supported, but that you might have to reproduce any problems directly on physical hardware if you needed support. That's no longer the case, and virtualization is supported as a first-class citizen.
>
> For your own purposes, you will probably want to evaluate whether there are any significant performance costs to the virtualization technology you have chosen. The safest way to evaluate that is under similar configuration and load as that of your intended production environment.

# How many domains?

This may be a question that surprises you, but how many P8 Domains do you need in your production environment? For most organizations, the answer is exactly one, but there are exceptions. Coordinating things across multiple Domains is harder than doing it within a single Domain, often involving custom development work or complex configurations. You should not use multiple Domains without a good reason. A single Domain can accommodate a lot of things before it becomes an interesting concern that you are inside a single domain.

*Planning Your Deployment*

> Of course, we're talking about the number of Domains in your production environment. In your parallel environments, discussed previously, you should not use the same Domains as your production environments, though you could use the same domain names if the networks are isolated from each other. Even without network isolation, you could reuse domain names, but you would run the risk of having a dependency that you didn't know about.

Here are some common reasons for considering the use of multiple Domains:

- With only a few exceptions, the CE servers in a Domain can talk to everything else in that domain. That means that each CE server can directly reach every other CE server, the GCD, and Object Store databases, and the filestores and other filesystem shares. If you cannot achieve that connectivity, due to either policies or purely technical factors, then you might consider partitioning your environment into distinct Domains.

- All authentication and authorization within a Domain is expected to have the same set of directories. If you have applications that need to use different user populations or group configurations, then having multiple Domains is probably going to help. (Here, we're talking about truly different sets of users and groups. We're not talking about just different subsets of the users needing access to different sets of data. Also, if it's just group memberships that are the problem, then you might be able to stay in a single domain by using access role objects instead of groups, as described in *Chapter 8, Security Features and Planning*.) Distinct directory requirements often come about when organizations or even entire companies are blended together, with each already having a distinct directory and Domain. Just as you would likely have a plan to consolidate directories in such a case, you probably want to develop a plan to consolidate the Domains.

- No matter how many applications you eventually have using your ECM platform, you will probably only need a few distinct Object Stores. If you find yourself needing several dozen individual Object Stores (again, unlikely, but not impossible), you may see reduced resource requirements in your CE servers if you partition things into multiple Domains. An Object Store, like most other entities, can be a part of only one Domain.

Unless you legitimately do fall into one of the above special cases, you probably do not need more than one Domain. As a planning factor, you should plan on a single Domain unless a clear reason arises to have more than one.

# How many Object Stores?

It's easy to start thinking of an Object Store as some kind of fancy database, and, from there, it's easy to start thinking that each application demands its own Object Store, just as it might have demanded its own database in years gone by. An Object Store has a couple of characteristics that greatly reduce the usual motivations for additional partitioning of data:

- Object Stores make use of fine-grained authorization. "Fine-grained" authorization operates in
  a couple of distinct dimensions: users and objects. It can be used to allow or deny a single user the right to perform a single type of operation on a single object.
- The population of users is usually selected from the enterprise directory. There is not an internal database of users independent of the configured directory servers.
- The CM data model allows for hierarchical, object-oriented design. Unrelated object classes can be defined independently within an Object Store while still sharing the common features afforded by CM.

There are definite operational trade-offs in deciding whether to partition the environment into multiple Object Stores:

- An Object Store is backed by a distinct database instance (or tablespace instance, depending on the database vendor). You may have policy or technical reasons for limiting the number of distinct databases.
- Using the techniques described in *Chapter 8*, it is usually straightforward to limit users to a subset of data within an Object Store, though there is a cost in administrative management. The CONNECT access right on the Object Store itself controls whether a given user can access anything at all inside that Object Store. Although this is theoretically no more secure than a limitation on objects within a single Object Store, you might wish to use this Object Store-level security control as an operational simplification or as part of a defense-in-depth security policy.
- Some enterprises have regulatory or legal constraints, usually involving national boundaries, for where data is physically stored. You can use multiple Object Stores to put different subsets of data in different locations. This policy requirement will frequently be at odds with performance and networking considerations, so you will have to decide how to make that trade-off. It also only directly solves the "data at rest" problem. The data can still transiently cross borders if you are not careful in your design.

- If you have multiple, geographically separate data centers, you may achieve a performance benefit—due to efficient network utilization—by placing Object Stores in different geographical areas. See the section describing *Distributed Deployments* later in this chapter.
- It is a CM best practice to do backups of the GCD and all Object Stores together, but there are some scenarios where you may find that you can individually back up logical subsets of the data. Partitioning those logical subsets into multiple Object Stores facilitates that.
- One popular reason for partitioning data into multiple Object Stores is that the data is date-oriented. That is, some types of documents are just naturally associated with a certain point or period in time. When enough time has passed, that data can become interesting only for occasional research purposes. The data can be made read-only (in effect, even if not in fact). A date-based partitioning of your data into multiple Object Stores can lead you to a situation of an active Object Store—in the sense of getting updates—and any number of archive Object Stores—in the sense of being read-only. A truly read-only Object Store would not need periodic backups.

As we did for domains, we lean toward using the smallest number of Object Stores you can. However, the number of factors to consider is significantly larger, and it is not unusual to see five to ten Object Stores in a particular Domain for various reasons.

# Network security

We assume you configure your network security according to some enterprise policy or at least according to the best judgment of your security architects. That may mean, for example, that network connections between servers within a single datacenter are trusted in terms of things like vulnerability to eavesdropping. It is likely that the connections between user machines and the datacenter are less trusted, and connections between your data centers may be completely untrusted without additional protection. Whatever your enterprise policies are, it is very likely that you will have to consider them when deciding how to deploy your ECM environment.

## TLS/SSL

When sensitive data passes over untrusted network connections, it should be protected by cryptographic means. There are protocol-specific cryptographic protection schemes, but in practice, network connections are usually protected with **Transport Layer Security (TLS)** or its precursor, **Secure Sockets Layer (SSL)**.

> The distinction between TLS and SSL is a little fuzzy to a lot of people. In fact, even though what you probably want is TLS, you might have never heard of it.
>
> SSL was developed by Netscape Communications Corporation in the 1990s and quickly became a *de facto* standard for securing HTTP and other kinds of network connections. It evolved through three versions, and SSLv3.0 is sometimes still seen in use.
>
> TLS was first standardized by the **Internet Engineering Task Force (IETF)** via RFC-2246. Although it is structurally very similar to SSLv3.0, it corrects some flaws and makes other protocol refinements. Because of some internal protocol numbering conventions, TLSv1.0 is sometimes incorrectly called SSLv3.1.
>
> We use the term TLS/SSL in the face of the reality that TLS is the proper term but SSL is the more widely recognized term.

As far as we are aware, it is possible to secure every connection used by and within CM with TLS/SSL. For example, all supported directories have a configuration provision for using TLS/SSL connections when doing directory lookups for authentication or authorization. There is computational overhead in using TLS/SSL (we typically use the rule of thumb of about 10% overhead, but it varies with the hardware), but it's good to know that TLS/SSL is available where you need it.

TLS/SSL also comes with a certain overhead in certificate administration. If you use certificates from mainstream certificate authorities, things will probably "just work". On the other hand, if you use self-signed certificates, certificates from a private certificate authority, or even certificates from lesser-known certificate authorities, you may have to spend some time exporting and importing certificates so that both ends of connections trust each other. This is exactly analogous to the action to accept an unrecognized certificate when visiting a web site with a browser. You've probably done that hundreds of times. The mechanics of importing certificates for automatic use by software components is a bit more complicated and varies by software component.

# Firewalls

You might have dedicated firewall appliances, you might use software firewalls on your server machines, or you might configure traffic rules in your network routers. In any case, you probably restrict traffic coming into your servers according to criteria such as originating IP address or destination TCP port numbers.

*Planning Your Deployment*

While protocols and port numbers for your custom applications are up to you, the CM-provided applications and APIs use these:

- When using the CE .NET API or the CE Java API with CEWS transport, the clients will connect to the CE server using HTTP or HTTPS connections. The port numbers used will be those configured on the application server that hosts the CE. Because of this single port orientation, CEWS transport lends itself well to firewall filtering.

- When using the CE Java API with EJB transport, the ports used are determined by the underlying protocol implementation. The wire protocol used for EJB transport varies by application server, but, in general, a range of ports is used. In some cases, the application server will let you tighten things down to a small number of destination ports. EJB transport can therefore be trickier to configure for passing through a firewall.

# Supported platforms

CM components are supported on a wide variety of different combinations of operating systems, applications servers, and so on. However, the list is not infinite, and not all CM components are supported on the same list of platform components. Considerable testing effort is used to make sure supported combinations work without functional or performance problems. The official guidance for supported platform components is documented in *FileNet P8 Hardware and Software Requirements*.

You probably already have enterprise policies for the platform components you use. In that case, you can just verify that your preferred components are supported for CM use. If, on the other hand, your choices are wide open, you will want to consider these factors:

- CM components are supported on most enterprise operating systems, including modern Microsoft Windows server versions and multiple flavors of Unix and Linux.

- Among J2EE application servers, CM is supported on IBM WebSphere, Oracle WebLogic, and Red Hat JBoss. The choice of J2EE application server is more significant than the choice of operating system for most CM components. That is, there is much more internal CM logic dealing with application server issues than with operating system issues.

- CM components support the following database servers: IBM DB2, Oracle, and Microsoft SQL Server. There are very few database-specific things that are visible to CM clients.

- Many directory servers are supported, including IBM Tivoli Directory Server, Novell eDirectory, Sun Java Directory Server, Oracle Internet Directory, and, of course, Microsoft Active Directory (both the full version and AD Lightweight Directory Services). The list tends to evolve over time, and you should also check for specific release numbers.
- CM supports a variety of storage technologies and vendors for content storage, including EMC Centera, NetApp Snaplock, and IBM System Storage N Series. That list also evolves over time.

# Integrating content with workflow

It's extremely common to use workflows as part of ECM. Whether you use the PE server bundled with CM or a more generally licensed BPM installation, you will want to consider the relative placement of these two engines when deploying your environment. We described workflow integration with examples from XT in *Chapter 6, End User Tools and Tasks*.

- The PE server need not be able to reach all CE servers, but it must be able to connect to at least one CE server in order to retrieve and update objects carried as attachments to workflows. For example, an update to a workflow property in a step processor may trigger a corresponding update to one or more document properties in CE.
- The CE must be able to connect to the PE in order to launch workflows in response to update events for documents and other objects. For example, the check-in of a new major version of a document may trigger an approval or publication workflow.
- Applications, particularly those involved with workflow step processing, will often need to connect to CE servers and PE servers.

# Content storage

You have several choices when it comes time to decide where to store your document content within CM. Properties for documents and other objects are always stored in the Object Store database, but the actual content bits for a document or annotation are stored according to configured storage areas and storage policies, as described in *Chapter 7, Major CM Features*. No matter where you choose to put the content, you will not be able to directly access it from your applications. Your applications will always go through a CE server to get the content as a stream of bytes. This makes the actual storage logistics transparent to applications and also ensures that CM security is not bypassed.

*Planning Your Deployment*

Where content is actually stored is dependent on two Document and Annotation properties: `StoragePolicy` and `StorageArea`, which point to Storage Policy and Storage Area objects, respectively. A Storage Area object represents a specific physical storage location. A Storage Policy object, on the other hand, represents one or more Storage Areas that are considered to be functionally and administratively equivalent. If the `StorageArea` property is set, then that Storage Area will be used. Otherwise, a Storage Area will be selected based on the value of the `StoragePolicy` property. Because of its administrative flexibility, it is a better practice to use Storage Policies. Either property can be set for a particular Document or Annotation, but the usual practice is to set values as class defaults on the Class Definition.

Let's look at different types of Storage Areas.

## Database Storage Area

Conceptually, the simplest storage choice is to put content into the Object Store database. Every Object Store is automatically configured with a **Database Storage Area** and policy. (The default content storage area you select during Object Store creation is only a default. The Database Storage Area is always there.) The content for a document is stored as a blob in a separate table, and referential integrity links to it are automatically maintained by the CE. The advantage of using database storage is that doing a database backup automatically does a content backup. With other storage types, the backups must be synchronized. The disadvantage of database storage is that databases sometimes have difficulty dealing with the sizes and quantities of blobs present in a production ECM repository. The database may require an inconvenient amount of tuning attention to provide reasonable performance. Also, for cost reasons, you may wish to use a different class of physical storage for your content.

## File Storage Area

The next simplest storage choice is the use of a filesystem as a storage device. For this **File Storage Area** case, the content is stored in actual files (one per content element), and the CE automatically maintains the links between the objects and the content.

A common question is how to find the file on the filesystem if you have access to the properties of the document in the Object Store. The answer is that you can't find it nor access the content directly. You must go through a CE server using an API. The pointers to the actual files are kept in non-exposed data.

> Folders used internally within a File Storage Area for content have no relationship to the folders used for filing objects within an Object Store. On reflection, this should be obvious, since you can store content for unfiled documents. Whereas the folders in an Object Store are an organizing technique for objects, the folders in a File Storage Area are used to avoid overwhelming the native filesystem with too many files in a single directory (which can impact performance).

All CE servers must be able to read files from every storage area. That usually means a File Storage Area should be defined as a network share, although you can get away with using a local directory for an all-in-one system that has only a single CE server. A common strategy is to use a NAS or SAN as the storage device and have the filesystem directory appear in the same location on all physical CE servers.

## Fixed content devices

The CE supports a number of specific storage devices collectively referred to as **Fixed Content Devices** (**FCDs**). Earlier, we mentioned the examples of EMC Centera, NetApp Snaplock, and IBM System Storage N Series. The term FCD originates in a type of vendor device that itself does some management of storage. Content put into such devices can generally not be changed, and it can often only be deleted in compliance with a configured retention policy. These device features complement similar features available in CM.

## Content Federation Services (CFS)

The last category of storage locations is a horse of a different color. Content is added to and stored within an external system. Selected properties of those externally stored documents are also present in the Object Store via a process known as **federation**. Cooperating background processes ensure that, when any of those selected properties is changed within the external system, the value is asynchronously copied to the corresponding property in the Object Store.

The Object Store does not hold the content for federated documents. When a CM application retrieves content for a federated document, the CE transparently retrieves it from the external system and delivers it to the caller.

CFS connectors are available for use with most IBM content repositories, whether FileNet heritage or not, and with EMC Documentum Content Server and Open Text Livelink.

*Planning Your Deployment*

# Clustering, High Availability, and Disaster Recovery

These three topics are related, but each represents a different aspect of managing the risks in your system. Each is a complex topic in its own right, so we can give only an overview here.

## Clustering

**Clustering** is a technique for reducing the risk of downtime and for optimizing resource utilization through load balancing. Clustering comes in a few flavors, but the common principle is that multiple equivalent servers are provisioned to handle a given load. In the CM case, we are usually talking about multiple instances of a J2EE application server at the application layer and the CE server layer.

> The version of IBM WebSphere bundled with a CM license does not include the *Network Deployment* feature. In other words, it doesn't include clustering and the accompanying administrative features. It's great for most development, functional testing, and even some types of production deployments, but it doesn't include that particular feature.

The most important thing to know about clustering in CM is that the best type of clustering to use for the CE servers depends on the API transport being used:

- For EJB transport, you should use software load balancing built into the application server. The reason for this is that the EJB address resolution tends to be done very infrequently and ties connections to some specific host in the cluster. This usually negates any intended load balancing from a hardware load balancer.

- For CEWS transport, hardware load balancers work well. You would typically configure a virtual host name for the load balancer and let it pass connections to physical servers. All hardware load balancers understand how to properly balance HTTP and HTTPS traffic.

> All API interactions with the CE are stateless. In other words, except for load balancing, it doesn't matter which CE server is used for any particular API request. Requests are treated independently, and the CE does not maintain any session state on behalf of the application. On the other hand, some CM applications do need to be configured for **sticky sessions**. A sticky session means that incoming requests (usually from a web browser) must return to the same copy of the application for subsequent requests.

With a simple clustering solution, failure of a single node in the cluster means that other nodes will take over a proportionate share of the workload, though sometimes with reduced performance.

# High Availability

**High Availability (HA)** takes clustering a step further and usually involves ensuring there is no single point of failure in the entire environment. Along the same lines, equipment is provisioned so that one or more redundant nodes can fail and the other nodes will be able to handle the workload without a degradation in performance. To a first approximation, HA is the over-provisioning of your resources and having a strategy for nodes to reliably cover for each other.

HA planning is generally a complex orchestration of budget availability versus risk tolerance.

# Disaster Recovery

**Disaster Recovery (DR)** is the ability to promptly resume operations after a catastrophic failure of a primary facility. To the uninitiated, that sounds a lot like HA, but it's qualitatively different. To be effective, a DR site must be located away from the primary site.

The definition of "away from" depends on what type of disaster you are planning for. Is it a flash flood in a nearby river? In that case, a DR site a few miles away might be fine. Is it an earthquake, volcanic eruption, terrorist attack, or asteroid strike? In that case, you probably want your DR site to be quite a bit farther away. Is it the sun going supernova and destroying all of the planets (including Pluto, even if it's not a planet)? In that case, hmm, we'll leave it to you to figure that one out.

DR planning should involve these factors:

- A DR site with a location chosen according to the disasters for which you are planning. The site will have sufficient equipment, networking capacity, and other resources to carry whatever percentage of the operational load you want.
- Some means of replicating the data from your primary site to your DR site. This could be as simple as periodic backups physically carried to the DR site, or it could be as complicated as near real time network copying over fiber links.

- A plan for how to actually do a recovery from a disaster. How will you actually load up the latest replicated data? How will you accommodate the gap, no matter how small it might be, between your replicated data and the transactionally committed data at your primary site before the disaster? How will you staff your DR site if staff from the primary site are incapacitated or otherwise unavailable for movement to the DR site? It goes without saying that the best plans are the ones that are practiced in DR drills and the like.

> We mentioned near real time replication for DR. It can be tempting to think of your DR site as your data backup, or at least eliminating the need for traditional backups. It seems too good to be true since all of your updates are almost instantaneously copied to another datacenter. The trap is that the replication can't tell desirable updates from mistakes. If you have to recover some of your data because of an operational mistake (for example, if you drop the tables in an Object Store database), the DR copy will reflect the same mistake. You should still do traditional backups even if you have a replicated DR site.

## Distributed deployments

Many enterprises operate with a single, centralized datacenter. This is often true even if the user population is geographically distributed. CM does not assume a single physical location, and many other enterprises use CM across multiple datacenters distributed globally. In this section, we'll describe some of the specific planning factors and CM features related to distributed deployments.

Cost and performance are the two driving factors in thinking about distributed deployments. Long distance networking is more expensive than local networking, and budget realities often constrain the network capacity you're willing to pay for. Long distance networking has two complementary characteristics of interest that can be partially solved with money: bandwidth and latency.

- **Bandwidth** refers to the amount of information your network can carry in a given period of time. There is no real technical difference between local networking and long distance networking for bandwidth except that long distance bandwidth is, in general, dramatically more expensive.

- **Latency** refers to how long it takes for a single piece of information to travel from one end of the network connection to the other end. It takes a certain amount of time for network signals to relay information over a distance and to be handled by intermediate pieces of networking equipment. Latency can generally only be influenced to a certain extent by provisioning faster switching gear between links or eliminating some switching points completely.

Given the realities of network expenses and physics, a distributed deployment plan will take into account the characteristics of conversations between different components and try to minimize overall costs and performance impacts on the system.

# CE topology

In a CM system, assuming a single domain:

- Every CE server must be able to reach the GCD, every Object Store database, every filesystem storage area, every Fixed Content Device, and every Content Search Engine.
- Each PE server must be able to reach at least one CE server, and *vice versa*. The PE server must be able to talk to the PE database.
- All CE servers talk to the same directory server. That really means that a single directory server address is configured in the CE, so any directory clustering could be hidden behind a virtual address. Directory traffic is relatively lightweight and highly-cached, so directory location is usually not performance-critical. Reliable connectivity to the directory, on the other hand, is very important.

Topologically, CE server components can be described with these operational tiers, which is a recap of more detailed explanations given in *Chapter 4, Administrative Tools and Tasks*:

- **Domain**: All CE servers sharing a given GCD and set of Object Stores.
- **Site**: Geographically close systems. Servers within a site are typically LAN-connected.
- **Virtual Server**: A collection of systems which appear topologically as a single system. This usually means a cluster.
- **Server**: A separately administrable physical server.

Most configuration settings of CE servers can be done hierarchically according to the operational tiers just described. You can configure settings to apply to an entire domain, a single CE server, or something in between. For example, we illustrated that in the *Trace Logging* section of *Chapter 4*.

*Planning Your Deployment*

For the purposes of distributed deployments, we are generally interested in the sites. It's common to describe a distributed deployment in terms of a central site and one or more remote sites. However, the CE itself does not have the concept of a central site. For the actual mechanics of CE behavior, it makes more sense to talk about the local site and a remote site. Which one is which really depends on where the Object Store or other resource lives.

## PE considerations

For PE, the objects involved are very dynamic. Because of the high rate of change, there is very limited caching of PE objects. PE activity tends to be database intensive, so it makes sense to locate the PE server near the PE database. That should be within the same physical datacenter.

The PE and CE converse for a limited number of things: PE's delegated authentication (typically lightweight in terms of network traffic), retrievals and updates of workflow attachments (can be heavyweight if content fetches are involved), and CE calls to PE to launch workflows. It is not a requirement that the PE and CE have the same physical location, but performance will be improved if they do.

## CSE considerations

The **Content Search Engine** (**CSE**) does full-text indexing and responds to full-text queries. Calling applications do not connect directly to the CSE. The CSE is accessed only through a CE server that is making CSE API calls. CSE must see its storage as being local to the CSE server even if that storage resides on some kind of network share.

It's probably easiest to think of the CSE as just another kind of database server. Since all CE servers must be able to talk to all CSE servers, it makes sense to centralize CSE servers unless you're lucky enough that your content naturally partitions for particular sites.

# CE distributed deployment features

There are two specific features of the CE that are meant to facilitate distributed deployments. If you are not using a distributed deployment, there is no advantage to using either of these features.

## Content cache

Content caching is interesting for two reasons: Database transactions and other chatter are relatively small compared to document content. There is also a reasonable chance that once a piece of content becomes interesting for some reason, it will stay interesting for a while and be retrieved additional times (perhaps the reason is that the document was just added).

The CE includes a **content cache** feature that does pretty much what you would expect, based on the name. It caches document content, but it does not cache document properties. Content caching is not implemented in a separate server. It's part of every CE server, but it is not enabled by default. When it is enabled, it is usually configured at the site level so that all CE servers at that site (and no CE servers at other sites) can use that content cache.

> Even though it's only the local CE servers that retrieve content from a content cache, all CE servers must have access to it for administrative housekeeping purposes. Therefore, it must be visible over the network, just like a filesystem storage area.

When a local CE server needs to access content that resides at another site, it can instead read the content from a locally configured content cache. On a cache miss (that is, a request for content that is not in the cache), the content is fetched and dropped into the cache. The protocol used is whatever would be used by the CE for reading content if the content cache didn't exist (usually NFS or SMB).

Before fetching any content, the CE, whether local or remote from the content, first checks the document properties in the Object Store. This ensures that the document content still logically exists in the Object Store and that the calling user is authorized to retrieve it. Therefore, data in a content cache is never stale from the point of view of the calling application. Currency and security have always been checked, just as if there were no content cache. Stale content can still literally exist temporarily in the content cache, but it will never be served to a caller; it will be effectively invisible outside of the CE server itself.

A content cache has a configured limit on how much space and how any pieces of content it can hold. When it gets full, it uses a **Least Recently Used** (LRU) policy for discarding content from the cache. A CE background thread purges stale content.

*Planning Your Deployment*

# Request Forwarding

The requests made from a CE client to a CE server are usually at a higher level of abstraction and less chatty than the resulting conversation between the CE and an Object Store database. It can often be more networking-efficient for one CE server to ask another CE server to perform a particular update or retrieval. This feature is called **Request Forwarding (RF)**.

The idea behind RF is to get to a CE that is closer to the Object Store database. Every Object Store is associated with some CE site. Every CE server is associated with some CE site. When the Object Store and the CE server are in different CE sites, it might make sense to use RF. RF is disabled by default. To use it, you must configure it at both the sending and receiving sites. RF always uses EJB transport and is essentially indistinguishable on the wire from a client request using EJB transport.

When a request is received by a CE server with RF enabled, it calculates the best target CE site, determines if RF should be used, forwards the request to the configured address, receives the results from the remote CE server, and relays the results to the original caller. There are a handful of conditions that will disqualify an incoming request from being forwarded:

- If the request references an Object Store at the same local site, then no other site will be better for handling it.
- If the request contains a content upload or retrieval, it will not be forwarded because direct access to content storage is more efficient than RF.
- If the request contains references to GCD objects, it is not forwarded.
- If the request asks for metadata (class or property descriptions, not properties of objects themselves), it is not forwarded. Every CE server has an in-memory cached copy of the metadata for all Object Stores. Again, we're talking about the class and property descriptions, which is a relatively small number of objects per Object Store.
- In incoming call can consist of a batch of requests. When a batch of requests is received, they will all be forwarded to the same distant CE site or none will be. All requests in a batch will be serviced by the same CE server.
- A request that has already been forwarded to a CE server will not be forwarded again.

These rules sound a little complicated, but they boil down to trying to make sure that using RF does not result in a net loss in response time. You might be wondering what sorts of requests do qualify for RF. Most requests seen by a CE server deal with objects inside a single Object Store. That's true even if there are several items in a batch request. It's fair to say that most requests are candidates for RF if the Object Store is located at another site.

## Typical distributed deployments

Here are brief descriptions of the two most common configurations for distributed deployments. Obviously, there are many other possibilities. These are just the most commonly used. The first one is probably common because it is conceptually very simple and tends to isolate the CM server tier and data at a central site. The second is a more complex configuration but is more likely to benefit from the distributed deployment features described above.

## Remote application tier

In this configuration, the clients talk locally, perhaps over a LAN, to applications. The applications talk over long distance networking to CE and PE servers. There is no content caching or request forwarding because there is only a single CE site. It is the application's responsibility for making the best use of the network.

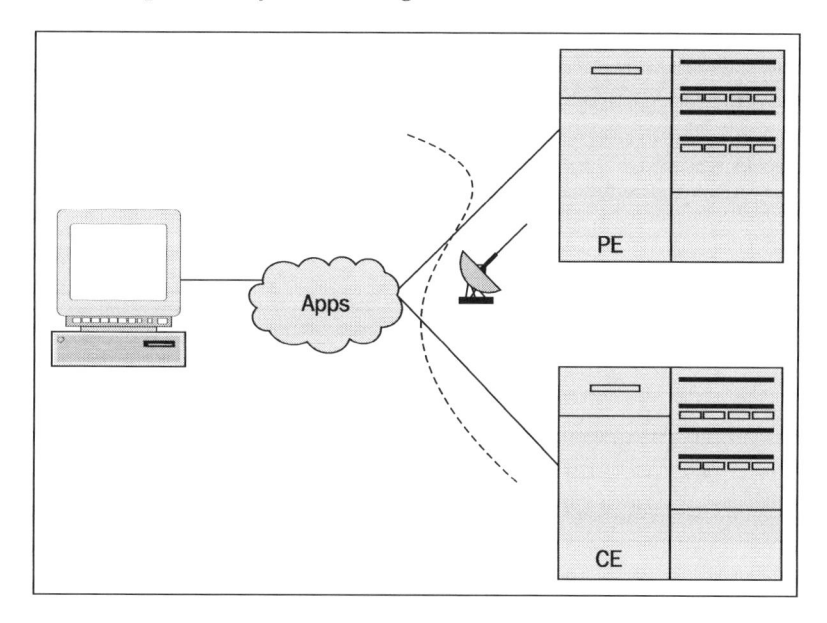

*Planning Your Deployment*

## Remote application and CE tier

In this configuration, clients again talk locally to applications. The applications and the CE talk over long distance networking to the PE server. The applications talk locally to a CE server that has a content cache and that uses request forwarding to send requests to a remote CE server.

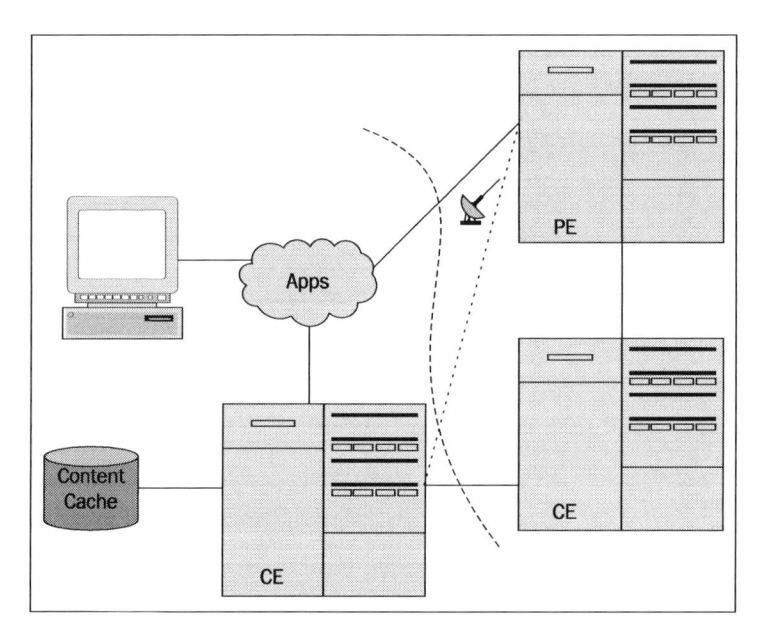

# Summary

In this chapter, we moved on from discussing individual features to looking at the big picture of how you would plan for and deploy the components of an ECM platform to a real environment. In many cases, we merely presented planning factors because you will have to decide on your own if those things apply or how you will make decisions on the trade-offs.

Your next step would be to come up with a plan for your own deployment. If you are new to ECM in general or FileNet in particular, it might make sense to arrange for some expert review of your plan before committing significant resources to rolling it out. It's probably a good idea to get additional opinions because of the effort it takes to rearrange things after the deployment is done.

In the next chapter, we'll move beyond the boundaries of CM itself and take a look some of the other software products and components commonly used along with CM.

# 10
# Included and Add-On Components

Most of this book has been about features and capabilities of IBM FileNet Content Manager (CM), an IBM product that includes specific software components. There are many enterprises that license CM and no other FileNet component. There are as many (probably more) enterprises that combine CM with other components, either as a different product offering or as add-on components that integrate with CM.

This chapter surveys the most popular of those other components. It would be easy to view this chapter as some kind of sales pitch, but we hope you don't see it that way. We're not trying to "up-sell" you a sandwich with your cup of coffee. These really are commonly-used configurations, and each is worth considering as you develop your ECM strategy.

This chapter includes discussions of the following:

- Standard CM components (things included with CM)
- Compliance management components (including records management and electronic discovery)
- IBM Smart Archive Strategy
- Business Process Management

We also discuss additional components that don't quite fit into those major categories but are nonetheless interesting.

*Included and Add-On Components*

# Standard CM components

The standard IBM license for CM 4.5.1 includes quite a few components, and we'll start with a look at those. Since we have discussed most of them at length in other chapters, we'll just list them all briefly here for completeness. In a few cases, where we haven't gone into much detail elsewhere, we'll give a more detailed description.

The licensing is revised from time to time (usually to tweak version numbers of included components) and is definitely revised for every product release, so you may want to check your license for the specifics if there is any doubt. Information in this section is based on the CM 4.5.1 license published in June 2010.

> We are engineers. We are not lawyers nor even specialists in software licensing. If you have any questions about the particulars of your license for IBM products, we're not the ones to ask. Information in this section is presented to the best of our understanding. Yes, we have read the CM 4.5.1 license from head to toe. *Chapter 13, Support, Fix Packs, and Troubleshooting* contains information for finding CM license information online.

Several of these components include **limited use licensing**. You will have no problem developing fairly sophisticated applications and deployments with this set of components, even with the license restrictions. When it comes to planning for deployment to a production environment, you should evaluate whether you need capabilities of the fully-licensed, non-bundled versions of those components.

# Server components

Some FileNet components are designated as **servers**. The distinction can be a bit murky because of the more general use of the term server in the computer industry. For example, you could make a reasonable case that just about anything running inside a J2EE application server is a server in the more general sense.

- **IBM FileNet Content Engine 4.5.1**. The CE, of course, is the main server in the CM product. It puts the "content" in Enterprise Content Management.
- **IBM FileNet Content Search Engine 4.5.1**. The CSE provides full-text indexing and searching. CM licensing does not include using CSE except for its integration with CE.
- **IBM FileNet Process Engine 4.5.1**. The PE is the main server for the IBM FileNet **Business Process Management** (**BPM**) product. The PE is included with the CM product to support the pre-defined workflow definitions available in CM, as described in *Chapter 6, End User Tools and Tasks*. The CM license does not include running other workflows on the PE.

# Applications and connectors

The next group of components we'll look at is a combination of two related categories. We've combined applications and connectors because an application can sometimes require a connector or adapter layer on its way to talking to CM server components.

- **FileNet Content Federation Services 4.5.1** and **IBM Content Integrator 8.5.1**. The CFS and ICI components enable you to federate content from other IBM ECM repositories to the CE, which acts as the central catalog. (We mentioned CFS in *Chapter 9, Planning Your Deployment*.) The IBM repositorics include IBM Content Manager, IBM Content Manager On Demand, IBM FileNet Image Services, and IBM FileNet Content Services. Interestingly, it is also possible to federate content from another P8 Domain (this need usually arises as a transitional step when it is desired to combine multiple P8 Domains, as during a corporate aquisition). The CM license does not include connecting to non-IBM repositories, though connectors for other repositories (as well as an SDK for writing custom connectors) are available under separate licensing.

- **System Dashboard for Enterprise Content Management 4.5.1**. System Dashboard provides instrumentation and a graphical application for monitoring the health and performance of individual components and the overall CM system.

- **IBM FileNet Application Engine 4.0.2** and **WorkPlace XT 1.1.4**. These web-based applications can be used productively for common document management tasks and also demonstrate many features of the CM product. We described many of those features in *Chapter 6, End User Tools and Tasks*.

- **IBM FileNet Integration for Microsoft Office 1.1** and **IBM FileNet Application Integration**. FileNet's integration with common office productivity applications has long gone under the nickname "AppInt" (for **application integration**). There are two distinct versions.

    ◦ The original package, used for Microsoft Office versions through Office 2003, is available for download from both Workplace and XT.

    ◦ The newer package, **IBM FileNet Integration for Microsoft Office (FIMO)**, is used for Office 2007 (and later, though no later versions are yet qualified by IBM). It includes complete integration with the Office ribbon bar and other UI panels introduced in Office 2007. It is available for download from XT or as a standalone installer.

*Included and Add-On Components*

- **WebDAV Server**. CM provides a WebDAV server as part of the Application Engine and XT applications. WebDAV is a standard protocol that uses HTTP for distributed authoring and is defined in IETF RFC-4918, *HTTP Extensions for Web Distributed Authoring and Versioning (WebDAV)* and related documents. That means that an application can use the WebDAV protocol for simple document management tasks in cases where documents reside in a repository. There are WebDAV clients built into Microsoft Windows Explorer, Internet Explorer, recent Office versions, and several non-Microsoft authoring tools. It would be nice to say that CM's WebDAV can support any WebDAV-compliant client, but WebDAV has historically suffered from problems of mutually incompatible client implementations. If you plan to use WebDAV, be sure to check that your specific clients and versions are supported by CM. It's also worth noting that most clients can do only fairly basic document management tasks via WebDAV compared to other integration techniques.

- **IBM FileNet Services for Lotus Quickr 1.1.0**. This component is an integration layer that enables the Lotus Quickr family of applications to seamlessly use CM as a repository for Quickr documents and other artifacts. Lotus Quickr provides a rich and general collaborative environment, and this integration layer enables the use of CM as a repository for Quickr document content.

- **IBM FileNet Connector for SharePoint Web Parts V2.2**. CM's connector for Web Parts is a component that integrates into a Microsoft SharePoint installation and provides access to CM features. From within SharePoint, you can create documents, browse for existing documents, and do other document management tasks for content stored in a CM repository. The connector also allows users to directly initiate workflows and check workflow inboxes without leaving the SharePoint environment. Content originally residing in a departmental SharePoint repository can be migrated into the CM repository to take advantage of archiving and compliance tools.

# Environmental components

In this section, we'll list the bundled environmental components. The environmental components are infrastructure upon which CM components are installed.

- **WebSphere Application Server 6.1 and 7.0 for FileNet Content Manager 4.5.1**. This provides the J2EE application server for hosting CM components. This is the WAS Base Edition and does not include WAS Network Deployment. The CM license limits the non-CM use of this WAS component. Both WAS 6.1 and 7.0 are included. Unless you have a specific reason for using WAS 6.1, we recommend you use WAS 7.0.

- **DB2 Workgroup Server Edition 9.5 for FileNet Content Manager 4.5.1**. This provides a database server for storing CM repository data for CE Object Stores and PE workflow artifacts. The CM license limits the non-CM use of this DB2 component.

## Initiatives and scenarios

There are many motivations for getting involved with ECM and many roads to a strategy and a solution for meeting your enterprise's needs. In the subsections that follow, we'll consider some of those scenarios and the components that are a logical part of them. In most cases, those scenarios represent specific IBM initiatives based on observed customer needs, but that is almost incidental. What you want to look at is whether those scenarios apply to your enterprise and whether you need to develop a strategy for meeting needs in those areas.

In terms of software components, many technical product components can serve well in multiple scenarios. Rather than repeat the descriptions in those cases, we'll just refer to the earlier description. Although we will mention them where appropriate, we've tried to avoid concentrating the discussion on specific IBM product bundles. Not only do those change from time to time, and so perhaps might be irrelevant when you read this, but we also want to concentrate on the functional areas that make up the scenarios. You can then choose how to develop your solution. We're sure your local IBM account team will be glad to work with you to package things in the way that is best for you.

> Many IBM ECM products carried IBM InfoSphere branding for a year or so. Much of that branding has been reverted and the word "InfoSphere" removed from the product names, though IBM InfoSphere remains a vibrant brand for other products. You may occasionally see these ECM products referred to with the IBM InfoSphere naming. If it doubt, visit the appropriate product pages on IBM's web site, where renamed products usually have a parenthetical mention of previous names.

## Compliance management

There was a major uptick in interest in ECM starting a few years ago due specifically to worries about compliance. Whereas compliance issues had traditionally been limited to government agencies and a relatively few regulated business areas, the passage of the Sarbanes-Oxley Act in the US in 2002 (and analogues in many other countries around the same time or later) greatly expanded the scope of compliance requirements to cover essentially all public companies.

*Included and Add-On Components*

Compliance measures take many forms. In ECM terms, it usually boils down to robust record keeping mandated by some law, regulation, or recognized industry standard. IBM has several ECM products to address aspects of compliance.

# IBM Enterprise Records (IER)

**IBM Enterprise Records (IER)** was formerly known as FileNet Records Manager and is tied to the IT practice of **records management**. Records management sounds like a rather tame subject, but it is actually one of the more rigorous and demanding fields in IT today. A major standard in records management is US Department of Defense (DoD) standard 5015.02, Electronic Records Management Software Applications Design Criteria Standard.. Even though it is a US military standard, it is mandated for use by many non-military and non-US government organizations. It also provides guidance for many non-government organizations. IER is certified against DoD 5015.02 v3 as well as the major Australian standard, the **Victoria Electronic Records Strategy (VERS)**. There are other popular records management standards or best practices, but not all such standards have formal certification processes for software vendors.

Records management software performs several functions, but, in broad strokes, those functions can be summarized with the following characteristics. More extensive coverage is available in the IER product documentation and the IBM Redbooks publication *Understanding IBM FileNet Records Manager*, available at `http://www.redbooks.ibm.com/abstracts/sg247623.html`.

## Declaration

To **declare** something as a record is to bring it formally under records management control. Regardless of the inherent importance of a particular document to an enterprise, the declaration step is the point at which the document becomes a permanent business record in the records management sense.

IER has a few interesting aspects related to declaration.

Using what IBM calls ZeroClick technology, all or many actual declarations can be done automatically. Eliminating human action and decision making leads to a more robust records management process and also reduces the burden on users. ZeroClick works through a combination of different mechanisms. In some cases, IBM-provided applications (for example, IBM Content Collector) are explicitly aware of records management and transparently perform the declaration at appropriate points in their own logic. In other cases, the CE event system can be used to do declarations in response to updates to documents. Finally, records declaration can be tied into workflows managed by the PE. In all of these, there is flexible configuration and rules-based processing so that you can automatically declare just the records appropriate to your scenario. Of course, manual declaration of a record is always available.

IER used with CM is not limited to records management of documents stored directly in a CM repository. Using the federation services built into CM, IER can manage records stored in many other types of repositories, both from IBM and from other vendors (additional connector licensing is required for non-IBM repositories).

IER is not even limited to records management of electronic documents. It has features for managing physical objects: a hardcopy document, a video tape, or even a box of cookies. (We're not really sure about the box of cookies, but we think IER's auditing and reporting would be very helpful in certain domestic situations when the last cookie has gone missing.) Records management of physical objects must also involve non-technical policy enforcement since there is no practical way that a software system can know that a physical item has been changed or moved.

## Classification

Records are organized according to a **file plan**. The file plan is realized in IER through the creation of record information objects. They contain security, disposition, and other information about one or more records. Therefore, classification of documents in the records management sense is usually more closely aligned with the type of document or the organization responsible for it than with the actual content of the document. IER works hand in hand with other IBM tools to do automatic classification at the same time as automatic declaration.

## Protection

When a document is declared as a record, it is no longer controlled directly by the author or other previously-authorized users. The record is controlled completely by the records management system under the control of records administrators. In IER, that control is implemented through the record information object in the file plan. For records residing in CM, a special form of CE security inheritance called full proxy is used. (We described proxy objects in general and full proxies in particular in the discussion of security inheritence in *Chapter 8*.) For records residing in federated repositories, the details vary, but in all cases the records administrator controls security access to the records.

## Disposition

A critical aspect of records management protection is that a record cannot be deleted except by a **disposition** process. That is easy to understand as a critical requirement when you consider the motivation for formal records management in the first place. It would not be very useful for uncovering fraud if the defrauders could simply delete incriminating documents.

Conversely, enterprises are generally interested in getting rid of records promptly when they no longer have business value (and assuming regulatory retention periods have been met). IER includes a disposition feature which can automatically do the job of deleting records when their policy-driven retention periods are exhausted. Retention periods are usually defined in terms of some interesting date or event. Examples include "five years after creation" and "three years after last update".

> An organization that wants to reduce litigation risk by meticulously disposing of records on schedule is not necessarily trying to cover up wrong-doing. Even a completely innocent actor can face substantial costs in defending itself against meritless charges. Documents can be misinterpreted or be embarrassing when taken out of context. Just because a document no longer has business value to an enterprise doesn't mean that it doesn't have value to someone on a litigation fishing expedition.

Although we have so far described disposition as the deletion of records, there are several other possibilities. A record might be brought to the attention of records administrators for review and appropriate action, it might be exported from the repository into some kind of archive storage, or it might be subject to one of the other disposition actions available in IER.

An interesting special case for deletion is the requirement that some electronic records have their contents affirmatively purged from the system. That usually involves over-writing the physical storage some number of times with prescribed patterns of bits so that the content cannot be recovered, even with forensic analysis of the media.

Just as organizations are eager to dispose of records as soon as possible to reduce costs and limit regulatory or litigation risk, there is a recognition by the legal system that potential evidence must be preserved. This also occurs for strictly internal reasons, such as the preservation of quality control samples. We'll talk more about this general topic below when we describe electronic discovery. For now, it's sufficient to say that IER has a feature for marking records with **holds**. A record with one or more holds cannot be deleted from the system, automatically or manually. The holds must be cleared first.

> Some records management systems use the term "freeze" for the process of applying what we have just described as a hold. This should not be confused with the CE feature of the same name (which prevents all application updates to the properties of a document version). They are unrelated.

# Audits and reporting

You want auditing in your records management system for two reasons that are so related you might think of them as the same thing. First, for your own internal or regulatory reasons, you want to know that your records management solution is doing what you think it should be doing. Second, if you ever have to produce documents (or claim the absence of documents) in a regulatory proceeding or legal dispute, the inherent trustworthiness of your evidence is boosted when you reliably show robust records management practices.

For example, suppose someone challenges your claim that some set of records was destroyed as part of a routine records management retention policy (and not as part of a nefarious plot for world domination). Someone could cast doubt on your claim about the retention policy, but it's obviously legitimate if you have records management audit records showing your regular destruction of such records over time.

IER auditing is implemented on top of and augments the CE audit logging feature, but IER provides tools and sets of predefined configurations for common records management scenarios. These can be customized for your particular circumstances.

Part of the tooling that IER provides is a reporting capability for records management activity. The tooling provides several pre-defined report templates. You can customize those or even create completely new reports.

# IBM eDiscovery

**Electronic discovery** (eDiscovery) is the legal process of searching electronic records for information relevant to a court case, regulatory proceeding, or similar matter. It seems logical that searching through electronic information should be faster, cheaper—better—than the equivalent process of searching through file cabinets and boxes of paper documents.

It seems logical until you consider how the volume of electronic information has grown in recent years. How much email is generated in your enterprise in a given day, month, or year? Hmm, we thought so: it's quite a pile. Do you have a compliance reason to keep all those emails, at least for some personnel, for a couple of years?

Make no mistake about it: electronic discovery is still an expensive process. Courts know all about electronic information and presume you can manage it effectively and produce relevant items on demand. You can no longer claim that something was "just email" and so you no longer have a copy. Email is just one piece of the puzzle, and you probably have significant volumes of other electronic information, whether it's client contact records, employee interview notes, engineering change records, or whatever is pertinent to your business.

IBM **eDiscovery** (eD) is a suite of applications to help you efficiently manage the eDiscovery process. It can be used in conjunction with IER or on its own. It can be used for both internal discovery and audit purposes, as well as for responses to actual externally mandated legal discoveries.

The efficiency of eD can be seen in in both time and cost.

External discovery mandates generally come with strict timelines, and the ability to provide complete information within those deadlines can have a big impact on whether you are considered to be responsive. You could make a mad scramble to put all available employees on the hunt for particular information, but that itself is an expensive undertaking. Large enterprises can often have several or even dozens or more different legal cases at different points of progression at any point in time. After one or two *ad hoc* discovery efforts, you will certainly want a more organized solution.

Discovery seeks to find internal information relevant to a legal case. No organization wants to provide more information than the legal requirements. There is too much opportunity for valuable business information to escape the enterprise, and there is also the risk of widening the litigation based on information found through discovery. It is as important to limit irrelevant material as it is to provide relevant material. Material provided as a result of discovery is usually reviewed by staff legal counsel and possibly outside counsel, all of which adds to costs.

## IBM eDiscovery Analyzer (eDA)

eDA, as its name suggests, is an analysis tool. What exactly is relevant to a particular discovery request? A discovery mandate will spell out the subject matter for the discovery, but it probably won't be in the same terms as you might use when looking for relevant material. It is usually an iterative process to zero in on the correct search terms, the lists of involved individuals, and so on, before you can arrive at something you can reliably use to be truly responsive in the discovery but also exclude irrelevant material. eDA is a graphical tool that helps a knowledgeable person perform that iterative process. By exactly honing in on the responsive documents and excluding irrelevant documents, you can greatly reduce the costs of document reviews.

## IBM eDiscovery Manager (eDM)

eDM is a tool for managing the information actually being used in discovery. Each individual discovery process is managed as a discovery case in eDM. The search terms used, the manual inclusions and exclusions—all types of information related to the actual production of documents for discovery—are managed. This is important in case there is a challenge to the thoroughness of your discovery efforts. If you can produce the actual searches that you used, and they are deemed reasonable, and, further, if you can show—in a repeatable way—that the information produced by those searches is the information you produced, then risks from challenges are greatly reduced.

An additional important feature of eDM is that it produces its own legal hold for documents. This is conceptually similar to the holds used by IER, but they can be done by eDM without IER being present (the CE mechanisms used are related but not identical). A document with a legal hold cannot be deleted from the repository until the hold is cleared from the discovery case. If there are multiple holds from different discovery cases, they all must be cleared before the document can be deleted.

## IBM Content Collector

Things would be simple if all content were created by applications that were aware of ECM repositories and its associated features. At least, things would be simple for the ECM system, but things would be a lot more complicated for the users. A lot of interesting content is created by other applications and typically stored directly in files in the filesystem or non-CM repositories of various types.

**IBM Content Collector** (ICC) provides a flexible, rules-driven application for finding this content and storing it in an ECM repository. ICC can find content in many locations, and it can perform a configurable set of processing steps on the way to and as part of ingestion into an ECM repository. In addition to the three source connectors inherent in the configurations described below, there are additional source connectors available from IBM and third parties, and ICC has an API for writing custom source connectors.

> ICC can be thought of as an evolution of and replacement for older products (FileNet Email Manager and IBM CommonStore) that performed similar functions, though technically (and in licensing and support terms) it's not an exact replacement for either product.

## ICC for File Systems

ICC for File Systems is somewhat analogous to the web spiders used by most Internet search engines. A configurable list of directories is periodically scanned for new content. This is a popular option when business content is stored in common shared filesystems. A centrally running ICC process can efficiently look for content even if user workstations are powered off or unavailable.

## ICC for Microsoft SharePoint

ICC for Micosoft SharePoint scans SharePoint repositories and moves selected content into a CM repository. The original SharePoint content can be deleted, left as-is, or replaced by a link that points to the CM copy of the content. This is a good solution when you can write rules describing which content to move automatically. Due to the informal, collaborative nature of most organizations' use of SharePoint, whether you can do this in your organization depends on a lot of factors. You should consider using this in tandem with the IBM FileNet Connector for SharePoint Web Parts, mentioned above, for manually selected migrations.

## ICC for Email

ICC for Email, which can work with either Microsoft Exchange environments or Lotus Domino environments, is used for archiving email messages and attachments. It can be configured to operate off master copies of messages on the email server or by scanning individual user mailboxes. The centralized server mechanism is more robust since there is no opportunity for users to have deleted messages before the scanning process sees them. ICC understands how to find both the basic message and its attachments, and it treats them as separate but related objects when it stores them in the repository. Even though a message has been moved to the repository, the users can still access it via a stub link left behind.

## Task connectors

With any of the above configurations, processing steps can be enabled for a variety of useful tasks, which ICC calls **task connectors**. An API is available for writing custom task connectors. ICC task connectors work with other ECM products to enable things like automatic classification, ZeroClick records declaration, and one of our favorites: deduplication.

The **deduplication** feature of ICC detects when identical copies of content are being ingested. It automatically reduces the multiple copies to a single instance. This is especially valuable in email archiving because of the prodigious duplication of email attachments. If you forward a message with attachments, the forwarded copy will be treated as a new message by the email system. The attachment, which probably makes up most of the size of the message, is completely identical to the copy you received. ICC can detect duplicate attachments and store them only once. The really nice part is that it can detect that an email attachment is the same as a document that it earlier found in a filesystem, SharePoint repository, or some other source. For many archiving use cases, there is a lot of content, and deduplication can result in substantial hardware and operational cost savings.

> Other names for deduplication include **single-instance storage** and **duplicate suppression**. Deduplication is also available at other points in the architecture for a CM system. The CE server can do deduplication within a single Storage Area, though it is not available for Fixed Content Devices. On the other hand, many of the Fixed Content Devices supported by CM have their own native deduplication features.

# IBM Classification Module

There are many cases where unstructured content must be categorized or classified in various ways. Perhaps it should be organized into folders in a certain way, or perhaps certain keyword properties should be filled in. From the compliance point of view, decisions must be made about whether a particular document meets the criteria for being archived or not. Even without compliance motivations, there can be many documents with little or no business value in your environment. Relying completely on users to make these decisions is costly and can lead to inconsistencies, so automated help is something to welcome.

**IBM Classification Module (ICM)** uses a combination of techniques to make classification decisions. Although we're discussing it here in the context of content in ECM repositories, it can also be operated as a standalone system. It can act on new content as it's being ingested into the CM repository or it can process existing content.

If there is some structure to your data (for example, purely internal email messages versus external email messages), ICM can act on that. In cases where business rules can be written, that is typically the most accurate classification tool and saves users a lot of effort. Rules can be based on keyword, proximity, and pattern matches.

For cases where the data has less structure, sophisticated textual analysis can be used to suggest a classification for a document. ICM's classification suggestions can be subjected to a user review, and that review can be tailored to a certain confidence level. For example, you might choose to bypass user review for cases where ICM says it's 90% confident. In cases where there is user review, ICM instantly learns from the confirmation or from the user's alternative classification. That makes it very easy to initially train ICM by using sample documents taken from the real content set.

For the compliance and legal realms, using a robust automated system as a tool for deciding which content must be archived and which can be discarded can be viewed positively during later challenges. ICM refers to this concept as **defensible disposal**.

# Smart Archive Strategy

The IBM Smart Archive Strategy is a big-picture look at an enterprise's storage and archiving needs. The ideal outcome is that you have the right solution in place. That solution is likely to be a combination of hardware, software, and services, but exactly what that mix is will depend on many factors. The idea is to get you to look at how you might best use available technologies to solve your problems in a strategic way. Like so many other areas, storage and archiving needs can likely be most cost effectively met if they are approached with an enterprise-wide strategy rather than a piecemeal approach.

IBM's goal is to have best-of-breed offerings for all of the possible solution components and to have those components work smoothly together, but the components also work well in a mixed environment. ECM is certainly one part—perhaps a large part—of your overall storage and archiving landscape. Just as certainly, there are likely non-ECM aspects for you.

The three pillars of IBM Smart Archive Strategy are:

- Finding content throughout your enterprise (ingestion)
- Storing the content on a robust infrastructure (infrastructure)
- Being able to find and capitalize on your content in ways that have business value for you (management)

Let's look at each of those points.

## Ingestion

Finding content throughout your enterprise means more than just exhaustively searching all the hard drives you can find and making a copy of everything on them. It costs too much and leads you to archive things with little value to you. Components we've described earlier in this chapter can help you efficiently analyze and organize your content while bringing it under enterprise control. A good strategy is to analyze content, organize it, weed out duplicate or irrelevant material, and then store it in ways that will be useful as you continue to use the content.

## Infrastructure

There are a lot of things to consider when you plan your actual storage infrastructure. Do you need records management, retention management, high-availability, disaster recovery, generational storage, and so on?

In the hardware realm, IBM components can work with third party storage devices that you already have or plan to acquire. If you are looking for a self-contained, low-hassle solution, IBM Information Archive is just such a solution. It works as an appliance for storage of both structured and unstructured content, so you can have it up and running on your facilities in short order. The IBM Information Archive is available in configurations of up to more than 600 terabytes of raw capacity. It can be used as a storage solution for CM via the IBM FileNet P8 Connector to IBM System Storage Archive Manager (SSAM) for IBM Information Archive.

The IBM Smart Archive Strategy also includes components to enable cloud-based storage, whether in your own privately-run cloud or in IBM's cloud services.

## Management

Once your information is stored on a secure infrastructure, you still have to manage it securely and flexibly for operational and compliance reasons. You want to be able to put your hands on information when you need it, confident in its integrity. The many ECM components described in this chapter can be integral parts of your storage and archive solution.

*Included and Add-On Components*

# IBM FileNet Business Process Manager

This book is about the content management aspects of ECM, but another very important area is Business Process Management (BPM). People used to talk about automated workflow, which is a great cost saver in its own right. BPM has grown well beyond workflow and affects and influences how an enterprise actually accomplishes it mission. The usual emphasis is still on cost efficiency, but there are other measures of success, such as speed of service and accuracy of the end results.

In this section, we'll describe a few components that are commonly combined with CM but which have a leaning more toward the BPM world.

We showed some aspects of IBM FileNet BPM in other chapters. In particular, the Process Engine (PE) server component is included with CM along with two pre-defined workflows for document approval routing. The full BPM suite has many more capabilities beyond that. BPM is integrated bidirectionally with CM. Not only can workflow steps update content in a CM repository, but the CM event framework can be used to automatically launch workflows in response to content updates.

> In addition to IBM FileNet BPM, IBM also offers other BPM products: WebSphere Process Server and WebSphere Lombardi Edition (and related products for each of those). All three of these products have strengths that make them appropriate for particular scenarios. For the purposes of our discussion here, we'll just note that as of CM 4.5.1 only IBM FileNet BPM has the out-of-the-box technical integration just described. Integration with either of the other BPM engines is possible but requires more integration work.

# IBM FileNet Business Process Framework

**Business Process Framework (BPF)** is a framework for rapidly developing and deploying end-user applications for a variety of BPM scenarios. It has a web-based user interface that is highly customizable through configuration to suit the needs of many enterprises. It features reusable and customizable components that help easily show workflow inboxes, content attachments, and other business artifacts. It's especially well-suited to basic case management applications (claims processing, customer contact records, and so on). It even includes tight integration with FileNet eForms for a great-looking and highly functional user experience.

# IBM Enterprise Content Management Widgets

The popularity of rich Internet applications is well-deserved. They provide the tools for building an attractive and responsive user interface in a web environment. The IBM ECM Widgets product is a collection of reusable user interface components which are tuned to various BPM and CM features. The ECM Widgets do more than just small windows of isolated interaction. They can be combined together—without coding—to interact with each other and with compatible IBM and third party widget technology. This combining process, called wiring, allows rapid application development and rollout. Even non-IT personnel can quickly create a customized page of widgets for specialized tasks, perhaps even for an audience of one person.

BPM also includes Business Space powered by WebSphere and IBM Mashup Center with InfoSphere MashupHub as infrastructure for widget-based applications.

# Other components

This final section is a brief description of a few more components that don't happen to fit in the above sections. As the saying goes, they are last but not least.

# IBM FileNet System Monitor

Earlier, we described IBM System Dashboard for ECM (SD), an application included with CM to provide information about the health and performance of a running CM system. IBM **FileNet System Monitor (FSM)** is a fully-featured system management component. It provides real-time monitoring of ECM components and has built-in alerting and automation features. It includes features for a variety of reports of historical system health data and has an integrated knowledge base of common anomalies and corrective actions. The knowledge base can be locally extended to capture information for your specific deployment details. For dozens of commonly-occurring problems and maintenance activities, FSM provides automation to save time and reduce errors. FSM can be used as a standalone tool or integrated with one of several popular enterprise systems management solutions.

# IBM FileNet Image Services

You may recall from the miniature history lesson in *Chapter 1, What is ECM?* that FileNet got its start creating products that were optical imaging solutions. The imaging segment remains strong and is still an extremely popular way to brings faxes and scanned paper documents under control. IBM FileNet **Image Services (IS)**, often combined with IBM FileNet Capture products and BPM, is a high volume and robust imaging solution.

*Included and Add-On Components*

It may seem strange to talk about IS as an "add on" for CM. Of course, it's often the other way around, with CM being combined with an existing IS deployment. CM's included **Content Federation Services** for **Image Services (CFS-IS)** makes it easy to bring additional features to bear for image content. This is ideal for enterprises that have a large investment in IS but want to add features such as records management and other capabilities of the CM product.

# IBM FileNet Capture and Datacap

A very common ECM use case is the ingestion of documents that arrive either as faxed images or as paper documents that are immediately scanned. Once converted to a computer file, these images usually need immediate processing before being committed to an ECM repository. That processing can include cleaning up the images (straightening, rotating, and so on), extracting property values and other text, marking with account numbers or other batching information for downstream processing, adding annotations of various kinds, and other site-specific procedures. After local processing, the image documents must be reliably submitted to the ECM repository.

IBM FileNet Capture software is a popular solution for this scenario. It comes in a Desktop edition (usually for low-volume or *ad hoc* use) and a Professional edition for higher volumes or for scenarios that require additional automation. Advanced Document Recognition is an add-on package for Capture Professional that further assists with and automates the extraction of metadata and text from images.

IBM recently acquired Datacap, Inc., an IBM business partner and a vendor of high-end capture solution software.

# Content Management Interoperability Services

**Content Management Interoperability Services (CMIS)** is an OASIS standard for a set of web services for common document management tasks. What does that mean for you? CMIS is an integration layer with support from many repository vendors. You can build applications that know how to talk to the repository via CMIS and then use that same application to talk to many different repositories. Because CMIS is a specification for web services, the inherent loose coupling allows you to use whatever software stack you choose to write your application.

For a couple of years, while awaiting OASIS ratification of the CMIS standard, IBM has had a technology preview of a CMIS connector for CM available for download. That CMIS connector is a web servlet listening for requests and translating them into native CE API calls. The productized CMIS connector was shipped in the last quarter of 2010 and is bundled with CM 5.0. It does not support earlier releases of CM.

## Darwin Information Typing Architecture

**Darwin Information Typing Architecture (DITA)** is a system for creating documents in a modular way. The concept is to divide large pieces of content into reusable topics, generally of about only a paragraph or two. Topic titles, keywords, and other structured data are managed with mechanisms that let you combine topics in a variety of different ways without having to copy and modify that content.

DITA was originally created by IBM but is now controlled by an OASIS technical committee. It had its origins in technical documentation—product manuals, programmer documentation, and so on—where the opportunities for content reuse were plentiful. It has seen great success in that area but is also usable for other types of documents. Even where content reuse is not very high, DITA structure can help with organization of complex documents.

There are DITA features in CM that are an expansion of the basic CE compound documents feature. The CE can be used to assemble and render finished documents via the DITA Publishing feature and integration with the popular DITA Open Toolkit. Third party authoring tools, including Quark XML Author for Microsoft Word, can be used to create and edit DITA documents in CM.

## IBM Content Analytics

For decades, sophisticated tools have been available from many vendors for performing *ad hoc* analysis of highly structured database content. IBM Content Analytics (ICA) provides an analogous capability for unstructured content. It provides a graphical user interface for rapidly and flexibly exploring relationships, trends, and gaps in information stored in unstructured data. The intelligence behind ICA recognizes conceptual information through sophisticated textual analysis. It does not merely rely on simplistic keyword matching.

An IBM Redbooks publication, *IBM Content Analytics: Discovering Actionable Insight from Your Content*, goes into great detail about how to set up and operate an ICA environment. You can find it at `http://www.redbooks.ibm.com/abstracts/sg247877.html` or by searching on the IBM Redbooks website.

## Summary

In this chapter, we described some of the other components that are parts of CM or are popular in combination with CM. We could only give a brief description of them, and in fact we could have listed dozens more. Even from this glimpse it is obvious that, in addition to the main built-in CM capabilites, it also integrates well with a vast array of components from IBM and third parties. You should be able to easily find extensive product documentation for each of these components.

In the next chapter, we will give an overview of the development environment for writing custom CM applications.

# 11
# A Taste of Application Development

This chapter provides a short overview of application development for IBM FileNet Content Manager (CM). We can only give a glimpse here since this is the kind of topic that could easily merit its own book of this size or larger. We're not trying to make you into CM developers just by reading this chapter.

Since this isn't a book about application development and is just an introductory book on the overall topic of CM, why include this chapter at all? It's useful for a few reasons. First, a fairly large percentage of CM customers do develop custom applications, and we think it's important that you know generally what's available. Second, it can help you to understand custom or off-the-shelf components provided by IBM Lab Services or IBM business partners. Frankly, we think it will help you better understand the nuts and bolts of the standard CM-provided applications. It should also help in understanding the sample application described in *Chapter 12, The DUCk Sample Application*.

In this chapter, we'll cover:

- The CE Java and .NET APIs
- The CE Web Services protocol
- Other APIs that are often used in CM solutions
- A very small sample program using the CE Java API in Eclipse
- The same small sample program using the CE .NET API in VS C# Express.

*A Taste of Application Development*

# The Content Engine APIs

We start our development story with the most fundamental piece of the picture, the CE APIs. The other components described in this chapter add significant functionality, but all interactions with the CE ultimately go through one of these CE APIs. The CE philosophy is to expose all features as part of documented APIs. There are no hidden, insider-only APIs (though there are lots of non-exposed API implementation details beneath those APIs). To be sure, there is plenty of complex logic locked up inside applications and toolkits, but everything they do goes through a documented CE API. You could, in theory, build for yourself anything you see a CE application doing.

## Don't bypass the APIs

Everything can be done through CE APIs. The corresponding restriction, however, is that the CE insists that everything go through its APIs. If it's not available via a CE API, it's basically not available.

The most important question related to this is whether you can do things directly to the underlying relational databases and filesystems—the Object Stores, the Global Configuration Database, and the file storage areas—that hold CE's persisted data. We'll consider the reading and updating cases separately.

> The following subsections discuss technical and supportability constraints. If you are using DB2 software bundled with CM with a limited use license, there are licensing constraints on the operations you are allowed to do in database applications. That kind of constraint is out of of the scope of this chapter.

## Reading

That actual data in the CE is your data. They're your documents, your properties, and so on. Are you entitled to read that data back out without the mediation of the CE server? Yes, you are entitled, but it's still a generally bad idea.

- The CE is enforcing security access checks for objects and properties. The mere existence of an object (say, a folder called `Plans for Selling the Company`) can be hidden from unauthorized eyes.

- For referential integrity and other operational reasons, the organization of some data can seem a little convoluted. Many of the details of that convolution are not publicly documented, and that means it's subject to change any time you apply a new release or patch from IBM. Some small changes are almost always made for major CE releases, but the CE server layer smooths out the upward compatibility issues.

Having said all that, if you still want to directly access the data (a popular reason is for running reports and gathering statistics), the CM product documentation does include a section that briefly describes the database tables and columns used by the CE. Remember, though, that directly accessing the data is going against the grain of all the product development effort put into the CE, and don't be surprised if it's difficult to get any particular piece of detailed information about it.

## Updating

This one is easy: IBM never supports bypassing the APIs to do direct updates to the data underlying the CE. Well, okay, there are occasional exceptions, but they all have these characteristics:

- Each exception is considered individually, on a case-by-case basis.
- The answer is almost always no.
- For the yes cases, each is a one-time update to some simple property value that cannot be tractably done via the APIs. Notice that we didn't say it couldn't be "reasonably" done via the APIs. It has to be essentially impossible to do it via the APIs but very easy to do it directly with database tools.
- You will be strongly urged (perhaps it would be better to say coerced) to engage IBM Lab Services to supervise or actually do the change.

Why all this discouraging news about direct updates?

The CE makes a lot of guarantees about your data. Most of these are simple data validity things. Others are referential integrity guarantees. In any case, things can be quite complex. Because the CE knows about these guarantees, it also depends on them. Sometimes a little bit of off-color data added to the mix can have devastating effects. Simple mistakes can destroy or render inaccessible large segments of your data. It can also be the case that you won't notice problems right away; you'll notice it later after fresh, new data has been blended in.

Take our advice: just forget about this possibility completely.

# API transports

Whenever there is a client API accessing a server, there has to be a communications path and some protocol between them. In the CE case, this is explicit and is called the **transport**. There are two transports available for the CE APIs: CEWS and EJB. Though very different in nature, they are, with only two exceptions, functionally equivalent.

As you can see from the following architectural drawing, the Java API has a choice of either transport, but the .NET API always uses CEWS transport.

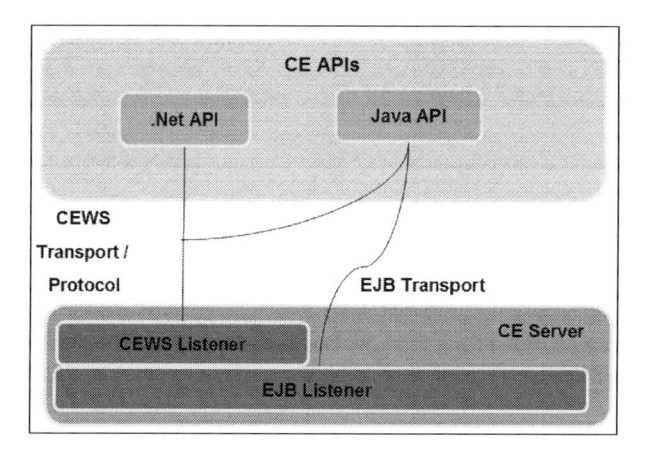

# CEWS transport

Because of its name, you will not be surprised to learn that **Content Engine Web Services (CEWS)** transport uses web services technologies to connect clients with the server. It is XML (in the form of SOAP requests and responses) over HTTP (or HTTPS). It therefore shares with web services in general these operational characteristics:

- Because it uses only one or two well-known TCP ports, it's relatively easy to configure firewalls and other filters to allow web services traffic to pass through.

- Because it's textual, it is easy to examine in a network trace during troubleshooting. Even someone who knows nothing about CE in particular can deduce quite a bit from the XML contents.

- Because it's textual and follows XML conventions, it tends to be somewhat more verbose on the wire and takes a little more effort to decode on the receiving end. In most environments, this doesn't add up to anything you probably care about, but it's a possible performance difference you can easily measure for yourself in most cases.

The CEWS transport is exactly the same thing as the CEWS protocol that will be described later in the *CEWS Protocol* section. It conforms to the published **Web Services Description Language** (**WSDL**) schema for CEWS. It's not some secret version of it or some abominable use of web services technologies.

> For historical reasons, CEWS transport is sometimes called **Web Services Interface** (**WSI**) transport. The most obvious place where that naming lives on is in the CE connection URLs that you have seen occasionally throughout this book. The URLs for CEWS transport always contain the string /wsi/.

## EJB transport

**Enterprise JavaBean** (**EJB**) transport uses the inherent remoting technology of EJB calls to connect client to server. That means that an inner layer of the API makes EJB calls to the CE. The specific EJB calls that are used are not exposed for you to call from your applications, and it's not safe for you to reverse engineer them and use them anyhow. Like most undocumented details, they are subject to change from release to release.

EJB transport is a little strange in that it's different in its underlying implementation for every supported application server type. The J2EE specifications leave it up to the vendors to implement whatever wire protocols they want as long as the higher-level EJB constructs meet the specified programming models. The vendors generally use compact, binary wire protocols for EJB remoting. There is a prescribed wire protocol that all vendors must implement for interoperability with other vendor products (the Internet Inter-ORB Protocol, IIOP), but, in practice, authenticated mixed-vendor EJB calls are difficult for other reasons.

In theory, the CE APIs depend only upon the J2EE-specified vendor-independent behaviors for EJB calls. In practice, each vendor has quirks and edge cases that need specific workarounds. None of this matters to you, the caller of the CE API, because the CE API smooths over those differences. You will just make ordinary method calls on objects representing things like documents and folders, and the CE API takes care of the rest.

EJB transport can only be used with Java technologies, and so it is only available for the CE Java API. On the other hand, the use of EJB transport automatically enables two features that are not available with CEWS transport, described in the next two sections.

## User transactions

All CE server updates are done transactionally. Every update submitted is committed or rolled back atomically. The CE takes care of starting a transaction, performing the operations, and concluding the transaction.

The CE APIs do not have any features to allow your application to start the transaction. You might want to do that if you had multiple operations you wanted to do atomically (and those operations would not be suitable for a single CE API batch update). You might also want to do it if you wanted to include updates to something else (something other than CE objects) in the same transaction.

J2EE APIs include facilities for creating and managing a transaction within an application. The principal interface is UserTransaction. It is because of these J2EE APIs that there are no transactional classes or methods in the CE Java API—they are not needed because they are available from the J2EE container. When you have started a UserTransaction and are using EJB transport, the necessary context for that transaction can be automatically carried to the CE server. In that case, any CE updates will be part of your UserTransaction and will be committed or rolled back based on J2EE transaction calls your application makes.

There is no need to inform the CE Java API about individual transactions because the propagation is automatically taken care of by the EJB programming model. However, to provide symmetric behavior with CEWS transport, the CE server will ignore any incoming client-side UserTransaction context unless the client connection is flagged to participate in the transaction. This is easily accomplished in application code by using ConfigurationParameter.CONNECTION_PARTICIPATES_IN_TRANSACTION.

> The use of a UserTransaction is a powerful feature, but it shouldn't be used casually. It tends to lead to longer lock hold times at the database level, and that in turn can lead to a variety of well-known negative database consequences. Most of these are not specific to the CE.
>
> For multiple CE updates, it is rare that they can't be accomplished via a single UpdatingBatch in the CE API. For enlisting additional resources, there is not much choice but to use a UserTransaction. In that case, structure your application so that the elapsed time while the transaction is open is as short as possible.

## JAAS context

The J2EE mechanism for keeping track of user authentication context ("being logged in", in simplified terms) is the JAAS Subject. In *Chapter 8*, Security Features and Planning, we described how the CE uses JAAS. When you make a call to the CE using EJB transport, the EJB infrastructure automatically and reliably propagates the user authentication context to the server side. The CE then uses the user identity from the JAAS Subject to make its authorization decisions.

The important part about this is that the EJB infrastructure does the propagation and the CE Java API infrastructure doesn't participate beyond actually making the EJB calls. Furthermore, JAAS already decouples the application (and the CE Java API) from the authentication process. When you combine these two things, the result is that neither the CE Java API nor the CE server care what techniques were used to create the JAAS Subject, nor (for the most part) do they care what is contained within the JAAS Subject. Anything that is acceptable to the application server is going to be acceptable to the CE Java API and CE server. The mechanics of it all are someone else's problem.

> EJB calls across multiple application server vendors are difficult because of JAAS Subjects. Although the Subject will indeed be transported by the EJB infrastructure if IIOP or another mutually supported wire protocol is used, the different vendor application servers don't understand and don't trust each others' JAAS Subjects. This isn't just vendor parochialism; it's a real and difficult technical issue.

Contrast that with CEWS transport, where the user authentication context has to fit within an XML schema structure. To fit into that structure, and to be unpacked from it and actually used on the CE side, the information in the context must be understood by both sides of the communication. So, CEWS is more limited in the types of authentication schemes it can support.

## Transport-specific coding

You might be getting worried because of all the talk about transport differences. Do you have to take all that into account in your application? If you want to be able to run your CM application and change your choice of transports later, will you end up with a lot of conditional code?

The good news is that you pretty much won't care, at the time you are writing your code, which transport will be used in the deployed application. You may or may not have some special case code in your application related to authentication, but the transport used can be purely a matter of configuration.

*A Taste of Application Development*

The CE APIs are given a connection URI by applications (for example, `http://wjc-rhel.example.net:9081/wsi/FNCEWS40MTOM/` or `iiop://wjc-rhel.example.net:2810/FileNet/Engine`). In the case of the CE Java API, where multiple transports are available, the API decides on the transport based strictly on the URI it's given. Anything that begins with `http:` or `https:` is CEWS transport. Anything else is EJB transport. It's as simple as that.

You might want to use TLS/SSL to secure the connections between the application and the CE. For CEWS transport, that is as simple as using `https:` instead of `http:`. For EJB transport, you should consult the application server's documentation for how to secure EJB connections. The technique is different for each vendor.

## CE .NET and Java APIs

The CE .NET API is aimed at applications using Microsoft-related technologies. The implementation language for the API is C#, but you can write .NET applications in any Microsoft **Common Language Runtime** (**CLR**) compatible language. Besides C#, the other common choice is Visual Basic .NET. Applications written with the CE .NET API must run in an environment which includes either Microsoft Web Services Extensions or Windows Communications Framework. The .NET Framework is also needed. Check the *IBM FileNet P8 Hardware and Software Requirements* for the latest precise required versions of supporting software.

The CE Java API is aimed at applications using Java-related technologies, and the obvious choice is Java for applications. The CE Java API supports, as of CM 4.5.1, Java Runtime Environment (JRE) versions 1.4.2, 1.5 (also known as Java 5), and 1.6 (also known as Java 6). Since Java 1.4 is considered to be obsolete, it will not be supported in future CM releases. Only official, Java logo-certified implementations are supported, though they need not be Sun implementations. The CE Java API makes a very full use of the Java runtime, so not only are Java clones not supported, they are very unlikely to work properly. When EJB transport is used, there is a supporting software requirement according to the instructions of the CE application server vendor. This is generally in the form of one or more JAR files, but there can be additional requirements. For example, for WAS, a thick Java client is required to use the WAS JRE.

The CE .NET and Java APIs differ mainly in the stylistic conventions specific to each environment. For example, interfaces in the CE .NET API start with the prefix letter "I", but in the Java API they do not. Method names in the CE .NET API are in `CamelCase`, whereas method names in the CE Java API are in `camelCase`. There are many of these minor stylistic differences, the aim being to make users of a given API feel comfortable with the look and feel of the CE API they are using.

When you get beyond the obvious implementation language differences, the style considerations, and the supporting software stack differences, you will find the CE .NET and Java APIs to be remarkably similar. In fact, except for their handling of authentication (where things are matched to the environment), the two APIs are functionally identical. That's not too surprising when you find out that a large percentage of both APIs is generated from a common database of CE metadata classes, properties, and relationships. That's the basis for the many API classes that directly represent CE metadata classes (for example, `Document`, `Folder`, and `CustomObject`) and the accessor methods for their system properties. As features are planned for the CE or for the APIs, manually-coded changes are implemented in parallel in both the CE .NET and Java APIs.

## CEWS protocol

The CE also supports the direct use of the CEWS protocol. Of course, this isn't really an API, though it's common to hear it referred to informally as an API.

There is no CM-provided software on the client side when you are using the CEWS protocol directly. You will be using a web services toolkit that can translate the CEWS WSDL into a set of programming language bindings that you can use. The list of supported web services toolkits is surprisingly short. Check the *IBM FileNet P8 Hardware and Software Requirements* for the latest list.

The reason the list is so short is due to the practical reality that all web services toolkits have quirks and shortcomings. This hardly matters at all for typical magazine article examples, where the example tends to ask a simple question with a simple answer. The CE WSDL is complex, and it has already been adjusted several times to work around quirks of supported toolkits. Making the adjustments is a tricky business because what makes one toolkit happy as often as not makes another toolkit unhappy. We wish it were not so, but the magical power of our wishing only carries so far.

We said earlier that the CEWS transport used by the CE APIs is exactly the same as the CEWS protocol supported for direct web services calls. That is literally true. The CE, when it receives a request at its CEWS listener, doesn't know or care whether the request came from a CE .NET API application, a CE Java API application, or a direct use of the CEWS protocol. (Okay, that last sentence is not literally true. The CEWS listener component also has a number of special cases where it adjusts some details of the HTTP headers and SOAP envelope of the response based on observed quirks of client-side software. The special cases are necessarily triggered by things seen in the corresponding places in the incoming request.)

*A Taste of Application Development*

Does it sound like we are trying to discourage you from directly using the CEWS protocol? Good, because we definitely are. The reason for supporting CEWS protocol is that there are a few cases where it is indispensable. You might be integrating with some other components that demand to use web services as their integration technology. In such instances, there may be no opportunity for you to include custom coding for the integration. CEWS protocol may be your only option.

What's the alternative to using CEWS protocol? It's the CE .NET and Java APIs, of course. If you use a web services toolkit for any complex interaction, you are likely to develop, on the side, a little basket of utilities, abstraction layers, helpers, caches, and so on, to improve the overall performance and quality of the custom components you develop. The CE developers have already done all of that in the CE APIs. The result is that the CE APIs are completely type-safe and have a modern, object oriented look and feel. They have conveniences galore that developers would take for granted. Assuming that you are not caught in a place that forces you to use CEWS protocol for integration, you will be saving yourself a lot of work (and probably a fair amount of frustration) by using the CE APIs.

## Attachment formats

When using CEWS as an API transport or directly using CEWS protocol, you have to give at least a small amount of thought into how document content will be uploaded to or downloaded from the CE. In the argot of web services, content is carried as **attachments** to a SOAP request or response.

There are three possibilities, all of which are functionally equivalent in terms of getting content from one end of the connection to the other. If you are using a CE API with CEWS transport, the attachment format is completely determined by a rather obvious detail of the connection URI; the example given earlier was for MTOM. If you are using CEWS protocol directly, consult your toolkit documentation to see which attachment formats are supported and how to use them.

- **MTOM**: **MTOM** is **Message Transmission Optimization Mechanism** and is the preferred attachment format in all cases. It bears some mechanical similarity to the Internet standard for email attachments, **Multipurpose Internet Mail Extensions** (**MIME**), but is different from the "MIME" attachment format supported by some older CM releases. If you are using CEWS protocol and adding the attachments yourself, there is a modest decoding performance advantage to adding the attachments in the same order they are referenced in the SOAP request (the CE APIs and CE server do it that way automatically).

- **DIME**: DIME was **Direct Internet Message Encapsulation**, an attachment format created by Microsoft. It has since been abandoned in favor of MTOM and is no longer supported by Microsoft infrastructure. In fact, it's a bit of a chase to even find the actual specification these days. Because Microsoft does not support DIME, it is not available when using the CE .NET API. It is supported by the CE Java API and the CE server only for backward compatibility reasons in CM 4.5.1. It is deprecated and will not be supported in the next CM release. You should not use this format at all with CE APIs. If you have CEWS protocol applications that use it, you should promptly convert them to MTOM.

- **SOAP**: SOAP is a nickname for something that is not really an attachment format. When SOAP was first defined, it was pure XML. There are difficulties in carrying arbitrary binary data within XML. SOAP has a data type of `base64binary` to carry binary data as text after first base64-encoding it. All SOAP software understands this data type and automatically decodes the values back into binary. This scheme works well, but it has a performance disadvantage for large content. The document content must be encoded on transmission and decoded on reception. That costs processing time, of course, but many components that deal with SOAP `base64binary` data expect it to be small and manipulate it completely in memory. This can lead to unexpectedly wild memory usage or outright failures in the case of large content.

- You should generally avoid using SOAP attachment format, but it can be useful for occasional troubleshooting. If you are getting mysterious errors or problems with MTOM attachment format, you can temporarily switch to SOAP as a way to gather additional clues. For CE API applications, the switch should be as easy as changing a few characters in your connection URI. Once the troubleshooting is completed, you will want to switch back to MTOM to avoid the performance cost of SOAP.

# Compatibility layers

We'll conclude this section about the CE APIs with a brief discussion of API compatibility layers.

The CM 4.0.0 release signaled a completely new architecture for the CE. It moved from being built on top of DCOM and other Microsoft technologies to being J2EE-based. Along with that CE server re-architecture came the opportunity to create a powerful set of new CE APIs. The CE Java API, CE .NET API, and CEWS protocol were discussed previously.

*A Taste of Application Development*

Members of the CM team are strong believers in backward compatibility, and it was not acceptable to strand applications written with earlier CE APIs. Two API compatibility layers and a CEWS protocol compatibility emulation were developed and have been supported since CM 4.0.0. These are all formally designated as deprecated, but IBM has made no public statement about when they will actually become unsupported.

## Java Compatibility Layer

Even when the CE server was based on Microsoft technologies, a majority of custom applications were written in Java and used the CE 3.x Java API. The Java Compatibility Layer presents the same programming interface in a CE 4.x environment. Internally, its implementaiton was changed from calling the CE 3.x COM API to calling the new CE Java API.

> The internal development code name for the CE 3.x Java API was *Buzz*, though, of course, it wasn't called the "3.x" API at the time. "Buzz" was never any part of any official product or component name, but you might hear it mentioned in unguarded moments by IBM support personnel ("gather Buzz logs") or see it mentioned in forum postings and the like. These days, it has come to also mean the Java Compatibility Layer in a CE 4.x environment.
> Shhh! Don't tell anybody we revealed this high-powered insider information to you. Do feel free to use it in casual conversation at any CE Java API cocktail parties you happen to attend.

The fidelity of the backwards compatibility of the Java Compatibility Layer is very good. Naturally, there are changes in administrative and configuration details due to the new architecture, but most applications are able to run without code changes or even recompilation. The minor differences, for the unlucky, are listed in the official product developer documentation in a developer guide section called *Upgrade Custom Applications*.

You should not use the Java Compatibility Layer for new work. The native CE Java API is more powerful and flexible. Also, because of the ways you can combine some operations in the CE Java API, you can write more performance-efficient applications than you can with the Java Compatibility Layer.

# COM Compatibility Layer

Before CM 4.0.0, the most fundamental CE API was the CE COM API. The **COM Compatibility Layer** (CCL) presents a subset of the same programming interface. Internally, it now calls the CE .NET API (using a technology Microsoft calls *COM Interop*). Because of this flipping of its position, from the bottom of the software pile to an emulation layer at the top, the CE COM API is not nearly as performant in the CCL as it was when it was the native CE API.

Many mainstream COM API applications can work with the CCL with just administrative and configuration changes; it's essentially swapping out some DLLs. However, there are some significant functional restrictions in the CCL, and you should review those in the product developer documentation if you plan to use the CCL.

You should not use the CCL for new work. The native CE .NET API is more powerful and flexible, on par with the original CE COM API. The CE .NET API is also more aligned with current technology trends in a Microsoft development environment.

# CEWS 3.5 protocol

The CEWS protocol used in the CM 4.5.1 release is an evolution of earlier versions of the same protocol. It differs in small but important details. As with most web services, you identify which variant you want to use by the **endpoint** you choose for your connection. Current CEWS endpoints contain `FNCEWS40` in the endpoint name (and connection URI), whereas the CEWS 3.5 endpoints contain `FNCEWS35` in the name. You might sometimes hear the shorthand terminology of "the four-oh endpoints" or "the three-five endpoints".

When using the CE APIs with CEWS transport, only the current generation of endpoints is supported. This is of no backward compatibility concern because the CE APIs take care of all of the details of formatting and reading the XML of requests and responses. To provide backward compatibility for applications written with direct calls to the earlier generation of the CEWS protocol, the CE server will accept requests in that format and respond in kind.

You should not use the CEWS 3.5 endpoints for new work. If you have applications written with the CEWS 3.5 WSDL, you should make plans to promptly migrate to the current generation of the WSDL.

*A Taste of Application Development*

# Other APIs

One thing is entirely certain—there is no shortage of APIs in CM. In the previous section, we described at some length the APIs available directly at the CE layer. There are many other APIs provided by other CM components and layers and add-on products. We refer to some of those as *boutique* APIs because of their highly specialized natures. Others are relatively full-featured and general purpose. We cannot describe all of them in this space, but we will briefly describe a few that are general purpose, widely used, or both.

# PE APIs

The Process Engine includes its own set of APIs, and you will find the JAR files for the PE Java API if you look around a bit in a CM installation. You could, in theory, write a custom BPM application using the PE APIs, but the normal CM license only entitles you to run workflows based on the pre-defined CM workflow definitions. It's not really going to be worth the effort to do custom PE development unless you also have the CM sibling product, IBM FileNet Business Process Manager (BPM).

# CMIS

We mentioned the Content Management Interoperability Services (CMIS) standard in *Chapter 1, What is ECM?*. It defines a set of REST-ful APIs and web services that can be used for most common document management operations. It was ratified by OASIS and published as a standard in May 2010.

Several ECM vendors have already announced support for CMIS interfaces to their repositories. IBM expects to ship its CMIS interface to the CE in the fourth quarter of 2010. In the meantime, there has been a CMIS technology preview for CM, publicly available from IBM's web site since October 2008. The latest iteration is based on an the ratified version of the CMIS specification. If you do an Internet search with the terms "IBM" and "CMIS", you'll find it among the first few results.

> Once the CMIS connectors are released as a product, the technology preview code will almost certainly be removed from the web site and will not be available.

Like most industry standards, the key story for CMIS is about interoperability. For common document management needs, you should be able to easily mix and match CMIS repositories from different vendors. In a practical sense, CMIS is likely to give you all the features you need for routine applications. It's still early days for this standard, but so far the support from vendors looks promising.

In many discussions with customers and partners, we have suggested they solve particular architecture problems by implementing a small set of custom web services that do exactly the handful of things they need. The web services layer then turns around and implements those things by making calls to CE APIs. This is a relatively well-received solution since it puts the customer or partner in direct control of their own environment. When a CMIS layer is available for CM, it can serve in exactly this role. The implementer can then concentrate on the business logic on the client side and use an off-the-shelf server side component as an adapter layer.

# ECM Widgets

Our discussion so far has been about APIs for implementing specific functions. In many cases, you might wish to avoid the low-level details and would like to find pre-built user interface components that you could work into an application of your own.

ECM Widgets is intended to fulfill this role. It is a set of reusable UI components for building Web 2.0-style applications. The aim is that a non-IT business analyst could combine ECM Widgets with other similar technologies in a portal-like application. Using a simple, graphical design application, widgets from various sources are selected and combined together in combinations suitable for some particular business situation. These are not merely unrelated post cards on a screen, though. Widget technology allows you to **wire** widgets together. Wiring means that one widget can pass data to another widget. The receiving widget acts on the data by rendering it or performing some other widget-specific action.

> The ECM Widgets are included with CM's sibling product, IBM FileNet BPM, and are not included in the CM licensing. We're including a mention of them here because it is so common for enterprises to use CM and BPM together. Future releases of ECM Widgets might include more CM focus, but no specific plans have been announced by IBM.

There are, depending upon how you count them, about ten separate components in the ECM Widgets 4.5.2 release. The depth and breadth of the components available have been growing over the last few releases. Most of the current ECM Widgets components are concerned directly with aspects of Business Process Management (BPM). For content-related operations, the ECM Widgets communicate with the XT application (which in turn communicates with the CE).

*A Taste of Application Development*

## AE/XT customization and integration

The IBM FileNet **Application Engine** (**AE**) and Workplace XT components include a collection of complementary components for both customizing the user experience and for integrating custom or third-party applications. We'll mention just a subset of those here.

The **Workplace Application Engine UI Service** (**AE UIS**) is a small collection of servlets that can be exploited by external applications to use parts of the pre-built Workplace UI. The technique is to do call-outs via easily constructed URLs that pass parameters to the servlets. For example, it's very common for other web applications to make call-outs to AE UIS for content download and rendering. The AE layer includes features for customizing handlers for different content types, and the outside application automatically benefits from that.

The **Web Application Toolkit** (**WAT**) is an AE-only toolkit for building model-view-controller (MVC) web applications. Workplace (but not XT) is built on top of WAT, and custom applications can also be built using it. In addition to MVC dispatching and customization, WAT provides various other application services. For example, there is an API for manipulating site and user preferences.

> WAT and AE UIS are not supported with XT. To use them, you must install AE and Workplace "classic". XT does support the `GetContent` servlet with the same usage and semantics as in AE UIS.

AE provides a form of single sign-on (SSO) where AE mediates the authentication process. The feature is called **User Tokens** in reference to opaque textual tokens passed back and forth as a credential between application components. One popular use of the User Token feature is to bypass the normal Workplace login screen when making use of the AE UIS. Including a valid User Token in the request suppresses the login screen. XT does not support User Tokens (except for its own internal use) because it is more thoroughly oriented to container-managed authentication for SSO.

## Development environments

We're not trying to make you into a developer if you aren't one already, but we'll conclude this chapter on application development by showing you how to set up a couple of development environments and run an extremely simple application using the CE APIs.

*Chapter 11*

There is a recurring irony in initial introductions to the CE APIs. Although a hefty majority of applications these days are web-based, everyone wants to do his/her initial experiments in the slightly simpler world of console applications. We're here to accommodate you, and we'll show you how to do a simple console application in both the CE Java API and the CE .NET API. In both cases, the point is not to show a really exciting application, but to show how to configure the development environment specifically for CE API work.

The application is logically the same in both Java and C#, so it's no coincidence that the explanations of them bear a strong resemblance to each other.

## CE Java API in Eclipse

For using the CE Java API, there aren't too many constraints on the development environment. Aside from using a supported **Java Development Kit (JDK)**, you could even do everything with command line utilities and a simple text editor. However, to make life easier and more efficient, most development is done using an integrated development environment (IDE). There are many Java IDEs available, and if you already use one, you should probably just continue using it.

For those making a fresh start of things, we'll use the popular Eclipse IDE, which can be downloaded at no cost from `http://www.eclipse.org`. Eclipse is available in several different bundles to suit various anticipated needs. That's mostly for your convenience. Since Eclipse has a plug-in architecture, most features can be added to an Eclipse installation at a later time.

> IBM's flagship tool for J2EE application development is Rational Application Developer (RAD). If your enterprise is already using WebSphere, there is a good chance you are already also using RAD, which used to be called WebSphere Application Developer (WSAD). Far from being a WAS-only tool, RAD is a powerful IDE for creating J2EE (and J2SE) applications for any J2EE application environment. RAD shares much with Eclipse because they come from a common heritage. The technology that IBM donated to seed the Eclipse Foundation also lay within the Rational tools family. Eclipse, with its plugin model, can be viewed as a framework upon which other tools can be built, and RAD exploits that model. If you use RAD, you should have no trouble following the descriptions of the steps done in vanilla Eclipse.
>
> In addition to RAD, IBM has a number of companion tools under the Rational and InfoSphere brands for assisting architects, developers, testers, and project managers in all phases of the product development cycle: data modeling, component design, project tracking, and others.

*A Taste of Application Development*

As of this writing, the current Eclipse release is 3.6, code-named Helios. We'll be showing examples using a non-customized download of a bundle called Eclipse IDE for Java EE Developers (in anticipation of expecting some of you to move on from simple console applications to J2EE applications, giving up your lives of idle comfort for the fast-paced world of Java in the enterprise). We won't take you through the steps of downloading and installing Eclipse since the Eclipse web site explains that well enough, and it's a fairly simple process.

When you run Eclipse for the first time and then dismiss the welcome screen, you will be left looking at a mostly empty tool configured in what is called the **Java EE** perspective. Since we're going to be doing a simple Java console application, let's switch to the **Java** perspective. From the toolbar, navigate to **Window | Open Perspective | Java**.

## The project

Let's start by creating a project and adding a class to it.

Create a new, empty project by navigating to **File | New | Java Project**. A Java project creation wizard will appear, as seen next:

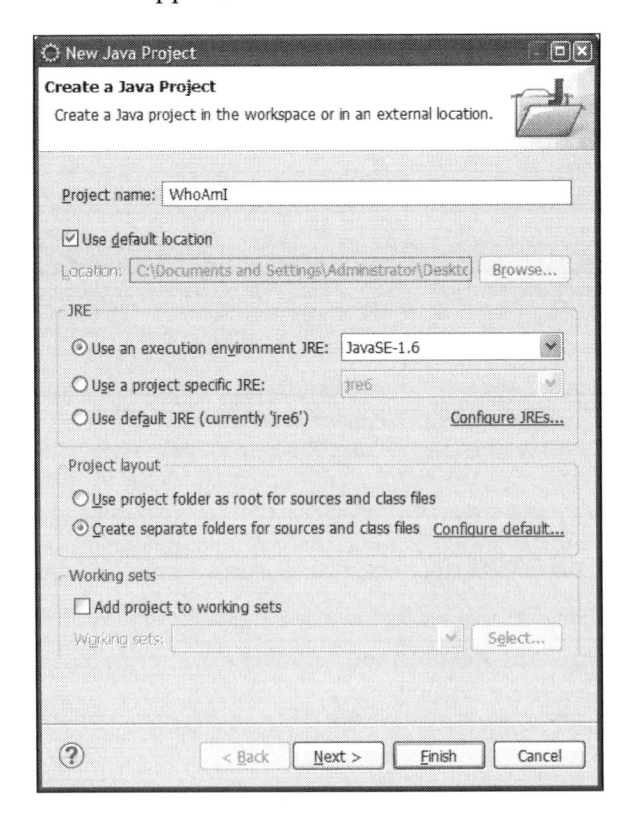

You can name the project anything you'd like. We'll use the project name `WhoAmI` in this example. You can take the defaults for all the other fields and click the **Finish** button. Your new project will appear in the left-hand **Package Explorer** panel with a small, skeletal structure.

Select the project name in the tree, right click and navigate to **New | Class**. A class creation wizard will appear, shown next. Java uses a construct called packages to prevent naming conflicts between classes. We don't really need that for this simple sample, but it's a good habit to get into. Use the package name `wjc` and the class name `WhoAmI`. (There's no actual requirement to use a name related to the project name.) Check the box to generate a `main` method, take the defaults for everything else, and click the **Finish** button.

You can expand the nodes in the **Package Explorer** to see that your class has, indeed, been created. It will also be visible in an editor tab in the center of the application. It has a minimal structure and stubbed contents. We'll return to this class is a moment.

*A Taste of Application Development*

## CE API dependencies

Obviously, Eclipse does not automatically know about CE APIs, so you will have to tell it a few things. The first thing you will need is a small collection of CE JAR files. If you are running Eclipse on a machine where you already installed the CE server or a Java-based client, you can find the necessary JAR files within that installation tree. However, for Java development, it's okay to simply copy the JAR files from another machine. You will want to make sure that your client application is using the same versions of those JARs as your CE server. The CE JAR files are not operating system specific.

The set of JARs needed is different for CEWS transport and for EJB transport. For a thick Java client (that is, for a console application), it is simpler to configure the environment for CEWS transport, so that's what we'll be doing in the rest of this section.

We installed the XT client, so copying the JARs from that location isn't a bad idea. You will find them on the Linux server in directory `/opt/ibm/FileNet/WebClient/CE_API/lib/`.

You will need a local copy of the following JAR files:

- `Jace.jar`: The actual CE Java API components. This is the only CE JAR file you will need to compile your application, but you will need additional JARs at runtime.
- `log4j.jar`: A utility for trace logging (the JAR file name may also include a version number). In addition to Jace.jar, log4j.jar is needed for running a CE Java API client application. That's true even if you are not enabling trace logging.
- `stax-api.jar`, `xlxpScanner.jar`, and `xlxpScannerUtils.jar`: The three JAR files are needed for some specialized XML parsing and are only required if your application uses CEWS transport. They are not needed if you use EJB transport (because it has its own set of dependencies).

> Satisfying runtime dependencies for CE Java API clients using CEWS transport was significantly more complicated before CM 4.5.1. Don't be confused if you come across any configuration instructions for those earlier versions.

We put our copy of all of those JAR files into a local directory called `C:/CE_API/`. Now, we'll tell Eclipse about them. Right-click the project name and navigate to **Build Path | Add External Archives**. From the file selection dialog, browse to `C:/CE_API/` and select `Jace.jar`. It will appear in the project's list of **Referenced Libraries**. The other JAR files may or may not be automatically added. If they are not automatically added, there is no need to add them manually. They are runtime dependencies, but only `Jace.jar` is a compile-time dependency.

The following image shows the **Package Explorer** window after the CE JARs have been added to the build path:

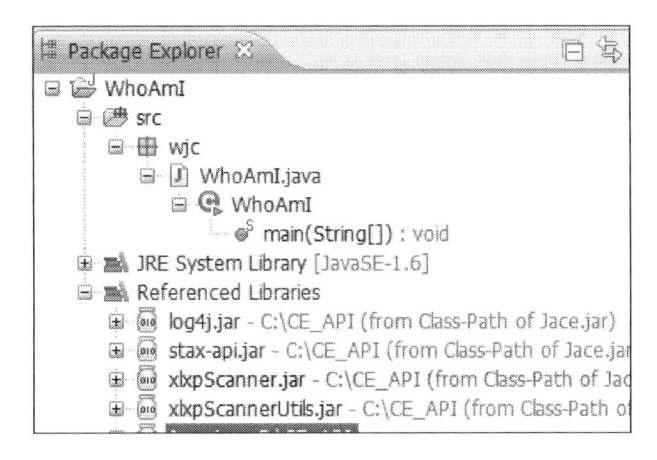

## The application code

The skeletal source code for `WhoAmI.java` should still be visible in an editor panel in the middle of the Eclipse window. Replace it completely with the following contents:

```
package wjc;

import java.util.Iterator;

import javax.security.auth.Subject;

import com.filenet.api.collection.ObjectStoreSet;
import com.filenet.api.constants.PropertyNames;
import com.filenet.api.core.Connection;
import com.filenet.api.core.Domain;
import com.filenet.api.core.Factory;
import com.filenet.api.core.ObjectStore;
import com.filenet.api.security.User;
import com.filenet.api.util.UserContext;

public class WhoAmI
```

## A Taste of Application Development

```java
{
  private static final String URI =
              "http://wjc-rhel.example.net:9081/wsi/FNCEWS40MTOM/";
  private static final String USERID = "gcd_admin";
  private static final String PASSWORD = "password";
  public static void main(String[] args)
  {
    Connection conn = Factory.Connection.getConnection(URI);
    Subject subj = UserContext.createSubject(conn, USERID, PASSWORD,
                                    null);
    UserContext uc = UserContext.get();
    uc.pushSubject(subj);
    try
    {
      doSomething(conn);
    }
    finally
    {
      uc.popSubject();
    }
  }

  private static void doSomething(Connection conn)
  {
    User u = Factory.User.fetchCurrent(conn, null);
    String uDisplayName = u.get_DisplayName();
    String uDistinguishedName = u.get_DistinguishedName();
    System.out.println("My name is:        " + uDisplayName);
    System.out.println("I am distinguished: " + uDistinguishedName);

    Domain dom = Factory.Domain.getInstance(conn, null);
    dom.fetchProperty(PropertyNames.OBJECT_STORES, null);
    ObjectStoreSet oss = dom.get_ObjectStores();
    for (Iterator it = oss.iterator(); it.hasNext();)
    {
      ObjectStore os = (ObjectStore)it.next();
      String oDisplayName = os.get_DisplayName();
      String oSymbolicName = os.get_SymbolicName();
      System.out.println("ObjectStore: dn='" + oDisplayName
                               + "', sn='" + oSymbolicName + "'");
    }
  }
}
```

> You can download this Java source file from the book's web site. See the preface for instructions.

Eclipse might report some warnings, but there should be no outright errors. You will want to replace the string values for the `USERID`, `PASSWORD`, and `URI` fields near the top of the file with values appropriate to your environment.

## Running the application

Eclipse automatically compiles the Java source file into an executable class file as you add source code text or make changes. You could take that compiled class file and run it from a command line. Instead of doing that, we'll run it from within Eclipse by creating a **Run Configuration**. From the main toolbar, navigate to **Run | Run Configurations**. In the wizard that pops up, select Java Application and click the **New** icon (it looks like a piece of paper with a small "+" sign). The resulting run configuration that appears, named after your project, should have automatically found your Java class with its `main` method.

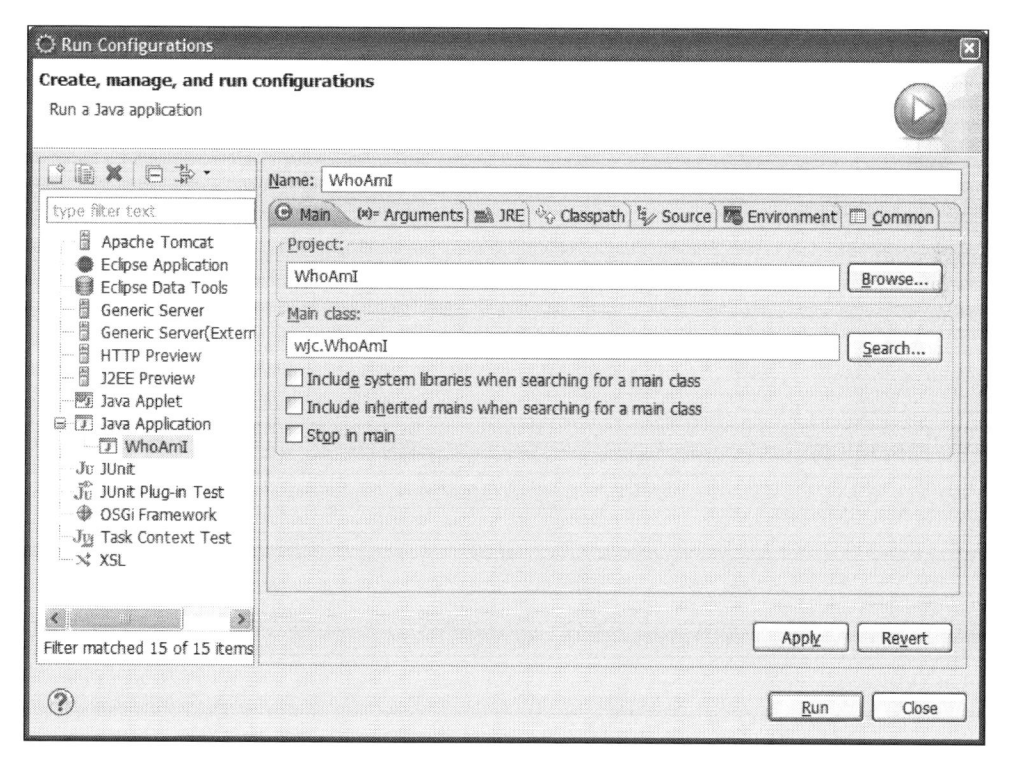

*A Taste of Application Development*

On the **Classpath** tab, check to see if it includes all of the CE Java API JAR files mentioned above. You may have to expand some nodes in the classpath tree to see them. If any are missing, add them manually by selecting the `User Entries` node, clicking the **Add External JARs** button, and navigating to `C:/CE_API/`. Click **Apply** and **Close** to configuration panel. If you didn't have to manually add more JAR files, the **Apply** button will be disabled, so just click **Close**.

With one of the nodes in your project selected, go to the main toolbar and navigate to **Run | Run**. If all goes well, you should see output in a **Console** tab that looks like this:

```
log4j:WARN The log4j system is not properly configured!
log4j:WARN All ERROR messages will be sent to the system console until proper configuration has been detected.
My name is:        gcd_admin
I am distinguished: cn=gcd_admin,cn=people,dc=whozit,dc=example,dc=net
ObjectStore: dn='Object Store One', sn='OStore1'
```

You can ignore the first couple of lines complaining about logging configuration. They are only there to annoy you (but you can get rid of them if you consult the developer documentation).

The simple sample connects to the CE, asks for information about the calling user, and then obtains and lists the names of all of the Object Stores (there is only one in our case).

## Some things we didn't show

We didn't show how to configure this application to run with EJB transport. Besides changing the URI value in the source code, you would also have to add more JARs to the runtime classpath, and you might have to do additional configuration as well.

We didn't show how to configure JAAS authentication. There is a defaulting mechanism within the CE Java API that tries to guess what you want. For simple situations like this, it is usually right. For more complex situations, you may have to explicitly tell it where your JAAS configuration file is.

We didn't show you how to liberally comment your source code, but we're sure you'll work that out for yourself.

## CE .NET API in VS C# Express

For using the CE .NET API, there are only a few choices for the development environment since there are many explicit and hidden dependencies on Microsoft components. Perhaps you already have some recent version of Microsoft Visual Studio .NET installed, in which case you can probably just use it. In any case, for convenience, you will want to use an integrated development environment (IDE).

For those making a fresh start of things, we'll use Microsoft Visual C# 2010 Express, which for brevity we'll call VC# for the rest of this section. It can be downloaded as a free trial version from `http://msdn.microsoft.com`. We won't take you through the steps of downloading and installing the VC# since the Microsoft website explains that well enough, and it's a fairly simple process. After a period of time, you will have to upgrade to a paid version or register for a free product activation key if you want to continue using this VC#.

When you run VC# for the first time, you'll be met by a few customary greetings and welcome screens. Once you've dismissed them, you will probably be left looking at a mostly empty tool awaiting the pleasure of your commands.

### The project

Create a new, empty project by navigating to **File | New Project**. A New Project creation wizard will appear. Supply a project name and select **Console Application**. You can name the project anything you'd like. We use the project name `WhoAmI` in this example. Click the **OK** button. Your new project will appear with a small, skeletal structure. A class will already have been created with a `Main` method.

We're going to do a few steps now just so things stay in parallel with the Java example above. You don't technically have to do all of these things, but for the rest of the example, we'll assume you have.

*A Taste of Application Development*

- In the **Solution Explorer**, highlight your project's name in the tree, right-click, and select **Properties**. In the configuration panel that appears, change the **Default namespace** to `wjc`. From the **Target framework** drop-down menu, select **.NET Framework 3.0**. (You might be prompted to save and reopen your project.) We used .NET Framework 3.0 because we already had it available on our development machine.

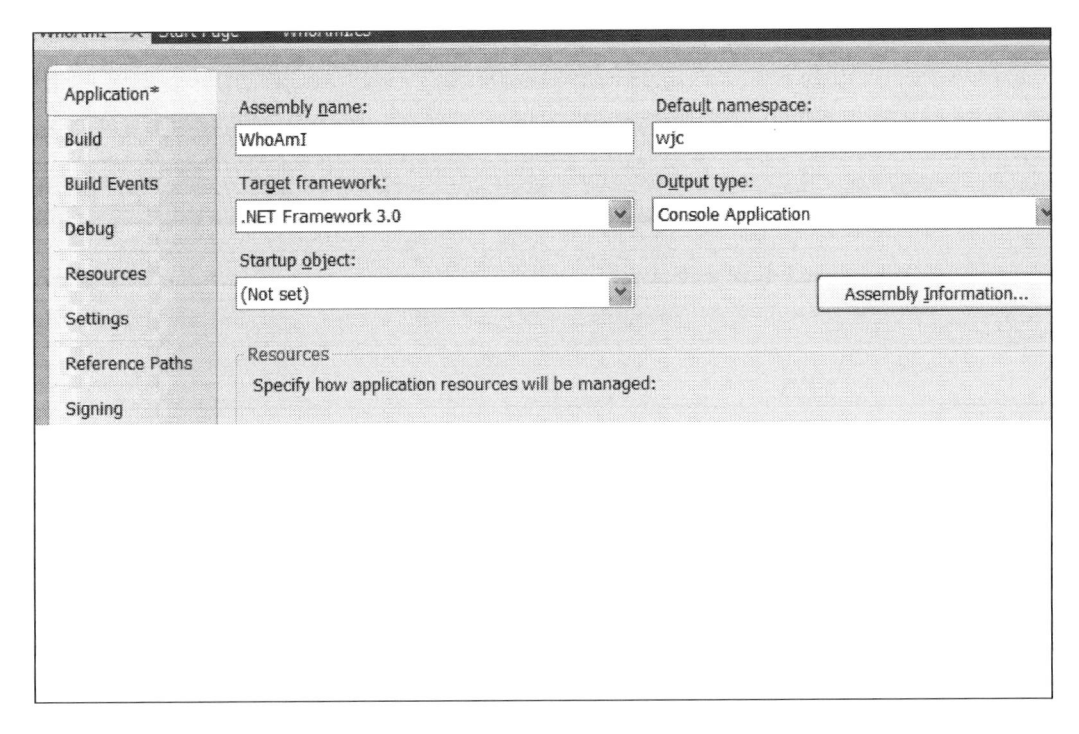

- In the **Solution Explorer**, select **Program.cs** in the tree, right-click, and select **Delete**.

- In the **Solution Explorer**, right-click the project name, **WhoAmI**, right-click, and navigate to **Add | Class**.

Give it a file name of **WhoAmI.cs** and click the **Add** button. The new file will be visible in an editor panel with stubbed contents. We'll return to this file in a moment.

## CE API dependencies

Obviously, VC# does not automatically know about CE APIs, so you will have to tell it a few things. The first thing you will need is the CE .NET API DLL file, named `FileNet.Api.dll`. If you are running VC# on a machine where you already installed FEM or another .NET-based client, you can find the necessary DLL file within that installation tree. However, for .NET development, you can also copy the DLL file from another machine. You will want to make sure that your client application is using a DLL that is the same versions as your CE server (although the CE server does not use this DLL).

We installed the FEM client, so copying the DLL from that location isn't a bad idea. You will find it on a Windows machine server in directory `C:/Program Files/IBM/FileNet/ContentEngine/`.

> In addition to the CE DLL file, you must also have Microsoft's .NET Framework (version 2.0 or later) and Web Services Extensions (WSE, version 3.0 or later). WSE is being phased out by Microsoft. You can use its replacement, Windows Communications Framework (WCF), as of CE 4.5.1 fix pack 2 if you are on a machine where WCF is supported, but there are some configuration steps that you should watch for, so look for that in the developer documentation. Our example will use WSE.

- In the **Solution Explorer**, within the **WhoAmI** project, expand the **References** node. Highlight all of the items beneath that node and delete them.

- We have our copy of that DLL file in a local directory called `C:/Program Files/IBM/FileNet/ContentEngine/` (not coincidentally the same directory used by FEM). Now, we'll tell VC# about it. In the **Solution Explorer**, within the **WhoAmI** project, right-click the **References** node and select **Add Reference**. From the **Browse** tab, browse to `C:/Program Files/IBM/FileNet/ContentEngine/` and select `FileNet.Api.dll`.

- Following a similar procedure, add a reference to the WSE DLL. It's default location (for WSE 3.0) is `C:/Program Files/Microsoft WSE/v3.0/Microsoft.Web.Services3.dll`.

*A Taste of Application Development*

# The application code

Replace the skeleton source code in `WhoAmI.cs` with the following contents:

```
using System;
using System.Collections.Generic;
using System.Text;

using FileNet.Api.Core;
using FileNet.Api.Util;
using FileNet.Api.Constants;
using FileNet.Api.Security;
using FileNet.Api.Collection;

using Microsoft.Web.Services3;
using Microsoft.Web.Services3.Design;
using Microsoft.Web.Services3.Security;
using Microsoft.Web.Services3.Security.Tokens;

namespace wjc
{
  class WhoAmI
  {
    static void Main(string[] args)
    {
      string uri =
                "http://wjc-rhel.example.net:9081/wsi/FNCEWS40MTOM/";
      string username = "gcd_admin";
      string password = "password";
      IConnection conn = Factory.Connection.GetConnection(uri);

      UsernameToken token = new UsernameToken(username, password,
                                 PasswordOption.SendPlainText);
      UserContext.SetThreadSecurityToken(token);

      try
      {
        DoSomething(conn);
      }
      finally
      {
        UserContext.SetThreadSecurityToken(null);
      }
      Console.WriteLine("Press enter");
      Console.ReadLine();
```

[ 340 ]

```
        }

    private static void DoSomething(IConnection conn)
    {
      IUser u = Factory.User.FetchCurrent(conn, null);
      string uDisplayName = u.DisplayName;
      string uDistinguishedName = u.DistinguishedName;
      Console.WriteLine("My name is:            "
                    + uDisplayName);
      Console.WriteLine("I am distinguished: "
                    + uDistinguishedName);

      IDomain dom = Factory.Domain.GetInstance(conn, null);
      dom.FetchProperty(PropertyNames.OBJECT_STORES, null);
      IObjectStoreSet oss = dom.ObjectStores;
      foreach (IObjectStore os in oss)
      {
        string oDisplayName = os.DisplayName;
        string oSymbolicName = os.SymbolicName;
        Console.WriteLine("ObjectStore: dn='" + oDisplayName
          + "', sn='" + oSymbolicName + "'");
      }
    }
  }
}
```

> You can download this C# source file from the book's web site. See the preface for instructions.

VC# might report some warnings, but there should be no outright errors. You will want to replace the string values for the `userid`, `password`, and `uri` fields near the top of the file with values appropriate to your environment.

> If you use an environment with WCF instead of WSE, one difference is that WCF insists on the use of secure connections. In that case, make sure you are using an HTTPS connection URI.

*A Taste of Application Development*

## Running the application

Running the application within VC# is quite simple. Right-click on the **WhoAmI** project node in the **Solution Explorer** and select **Build** to make sure all the latest changes have been compiled. Run the application by right-clicking the project node and navigating to **Debug | Start New Instance**. A console window will open up and you will see the output of the program. Press enter to end the program and close the window.

```
My name is:           gcd_admin
I am distinguished: cn=gcd_admin,cn=people,dc=whozit,dc=example,dc=net
ObjectStore: dn='Object Store One', sn='OStore1'
Press enter
```

The simple sample connects to the CE, asks if for information about the calling user, and then obtains and lists the names of all of the Object Stores (only one in our case).

## Some things we didn't show

We didn't show how to configure this application to run as a standalone executable. We'll leave that for you to work as as you explore VC#.

We didn't show how to run the application configured with **Integrated Windows Authentication (IWA)**. You can find those details in the product developer documentation.

We didn't show you how to liberally comment your source code, but we're sure you'll work that out for yourself.

## Summary

In this chapter, we provided a high-level overview of various APIs available with CM, and we discussed a bit of development methodology and philosophy. Our main focus was on the CE Java and .NET APIs, and we concluded the chapter by showing in detail how to configure popular IDEs for a very simple application in each.

In the next chapter, we'll be walking through a sort of case study for a small custom application. We'll start with requirements and work our way up to a functioning prototype of an application.

# 12
# The DUCk Sample Application

This chapter contains a complete, self-contained sample application that demonstrates some CM features. The application is called **DUCk**, which stands for **Documents Under Control** (the "k" is there just because we wanted to end up with the word "duck" in the grand IT tradition of creating expansions after favored acronyms have already been selected). This isn't really a development-oriented book, and the purpose of the sample is really just to show some things that are possible. For that reason, many of the low-level implementation details have been omitted for brevity but are available in the source code.

> Complete source code and other artifacts for this sample application are available for download from the publisher's website. See this book's preface for details for the download and also the usual disclaimers.

We'll go through a complete application design cycle, from concept to a first-round prototype. When we say prototype, we mean that the DUCk application is mostly functional but not necessarily polished for usability and other factors. There are also a few secondary functions that are left unimplemented. We'll mention the unimplemented things along the way. It might be fair to think of the application as a proof of technology in that it shows that things are possible without drilling down into every last detail. The DUCk application is focused mainly on the unique business requirements described in the next section and does not try to be a general document management application. It is assumed that administration and other tasks are done using IBM-provided applications or other custom applications.

*The DUCk Sample Application*

The specific things that we will look at in this chapter include:

- Business scenario and requirements
- Mock-up of the application from the user point of view
- Design of data and security models for the business scenario
- Implementation details for the prototype application

We'll conclude the chapter with information about how to actually deploy this application in your CM environment. If you are not a developer, you can download and deploy the application as-is to get a better feel for its operation. If you are a developer, source code is available so that you can tinker with it.

# Business requirements

Our enterprise has a large number of digital assets: documents, video files, images, and audio files. For simplicity, we'll refer to all of these things as documents.

Many of these documents are completely unrestricted. Perhaps they were developed in-house, or perhaps they were obtained from sources that did not impose redistribution restrictions. The enterprise refers to these generically as **unrestricted** documents:

- There is no particular extra processing required for unrestricted documents
- We will need the usual access checks: deletion and modification only by appropriate users, and so on

## Restricted quantity documents

Some documents, however, have licensing restrictions on the number of distinct copies that can exist in the enterprise. The enterprise refers to these documents generically as **restricted quantity** (RQ) documents and would like to honor the restrictions. There are enterprise policies related to intellectual property, but features of their CM-based ECM environment will be used for technical enforcement where it is feasible:

- The enterprise would like to use a model analogous to a lending library to control the number of copies in circulation. Although they only want to keep one master copy in the CM repository, users must do something equivalent to *borrowing* the item for use and *returning* the item when they no longer need it. (We're intentionally avoiding the terms *checkout* and *checkin* so that there will be no confusion with the same terms related to document versioning.)

- The system must not allow more copies to be in circulation than the quantity restrictions allow. The single copy in the repository does not count as being in circulation.
- It must be possible to find the identities of all the current holders of borrowed copies of a given restricted quantity document.

## Restricted circulation documents

Independent of the intellectual property restrictions, there are some sensitive business documents for which the enterprise would like extra control: who is authorized to access the document, and who has seen the content during its lifetime. The enterprise refers to these generically as **restricted circulation** (**RC**) documents. Again, part of that will be through policy (for example, you're not allowed to have someone watch over your shoulder as you view a video clip), and part will be via technical features of the platform:

- For each RC document, there is a specific list of users authorized to view the document content. Different documents can have different lists. The system must prevent any unauthorized user from getting a copy of the document content. There is no such restriction on the document properties.
- There must be a procedure for the owner of a document to modify the list of authorized viewers.
- Even if they have had access in the past, users removed from the list cannot get a fresh copy of the document.
- The system must keep a definitive list of who has accessed each RC document's content along with details like the date and time. It is not a requirement to track users who have merely viewed properties. If a document is deleted, this list must live on. (We will revisit this requirement during the data model design.)

The concepts of restricted circulation and restricted quantity are orthogonal. For a given document, none, both, or neither could apply.

## Design of end-user view

This section is a description of the overall end-user experience. It reflects not only the above business requirements, but also the conventions and practices of the IT department within our enterprise.

Most features will be implemented as parts of the DUCk web-based application. Because we have the magic of the writing process to help us, we can use screenshots from the actual, completed web application to illustrate things. If we didn't have that, we'd have to mock up the screens to show what we wanted. We have a few notes about details on some of the screens. We've presented those near the screenshots in this section rather than repeating similar screenshots later when we describe the implementation details.

## Common login screen

There will be a single, common login screen for all parts of the DUCk application. Any attempt at unauthenticated access will result in a redirect to the login page. All DUCk pages will feature a logout link that will result in the discarding of the security context and the transporting of the user to the login page pictured next:

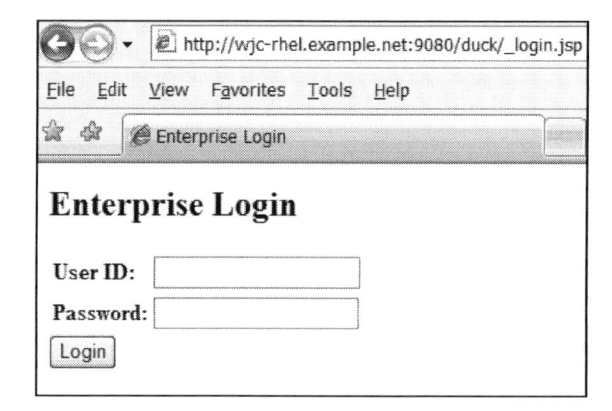

Although we are constructing the login page just for the DUCk application because of the logistics of making a standalone sample, it could be shared with other web applications deployed in the enterprise. What we are really saying is that our DUCk application will operate with common, enterprise-wide authentication, and the application will be oblivious to how the actual authentication was done. We'll illustrate with traditional form-based authentication with a userid and password, but it could be extended to any common login scheme used by the enterprise. The DUCk application has a fairly simple look and feel. The common login and related screens do not attempt to emulate that look and feel.

> In J2EE terms, we'll be using **container-managed authentication**, and we'll be using the a form-based login (in the previous screenshot) conforming to J2EE specifications. Unfortunately, the J2EE specifications don't provide a standard means for logging out, although most application servers provide proprietary mechanisms to achieve that. We wanted our sample application to be as platform-neutral as it could be, so we didn't use any of those proprietary mechanisms. Although every screen in DUCk application has a **Logout** button that takes the user back to the login screen, the user is not actually logged out at that point. The user could, for example, use the browser **Back** button to return to the previous screen and navigate from there because the session is still active.

## Find documents

The basic model will be to find documents by browsing the folder hierarchy, starting at the root folder, of a single configured Object Store. The browse process will honor the `Folder.IsHiddenContainer` property and will not show hidden folders. At each level, a list of subfolders and containees will be displayed in a predefined layout. Clicking on a subfolder name causes descent into that subfolder.

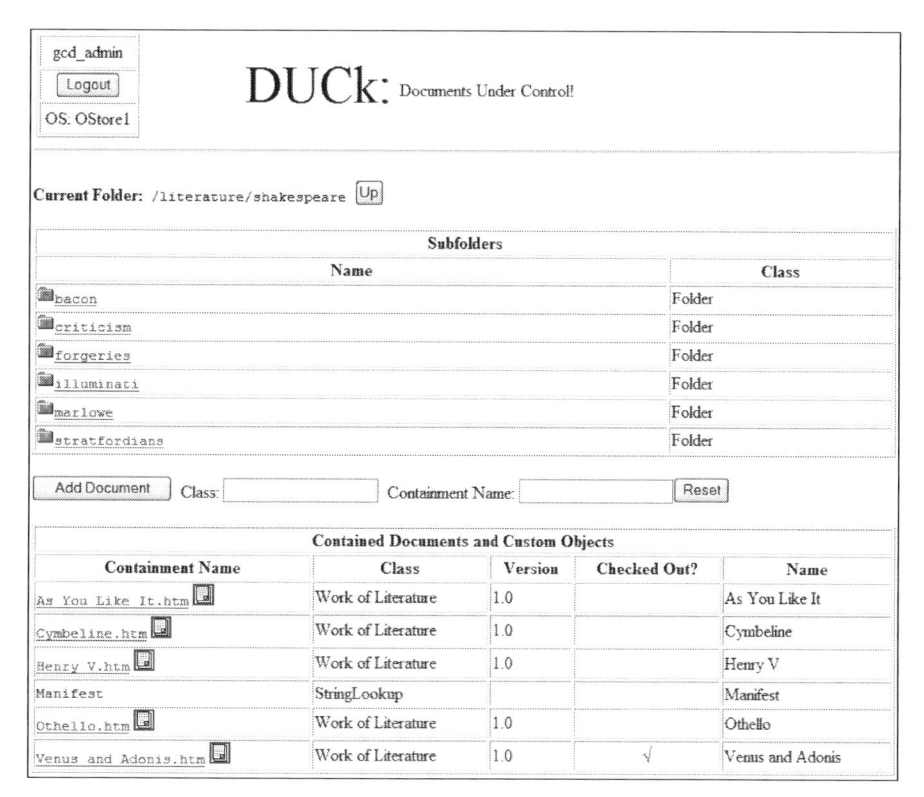

**DUCk:** Documents Under Control!

gcd_admin
[Logout]
OS: OStore1

**Current Folder:** /literature/shakespeare [Up]

### Subfolders

| Name | Class |
|---|---|
| bacon | Folder |
| criticism | Folder |
| forgeries | Folder |
| illuminati | Folder |
| marlowe | Folder |
| stratfordians | Folder |

[Add Document]  Class: _____  Containment Name: _____  [Reset]

### Contained Documents and Custom Objects

| Containment Name | Class | Version | Checked Out? | Name |
|---|---|---|---|---|
| As You Like It.htm | Work of Literature | 1.0 | | As You Like It |
| Cymbeline.htm | Work of Literature | 1.0 | | Cymbeline |
| Henry V.htm | Work of Literature | 1.0 | | Henry V |
| Manifest | StringLookup | | | Manifest |
| Othello.htm | Work of Literature | 1.0 | | Othello |
| Venus and Adonis.htm | Work of Literature | 1.0 | √ | Venus and Adonis |

There will also be a way to query for documents, and the results will be shown in the same (or similar) predefined format as for browsing.

For the query results view, the document `Name` will be shown. For the browse view, the relationship `ContainmentName` will be shown. The browse view also shows any contained Custom Objects (for example, the **Manifest** row in the previous screenshot).

In either form of the list, there will be a link on the name for each document row (this does not apply for custom objects). That link will lead to the detailed properties described above. Details of restricted quantity or restricted circulation status will be shown on the details screen, but it's not required to show those details in the list.

> If the user cannot view properties of any document, then the CE will automatically exclude that document from the results. This is normal behavior and no UI treatment is necessary. The document will simply be invisible to that user.

## Content download

Documents are also visually distinguished from custom objects by the presence of a small document icon near the containment name. The icon is always there for document rows. If the user has the right to view the content of the document, the icon is a link for displaying the content; otherwise, the icon is displayed without being a link. In the case of a disabled link, it is not required to distinguish among the cases of restricted quantity documents, restricted circulation documents, and documents for which the user does not have the right to view content for some other reason.

A document may have an arbitrary number of content elements. It must be possible to download any single content element individually. Since access control checks are at the document level, all content elements are available or all are unavailable.

Content handling on the client side is done by the user's web browser and will typically be an open/save-as dialog box provided by the browser. In the case of a `ContentReference` element, the `ContentLocation` URL is given to the user without any interpretation by the CE.

For the prototype, we use a redirect to XT for the display of content. XT provides a servlet, `GetContent`, specifically for rendering content using XT mechanisms. That servlet is accessed by constructing a URL with documented query parameters. This makes content download very easy to implement. It has the nice side-effect that graphical content is rendered by default in the Image Viewer applet included with XT. We could also have used Workplace "classic" since it has the same `GetContent` servlet. The document icon on the browse/query screen is used to open the content via XT. A new window is opened so that the navigation path in the DUCk application does not get confused.

> The `GetContent` servlet does not have a parameter for requesting a specific content element. It always assumes the caller wants the first content element. (As a special case, the Image Viewer applet knows how to navigate to additional content elements since it's common to store multi-page images that way.) To move beyond the DUCk prototype, we will either have to find a way to deal with multi-element documents or seek a relaxation of the business requirement.

## Adding a document

Authors/owners must be able to add documents into the repository. That includes the usual populating of properties, content upload, filing into a folder, and so on.

> The prototype does not implement content uploads. Doing a file upload with the standard JSF 1.2 components has well-known problems. (We'll discuss JSF below when we get to implementation details.) As a practical matter, many JSF implementations provide components to make file uploads straightforward, but we wanted to stick with the standard components for this example because this is not a book about JSF. Doing document creation directly in DUCk could be viewed as a convenience since DUCk's principal role is to facilitate access to RQ and RC documents. It is possible to add RQ and RC documents with routine actions in FEM, XT, and other tools.

*The DUCk Sample Application*

Additionally, it will include these features:

- A document may be designated as a restricted quantity document, in which case the number of authorized copies must be provided
- A document may be designated as a restricted circulation document, in which case an optional list of authorized users may be provided

If you look at the screenshot in the previous section, you will see the controls for adding a document in the middle section of the page:

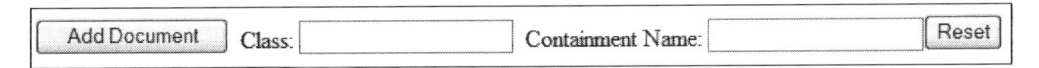

[Add Document] Class: [         ]  Containment Name: [         ]  [Reset]

The user may optionally supply the name of a specific `Document` subclass and a containment name. The user will be taken to a details page where property values can be supplied. The created document will automatically be filed into the folder currently shown in the browse/query screen.

> The list of available document subclasses should be presented to the user for selection instead of requiring that it be typed in. That's not implemented in the DUCk prototype.

## Viewing details for a document

There will be a detailed properties page where authorized viewers can see all properties of the document. Values for hidden properties (as indicated by `PropertyDescription.IsHiddenProperty`) are not displayed (this is configurable). This is also the page from which various activities related to the document are performed.

*Chapter 12*

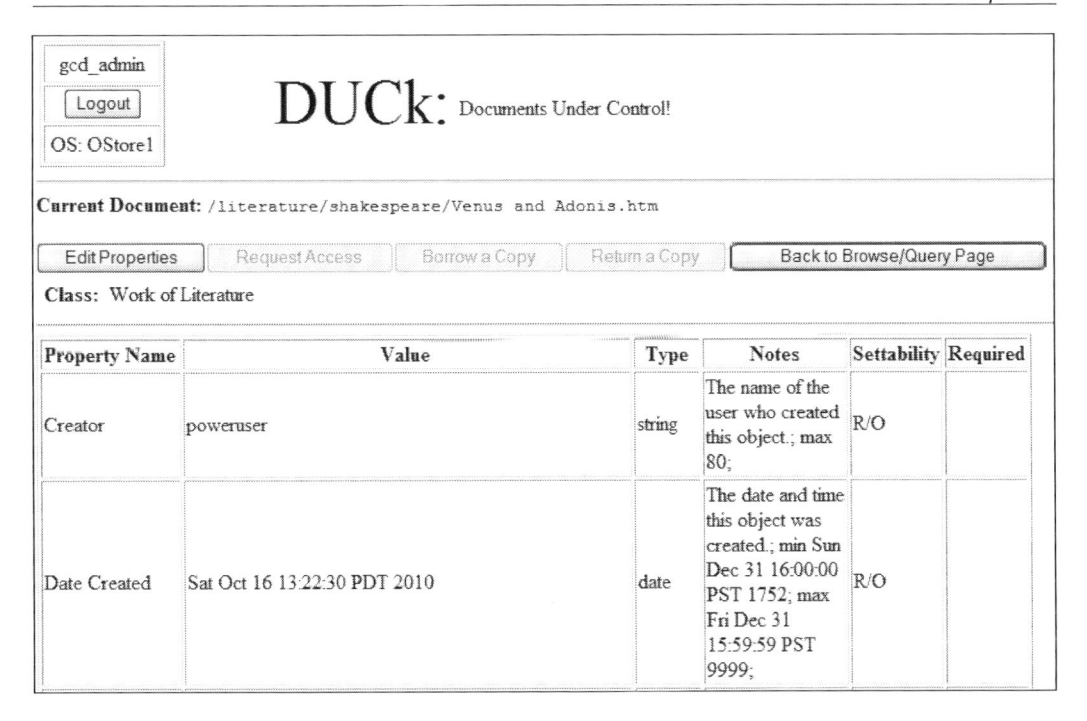

```
┌─────────────────────────────────────────────────────────────────────┐
│  gcd_admin                                                          │
│  ┌────────┐      DUCk:  Documents Under Control!                    │
│  │ Logout │                                                         │
│  └────────┘                                                         │
│  OS: OStore1                                                        │
├─────────────────────────────────────────────────────────────────────┤
│ Current Document: /literature/shakespeare/Venus and Adonis.htm      │
│ ┌──────────────┐ ┌──────────────┐ ┌──────────────┐ ┌──────────────┐ ┌────────────────────────┐ │
│ │Edit Properties│ │Request Access│ │Borrow a Copy │ │Return a Copy │ │Back to Browse/Query Page│ │
│ └──────────────┘ └──────────────┘ └──────────────┘ └──────────────┘ └────────────────────────┘ │
│ Class: Work of Literature                                           │
└─────────────────────────────────────────────────────────────────────┘
```

| Property Name | Value | Type | Notes | Settability | Required |
|---|---|---|---|---|---|
| Creator | poweruser | string | The name of the user who created this object.; max 80; | R/O | |
| Date Created | Sat Oct 16 13:22:30 PDT 2010 | date | The date and time this object was created.; min Sun Dec 31 16:00:00 PST 1752; max Fri Dec 31 15:59:59 PST 9999; | R/O | |

You can see that in this example, the buttons for **Request Access**, **Borrow a Copy**, and **Return a Copy** are disabled because this document doesn't happen to be restricted quantity or restricted circulation. (If we were looking at *Hamlet* instead of *Venus and Adonis*, we'd be tempted to say something about being neither a borrower nor a lender, but we must let that opportunity pass.)

Likewise, the **Edit Properties** button will be disabled if the user does not have the right to update properties on that specific document. The evaluation of that right does not include implicit owner/admin rights (described in *Chapter 8, Security Features and Planning*). From the screenshot, you can deduce that the document was created by **poweruser** and the logged in user is **gcd_admin**. Therefore, **gcd_admin** must have been explicitly granted `AcessRight.WRITE` (called **Modify all properties** in FEM) for that document.

## Restricted quantity documents

Recall that restricted quantity (RQ) documents are documents for which a limited number of copies may be in circulation at any given time. These requirements apply only to RQ documents:

- There will be a visible indication that it's a restricted quantity document and a way to display the list of current borrowers.

- If the user is a current borrower, there will be a link for returning the borrowed copy. There is no upload step in returning the copy, but the user is asked to confirm that he/she has deleted his/her local copy. After the return step, the page is re-displayed with the user not being a current borrower of the document.
- If the user is not a current borrower of the document but there is at least one copy available for borrowing, there will be a link for making the user a borrower.
- The download link will be disabled unless the user is a current borrower of the document.

> The DUCk prototype does not implement the display of the list of current borrowers. The list is available as a multi-valued string property on the document, so it can be viewed in any application that can display multi-valued string property values.

## Restricted circulation documents

Recall that restricted circulation (RC) documents are those for which content viewing access is tightly controlled. These requirements apply only to RC documents:

- There will be a visible indication that it's a restricted circulation document and whether or not the user is authorized to view the content.
- If the user is not authorized to view the content, there will be a link for requesting access from the owner. Access will be granted asynchronously by the owner (if granted at all).
- The download link will be disabled unless the user is authorized to view the content.
- For multi-element documents, the plan is to have a link for each content element on the details page. That is not implemented in the DUCk prototype because of the previously-described technique of using links to the `GetContent` servlet from the browse/query page.

## Modifying a document

For users authorized to update a document's properties, there will be an edit link on the document details page (see the previous screenshot). When a user clicks the edit link, the page will be redisplayed with updatable properties rendered with appropriate UI controls and a **Submit** link for the overall page, as in the following image:

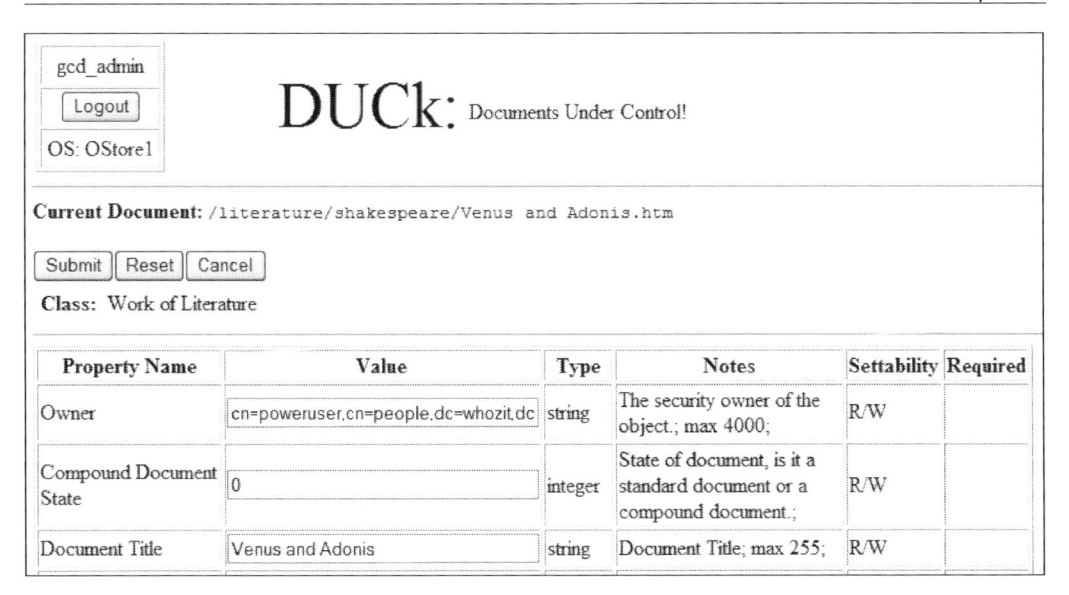

| | | | | | |
|---|---|---|---|---|---|
| gcd_admin [Logout] OS: OStore1 | **DUCk:** Documents Under Control! | | | | |

**Current Document:** `/literature/shakespeare/Venus and Adonis.htm`

[Submit] [Reset] [Cancel]

**Class:** Work of Literature

| Property Name | Value | Type | Notes | Settability | Required |
|---|---|---|---|---|---|
| Owner | cn=poweruser,cn=people,dc=whozit,dc | string | The security owner of the object.; max 4000; | R/W | |
| Compound Document State | 0 | integer | State of document, is it a standard document or a compound document.; | R/W | |
| Document Title | Venus and Adonis | string | Document Title; max 255; | R/W | |

The page will only display properties that can actually be updated, and current values will be supplied as defaults. As for the previous page for viewing details, the **Notes** column is a composite of the `PropertyDescription.DescriptiveText` property and a simple rendering of the property validation criteria (for example, minimum and maximum values for an integer property).

There are many aspects of full property editing that are not implemented in the DUCk prototype. These include: the use of choice lists to guide value selection, object valued properties, multi-valued properties, and binary (blob) properties. The processing of updated values from the UI is done via fairly simple parsers that don't have the user friendliness that would be needed for a production application (for example, we use methods `Integer.parseInt()` and `Date.parse()`).There will be a link for updating content in addition to the edit link. The content update will cause a document checkout, and the edit page will be for the properties of the reservation document. There will be a content upload link, and there will be the opportunity to commit the change (by doing a document checkin) or cancel.

> For the reason we described previously (in the description of adding a new document) the DUCk prototype does not implement content uploads.

*The DUCk Sample Application*

## Enterprise mandates

The DUCk application will be subject to the same mandates for localization, accessibility, and other standards that all of our enterprise applications must meet. The DUCk prototype does not implement most of those things.

Just to make a point about CM, however, it is easy to see partial localization if you change the preferred locale in your web browser. CE property and class display names are localizable, and localizations are provided by IBM for the display names of system properties and classes for several locales. Here, for example, is a screenshot of the edit screen for the same document as above, but with the web browser locale set to Chinese (locale `zh-CN`). No software changes are needed in the application to get those localized names because DUCk passes the browser locale into the CE API, and the CE automatically returns localized display names appropriate to that locale.

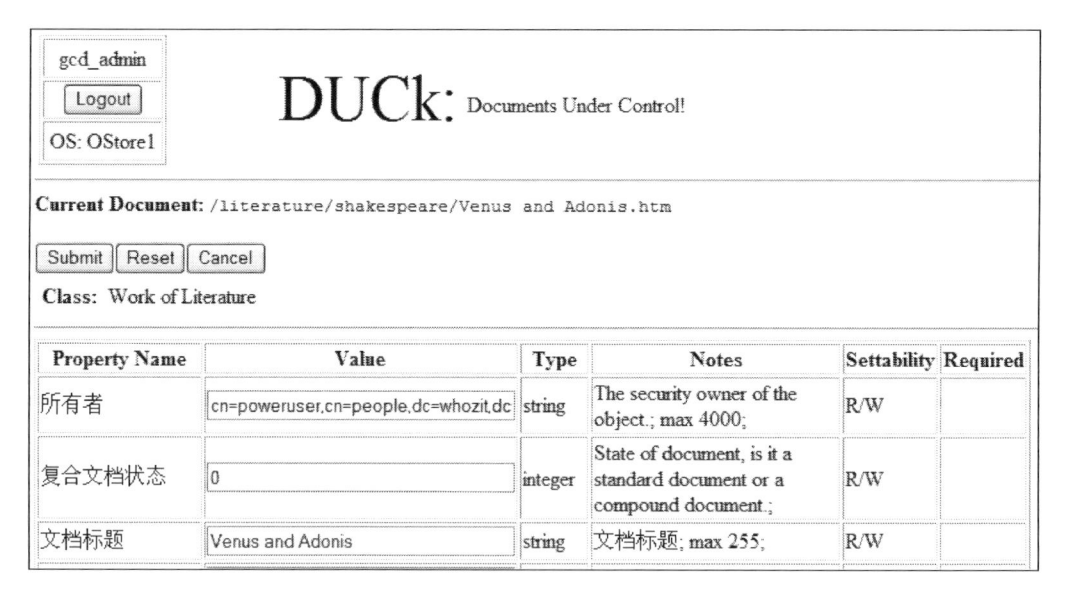

## Navigational overview

The following figure illustrates the basic navigational transitions between pages in the DUCk application. If you are familiar with editing JSF navigation rules, this may look familiar to you. The four rectangles (**BrowseQuery**, **AddDoc**, **ViewDoc**, and **EditDoc**) represent the principal screens of the DUCk application. The labeled arrows correspond to user actions which trigger transitions to another screen or back to the same screen.

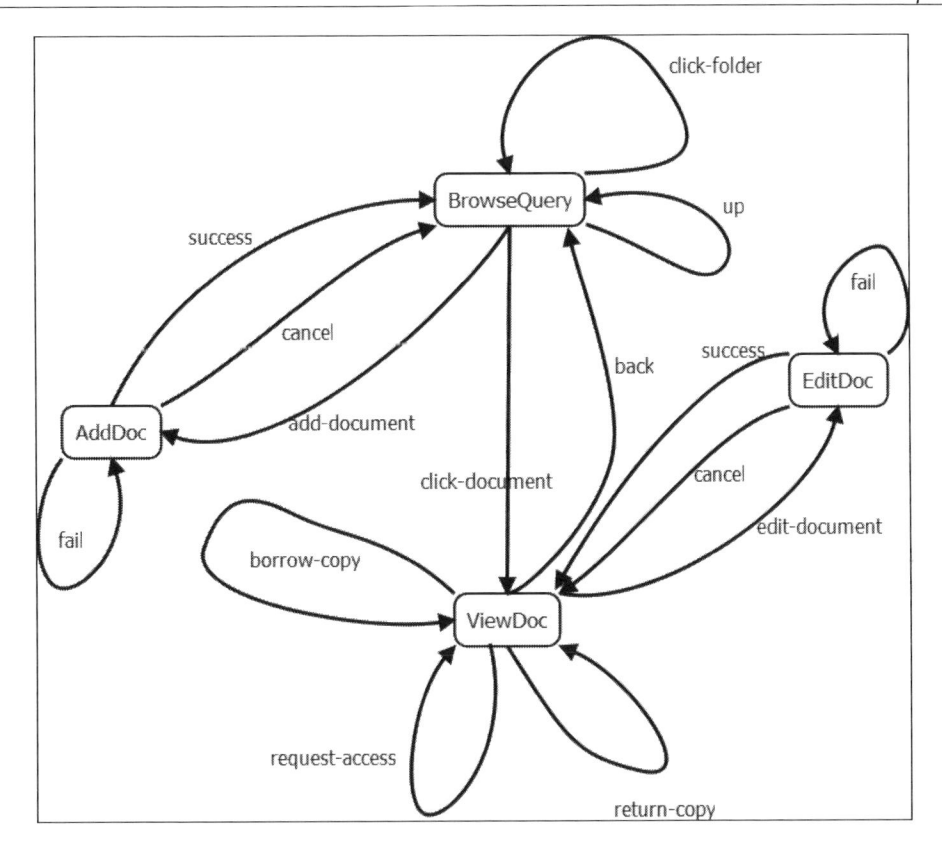

This diagram does not include the flow for the interstitial confirmation dialogs. We implemented those in the prototype as browser-native JavaScript pop-ups in the JSP pages, as in this example for the **Borrow a Copy** button (this is the Firefox version):

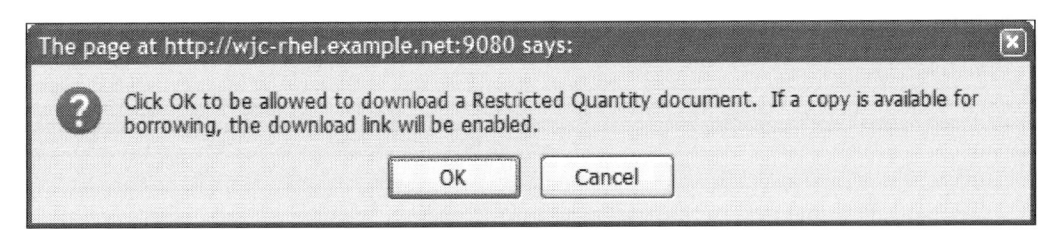

# Data model and security model

In this section, we'll delve into how CM features and application logic can be structured to implement the business requirements and the end-user application views described above. This decomposes into modeling the data—using CE classes and properties—and modeling the security—using CE security features. These are somewhat entwined, so we will describe them together.

We have designed the security and referential integrity aspects such that things won't get knocked for a loop if someone uses FEM, XT, or another application to attempt to directly modify an object. This demonstrates that you can use the CM platform itself to control those things and not rely on application logic for those critical functions.

When thinking about how your controls can be circumvented, you must always assume that someone can write an application directly with the CE APIs and bypass your application. Of course, you could say a similar thing about database access: that someone could bypass the CE and go directly the database. That's true enough, but most organizations have fairly tight controls via firewall rules or other mechanisms for who can directly access the databases.

## Document properties

Immediately, we sense that we will need one or more bookkeeping properties when a document has one of the two types of restrictions, RC or RQ. We could make a document subclass for each type of restriction, but since there are three combinations (plus the unrestricted combination), it would be awkward at best. Any other natural subclassing for document typing reasons would have to be replicated in each branch. It is simpler in this case to add any properties to the Document base class so that they will apply to all documents in the repository.

> In the following implementation details, we use symbolic names with a prefix of Wjc. That's in keeping with IBM's recommendations for using a prefix to avoid collisions with property names from unrelated projects. There is no need for such a convention for display names because display names do not have the same uniqueness requirement. Like most applications, DUCk manipulates things internally with symbolic names but uses display names in the UI. It's an unfortunate fact of naming things that short, generic, popular names are likely to be used by other parties.

## Restriction indicators

We have only two types of restrictions in our scenario, and that means that there are a lot of possible ways of indicating that any particular document has one or both restrictions. The two most obvious choices are:

- A multi-valued property (probably strings with a choice list) holding a list of applicable restrictions
- A set of individual properties indicating whether or not a particular restriction applies

There are certainly other possible approaches.

The multi-valued string property approach would give us the flexibility to add more types of special handling considerations in the future without perturbing the data model too much. On the other hand, adding new special handling types is likely to be an inherently big change for the application and data model, so we'll take the conceptually simpler approach of defining separate properties for each restriction.

We'll add the following properties to the `Document` base class:

- Symbolic name `WjcIsRestrictedCirculation`, display name `Is Restricted Circulation`. Boolean valued, default value false. If true, the document is a restricted circulation document. Value may only be updated by users with `AccessRight.WRITE_OWNER` so that the owner controls this status even if others have general rights to modify properties.

- Symbolic name `WjcRestrictedQuantityCount`, display name `Restricted Quantity Count`. Integer valued, default value 0. If the value is greater than zero, the document is a restricted quantity document with the indicated total number of available copies. Value may only be updated by users with `AccessRight.WRITE_OWNER`.

- Symbolic name `WjcRestrictedQuantityBorrowers`, display name `Restricted Quantity Borrowers`. Multi-valued string (unique and unordered) with no default values. Contains a list of the identities (directory distinguished names) of the current borrowers. Value may only be updated by users with `AccessRight.WRITE_OWNER`.

## Restricted circulation

There are two basic requirements for RC documents: controlling the actual content viewing, and keeping track of who has seen the content over its lifetime.

## Access logging

To create a historical record of who has viewed a restricted circulation document, it would be nice to use standard CE audit logging. By audit logging content retrievals, we would have a perfect record of accesses to the restricted circulation documents. Unfortunately, there is a pragmatic consideration that makes this a poor solution for our scenario.

Audit logging can only be enabled for an entire class, and we have already decided that a document of any class may be designated as restricted circulation. We must, therefore, enable audit logging of all content retrieval operations for all documents. Content retrievals are a large part of repository activity, and that would produce a huge number of audit log records. It would be likely to impact both performance and our ability to manage the audit logs themselves. We could revisit our decision to allow documents of any class to be designated as RC, but we'd like to keep that flexibility.

Instead of audit logging, we could instead turn to event subscriptions. There are two nice features to address the problems we saw with audit logging:

- An event subscription can be associated with an instance of a document rather than an entire class. If the number of RC documents were relatively small, instance subscriptions might be attractive.
- Event subscriptions have a filter expression. The filter expression is similar to a CE SQL WHERE clause (with some restrictions). If the filter expression evaluates to false, the event subscription handling is skipped. We could apply the subscription to all document classes but use a filter expression that would be true only if WjcIsRestrictedCirculation were true.

So, why not use an event subscription? The simple reason is that there is no subscribable event for content retrieval. The content retrieval event is only available as a trigger for audit logging.

Our use case requires only that we keep track of those users who have viewed the content of a restricted circulation document. We are not required to keep a list of those who have been authorized to view the document. It only matters if they actually took advantage of that authorization to actually download the content. As we have just seen, we can definitely achieve the business requirement, but the cost is very high. As a result, we have explained the situation to the business stakeholders, and they have agreed that it would be acceptable to record those who have been granted access to each document as long as we also record the date and time when they were given access or when it was taken away.

We can meet this revised business requirement by keeping track of restricted document creations, deletions, and security updates. Those operations are rare compared to content retrievals, but are they rare enough so that we're not worried about volume problems with audit logging? Probably so, but that's a judgment that has to be made for each environment. For our scenario, we will assume it is adequate.

> An alternative to audit logging would be to use an event subscription for those events along with a filter expression that limited them to restricted circulation documents. The event handler could log the security information to a private, non-repository location.

## Access control

The owner of a document controls access to it, and we will use the standard `AccessRight.VIEW_CONTENT` right to control who can see content for a restricted circulation document. We'll use directly applied user-specific ACEs to apply or remove that right.

## Requests for access

When a user requests access to a restricted circulation document, it will trigger an approval workflow targeted to the document owner. The actual workflow approval will do nothing of consequence, but the owner will not act on the approval until s/he has manually updated the access to the document. (It would also be possible to configure the PE Component Manger to make a call back into the CE repository and directly update the document permission as part of the workflow approval process.)

> Although we created the access request implementation for RC documents, it is decoupled from the RC document audit logging requirement and implementation. There's no reason the access request mechanism couldn't be used for any document for which the caller desires to see the content. In fact, DUCk only checks for the right to view content in deciding whether or not to enable access requests. DUCk doesn't care why the user doesn't have that right.

The DUCk application does not contain workflow inbox features. The standard XT workflow monitoring features or those of another application can be used.

*The DUCk Sample Application*

The implementation of the strategy for access requests consists of two parts—the approval workflow and the trigger for it:

- For the trigger, our application will use a custom event. A custom event is just a subclass of the CE `CustomEvent` class, created like any other subclass via FEM. This custom event has symbolic name `WjcRequestContentAccessEvent` (and display name of `Request Content Access Event`). At an appropriate time, the DUCk application will trigger the custom event by calling the `raiseEvent()` method on the document, passing an instance of the custom event as a parameter. Semantically, the raising of the custom event connotes "the calling user requests access to this document". A CE Class Workflow Subscription on the `Document` base class for the custom event launches the approval workflow.

> Using an event to launch the workflow is another interesting instance of decoupling components. The DUCk application does not have any workflow logic at all and includes no calls to the PE API. In fact, the DUCk application does not even know what the servers do in reaction to the `WjcRequestContentAccessEvent` custom event. It only knows that the custom event is the way that a user requests access to document content. This also makes it very easy to implement the same logic in other applications. They need merely raise that custom event.

- If the site is a BPM licensee, then the Process Designer can be used to create a workflow of any desired routing. Without a BPM license, one of the predefined approval workflows included with CM can be used. All that is necessary is that the approval workflow gets routed to the document owner for approval. The calling (requesting) user will be indicated as the originator of the work object.

> The DUCk prototype raises the `WjcRequestContentAccessEvent` custom event but does not implement the workflow subscription. The **Request Access** button in the UI does nothing interesting.

It's not part of the DUCk requirements, but we could use the same idea of a custom event and a workflow to request that the owner of the document remove a user's access to it.

# Restricted Quantity

The requirements for RQ documents are to manage the borrow/return process and to restrict content retrievals to current borrowers of a given document. That means that we must keep track of the total number of copies that may be borrowed and the list of current borrowers. The number of available copies for borrowing may be easily deduced from those two things.

We don't want users to be able to directly manipulate the properties that keep track of borrowing. Through carelessness or malice, users could disrupt the bookkeeping and hinder our ability to enforce the maximum copy count.

Our first inclination would be to have the bookkeeping done inside the server via an asynchronous subscription event handler tied to the RQ document. We'd use an asynchronous subscription because a synchronous subscription event handler is not allowed to update the triggering object's properties. There are a couple of problems with this approach:

- It's asynchronous, so there is a short but unpredictable delay between the user clicking a link to borrow a copy and the content actually being available for retrieval by that user. That's probably not too bad in practice since the delay will usually be significantly less than a second. The application could implement a loop with a short delay to smooth the user experience.

- There is a race condition. Suppose there is a single copy left to be borrowed, but two users simultaneously click the borrow link. Both users will believe they have been granted a copy, but the event handler that fires second will not add that user to the list since the copy count will already be at the maximum. This presents some tricky UI issues for the application. An asynchronous event handler has no built-in notification mechanism for failures other than the CE log file.

It will be easier to build the application and will lead to a better user experience if we can have some sort of synchronous commitment from the CE that the borrow operation has succeeded or definitely will succeed. The usual practice in such situations is to put the updating business logic into the application and rely on a synchronous subscription event handler to inspect the update and veto it if it isn't appropriate.

## The DUCk Sample Application

The solution we will use is to put the total count and list of borrowers on the RQ document as described above. We'll then use a satellite object to synchronously handle the events and update the RQ document properties. There are many implementation choices for this satellite object (by which we merely mean that it is secondary to the "real" object, the RQ document), but we like to use the handy built-in Annotation class when we can. It has instances with some favorable characteristics:

- An annotation is associated with a particular object called the annotated object. The annotation cannot be moved to another object (because the AnnotatedObject property can only be set at the time the annotation is created).

- The Annotation base class has only a few properties, most of which we do not care about. If we have to, we can give access to all of the annotation properties without worrying about strange side effects.

- An annotation is automatically deleted when its annotated object is deleted. That makes it easy to avoid referential integrity problems.

Naturally, if we didn't already have the Annotation class available, we could construct all of those same things from scratch using, for example, a CustomObject subclass and standard CE features.

We will define a custom subclass of Annotation called WjcRestrictedQuantitySatellite, display name Restricted Quantity Satellite. We don't need any custom properties for this annotation subclass since we're only using it in this satellite object capacity. In fact, the use of a custom subclass is only to distinguish the particular annotation we will be using from other annotations that may happen to be associated with the document.

The act of borrowing or returning a copy is implemented as updating the WjcRestrictedQuantityBorrowers list to add or remove, respectively, the calling user's identity. The business logic for this is implemented in handler for a WjcRestrictedQuantityBorrowReturnEvent raised on the annotation. The handler for that event (DuckRQB, described more fully below) performs the following actions:

- If the annotated document is not an RQ document, no action is taken.

- If the calling user's identity is on the list of borrowers, the operation is a return. The user's identity will be removed from the list of borrowers.

- Otherwise, it is a borrow operation. The user's identity will be added to the list of borrowers if there is at least one copy available for borrowing. If there is no copy available, the handler will throw an exception.

*Chapter 12*

> Assuming the consistency checks pass and the update is interpreted as either a borrow or a return operation, the event handler will also update the ACL on the annotated document to either create an ACE to ALLOW the `AccessRight.VIEW_CONTENT` right for the calling user or search for such an ACE and remove it. The removal requires looking for the access right in all user ACEs because the server may have combined that right with others when it consolidates ACEs. The DUCk prototype doesn't deal with `AccessRight.VIEW_CONTENT` granted or denied via a group ACE or an inherited or template ACE. Group ACEs can be dealt with via a more complicated calculation in the event handler, but inherited and template ACEs must be brought to someone's attention for manual correction.

The handler will also be associated with the standard `CreationEvent` and `UpdateEvent` for documents. If it detects the `WjcRestrictedQuantityCount` being changed to a positive number, it will create the `WjcRestrictedQuantitySatellite` annotation so that it can then be the target of the custom event. If it detects the count being changed from a positive number to zero or a negative number, it will delete the annotation.

# Technical implementation details

The entire DUCk solution consists of various unique pieces:

- CE metadata changes
- The DuckRQB event handler
- The DUCk web application

We'll describe each of those in this section.

## CE metadata changes

The metadata changes for the DUCk solution are fairly simple: a single custom class and a few custom properties. For a production application, you would be likely to create a CE AddOn (described in *Chapter 7, Major CM Features*), or perhaps one or more XML files that could be imported via FEM. The first step in doing those would be to manually create the metadata changes in a development Object Store, and that's what we'll describe here.

We showed some examples of metadata changes in *Chapter 4, Administrative Tools and Tasks* in the *Subclassing Example* section. You may wish to refer back to that section as you complete these metadata changes.

## The annotation subclass

Create a custom subclass of `Annotation` called `WjcRestrictedQuantitySatellite`. In FEM, in the tree view, navigate to **Object Stores | Object Store One | Other Classes | Annotation**. Right-click and select **New Class** to launch the **Create a Class Wizard**. Give this class a name of **Restricted Quantity Satellite** and a symbolic name of **WjcRestrictedQuantitySatellite**. On the **Select Properties** panel, there are no custom properties to add.

## Custom document properties

The custom properties applied to the `Document` base class are used to indicate whether a document instance is an RQ or RC document. In FEM, in the tree view, navigate to **Object Stores | Object Store One | Document Class**. Right-click and select **Add Properties to Class** to launch the wizard. On the **Select Properties** panel, click the **New** button and create the following custom properties:

- `WjcRestrictedQuantityCount`. Use a display name of **Restricted Quantity Count**. Integer valued with default value 0.
- `WjcIsRestrictedCirculation`. Use a display name of **Is Restricted Circulation**. Boolean valued with default value false.
- `WjcRestrictedQuantityBorrowers`. Use a display name of **Restricted Quantity Borrowers**. Multi-valued string property with no default.

All of those properties must have a **Modification Access Required** of **Modify owner** (`AccessRight.WRITE_OWNER`).

## Custom events

Create the following custom event subclasses. In FEM, in the tree view, navigate to **Object Stores | Object Store One | Other Classes | Event | Object Change Event | Custom Event**. Right-click and select **New Class** to launch the **Create a Class Wizard** for each of the following:

- `WjcRequestContentAccessEvent`. Use a display name of **Request Content Access Event**. In the DUCk prototype, this event is not used in any subscriptions.

- `WjcRestrictedQuantityBorrowReturnEvent`. Use a display name of **Restricted Quantity Borrow/Return Event**. This event will be associated with `DuckRQB` below.

Neither of these custom event subclasses has any custom properties.

## Audit logging configuration

We're going to keep track of access changes by doing audit logging of document creation, deletion, and security updates.

Enable audit logging for the Object Store by right-clicking on **Object Store One** and selecting **Properties**. On the **General** tab, check the box for **Auditing Enabled**.

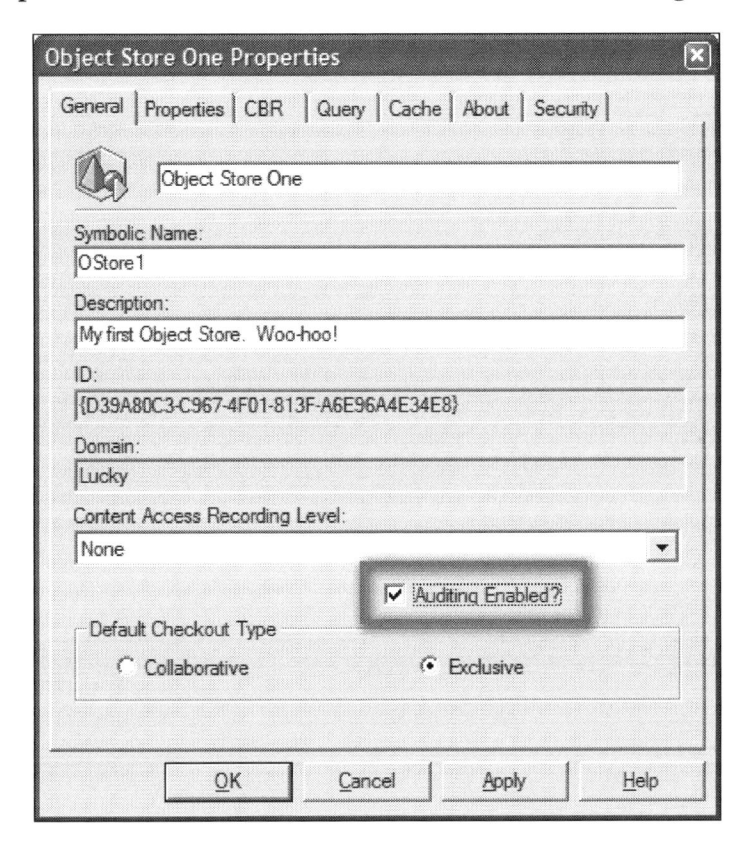

*The DUCk Sample Application*

In FEM, in the tree view, navigate to **Object Stores | Object Store One | Document Class**. Right-click and select **Properties**. From the pop-up panel, select the **Audit Definitions** tab. Create audit definitions for **Creation, Deletion,** and **Update Security** events. All should audit for **Success** and all should **Apply to Subclasses**.

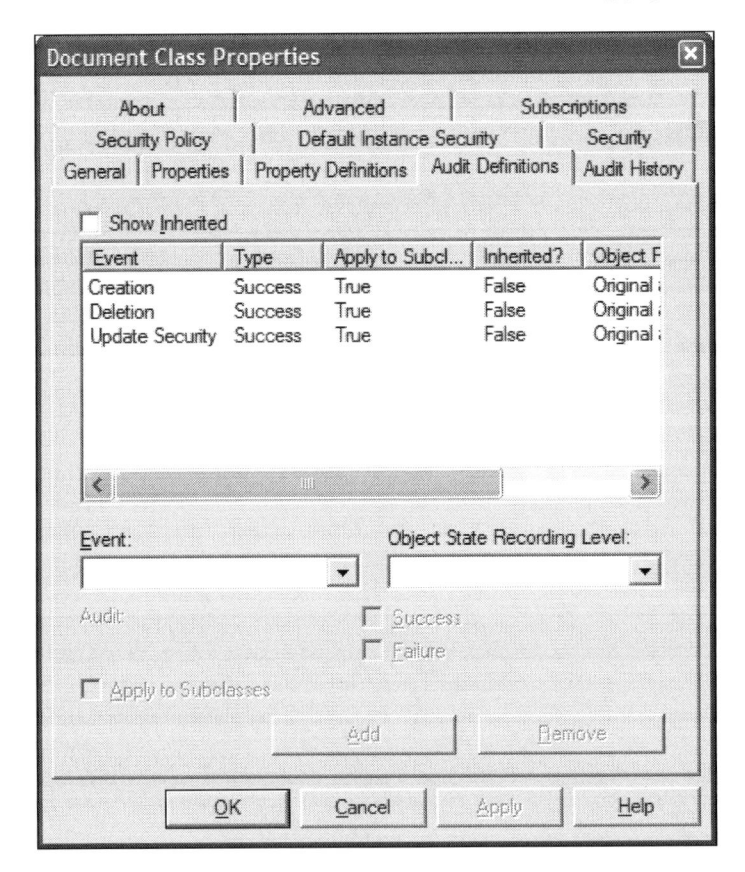

# Deploying the event handler code module

We've provided the event handler code as both an Eclipse project and as a JAR file that you can deploy without the use of any development tools.

> A CE event handler (actually, any code module in general) can be packaged as a standalone Java class file or as a JAR file. Either would work for this simple example, but we recommend getting into the habit of using a JAR file. It's not really much more trouble, and it gives you more flexibility for partitioning a more complex event handler into multiple classes. It also gives you a place to put resource files if you decide to localize your exception messages and other text.

# The DuckRQB project

The CE event handler code for dealing with Restricted Quantity borrowing and returning is in an Eclipse project called `DuckRQB`. Like most CE event handlers, it's just a single Java class: `net.example.wjc.duck.DuckRQB`. We have also included the compiled class, bundled inside a JAR file so that can use it as-is. Here are instructions for compiling it yourself in Eclipse in case you wish to do so (and which we hope will encourage you to tinker with it a bit).

Import `DuckRQB` as a project into Eclipse via the procedure described later for the `Duck` project. The filename for the project in the downloadable material is `duckrqb.project.ZIP`. You will need to have a copy of `Jace.jar` from CM to compile the sample code, and the `DuckRQB` project is configured to find it in the standard location for a Windows environment. However, when you deploy the event handler, the classes from `Jace.jar` are provided by the CE server runtime environment. You don't have to worry about packaging any CE JAR files with your event handler.

Right-click the project node in the Eclipse Project Explorer and select **Export**. Navigate to **Java | JAR File** and click **Next**. During development, we favor exporting pretty much everything, including the source code. That can help you keep track of what version is actually deployed as you iteratively modify things. For production, you may wish to include only the Java class files and any resources in your deployed JAR file. Save the JAR file in some convenient location with some suggestive name.

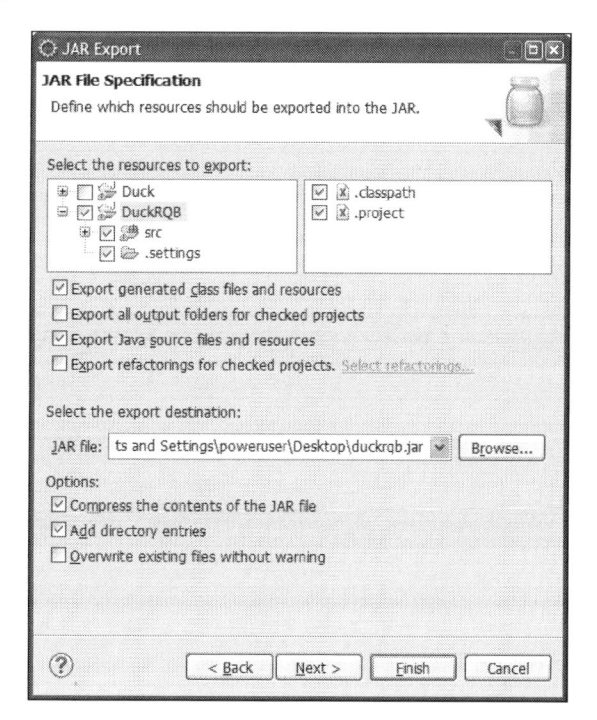

For the sake of discussion, we'll assume you have choosen `duckrqb.jar`, the same name as the pre-made JAR file that we've provided for you. Your exported JAR file should also have the same contents as ours.

## New code module

You have a choice of installing the JAR into a CE repository as a code module or placing it onto the application server classpath. Many developers prefer the classpath approach because it seems less complicated. It does, however, mean restarting the application server for any changes, and that can be an annoyance during iterative development. We use the code module approach and suggest that you use it, too, since that is the approach that you will use in production.

Deploying a code module for a new subscription is fairly painless since FEM has a wizard that will lead you through the steps. For our case, right-click the **Document** class node in FEM and select **Add Subscription** to launch the wizard to add a synchronous handler for **Creation Event** and **Update Event**. Click the **New** button to create an Event Action, and you'll be prompted for the location of the class or JAR file and the fully-qualified name of the Java class: **net.example.wjc.duck.DuckRQB**. FEM will create all the needed linkages and will file the code module object into the Object Store's `/CodeModules/` folder. The filing is for your convenience and is not a requirement for using a code module.

> You can also place a code module into the Object Store just like any other document, and you can file it or not, as you wish. If you do create a code module manually, be sure it is created as an instance of the `CodeModule` class or it won't be usable. See the product documentation for other code module considerations.

Right-click on the **Restricted Quantity Satellite** class node in FEM and select **Add Subscription**. This time, the event is **Restricted Quantity Borrow/Return Event**, and you should use the **DuckRQB** code module that we just created. The code module has conditional logic so that it can be used for multiple purposes. It will know what type of event is triggered and what the triggering object is.

## Modifying a code module

The process for modifying a code module, which you will surely do during development, is a bit more complicated because the internal linkages reference a specific document version as the code module. So, whether you create a completely new code module for each iteration or do a checkout/checkin cycle for a single code module's Version Series, the subscription linkage must be updated to point to it. We'll describe that process here.

Use FEM to locate your code module (probably in the /CodeModules/ folder). Perform a normal checkout/checkin cycle to update the content of your code module. For simplicity, we suggest that you do not use minor versions. FEM will now be displaying the latest version of the code module, but it is not yet referenced by anything. (If FEM is not displaying the correct major/minor version numbers, you may have to refresh the view of the /CodeModules/ folder.) Right-click on the code module and select **Copy Object Reference**. That puts a pointer to that specific object into a clipboard of sorts in FEM.

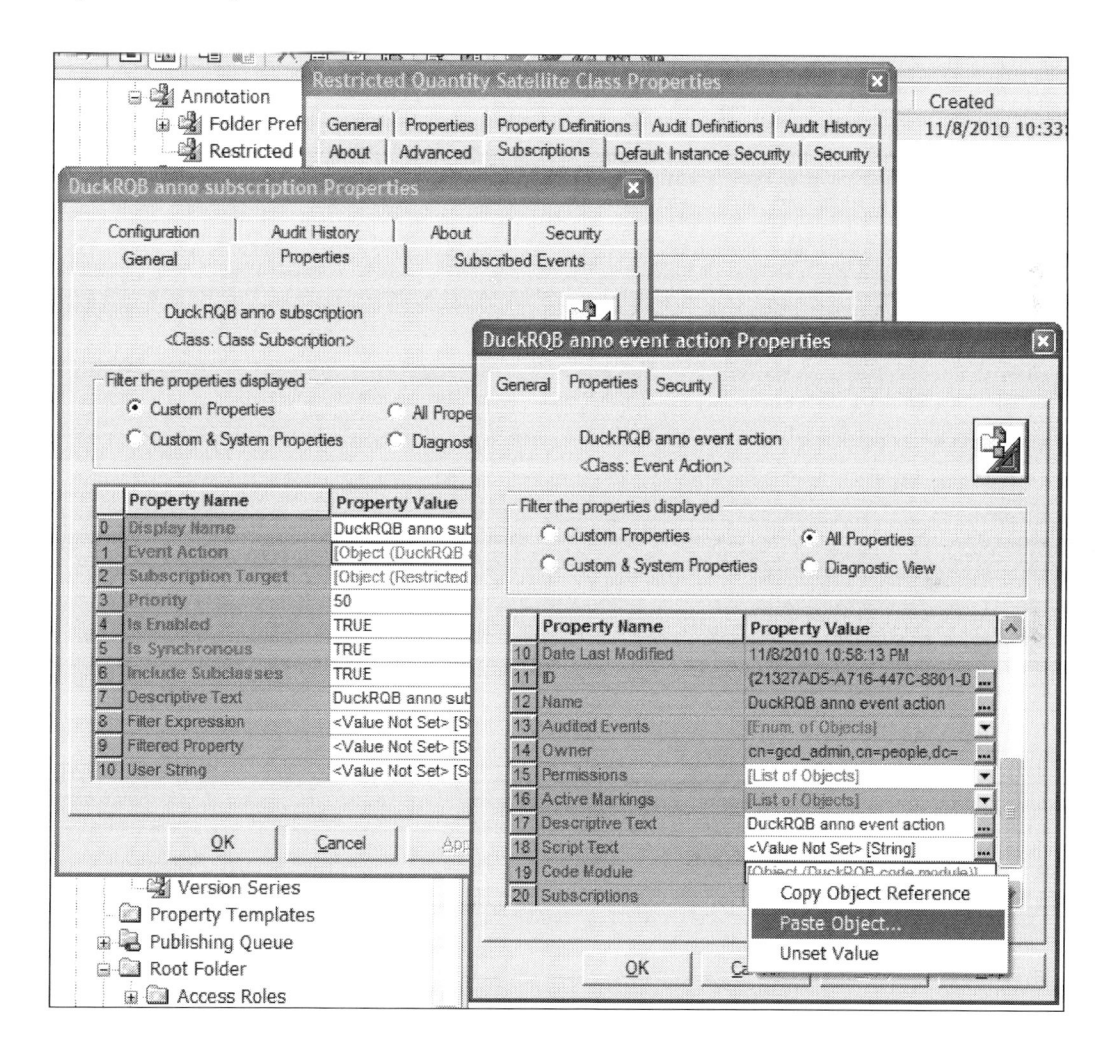

Refer to the previous figure for the following steps:

1. Right-click the `Restricted Quantity Satellite` class node, select **Properties**, and click on the **Subscriptions** tab.
2. You will see the subscription you created. Select it and then click the **Properties** button. The subscription properties pop-up will appear. Click on the **Properties** tab to get the generic property sheet.
3. One of those properties will be `Event Action`. Click on its row in the **Property Value** column. The event action properties pop-up will appear. Click on the **Properties** tab to get the generic property sheet.
4. Select the **All Properties** filter choice. One of the properties in the list will be `Code Module`. If you click on its **Property Value** column, the code module properties pop-up for the earlier version of the code module will appear. That's not what we want. Instead, right-click on the **Property Value** column for that row and select **Paste Object**. After a confirmation dialog, the previously copied object reference (the one we copied earlier) will be used to populate that `Code Module` property value.

Repeat the preceding steps for the **Document** class. We'll be the first to admit that this process seems a little arcane and arbitrary. It comes across that way because FEM doesn't have specific helper panels for this, so we used the generic property sheets. Of course, revising a code module in production is a pretty rare event. After you've done this a few times, and if you've used logical names for the subscription, the event action, and the code module, we think you'll forget about its arbitrary nature and be able to click through it quickly.

Once you've updated a code module, you can delete older versions of the code module at your leisure. The CE will not let you delete a code module that is referenced by any subscription, so you don't need to worry about that aspect.

## Debug logging

Our `DuckRQB` code module class has some rudimentary debug logging built in. The debug logging, if enabled, is simply written to standard output. For our WAS CE, that ends up in the file `/opt/ibm/WebSphere/AppServer/profiles/AppSrv02/logs/server1/SystemOut.log`.

Logging is disabled by default. You can enable it by setting the Java system property `DuckRQB.debuglog` to the value `true`. In WAS, you can do that via the WAS console by navigating to **Servers | Server Types | WebSphere application servers | server1 | Java and Process Management | Process Definition | Java Virtual Machine**. In the text box for **Generic JVM Argument**, add **-DDuckRQB.debuglog=true**. To disable logging, either remove that item or change the value to **false**. In any case, you will probably have to restart the application server for the new value to take effect.

Remember, you are controlling debug logging for the event handler running inside the CE, so you want to do these manipulations on the CE instance of the application server.

## The Duck project

We did the implementation of the DUCk web application using **JavaServer Faces (JSF)**. This isn't the cutting edge technology that it was thought to be a few years ago, but it's still a fast way to create an application. It has reasonable component libraries, especially for the straightforward things we want to do, and it works with all of the application servers supported by CM. We'll leave it to you, if you are so inclined, to re-implement the application as an in-browser AJAX application or whatever else would make it look slick and modern in your enterprise's eyes.

We'll be using the popular open source integrated development environment Eclipse to create the application. We're using Eclipse 3.6.0 (http://www.eclipse.org; specifically, we're using the bundle called Eclipse IDE for Java EE Developers) and will be using the Apache MyFaces implementation of JSF (http://myfaces.apache.org). Although there is an Apache MyFaces release corresponding to JSF 2.0, we'll use the version corresponding to JSF 1.2 because our needs are simple and because there is a better guarantee that you will find support for it in your environment. For example, it's possible to install and use JSF 2.0 with WAS 7, but it has JSF 1.2 out of the box.

The downloadable material for this chapter includes complete Eclipse projects as ZIP files. You can put a ZIP file in any convenient location (it is not necessary to unZIP it) and import it into your Eclipse workspace by navigating to **File | Import | General | Existing Projects into Workspace**. Choose **Select archive file** and browse to the ZIP file. The project will be imported as a new project in your Eclipse workspace. The project names will be the ones we used when we created them.

*The DUCk Sample Application*

The filename for the DUCk web application Eclipse project is `duck.project.ZIP`. Import it into Eclipse as described just previously. In short order, the Duck project will appear in the Eclipse Project Explorer panel, as seen here:

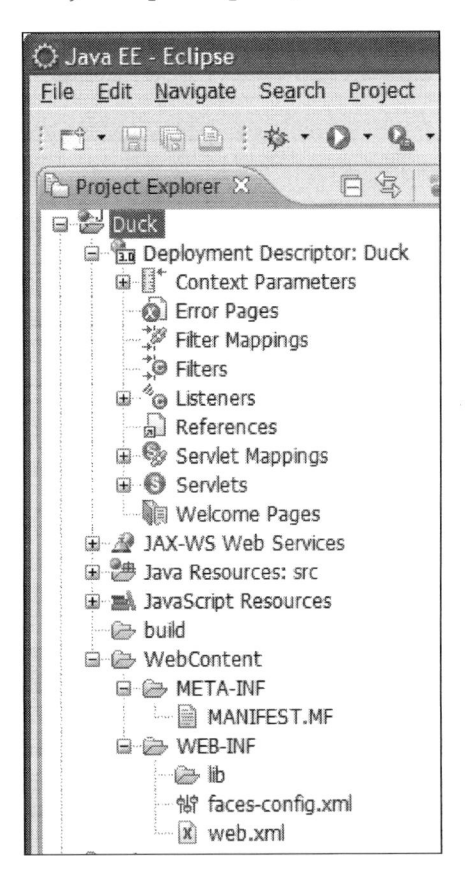

> You will also need references to `Jace.jar` and `log4j.jar` provided by the CE client installer. If your copies of those JARs happen to be in the same location as ours, then your project might be OK as-is. If they are in a different location, Eclipse will mention some build path errors to you, and you will need to correct the locations of those JAR files.

If you have not previously installed a JSF implementation package, you can easily download one from within Eclipse. Select the project name **Duck** in the **Project Explorer**, right-click and select **Properties**. In the pop-up dialog box, navigate to **Project Facets | Java Server Faces**. If you do not see an entry for JSF 1.2 (as in the following screenshot), click the download icon (the floppy disk with a down-pointing arrow).

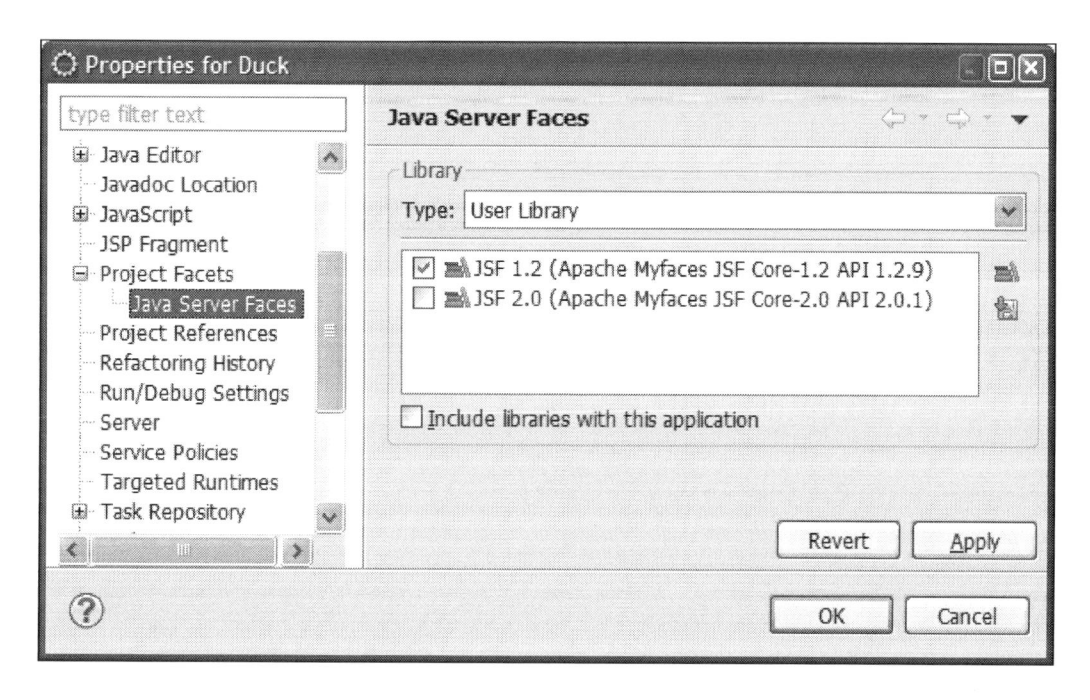

Select and download the Apache MyFaces implementation of JSF 1.2. Theoretically, any JSF 1.2 implementation should behave the same way as any other. We used Apache MyFaces for our sample DUCk implementation and suggest you do the same just in case practice doesn't match theory. Once it's downloaded, be sure the JSF 1.2 user library is selected and there is no selection for any other JSF implementation. The checkbox for **Include libraries with this application** should not be checked. That controls whether the JSF JARs are included in the WAR file that will be created. We won't need them since WAS 7 provides Apache MyFaces 1.2 automatically.

*The DUCk Sample Application*

# Exporting and deploying Duck.war

If you have imported the Duck project into Eclipse and done any latent configuration fix-ups so that things build correctly, you can recreate `Duck.war` by exporting it from Eclipse. Select the **Duck** project in the Eclipse Project Explorer, right-click and navigate to **Export | WAR file**. During development, we like to include the source files in the exported WAR file, but you would probably not do that for your production deployment.

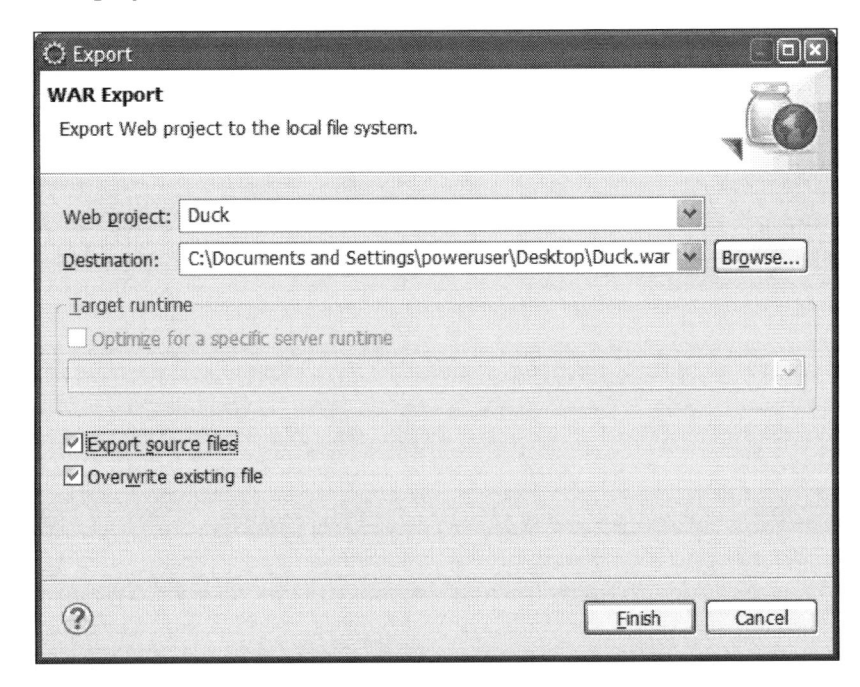

The exported `Duck.war` will be the same as the one we included with the downloadable material for this chapter, with one exception. Our copy does not include `Jace.jar` and `log4j.jar`. If you decide to use our copy, you must add those two JAR files to the `WEB-INF/lib/` directory inside the WAR file:

[ 374 ]

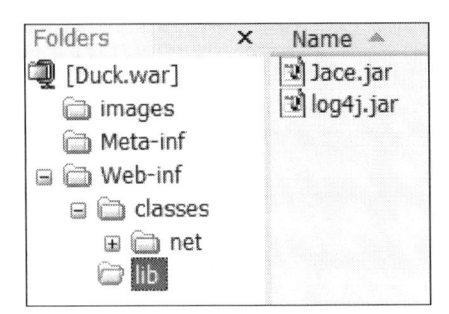

# Deployment descriptor

`Duck.war` contains an XML deployment descriptor at `WEB-INF/web.xml`. If you have used the same server configurations as we used in the examples throughout this book, then you may be able to use that deployment descriptor without any changes. Most of it is standarad JSF boilerplate, but there are a few `context-param` elements that are specifically for the configuration of the DUCk web application. If you want to change any of those values, you have a few choices:

- Application servers will sometimes let you directly modify those parameters for the deployed web application. This is usually not a very good choice except for temporary changes.
- You can modify `WEB-INF/web.xml` by extracting it from `Duck.war`, editing it, and replacing it in `Duck.war`.
- If you have the `Duck` project in Eclipse, you can use the Eclipse editor for `web.xml` before exporting the WAR file. This is probably the best choice since the changes are least likely to be lost.

All of the application-specific parameters have names starting with the prefix `duck`. If you modify anything in `web.xml`, be careful to not change anything other than the values for those parameters. Here is a complete list of parameters along with the values we have provided:

- `duck.ce.uri=iiop://wjc-rhel.example.net:2810/FileNet/Engine`: It gives the location of the target CE server. You should use the EJB transport form of this connection URI.
- `duck.ce.objectstore=OStore1`: It gives the name or Id of the Object Store that will be used for all operations.
- `duck.ce.showhiddenfolders=true`: It controls whether or not the DUCk UI will suppress folders whose `Folder.IsHiddenContainer` property value is true.
- `duck.ce.showhiddenproperties=true`: It controls whether or not the DUCk UI will suppress properties whose `PropertyDescription.IsHidden` property value is true.
- `duck.xt.baseurl=http://wjc-rhel.example.net:9080/WorkplaceXT`: It is a URL for connecting to the XT application. DUCk uses this when it constructs a URL for redirection to the `GetContent` servlet.

## Deploying to WAS

In keeping with our architectural tiers, we'll deploy DUCk to the same WAS profile that we used for XT since they are both web applications. This is not a requirement for the DUCk application, which merely needs to be able to connect to the configured CE server and the configured XT server.

> If you decide to deploy the DUCk application other than in the XT WAS instance, you will have to configure the WAS directory configuration and LTPA trust relationship using the procedure we described for XT deployment in *Chapter 5, Installing Other Components*.

Given **Duck.war**, prepared as just described, the first deployment into WAS is the routine adding of a new web application:

1. In the WAS console (for the XT WAS instance), navigate to **Applications | Application Types | WebSphere enterprise applications**. Click the Install button to launch the wizard for installing a new application.
2. When prompted, browse to your copy of `Duck.war`.
3. You can take defaults for things until prompted for the context root. Change the default value of **/** to **/duck**.
4. Complete the wizard and save the configuration. **Duck_war** will be listed among the **Enterprise Applications** but will not yet be started. WAS changes the period to an underscore when it creates the application name from the WAR file name.

You can use that same procedure for updating the DUCk application in place. All settings, including the context root, will be remembered and carried forward to the replacement WAR. There are, however, some additional configuration steps that must be done the first time DUCk is installed. Those are described in the following two subsections.

## Selecting the JSF Runtime

We want to make sure that we use the WAS-provided version of Apache MyFaces for maximum compatibility with our development environment (even though we did not intentionally use any non-standard JSF features).

From the **Enterprise Applications** screen, click on **Duck_war** and then click the link for **JSP and JSF options**. For **JSF implementation**, select **MyFaces 1.2**.

## Configure role mapping

The DUCk application uses container-managed authentication via form-based login. The `Duck.war` deployment descriptor restricts access for all of the application screens to users who are members of the `authenticated-duck-user` role. Users not in that role will be automatically redirected to the enterprise login screen by the web container. We'll now map the `authenticated-duck-user` role so that all authenticated users are in that role.

From the **Enterprise Applications** screen, click on **Duck_war** and then click the link for **Security role to user/group mapping**. Check the box next to **authenticated-duck-user**, and, from the **Map Special Subjects** drop-down, select **All Authenticated in Application's Realm**.

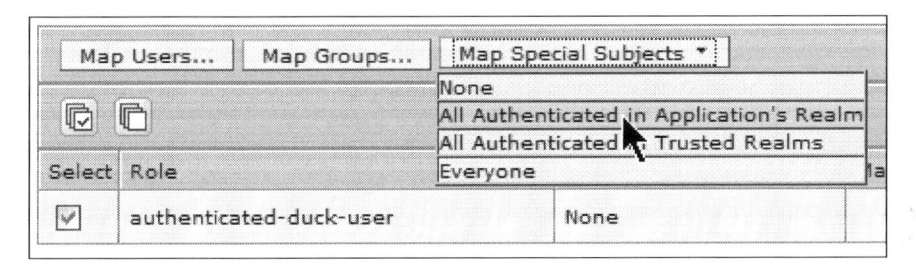

## Starting the application

After performing the above configuration steps and saving all settings, return to the **Enterprise Applications** screen, select checkbox for the **Duck_war** application, and click the **Start** button. The DUCk application should start successfully.

Log out of the WAS console and connect with your web browser to `http://wjc-rhel.example.net:9080/duck/`. You should be directed to the enterprise login screen. Log on with valid credentials (any of the LDAP directory users and passwords that you created in *Chapter 2, Installing Environmental Components* or later), and you should see the browse/query screen for the root directory of **OStore1**.

> Because the WAS console and the DUCk application both use container-managed authentication, you must first log out of the WAS console if you want to see the DUCk enteprise login screen. If you don't, you'll be taken immediately to the first browse/query screen, logged in as `was_admin`.

Congratulations! Your DUCk application is now running, and you can explore the features described earlier in this chapter.

## Summary

We presented the self-contained DUCk custom application. Along the way, we walked through the business requirements, the planned user experience, and the planning steps for various implementation details that exploit CM features. Because we also provide the artifacts for the DUCk solution as a companion download, you can run it and see for yourself that it performs as described. You can also inspect repository documents and their annotations directly using FEM or another application to see what the classes and properties look like in a low-level view. You can also try to use those tools to defeat the safeguards built into the design. We have our fingers crossed that you won't find any loopholes.

In the next chapter, we'll give some troubleshooting information for your CM environment, including a recap of many other information resources.

# 13
# Support, Fix Packs, and Troubleshooting

Earlier chapters of this book helped you to create a working IBM FileNet Content Manager (CM) system and even place a few sample items into it. If you followed along, you should have a complete system to tinker with and explore on your own. That in turn should give you confidence in constructing your production deployments.

Now comes the less glamorous part: you need to keep your systems up and running for the long haul. There are both routine and occasional things to do. We're not going to try to provide a detailed plan for you here. That would depend too much on circumstances specific to your enterprise. Instead, we'll present an overview of some things you will want to think about as you yourself develop such a detailed plan.

In this chapter, we'll cover these areas:

- We'll describe online and other resources to help you stay informed about product features, fixes, and updates
- We'll show you how to actually apply CM fix packs
- We'll discuss some common troubleshooting situations and techniques

## Resources

Whether you are just getting started with CM (which would make a great title for a book) or have considerable experience, you will want to take advantage of the gamut of documentation and other resources available, from IBM and from others, to make your ECM projects an ongoing success. In this section, we're going to list several such resources that you might think of as self-help.

We do want to mention, however, that there is a rich ecosystem of people who can help you do everything from developing a strategy, to planning your projects, performing implementations, and providing ongoing support. Those people include IBM Lab Services, IBM business partners, and other consultants. You can find information about IBM's business partners in the ECM area at this web page: `http://www-01.ibm.com/software/data/content-management/partners/`. Information about IBM's ECM Lab Services offerings is available here: `http://www-01.ibm.com/software/data/content-management/services/lab.html`.

While we're on the topic of people who can help you, we'll mention that IBM has a certification and assessment program called **FileNet Certified Professionals (FCP)**. You may want to take that into consideration when looking at the qualifications of any consultants. In fact, some of your staff may be interested in following an education and testing path to become FCPs. You can find information about the certification program if you visit IBM's main web page for ECM: `http://www.ibm.com/software/ecm`. Navigate to **Services | Training and Certification**.

On that same web page, you can also find information about IBM's extensive training courses for FileNet products, including CM. Courses are offered in a variety of formats and locations. Some courses are available online, and others are face-to-face at an IBM facility or at your location.

# Documentation

The IBM ECM link mentioned above is a good place to start looking for product descriptions, announcements, and marketing materials. In this section, we'll describe where to find in-depth technical documentation for CM.

## Information center

The starting point for technical documentation for CM is the information center, an online collection of complete product documentation. The information center for CM 4.5.1 is the *IBM FileNet P8 Version 4.5.1 Information Center* at `http://publib.boulder.ibm.com/infocenter/p8docs/v4r5m1`. The information there is hierarchically organized and fully searchable. The availability of this online resource means that many customers choose to skip having a locally installed copy of the product documentation.

There is a movement within CM applications to transition help links to be pointers to relative links in the information center. At this time, not all applications have been converted, but more are converted for every product release. At installation or configuration time, you can set the base URL for the information center. If you choose to do so, you can download and locally install a copy of the information center. In that case, you can choose to point to your own copy as the base for the help links. You can find information about the *FileNet P8 Version 4.5.1 Installable Information Center* here: http://www-01.ibm.com/support/docview.wss?uid=swg24025610.

## Standalone documents

There are several documents that are downloadable separately, usually as PDFs, even though they are linked to or included within the information center. An example is the *IBM FileNet P8 Version 4.5 Hardware and Software Requirements* document that we have mentioned several times in this book. The starting point for finding all of those documents is *Product Documentation for FileNet P8 Platform* located here http://www-01.ibm.com/support/docview.wss?uid=swg27010422.

> CM 4.5.1 was the first release to use the IBM information center framework for online documentation. The downloadable *FileNet P8 Platform Documentation* located on the page at the above link is in the pre-information center format. It is still useful, and it is the best documentation source for CM releases before CM 4.5.1.

You can look over the contents of that web page for yourself, but we'll just call to your attention a few of the more notable items available there. We've mentioned some of these elsewhere in this book:

- *FileNet P8 Release Notes*: These are release notes for full releases of CM and related components. The release notes include a list of all significant new features and fixes. This is handy because there can be significant planning involved before you do a full release upgrade. You can study the release notes at length to see if there are any areas that particularly affect you.

- *FileNet P8 Hardware and Software Requirements*: This is the official guidance on which environmental components are supported. We think it's advisable to check this document any time you plan an environmental change. Because this document is revised from time to time, you should always check that you have the latest version.

## Support, Fix Packs, and Troubleshooting

- *Fix Packs and Compatibility Matrices*: The documents are downloadable spreadsheets that tell you which combinations of releases and fix packs for CM and related components are supported together. It's good to check this document when planning to apply fix packs. You shouldn't generally expect a problem when you are bringing everything up to the most current levels, but there are occasional issues with mixing newer and older fix packs.

- *Installation and Upgrade Worksheet*: We used this spreadsheet extensively in *Chapter 2* through *Chapter 5*. It's a very handy way to gather and organize the many tiny bits of information you will need for configuring your environment.

- *FileNet P8 Platform Installation and Upgrade Guide*: Also look for the link that leads to customized versions of this document for specific combinations of components. If you happen to use one of those popular combinations, it will save you some jumping around past material that doesn't apply to your environment.

- *FileNet P8 Security Help Extract*: As you plan your environment, you'll come to have many questions about how CM components handle various aspects of security. This document is an attempt to gather all of that information together into a single place. If you are the one charged with "doing security", we suggest you read this document straight through to get a good foundation in the security features available.

- *FileNet P8 Platform Developer Samples*: There are numerous code samples spread throughout the product documentation and in various *IBM developerWorks* articles and *IBM Redbooks*. The samples available here are mostly small, standalone applications and are especially helpful if you are doing something in a less central area of CM APIs.

- *FileNet P8 Performance Tuning Guide*: You should at least look through this document as you plan your deployment. It is often revised and contains the best tuning advice for CM components and environmental components based on direct experience and testing. If you are troubleshooting a performance problem, you will definitely want to consult this document.

## Other links

This section is a collection of links to other documents that we have mentioned in the book outside of this chapter. We have gathered them here for your convenience, so the items that follow might seem unrelated to each other.

- For the specific combination of CM 4.5.1 and WAS 7.0, there is a small known issue that occurs at a certain point in the application server configuration panel of the Configuration Manager tool. The issue is described here: http://www-01.ibm.com/support/docview.wss?uid=swg21415627.

- In the event you have problems connecting from PE to CE, the PE team in IBM has published this *Troubleshooting the PE to CE Security Configuration* tech note: http://www-01.ibm.com/support/docview.wss?uid=swg21328045.

- Many subtle problems can arise in the configuration and ongoing operation of the full-text search engine. The CM support organization has consolidated tips for investigating and resolving many of these into a very detailed technical notice titled *Content-based Retrieval (CBR) Troubleshooting for FileNet Content Engine 4.x*: http://www-01.ibm.com/support/docview.wss?uid=swg27012912.

- We've referred to CM and other product licensing many times in earlier chapters. Someone in your enterprise will have a copy of the actual license agreements. However, most IBM software license files, including those for CM and related products, are also available online. Visit this web page and search for "**filenet content manager**": http://www-03.ibm.com/software/sla/sladb.nsf. The results will include both the current license file as well as several previous versions.

- In several examples, we use or refer to works of William Shakespeare. Shakespeare's works are readily available from many sites on the Internet. One of our favorite sites is at MIT: http://shakespeare.mit.edu. It's handy because it's really just the text without a lot of notes, criticisms, and so on.

# IBM Redbooks

IBM has a long tradition of publishing additional documentation as a supplement to official product documentation. These are called IBM Redbooks publications, and they really are books. They try to not overlap the product documentation too much. For example, they generally include a limited amount of reference material because they assume you can consult the product documentation for the latest lists of special values and so on. Instead, they are hands-on and tend to be focused on particular scenarios.

Complete IBM Redbooks can be downloaded in PDF format at no charge. If you are old school and would like a physical book, most are available for purchase in hardcopy. To find IBM Redbooks related to CM and other FileNet products, visit http://www.redbooks.ibm.com and search for "**filenet**". Additional titles are added all the time.

IBM Redbooks are written by a specifically empanelled writing team for each book. The writers can include IBM engineers who worked on creating the product in question, IBM field personnel who work with the product, or, in fact, anyone who has an interest in participating in writing such a book. Although most of the authors are IBM employees, that is not a requirement. You might find yourself interested in participating on an IBM Redbooks writing team. Visit the IBM Redbooks page and look for information about residencies.

## IBM developerWorks

IBM **developerWorks (dW)** is a collection of articles, code samples, and other resources on a variety of technical topics. Although we are introducing you to dW to point out to you the availability of several articles related to CM, the breadth and depth of dW coverage is quite striking. You will find articles on essentially every area of modern IT interest, and many of those articles are written by people outside of IBM.

To find dW articles related to CM and other FileNet products, go to this web page: `http://www.ibm.com/developerworks`. You can either search for "`filenet`" and related terms, or you can navigate to the dW ECM Zone at `http://www.ibm.com/developerworks/data/products/ecm`.

Be sure you don't overlook the dW forums. These forums are hosted by IBM but are not an official support channel. Instead, they are intended as a place where customers and business partners can help each other. If you have a question or want to discuss something, perhaps to get someone else's perspective, the forums are a great place. Nothing is guaranteed, but the price is right.

You can find a list of forums related to IBM Information Management products here: `http://www.ibm.com/developerworks/forums/im_forums.jspa`. The direct link to the specific forum for IBM FileNet Content Manager is `http://www.ibm.com/developerworks/forums/forum.jspa?forumID=1165`.

## Worldwide IBM ECM Community

The Worldwide IBM ECM Community is a collaborative center for the exchange of information and discussions about all aspects of IBM ECM. In addition to the forums and wikis hosted as part of the community, you will also find links to internal and external blogs, links to local and regional IBM ECM user groups, and pointers to IBM ECM presence on popular social networking venues like LinkedIn, Twitter, and Facebook. You can find the community via this link: `http://www.ibm.com/community/ecm`.

# Online support resources

The resources in this section are related specifically to support situations.

## Support portal

IBM maintains a support portal which can be used as a starting point for finding support resources for all IBM products. Visit `http://www.ibm.com/support`. To find the CM support area, use the drop-down menus on that page to navigate to **Information Management | FileNet Content Manager**. The resulting CM-specific support overview page, `http://www.ibm.com/support/entry/portal/Overview/Software/Information_Management/FileNet_Content_Manager`, gives links to many support resources, some of which we highlight next.

## PMRs and APARs

For reasons lost in the mists of time, when a customer reports a problem to IBM it is called a **Problem Management Report** (**PMR**). If it is determined that there is a product problem, the resulting fix or problem description is called an **Authorized Problem Analysis Report** (**APAR**). Now that you know what those acronyms stand for, our advice is to forget it and just use the acronyms like everybody else.

Most APARs are published on IBM's support site, though some are visible only to customers with certain contracts or product licenses. Often, when you are desperately searching the Internet for advice about some problem that has been vexing you, you will find search hits that lead to APAR pages. As just one example to see what they are like, here is an APAR we found by searching for **performance** in the CM area. It's called **PJ36972: POOR PERFORMANCE WHEN PERFORMING VARIOUS ADMIN FUNCTIONS IN FEM WITH LARGE # OF DOCCLASSES AND DEEP HIERARCHY** and can be found at `http://www-01.ibm.com/support/docview.wss?uid=swg1PJ36972`. The APAR number is `PJ36972`. By the way, this particular fix was included in CE 4.5.1 fix pack 2. You'll find that mentioned if you follow the link to the APAR.

## Technotes

We don't know how many technical notices IBM publishes, but we do know it's a lot. A technote is a brief description of a very focused topic. It is often generated as a result of customer or partner questions. The information in technotes generally finds its way into product documentation, but the turnaround time for technotes can be extremely short.

*Support, Fix Packs, and Troubleshooting*

You can search for technotes by key word within product areas from the support page. As just one example to see what they are like, here is a technote we found by searching for **authentication** in the CM area. It's called *How to configure Process Engine to work with Content Engine authentication that is secured by SSL* and can be found at `http://www-01.ibm.com/support/docview.wss?uid=swg21392767`.

## Personalized notifications

One of the links you will find on the CM-specific support overview page is for getting personalized notifications for a variety of information as it is published. It's called **My Notifications** and includes everything from product release notices to routine technical notes. To use My Notifications, you will have to register with `IBM.com`, but it's free and independent of any software or support contracts you might have. Anyone can register. If you follow the link, you'll get the usual sort of prompt for a login and opportunity to register. You'll be able to customize the notifications you get by type and by product, and you can also add other IBM products and information updates to your subscription list.

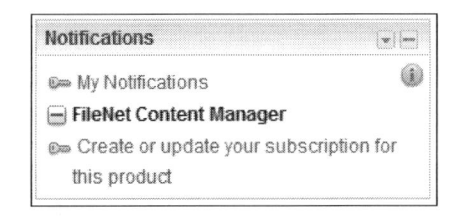

```
Notifications
   My Notifications
   FileNet Content Manager
      Create or update your subscription for
      this product
```

The small key icon next to a link indicates that you have to log on to `IBM.com` before you can access it.

## Fix Central

One support area that you should definitely remember is Fix Central at `http://www.ibm.com/support/fixcentral`. This is an easily navigated site for finding available fixes for most IBM Software Group products, including those from ECM. As the name implies, it's the central location for obtaining fix information and actual fix pack downloads. You cannot obtain product base images from Fix Central, only fix packs and other types of updates. Later in this chapter, we'll be installing fix packs for several components. We obtained all of those fix packs from Fix Central.

# Information on demand conferences

The premiere conference series for CM users and IBM business partners is IBM **Information On Demand (IOD)**. The conferences highlight the product lines of IBM's Information Management division and other closely allied organizations within IBM Software Group. It's a good opportunity to get information in a high-bandwidth setting. You can find detailed information about IOD conferences by consulting the events calendar at `http://www.ibm.com/software/data`. Of course, you can also find information about the conferences by doing an Internet search for **IBM Information On Demand conference**.

There are three varieties of IOD conference:

- IOD Global Conference is the largest gathering. It's held annually in October, and for the last few years has been held in Las Vegas. Several thousand participants from customer organizations, IBM business partners, and IBM itself meet to present and participate in hundreds of technical and business sessions. A large exposition area complements the conference. Information about the 2010 conference is available here: `http://www.ibm.com/software/data/2010-conference/`.

- Regional IOD conferences are held in the spring in Europe and Asia, and there are some IOD conferences for particular countries. These conferences usually have their programs tailored more to the specific interests of the regions or countries where the events are held.

- Within the United States, Canada, and in some other areas, local events are held under the umbrella name of Information On Demand Comes to You. These are generally one or two day events hosted locally and customized to the interests of customers and partners in a particular area.

If you can possibly make it, we urge you to attend whatever IOD events you can. Aside from the formal program, it's a good way to meet and share experiences with others who are using CM and related IBM products. You might even see us there.

# Releases and fixes

There are three categories of updates you might get from IBM for the CM product. It follows the same pattern as is used for most IBM Software Group product updates.

# Product releases

New formal versions of CM are released from time to time. The timing and content of each release is decided individually, so it's not really possible to predict future releases with any precision before they are announced by IBM.

*Support, Fix Packs, and Troubleshooting*

For pragmatic reasons, there is a historical pattern of no more than one or two releases in a calendar year. The relative infrequency of new releases is actually good news for you. You probably want to upgrade to most new releases (to avoid a feeling of falling behind), but there is probably considerable testing and qualification work for you when you do.

CM releases are numbered with a pattern of *VRMF*: version, release, minor release, fix pack. You can see this, for example, in the `v4r5m1` component of the CM InfoCenter URL that we mentioned earlier in this chapter. You shouldn't get too distracted by what a version is, what a minor release is, and so on, because, frankly, decisions about such things are a partial mystery to us, too. (Furthermore, don't be distracted by the fact that the "release number" includes within it a piece called "release". That's just part of the charm of recursion.) Instead, think mainly about the corresponding numbers. The release described in this book is CM 4.5.1.

Does CM suffer from the software industry's traditional "dot zero" problem? In other words, should you avoid a release with a second or third digit of zero and wait for the "dot one" release with all the fixes? We're biased, of course, but we think not. It's true that there were both CM 4.5.0 and 4.5.1 releases, but the "dot one" version was not constructed as fix-up releases for its "dot zero" sibling. For whatever reasons, IBM decided to use the "dot one" numbering, but each release had full development, test, and documentation cycles with plenty of new features. The actual, practical problem you are likely to be worried about for the "dot zero" problem is handled nicely by the fix pack mechanism described next. So, if we were you, we wouldn't particularly avoid "dot zero" releases. We'd treat them like any other available new releases. If you follow the plan we outlined in *Chapter 9, Planning Your Deployment* and have test environments separate from your production environment, you should have no problem installing an upgrade and safely testing it without the risk of your production environment having excessive downtime or functional problems.

We won't go into detail here about how to upgrade to a new release. Each CM release includes with it comprehensive instructions for how to actually do the upgrade, and most of it is pretty painless. Any exceptional circumstances will be called out in the installation and upgrade instructions. A release upgrade does
share some characteristics with a fix pack installation, which we'll cover in more detail below.

One thing in particular that you should always pay attention to is client compatibility. When there are client and server components to upgrade, you will want to upgrade the server components first (unless there are specific different instructions from IBM, but that should be pretty rare). A new server release usually brings with it new client components (JARs, DLLs, configuration files, or other artifacts). The PE and CE client installers usually find and automatically upgrade the CM-provided applications, but they usually cannot automatically do the same thing for custom applications.

As a rule of thumb, the servers will support client components that are one release older. For example, the CE 4.5.1 server will support CE 4.5.0 clients. The opposite combination is not supported: servers generally do not support client versions that are newer. Here, we mean it's supported in the sense of IBM's official support policies. Other combinations may work in a technical sense, but if something went wrong (which it certainly could, perhaps in a subtle way) you would not be in a supported configuration. In any case, for the least risk, you will want to move your clients to versions that exactly match the server as soon as you reasonably can. The "N minus 1" support is really intended as a temporary situation during upgrades.

> Here is a note of interest to those doing custom development and who might face multiple release environments. You want to do your development and testing in an environment that is the oldest release you will support. This helps you avoid both the temptation to use newer features and the possibility of doing so by accident.

## Interim fixes

If you have a specific problem with CM, there are many possibilities for what's going on. Of course, you will do due diligence by checking CM product documentation and examining your own custom applications for problems, but perhaps the problem you are seeing will be in the CM product itself. In some cases, what you might think of as a product problem is really that CM is behaving as designed, but it doesn't behave as you expect. In other cases, the problem might be a bug: CM isn't doing what it was designed to do.

In any case, after verifying a problem, one of the first things IBM support will often do is try to find a workaround so that you get the behavior you're looking for. This may be a configuration setting or, in the case of custom development, the suggestion of a different approach to a problem. (Support for custom development is handled by a different support area and under different terms than support for out of the box components.) This search for workarounds is not IBM trying to duck responsibility or avoid fixing problems. It's actually in your best interests because a workaround, if found, can often solve your problem immediately.

> Some workarounds will be the suggestion to set an undocumented configuration option to some value. Why are some configuration options undocumented and only revealed by IBM support in response to your call? Often they may have potential performance or functional side-effects that must be considered on a case by case basis. Others are configuration options put into the product by developers for conditions they don't think will occur in practice or that are only thought to be interesting for IBM's internal development process. Perhaps it is appropriate to think of these undocumented items like prescription medicine. Used the wrong way they can do more harm than good.

In the case of an actual product defect, one of these possible things could happen:

- If it's not too critical, or there is some reasonable kind of workaround, or other circumstances dictate (for example, a product on the verge of its end of support life), the bug may go unfixed. In our experience, this is relatively rare but not unheard of.
- With or without a workaround, you might agree that the bug is not too time-critical for you. The fix for the bug will be added to a future product fix pack or release. (Items added to fix packs are routinely added to the next product release.)
- IBM support might agree that a fix must be provided and that your circumstances are such that you can't wait for even the next fix pack. In that case, IBM will provide you with an **interim fix**. (Interim fixes are routinely added to next fix pack.)

The name interim fix is significant on two counts. First, it's intended to be used only until you get the product fix pack that incorporates a permanent fix. Occasionally, a permanent fix will have a different nature than an interim fix. This is typically due to the difference in time available for implementation. Second, an interim fix is not a vehicle for one-off features maintained for a specific customer. It certainly sometimes happens that a bug report and an interim fix will lead to a new feature or a change to an existing feature, but the interim fix still lives only until the next fix pack or product release.

Whether or not an interim fix should be produced is often subjective and a bit of a negotiation between you and IBM support. Should you always stick to your guns and demand an interim fix? We can't advise you about the difference, for you, between critical issues, inconveniences, and trivialities, but we do want to point out that there are some disadvantages to you in applying an interim fix:

- You might be the only one in the world running the exact configuration that includes the interim fix. That fact alone is a discouraging factor for many organizations.

- An interim fix gets tested, and that testing is based on the best judgment of IBM support and product development that the changes are isolated to certain areas. Still, the testing is not as rigorous as for a fix pack or product release. There is a minuscule—but not zero—risk of seeing some side effect.
- If you need an additional interim fix down the road, it may take longer for IBM to create and deliver it to you, even if there is already an existing interim fix for the same issue for a different customer. The reason for that is that the installed interim fix does not operate in isolation. It will generally be part of the same JAR, DLL, or other component with many other things. Installing a new interim fix in a component will usually wipe out any previous interim fixes in that same component. IBM must therefore create a product build for every combination of interim fixes delivered to a customer. Not only must this follow IBM's rigorous source control and other build practices, but it sometimes involves a specialized analysis by product developers to make sure that the combination of interim fixes can peacefully co-exist.

Nevertheless, if you need an interim fix, you need an interim fix. The preceding factors are just things to think about as you weigh things in your own mind.

# Fix packs

We've already mentioned fix packs a few times, and now it's time to describe them in more detail.

If modern, complex software were perfect, there would be no need for fixes. But perfection in something with as many moving parts as enterprise software is rare (some say nonexistent). In recognition of this practical reality, all major software vendors plan for providing software updates after a product has shipped. Different vendors use different names and numbering schemes.

The IBM term is **fix pack**. (Informally, fix packs and interim fixes are also called patches, but that terminology suggests an obsolete process that doesn't really apply these days.) For CM and most other IBM Software Group products, fix packs are numbered sequentially using the fourth digit of the VRMF pattern. For example, as of this writing, the latest CE fix pack is number 4, so the full release number for the CE components is CE 4.5.1.4. The actual fix pack name is something different: you would apply a fix pack named P8CE-4.5.1-004 to bring your installation to release number CE 4.5.1.4.

It is rare for a fix pack to contain new features. When it does happen, it is usually because the new feature is a generalization of some fix being included in the fix pack and it is less effort (or less confusing) to just include the new feature. It is not unusual for a fix pack to introduce new supported platform components. These are typically newer versions of already-supported components like directory servers, databases, and application servers. Fix packs never intentionally remove features or introduce backward compatibility problems. The reasoning is simple: it's in IBM interest and the customers' interests to rapidly move to new fix packs as they are published. For the same reason, IBM support and product development very closely control what fixes go into a fix pack. With only occasional exceptions, fixes come from customer-reported problems that are evaluated as being of sufficient seriousness or applicability that all customers should get the fix. The release notes document for a fix pack includes a concise list of all included changes.

> An important special case of features added in a fix pack are items called **post-qualification** efforts. Sometimes complete testing of a feature or supported platform would unacceptably delay a product release, so a decision is made to qualify it after the formal product release. The decision is made with the expectation that testing will merely prove that development was as it should be. In that case, IBM merely announces support for the feature or platform. If product changes are needed as a result of testing, they are rolled into a fix pack.

Fix packs are cumulative. That means that if you install a particular fix pack, you will automatically have all of the changes from previous fix packs for the same product release. It is not necessary to install all fix packs in order. By the same reasoning, earlier fix packs are obsolete for most purposes as soon as a later fix pack is published. Earlier fix packs remain downloadable, as a general rule, for testing and other special purposes. You will certainly want to get the latest available fix pack whenever you are looking at installing any fix pack unless you have some special reason (for example, perhaps you are trying to match an existing environment).

Different components of the CM product tend to operate on different fix pack schedules. The reason is that those same components may be part of multiple product bundles from IBM, and a synchronized fix pack schedule is pretty much impossible. This can be a bit confusing, so IBM support publishes the *FileNet P8 Fix Pack Compatibility Matrices* (see the previous link). Those are spreadsheets which go into great detail about which fix pack combinations for all the components can be installed together, including any special circumstances for particular combinations. (The matrices do not include information about interim fixes.)

# Installing fix packs

To further illustrate the fix pack process, we'll take the opportunity to install the latest fix packs for all of the CM components that we have installed.

## Supporting components

We won't be illustrating the procedure for updating other components, like the application server, but we will just note the versions of those components that we got when we brought everything up to the latest fix packs:

- **DB2**: We installed the latest DB2 fix pack, moving from 9.5.0.0 to 9.5.0.6. When applying fixes or upgrading your database, don't forget that you may have machines with database client software components. In our case, that's the Windows server, `wjc-w2k3.example.net`, where we installed the PE server. Unless instructed otherwise by the database documentation, it's a good idea to keep all of the database software components in sync.

- **TDS**: We installed the latest TDS fix pack, moving from 6.2.0.0 to 6.2.0.13. Because our installation of TDS is using our main DB2 installation, the updates we did for DB2 are automatically picked up for TDS. Our TDS is using an embedded copy of WAS and is not using our main WAS installation. We installed the latest embedded WAS fix pack recommended by the TDS support site, moving from WAS 6.1.0.13 to 6.1.0.31.

- **WAS**: We installed the latest WAS fix pack, moving from 7.0.0.0 to 7.0.0.13. If you have installed the WebSphere Application Client (for example, if you took our simple development example further and configured it to use EJB transport), you will want to also update it to the latest fix pack. WAS server and client fix packs are typically released simultaneously.

> If you followed our example in *Chapter 2, Installing Environmental Components*, and are running your WAS profiles as a non-root user (for example, user `ecmuser` and group `ecmgroup`), then you will probably have to repeat the directory and file ownership adjustments that we described in *Chapter 2*, in the section WebSphere Application Server. If you don't, you're likely to get mysterious complaints about incompatible transaction types. We'll repeat the exact instructions below, after we have installed the CE fix pack.

- **RHEL**: We did not upgrade our version of Red Hat Enterprise Linux. Instead, we used the RHEL package management software to apply fixes and upgrades to individual software packages as they were made available.

*Support, Fix Packs, and Troubleshooting*

Our methodology for installing updates to this supporting software was to do it in the order described above, but also to reboot the RHEL server after installing each item and run a few tests to make sure we hadn't made any blunders. Whenever we are upgrading an environmental component, we stop all of the CM components first so that things are as idle as possible. The reboots and testing are theoretically not needed, but we wanted to have an easier time pinpointing a cause if something went wrong.

## CM components

Different FileNet-provided components of CM have their own fix pack cycles and fix pack installers. We will upgrade our installation with the latest fix packs for all of the components that we have installed. (The PE didn't happen to have any fix packs for PE 4.5.1, but it did have some interim fixes available. We will not be installing the PE interim fixes here, but you can download and install them at your own discretion.) The resulting version numbers for individual components are summarized in this table:

| Component | Fix Pack Level |
| --- | --- |
| CE | 4.5.1.4 |
| CSE | 4.5.1.1 |
| XT | 1.1.4.8 |

For CM server components, there is usually a server fix pack installer and a client fix pack installer, issued simultaneously. We will use both in appropriate places to update related components. The idea of the separate installers is that the client-side API components can be kept in sync with the updated server components.

> The CE 5.0.0 release includes a feature called Downloadable Client Components. Using a small and stable API, client applications can obtain CE JAR files and other artifacts directly from the running CE server. That's a good way for applications to ensure they always have client pieces matching the CE server. However, because it's a new feature, it will be a while before most applications have adopted it.

The first step in planning for CM fix pack installation is to make sure that all of the contemplated fix packs are compatible, and that means checking the *FileNet P8 Fix Pack Compatibility Matrices* mentioned previously. Be sure to get a fresh copy of the spreadsheet since it is frequently updated. If you are installing a recently released fix pack, it might not yet be mentioned in the matrix. Most combinations of "the latest stuff" will be compatible, but you can always check with IBM support if there is doubt after you've checked the spreadsheet.

A fix pack will include a set of instructions for installing it. We won't go over that in detail, but you should read through it for the particular fix packs you are installing. The procedure we will illustrate next is fairly generic, and fix pack instructions sometimes include important special case items or limitations. A fix pack usually cannot be uninstalled, so it's important to have backups or some other recovery plan in case you run into problems or decide to abandon the installation of a fix pack.

## CE 4.5.1.4 server

Our first stop will be upgrading the CE server and client components. The CE server is running on our Linux server in a WAS profile. CE client updates must be done for the XT installation in a separate WAS profile, the PE server running on our Windows server, and any Windows machine where FEM is installed. If you set up the Java or .NET development environments, then those machines need the client update as well. We'll update the CE server first and then apply the client updates. That's the supported order for CE updates.

> Before making any change to your CE server, make sure you have safely saved a copy of your bootstrapped CE EAR file. If you didn't do that in *Chapter 3, Installing the Content Engine* do it now. The CE EAR file will be named Engine-ws.ear, Engine-wl.ear, or Engine-jb.ear, or Engine-jbc.ear, depending on your application server brand (WebSphere, WebLogic, or JBoss, respectively). If you are taking a copy from a deployed location, your application server may have renamed the CE EAR to something else. You should not skip this step. There are a lot of recoverable mistakes that can become unrecoverable if you have lost your original bootstrap settings.

Download and unpack the CE server fix pack update. One of the files you will find in the unpacked directory is version.txt. This short file precisely describes the exact builds of the included components. Here are the contents of version.txt from our CE fix pack:

```
P8 Content Engine 4.5.1.4 build dap451.004.002
Using pui451.057
Using pch455.004
Using cm451.002.008
Using dep451.074
This build includes cambridge14.mdb revision
```

It's not too important to know what each of those things means. They're just internal build number designations for subcomponents, not all of which are actually visible in the installed product. We'll use this information later to double check that the fix pack installation went as expected.

*Support, Fix Packs, and Troubleshooting*

With the CE server shut down, run the CE server fix pack installer. In our case, the name of the executable is `4.5.1.4-P8CE-FP004.BIN`. Even though it's a graphical installer program, we recommend launching it from a shell window in case any important console messages are printed. Several of the installer panels are applicable only to a Windows environment, and you probably want the default location for the CE installation. That means you can click through most of the panels.

On the final panel, the installer suggests that you run the client updaters for PE and CSE if you are using those components and have updates for them. In other words, it is telling you to update those components if they are used by the CE server. We are using both but only have an update for CSE, so we'll take care of that next. Make sure you uncheck the box for **Launch Configuration Manager** and click the **Done** button.

You should look through the installation log file (in directory `/opt/ibm/FileNet/ContentEngine/`) to see if any problems occurred.

## CSE 4.5.1.1 client

Unpack the Linux client package for CSE fix pack 4.5.1.1. The installer executable name in this case is `4.5.1.1-P8CSE-CLIENT-LINUX-FP001.BIN`. Again, we recommend running this from a shell window to launch the graphical installer. This installer will be updating the CSE client files inside the CE server EAR file. Assuming you are using the default paths, you can click through the installer panels and it will finish without incident.

> One thing you should look for in release notes for a CSE fix pack is whether or not it requires a re-index of your content. Typically, they do not, but it is possible that one would. For our tiny all-in-one site, that wouldn't be an issue. For a production site with a few million documents or more, the re-indexing time would be significant.

The CSE client file updates will be placed in `/opt/ibm/FileNet/ContentEngine/CSEClient/`. You will want to glance through the installation log file in that directory to check that no problems occurred.

## CSE 4.5.1.1 server

Since we just installed the CSE client update, we'll install the CSE server update to keep things in sync. Unpack the Linux server package for CSE fix pack 4.5.1.1. The installer executable name in this case is `4.5.1.1-P8CSE-LINUX-FP001.BIN`. Again, we recommend running this from a shell window to launch the graphical installer. If you don't have an environment variable setting already for this, you will need to set a value for `JAVA_HOME` before running the installer. Here is the setting we used in *Chapter 5, Installing Other Components*:

```
# export JAVA_HOME=/usr/lib/jvm/java-1.5.0-ibm-1.5.0.11.2.x86_64
```

> You must shut down all CE and CSE servers during the update to CSE server software. Otherwise, the CSE may be trying to service CE requests during the update, and corruption of your text index can result.

The installer will be updating software in the CSE server itself, so we will first stop the CSE server. If you are using something like our up and down scripts from *Chapter 2*, you can just run the down script to stop everything. Otherwise, go to the CSE software location (the default is `/opt/ibm/FileNet/ContentEngine/verity/k2/_ilnx21/bin/`), and run the `k2adminstop` command.

> A quick way to see if any CSE software is running on a Unix or Linux server is to run the command `ps -ef | grep k2`. If nothing shows up (except perhaps the `grep` command itself), then no CSE software is running.

The fix pack files include scripts for backing up and restoring your CSE configuration files. You'll need a target directory for storing these files (they'll total 30-50 MB). You can safely put them into a directory under `/tmp/` only if your system doesn't automatically clean up `/tmp/` during a reboot. A safer policy would be to store them in a new subdirectory of the location where you unpacked the fix pack files. You should run the backup (and the later restore) as the user we designated in *Chapter 5* as the `k2_os_user`.

```
# su - k2_os_user -c "/some/path/backup_k2.sh /opt/ibm/FileNet/
ContentEngine/verity /some/path/k2save"
```

In a production environment, you might be splitting up the various CSE functions among multiple servers. If that's the case, you should run the backup procedure and the CSE installer on each separate server.

Run the graphical installer program. The installer will supply the correct defaults for most items. You can consult the original CSE installation steps in *Chapter 5* for any information that is not obvious or that you don't remember.

There are a couple of steps to do after running the graphical installer. You may recall from the original CSE installation that we had to manually adjust the ownership and permissions for the `vspget` command. The installation we just did will have undone that, so we have to do it again. Here's a repeat of that procedure. From a Linux command prompt, while logged in as `root`, do the following commands:

```
# cd /opt/ibm/FileNet/ContentEngine/verity/k2/_ilnx21/bin
# chown root vspget
# chmod u+s vspget
```

The installation steps above cause the CSE servers to restart, so shut them down again before doing the restore of the configuration files:

```
# su - k2_os_user -c "/some/path/restore_k2.sh /some/path/k2save /opt/ibm/FileNet/ContentEngine/verity"
```

At this point, you could restart your CSE servers, but let's wait and restart them when we restart the CE server.

## Redeploying the updated CE server

With those side excursions out of the way, we can get back to the CE server update. (If we had any PE fix packs to apply, we would do that first.) When we ran the graphical installer for the CE server fix pack, it installed things in the sense of putting the files on the disk in the CE server installation area. We will now go through the process of creating an updated EAR file and deploying it to the application server.

CE server fix pack installation instructions direct you to gather information so that you are ready to answer installation questions in the following steps. That's good advice because you will typically be installing a fix pack months after you initially installed the CE or installed the previous fix pack. You may have lost track of the information you recorded in the *Installation and Upgrade Worksheet*. Luckily, in this case, someone has conveniently provided a book with all of that information in it, at least for our example installation. You may wish to review *Chapter 2* and *Chapter 3* and make sure you have the information where you used something different from our choices.

For the best redeployment scenario, you can get rid of your existing deployment of CE server. (If you didn't take our advice about making a backup copy of that EAR, do it now, before going any further.) Technically, you don't have to do this undeploy step, but every once in a while some piece of lint or foam rubber from the old copy will interfere with the deployment of the new copy.

Restart the CE WAS profile. (If you stopped the WAS profile by shutting down everything, you will also have to restart the directory server.) From the WAS console, navigate to **Applications | Application Types | WebSphere enterprise applications**. Select the CE server (usually called `FileNetEngine`) and click the **Uninstall** button. Follow the prompts and **Save** the changes to the master configuration.

If your CE server application was called `FileNetEngine`, then the WAS cache files for it will be `/opt/ibm/WebSphere/AppServer/profiles/AppSrv02/temp/localhostNode02/server1/FileNetEngine/`. The most likely situation is that you will find only empty directories in that location. Stop the WAS profile, and delete everything in that `FileNetEngine` directory and below.

Restart the WAS profile. All vestiges of the CE server application are gone at this point.

When we initially installed the CE server in *Chapter 3*, we did so as the `root` user. We'll also run the P8 Configuration Manager as the `root` user. We'll fix up the file and directory ownerships later, just as we did in *Chapter 3*. Run the P8 Configuration Manager with the following command:

```
# /opt/ibm/FileNet/ContentEngine/tools/configure/configmgr
```

Navigate to and open the configuration profile (`wjc-rhel`) saved from the initial install. You may recall from *Chapter 3* that we changed the WAS console administrator login from `administrator` to `was_admin`. The configuration profile probably still reflects the earlier `administrator` user. Click the icon that looks like a computer to open the panel for application server configuration settings. Supply the `was_admin` user name and password. Use the **Test Connection** button to make sure your settings are correct.

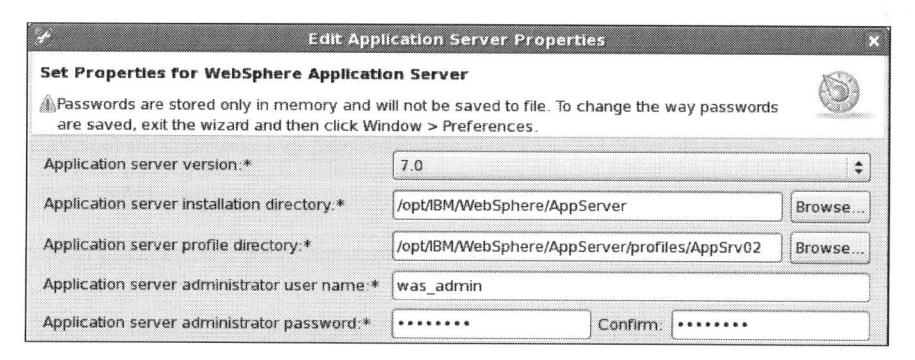

*Support, Fix Packs, and Troubleshooting*

Because we haven't changed any fundamental configuration items for our CE server installation, we have only a couple of real steps to perform in applying the fix pack. If you have not kept the original configuration profile, you will have to consult the product documentation mentioned in the fix pack instructions and do a more detailed procedure. We'll assume you were either smart or lucky, and we'll just describe the short procedure:

- **Bootstrapping**. Double-click the **Configure Bootstrap Properties** task in the configuration profile tree view. Change the **Bootstrap Operation** to **Upgrade**. Right-click the **Configure Bootstrap Properties** task and select **Run Task**. This will modify the fix pack CE EAR file to include the bootstrap information from the initial installation.

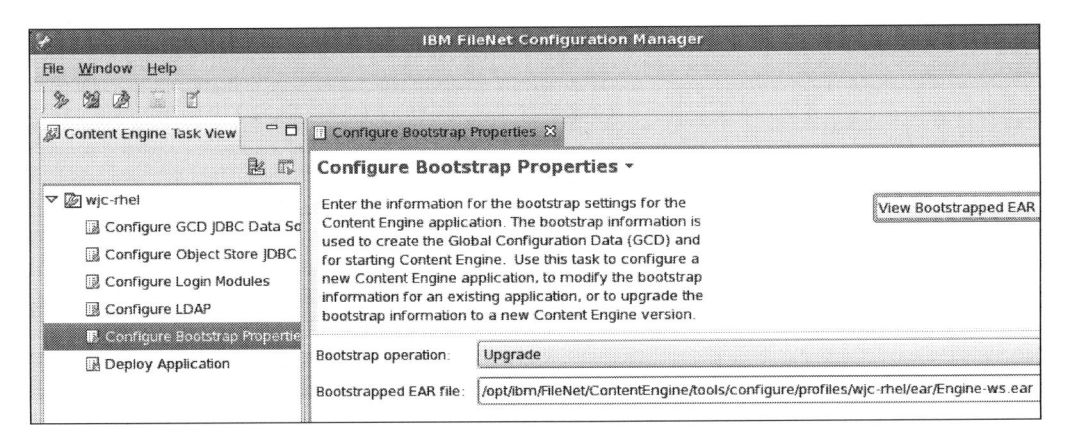

- **Deployment**: Right-click the **Deploy Application** task and select **Run Task**. This will deploy the bootstrapped CE EAR file into the application server. If all went well, you are done.

> We are often unlucky in the deployment step and have experienced failures for a variety of reasons. If that happens to you, you can easily deploy the CE EAR with your application server's tools. From the WAS console, navigate to **Applications | Application Types | WebSphere enterprise applications**. Click the **Install** button, navigate to the bootstrapped CE EAR file (using the **Remote file system** option unless you are running your browser on the CE server machine), and follow the additional steps to deploy the CE EAR.

- From the WAS console, check to see if the `FileNetEngine` application is running. If not, start it.

You may recall from the original CE installation that we had to manually adjust the ownership of the directory trees for the WAS profiles. The installation we just did will have undone parts of that, so we have to do it again. Here's a repeat of that procedure. From a Linux command prompt, while logged in as `root`, do the following commands:

```
# cd /opt/ibm/WebSphere/AppServer/profiles
# chown -R ecmuser:ecmgroup AppSrv02 AppSrv01
```

To verify that you are now running what you think you are, use your browser to connect to the CE "ping page": `http://wjc-rhel.example.net:9081/FileNet/Engine`. You should see the correct VRMF in the startup message, as in the following image:

| Key | |
|---|---|
| Process Engine | 4.5.1.0 pui451.057 |
| Server Instance{s} | server1 {server1} |
| Startup Message | P8 Content Engine Startup: 4.5.1.4 dap451.004.002 Cop... |
| J2EEUtil | com.filenet.apiimpl.util.J2EEUtilWS |
| Start Time | Wed Aug 04 11:50:39 PDT 2010 |
| P8 Domain | Lucky |
| Log File Location | /opt/ibm/WebSphere/AppServer/profiles/AppSrv02/FileNe... |
| Classpath | /opt/IBM/WebSphere/AppServer/profiles/AppSrv02/prope.../AppServer/lib/jsf-nls.jar:/opt/ibm/WebSphere/AppServer/.../deploytool/itp/batch2.jar:/opt/ibm/WebSphere/AppServe... |
| JDBC Driver | IBM DB2 JDBC Universal Driver Architecture 3.59.81 |
| Working Directory | /opt/ibm/WebSphere/AppServer/profiles/AppSrv02 |

## CE 4.5.1.4 clients

We won't walk through running the CE client fix pack installers. They are pretty straightforward and are likely to have correct default values for all of the questions they ask. Let's just recap which installers to run where:

- You must run the CE client installer specific to the operating system platform of the client application. It is sufficient to run the CE client installer once on a given machine.

*Support, Fix Packs, and Troubleshooting*

- For FEM and other CE clients based on the CE .NET API, you run the CE server fix pack installer to update those client components. That can be a bit confusing (because you are probably expecting to use the client fix pack installer), but it's done that way for historical reasons.
- For all CE clients based on the CE Java API, which includes most of the applications provided with CM, you run the CE client fix pack installer.
- The previous bullets also apply to any custom application development environments. In those cases, you may have to copy CE client components or reference them from a common location. The CE installer will tell you where it is placing the updated components.

## XT 1.1.4.8

The final CM component that we will upgrade is Workplace XT. XT fix packs are unusual in that they include a complete XT installation, so they can be used to install from scratch or as an update to an existing installation. In fact, one option you could take would be to completely remove your existing XT installation and install the new one from scratch. We'll describe the process of doing the in-place update.

> As for the initial installation, in consideration of the size of the XT WAR and EAR, we suggest that you have at least 3-5 GB of disk space available for any kind of XT update. Most of that space is only used temporarily and can be recovered at the end of the XT update.

As with the CE server fix pack installation, the first step is to make a safe backup of your XT deployment so you can recover if anything goes wrong. The XT EAR file is quite large, and you may be willing to accept the risk of applying the fix pack without a backup. Most XT (and AE) configuration information is stored inside one of the Object Stores, but there is a small amount of configuration needed to get the XT application to the point of being able to read things in that Object Store.

There are three small files that you should back up before doing an XT upgrade. Those files and their default locations are as follows:

`/opt/ibm/FileNet/Config/WebClient/bootstrap.properties`, `/opt/ibm/FileNet/WebClient/WorkplaceXT/WEB-INF/web.xml`, and `/opt/ibm/FileNet/WebClient/WorkplaceXT/WEB-INF/WcmApiConfig.properties`.

It is not unusual for users to make tweaks to those last two files in the deployed XT application. You might wish to compare those files with the deployed versions, which are by default located in `/opt/ibm/WebSphere/AppServer/profiles/AppSrv01/installedApps/localhostNote01Cell/WorkplaceXT.ear/web_client.war/WEB-INF/`. (We find the length of that path to be discouragement enough to keep us from ever changing those deployed files, but it is sometimes a possibility.) If there are changes in the deployed copies that you wish to preserve, you must copy them to the `/opt/ibm/FileNet/WebClient/WorkplaceXT/WEB-INF/` directory. The XT fix pack installation process will manipulate files in that location.

Start the WAS profile containing the XT application and use the WAS console to uninstall the `WorkplaceXT` application. Stop that WAS profile, and remove the application server's cache files for the `WorkplaceXT` application. You can consult the earlier section describing the removal of the `FileNetEngine` application for guidance on how to do that.

Unpack the XT fix pack and run the installer program. In this case, it's `WorkplaceXT-1.1.4.8-LINUX.bin`. We recommend running the graphical installer from a shell window in case any messages are logged to standard output.

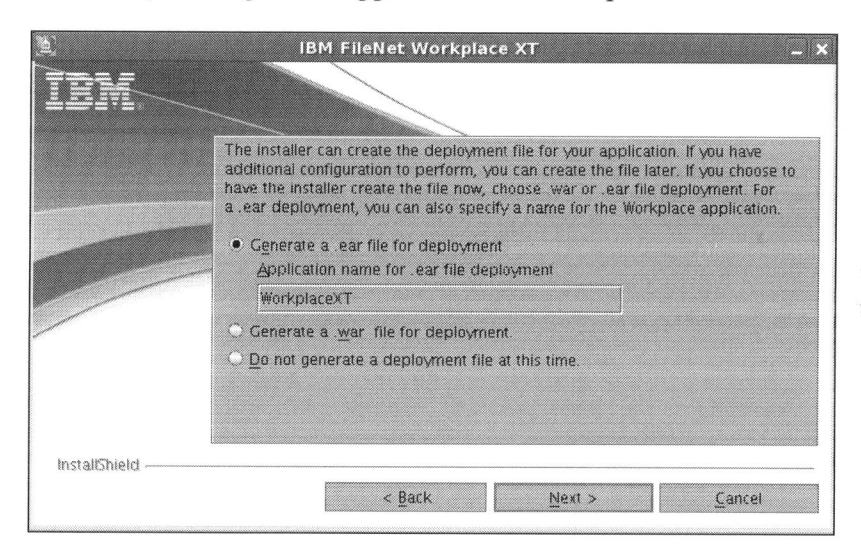

The installer will offer to generate the EAR file for the updated application. Because we have already installed the CE client file updates, go ahead and generate that EAR.

You are now ready to deploy the XT application into your application server. Restart your WAS instance for XT, and head back to *Chapter 5* to find the XT pre-deployment and deployment steps from the initial installation. They're just a bit long, and we won't repeat them here. Some of the settings will have automatically been kept from the initial installation, but others will need to be set again. Check each step to be sure.

*Support, Fix Packs, and Troubleshooting*

After deploying the new XT version, perform the same file ownership tweaks as we did after deploying the CE server earlier in this chapter. There is an additional step for the XT log file location. Make sure that it is writable by the operating system user and group under which the WAS profile is running.

```
# chown ecmuser:ecmgroup /opt/ibm/FileNet/WebClient/LogFiles
```

Use your web browser to connect to XT at `http://wjc-rhel.example.net:9080/WorkplaceXT/`. You should be able to log in and perform all operations as before.

# Troubleshooting

Sooner or later, your perfectly happy world of ECM will stumble a bit, and your goal will be to get things working as soon as possible. If trouble happens in your development or test environment, you'll be uneasy with the lost productivity until you can use your full setup again. If trouble happens in your production environment, you might rapidly move beyond being in a panic.

We could present quite a long list of specific things to check or try when you run into problems. That could fill a book of this size by itself, and we might not happen to cover the circumstances of your particular situation. We will instead describe some general troubleshooting techniques that may help you zero in on the problem.

## Prevention

If you are reading this chapter because your production system is down, please skip this section. We don't want to risk you becoming violent when we tell you that the best troubleshooting technique is to avoid trouble in the first place. It's true, of course. Despite the best intents of a disciplined process, sooner or later you might be able to subvert one of these obviously good ideas.

## Configuration Control

Configuration control is essential for a smooth running production environment, but it's also a good idea for important non-production environments. Don't make changes without recording them in a reliable way. Here, reliable can mean anything from rigorous note-taking to a full-fledged software configuration management system. Some sites have a policy that no change can be made to a production environment unless it is scripted. Nothing is left to human hands except running the script itself.

The purpose of recording changes, including the order in which you made the changes and things like reboot/restart steps, is two-fold. First, you want to be able to reproduce the change in exactly the same way in multiple environments. Second, if things don't go the way you expect them to go, it's a lot easier to solve the resulting puzzles if you know exactly what you did.

(By the way, we are terrible at following this advice, which is why we are in development instead of operations.)

## Snapshots

If you can arrange to test your changes in a virtual machine environment, then your virtual machine manager will surely have the capability to make at least one snapshot. A snapshot for a virtual machine is a file-based capture of the entire virtual machine state at a given point in time. Some platforms will allow a single snapshot while others will allow arbitrarily many in a branched, hierarchical topology.

The idea of a snapshot is that you can discard all changes back to the point of the snapshot. All mistakes are conveniently erased. That's good and bad. You get a chance to start over, but you should first capture as much information as you can about what went wrong so that you don't waste too much time re-making the mistakes.

## Backups

We're not going to say too much about backups because the benefit is pretty obvious. If your configuration management system doesn't include doing a backup of configuration data before a change is made, you should definitely do it manually in any environment that is important enough that you don't want to lose it.

Backup of business data is often a decision made based on a risk assessment if there is significant downtime involved. The sheer volume of data and complex relationships can make planning for business data backup a complicated matter. For many good suggestions and best practices, there is an IBM Redbooks publication called *Disaster Recovery and Backup Solutions for IBM FileNet P8 Version 4.5.1 Systems*, available at `http://www.redbooks.ibm.com/abstracts/sg247744.html`.

*Support, Fix Packs, and Troubleshooting*

# Looking for trouble

There are a lot of ways to categorize problems, but the most useful in our experience is to separate out initial "get it running" problems from problems that suddenly occur in what was a healthy environment. When you ask an experienced troubleshooter why something doesn't work in your environment, among the first questions they will ask is whether it was working before. If it was working before, the very next question will ask what changed. There is a rich history of people saying that, ahem, *nothing* changed. There's probably no reason for you to have a different answer unless you want to get your problem solved.

# Initial configuration

The odds are pretty good that your business situation is at least a little bit unique. The odds are equally good that the fundamentals of your technical environment are not so unique. That's good news because it means that the documented configuration steps are likely to fit your environment.

We're not going to admonish you to read the documentation. We honestly assume you actually do that. However it presents itself to end users, ECM software is complex. It does fundamentally complex things and often interacts with other complex software components in the environment. Seemingly small errors in configuration, which you might reasonably expect to result in a concise and enlightening diagnostic, can instead result in silence or a frustratingly uninformative error message.

CM applications depend upon the CE (and, in some cases, the PE) functioning properly. The PE depends upon the CE and the database functioning properly. The CE depends upon the J2EE application server, the database, and the enterprise directory functioning properly. The CE also depends upon the operating system and physical hardware, but problems in those areas are less common.

You will want to double and triple check your CM installation and configuration steps. Depending upon the particular environmental components you are using, those steps can be quite complicated. Although you may have used the steps in the early chapters of this book as a quick way to get things going, you will want to consult the IBM product documentation if something goes wrong. Pay particular attention to the specific releases and fix pack (or equivalent) versions in use. Check each one in the hardware and software guide to make sure they are supported for CM. For example, a common source of mysterious problems is the use of an unsupported JDBC driver.

It may sound like passing the buck, but one useful thing you can do is to check that those infrastructure pieces are healthy on their own. Each has native tools and can support applications outside of the CM usage. For example, every database has graphical or command line tools for issuing SQL commands and queries. If you can't reach the database behind an Object Store with native tools, then the CE will likely do no better. Become familiar with those native tools and troubleshooting techniques for the individual components so that you can quickly tell if something is wrong with them independent of CM.

CM and all of the environmental components have built into them a fair amount of trace logging of various sorts. By its nature, trace logging for a component tends to produce a lot of output. Since it's expected to be used primarily by support and engineering personnel for the component in question, the specific logged items are generally not well documented. Still, even without documentation for what various trace log entries mean, we find it is often quite useful to look through those log files in our search for additional clues about what the problem might actually be. The sizes of the log files can make this a time-consuming process, so you have to decide for yourself when you have reached the point of diminishing returns.

> One word of caution: Beware of false alarms. Trace logging will often contain statements that some things were not found or defined or available or whatever. You really can't tell from that whether that is a routine condition that the software deals with or whether it's a dire emergency. As we said, you're just looking for clues, not a line that has your name on it and a mention of the specific line in a configuration file that you need to change.

For IBM components in particular, there is almost always a published "must gather" procedure. For example, see *MustGather: Read first for FileNet Content Engine*, http://www-01.ibm.com/support/docview.wss?uid=swg21308231. That is a document that describes a collection of information and log files that IBM support may need before diagnosing a problem. You can often use documents like that as a guideline for what to look at for your own troubleshooting purposes.

# Authentication

One very common problem we come across, usually in an initial configuration but sometimes as a result of a configuration changes, is general authentication failure. If an isolated account has an authentication problem, you don't need us to tell you how to check it out in the directory. If all accounts are having authentication problems, and if the enterprise directory itself is healthy, then it is likely a CM configuration problem.

*Support, Fix Packs, and Troubleshooting*

The CE insists on authentication for all requests, and authentication failures fall into two categories: authentication failures (E_NOT_AUTHENTICATED, FNRCE0040E) and anonymous requests (SECURITY_ANONYMOUS_DISALLOWED, FNRCS0001E). Those codes we just mentioned appear as part of CE-generated exception messages. If a failing application doesn't display them, then you will have to consult CE trace logging.

Authentication failures are fairly straightforward and most often occur in isolated cases for individual accounts. These can be cases of expired passwords or other directory conditions. The CE intentionally avoids giving details of the reason for an authentication failure in exception messages because information that is helpful to a user or an administrator is also helpful to a security attacker. You may find additional information about authentication failures logged in the CE error log.

Anonymous requests are very simple to understand, but it can be tricky to track down the thing that needs fixing. The CE considers a request to be anonymous if there is no JAAS Subject, if the JAAS Subject has no user Principal, or (in the case of some application servers) the JAAS Subject contains a special Principal that the application server uses to indicate anonymity. If you haven't guessed already, these cases occur when using EJB transport. Authentication is usually done on the client side for EJB transport, and it will usually result in a simple authentication failure if the problem is something like bad credentials. Here are some things to check in the case of failure due to anonymous requests:

- If a custom application is failing, it might not be performing authentication at all. Authentication is done via an explicit JAAS login, a call to UserContext.createSubject, or container-managed authentication. Problems with the first two will be found during development and routine testing. For container-managed authentication, check that whatever mechanism you are using is actually wired up correctly. For example, we showed steps for configuring XT's container-managed authentication in *Chapter 5*.

- You may have an inappropriate JAAS configuration file. The application servers all have their own login modules for use with EJB transport. It would be unusual to have the modules for more than one application server actually available in a given environment, but it's not impossible. More commonly, CEWS transport uses a CM-supplied JAAS login module that won't work with EJB transport. In all of these cases, the legitimate JAAS Subject created in the client will not be recognized by the application server's EJB container, and the Subject will be discarded.

- If your client runs inside an application server, you might have neglected to establish a trust relationship between the client application server and the application server where the CE runs. In the absence of a trust relationship, the CE application server's EJB container will not accept a JAAS Subject created on the client application server. Different application servers have different procedures for creating trust relationships. Whatever the mechanism, if things were working and suddenly stopped working, check for expiration of security certificates or other artifacts of the trust relationship. They sometimes have a defined validity period that can sneak up on you.
- See if your application server has specific trace logging for authentication matters. The authentication handshake can often be more complex than you imagine, and there could be sand in the gears of any one of several moving parts.

## WAS bootstrap information

The flexibility of possible WebSphere configuration topologies can lead to a misunderstood failure mode in authentication or even basic connectivity for EJB transport. Have a look at the port assignments information for WAS in *Chapter 2*. It quite often happens that the names in the **Host** column will be `localhost` or another simplified form of the server name where WAS is installed. You should use the fully-qualified host name in that column. The important part is that the name that appears in those entries can be resolved properly in DNS from the client machines. It is not enough that they are correct names from the WAS server's point of view. In some exchanges, the WAS client will ask the WAS server for one of those host names and port numbers. If it cannot be resolved from the client side, the subsequent connection will fail.

## Performance

There are a lot of different ways that performance problems can arise. For a newly deployed custom application, there could certainly be less than optimal development practices that lead to performance problems. In this section, however, we will focus on troubleshooting performance problems that arise in a previously healthy system.

In addition to the items mentioned here, you will want to consult the *FileNet P8 Performance Tuning Guide* mentioned previously.

## Trace logging

It's not the most frequently occurring performance problem, but we have seen cases where this baffled clever people. Since it's reasonably easy to look for it once you think of it, we'll describe it first.

Trace logging, of CM components and of environmental components, can have a moderate to severe impact on performance. You might think it's an obvious thing to check—if you turn on trace logging and performance suffers, there is a pretty obvious link. In an environment where there are multiple hands doing administrative tasks, it's easy for one person to turn on logging for some temporary reason. Later, someone else is investigating a performance problem and doesn't know anything about the forgotten logging.

CE trace logging has an additional factor to beware of. You can be fooled by the hierarchical configuration scheme. The usual practice is to use FileNet Enterprise Manager (FEM) to enable or disable CE trace logging at the P8 Domain level, but it is also possible to selectively enable trace logging at the site, virtual server, or server levels. If you just look at the Domain level trace logging configuration, you can be fooled into thinking it's all disabled when it is actually enabled at a different point in the hierarchy. Check all the levels.

The CE Java API and many applications use a popular package called **log4j** for trace logging. There is no logging by default for the CE Java API, but it's readily enabled via a log4j configuration file. Unfortunately, a carelessly created log4j configuration file for the application or some other included library can accidentally trigger massive logging for the CE Java API as well. This can be tricky to track down because the log4j configuration file might be supplied by someone else and not even be known to you. You can set a Java system property `-Dlog4j.debug=true` to have log4j report where it finds its configuration file and many other internal details.

## Isolation

Among the first things you want to do when looking at a performance problem is to isolate the poorly performing component. It can certainly be the case that your load has increased so that most components are pretty busy. In that case, the only cure might be to add more hardware to handle the load. Often, however, one or a few components will become performance-critical while other components are having a relaxed time.

Native operating system or environmental component tools can be used in many cases to find the performance bottleneck. For CM components, you can also use the FileNet System Dashboard to get a glimpse into instantaneous and average operation rates. You can also use selective trace logging to see what operations are taking a long time or otherwise tying up resources. Because you don't want trace logging to have any more impact on performance than is necessary, start by looking for trace logging options that will provide minimal information.

## Database tuning

A modern database system does a lot of things to take care of itself automatically. You could be forgiven for thinking that you never really have to look into what it's doing. This can backfire on you, though, because the data in a database can greatly affect the automatic tuning that it does and the decisions it makes when performing operations. A database that was finely tuned at one time can fall into a degraded state over time.

If you have a large IT organization with on-staff database specialists, you don't need us to tell them what performance measures to look at periodically, what metrics to gather, what reorganizations to do from time to time. If you don't have on-staff database specialists, it may be worth considering having a consultant on retainer. A couple of hours a week of routine database housekeeping can go a long way in avoiding an eventual performance crisis.

A particular case of degraded performance in the database catches many people off-guard because of the sudden shift in behavior. We often hear distress calls related to "bad queries" that used to be just fine. With CE trace logging, you can find out what native database SQL is used for a given CE SQL query. With that information and native database tools, you can find out how the database executes that particular query. You may be surprised to find out that the database is deciding to ignore an index that you specifically created to make the query perform well. The database is keeping track of the actual values in the indexed columns, and it can decide that there is not enough variety in the indexed values to make it worthwhile to use the index. If 95% of the values in a given column are the same, it's not a very good candidate for narrowing the search. If the database doesn't find a useful index for a given query, it will do a table scan. That is, it will read every row in the table to look for values matching the query conditions. That's bad and gets worse as the table gets larger and the number of concurrent searches grows. The surprising part about all of this is that the database server can suddenly switch its strategy from using the index to doing a table scan. The accretion of data leading to the problem happens over time, but the performance change is sudden.

Database performance problems can lead to a lot of different strategies for a cure. There are too many possibilities for us to list them here. Awareness of the problem is more than half the battle, but it will often need a database specialist to look at the particular circumstances and come up with a solution.

# Summary

This chapter was about keeping your system running and in good health. It included discussions of support resources, how to install fix packs, and some troubleshooting methods for when things go wrong.

# Index

## Symbols

#CREATOR-OWNER 250
.NET clients
  and CEWS users 233
/opt/ibm/ldap/V6.2/bin/ldapsearch command 64

## A

Access Control Entry (ACE) 241, 242
Access Control List (ACL)
  about 241
  levels 244, 245
  rights 243, 244
  unused bits 245
  user and group access 243
Action.CodeModule property 220
adapter object 258
AddOns
  about 221
  advantages 221
  authoring 223
  components 222
  creating 222
  installing 223
AE
  about 46, 73, 127, 151, 328
  and XT 151
AE UIS 328
AIIM
  about 17
  DMA 17
  ODMA 18
AnnotatedObject property 255
Annotation base class 213

annotations 213, 214
Annotation subclasses 214
anonymous 236, 237
API transports
  about 316
  CEWS transport 316, 317
  Enterprise JavaBean (EJB) transport 317
  JAAS context 319
  transport-Specific coding 319
  user transactions 318
Application Engine. *See* AE
applications, CM
  FileNet Content Federation Services 4.5.1 295
  IBM FileNet Application Engine 4.0.2 and WorkPlace XT 1.1.4 295
  IBM FileNet Connector, for SharePoint Web Parts V2.2 296
  IBM FileNet Integration for Microsoft Office 1.1 and IBM FileNet Application Integration 295
  IBM FileNet Services, for Lotus Quickr 1.1.0 296
  System Dashboard, for Enterprise Content Management 4.5.1 295
  WebDAV Server 296
application server trust relationships 230, 231
ApplyStateId property 251
Association for Information and Image Management. *See* AIIM
asynchronous subscription 218
audit logging 219
authentication 226
authentication, in CM
  about 226, 227

anonymous and guest access  236, 237
application server trust relationships  230, 231
CEWS clients  232
impersonation and run-as  237, 238
Java Authentication and Authorization Service (JAAS)  227-230
Java clients with CEWS  232
Single Sign-on (SSO)  235, 236
thick EJB clients  231
**authorization  226**
**authorization, in CM**
  #CREATOR-OWNER  250
  about  240
  Access Control List (ACL)  241, 242
  default instance security  249, 250
  discretionary access control  240
  document lifecycle policy  250
  dynamic security inheritance  252
  extra access requirements  247
  hypothetical scenario  263
  implicit rules  245
  mandatory access control  240
  marking-controlled property  259
  Modification Access Required (MAR)  247, 248
  security policy  250, 251
  security templates  251
  Target Access Required (TAR)  248
**Authorized Problem Analysis Report (APAR)  385**
**autoclassification  197**

# B

**BM Content Manager  70**
**Bootstrapping  400**
**boutique  326**
**BPF  308**
**BPM  11, 294, 308**
**Business Process Framework.** *See* **BPF**
**Business Process Management.** *See* **BPM**
**business, requisites**
  restricted circulation (RC) documents  345
  restricted quantity (RQ) documents  344, 345

# C

**CCL  85**
**CCL** *See also* **COM Compatibility Layer**
**CE**
  client installation  146, 147
  configuration, for PE  150
  deployment features  289
  enterprise directories  239
  installing  75
  WAS console tweaks  81-83
**CE 4.5.1.4 clients  401, 402**
**CE 4.5.1.4 server  395, 396**
**CE APIs**
  about  314
  API transports  316
  CEWS 3.5 protocol  325
  COM compatibility layer  325
  compatibility layers  323
  data, reading  314, 315
  data, updating  315
  Java compatibility layer  324
**CE client software  156**
**CE, configuring for CSE**
  Object Store, configuring  138-141
  P8 Domain, configuring  137, 138
**CE installation**
  about  75
  CE server installer, running  76
  Configuration Manager  76-80
  FEM, installing  83-87
  ObjectStore, creating  90-92
  P8 Domain, bringing up  88-90
  software, obtaining  75
**CE Java API  320**
**CE Java API, in Eclipse**
  about  329, 330
  application code  333-335
  application, running  335, 336
  CE API dependencies  332, 333
  project  330, 331
**CE metadata changes, DUCk solution**
  about  363
  annotation subclass  364
  audit logging configuration  365, 366
  custom document properties  364
  custom events  364

CEMP 23
CE .NET API
  and Java APIs 320
CE .NET API, in VS C# Express
  about 337
  application code 340, 341
  application, running 342
  CE API dependencies 339
  project, creating 337
CE server
  updated CE server, redeploying 398, 399
CE SQL 125, 199
CE Toplogy
  domain 287
  server 287
  site 287
  virtual server 287
CE Web Services (CEWS)
  .NET clients and Direct CEWS users 233
  about 232
  custom authentication and tunnelling 233
  delegated authentication 234, 235
  Java clients with 232
CEWS 3.5 protocol 325
CEWS protocol 321, 322
CEWS transport 316, 317
CFS 283
CFS-IS 310
checkin model 192
checkout model 192
class definitions
  properties 210
classloader configuration 159
class subscription 217
clustering
  about 284
  in CM 284
CM
  about 93, 313
  components 394, 395
  documentation 380
  initiatives and scenarios 297
CM components
  about 294, 394, 395
  applications 295, 296
  connectors 295, 296
  environmental components 296, 297

limited use licensing 294
server components 294
CMIS 310, 311, 326, 327
CMS 19
Collocation 29
COM compatibility layer 325
COM compatibility layer. *See also* CCL
COM Interop 325
Common Language Runtime (CLR) 320
compliance management, ECM
  about 297, 298
  audits and reporting 301
  classification 299
  declaration 298, 299
  disposition 299, 300
  protection 299
Component Integrator 173
compound documents 197
CompoundDocumentState property 197
configuration objects, GCD
  directories 96
  system configuration 96
connectors. *See* applications, CM
Container-Managed Authentication (CMA) 160, 235
content access recording level 219
ContentAccessRecordingLevel property 110
content-based retrieval (CBR) 129, 201
content element numbering 190
content elements 188
Content Engine. *See* CE
Content Engine APIs. *See* CE APIs
Content Engine (CE) 23, 187
Content Engine Multiplatform. *See* CEMP
Content Engine, P8 platform architecture
  about 73
  content 72
  domain 72
  Global Configuration Database (GCD) 72
  metadata 72
Content Engine Web Services. *See* CEWS transport
Content Extended Operations 173
Content Federation Services for Image Services. *See* CFS-IS
content integration

with workflow 281
ContentLocation URL 349
Content Management Interoperability Services. *See* CMIS
Content Management Systems. *See* CMS
Content Manager. *See* CM
content reference 189
ContentReference element 349
Content Search Engine. *See* CSE
Content Search Engine (CSE) component 201
content storage
  about 281
  Storage Areas, types 282
content transfer 189
ContentType property 190
contributed ACE 253
CopyToReservation property 210
Create a Class Wizard 123
Create a Property Template wizard 118
Creator property 246
CRUD 188
CSE
  about 74, 129
  CE configuring, via FEM 136
  command line configuration, steps 133, 134
  configuring, via K2 Dashboard 134, 136
  considerations 288
  installer, running 130-132
  Object Store, configuring 138-141
  P8 Domain, configuring 137, 138
  user 130
  working, steps 129
CSE 4.5.1.1 client 396
CSE 4.5.1.1 server 397, 398
custom application
  considerations 273
custom objects 212

# D

Darwin Information Typing Architecture. *See* DITA
Darwin Information Typing Architecture (DITA) publishing 198 198
database engine (DB2) 127
database tuning 411, 412

data model 356
DateContentLastAccessed property 219
DB2 393
DB2 client software 144, 145
DB2 Database and Tablespaces 143
DB2 installation, environmental component configuration
  about 40, 41
  and WAS 51
  buffer pool definition, creating 42
  drop default user tablespace 42
  new databse, creating 42
  OSTORE1 database, creating 45
  parameters, setting 45
  specific points 40
  tablespaces, creating 43
  user, adding to database 44, 45
DB2 User Permissions 144
DB2 Workgroup Server Edition 9.5
  for FileNet Content Manager 4.5.1 297
deduplication feature, IBM Content Collector (ICC) 305
DefaultInstanceOwner 210
DefaultInstancePermissions 210
DefaultInstancePermissions property 249
DeletionAction 212
DeletionAction properties 212
Deployment 400
deployment features, CE
  content caching 289
  request forwarding 290
desktop shortcuts 66
Development Kit (JDK) 329
DIME 323
Direct Internet Message Encapsulation. *See* DIME
directory, environmental component configuration
  CE-specific entries 63
  groups 62
  manual TDS queries 64
  populating 55
  server-side sorting 59
  suffix 59
  TDS web console setup 56-58
  users 60-62
  using 54

**Disaster Recovery (DR)**
  about 285
  planning factors 285, 286
**discretionary access control 240**
**distributed deployment**
  bandwidth 286
  CE Toplogy 287
  common configurations 291
  CSE considerations 288
  latency 287
  PE considerations 288
  planning factors 286
**DITA 311**
**DMA 17**
**DNS 37**
**document**
  about 188
  adding 349, 350
  autoclassification 196
  Autoclassification 197
  checkin model 192
  checkout model 192
  compound documents 197
  content element numbering 190, 191
  content elements 188
  content reference 189, 190
  content transfer elements 189, 190
  Darwin Information Typing Architecture (DITA) publishing 198
  details, viewing 350, 351
  lifecycles 195, 196
  MajorVersionNumber 194
  MinorVersionNumber 194
  modifying 352, 353
  multiple content elements 189
  rendition engine 198
  restricted circulation (RC) documents 352
  restricted quantity (RQ) documents 351, 352
  version, freezing 193
  versioning 191, 192
**documentation, CM**
  IBM developerWorks 384
  IBM Redbooks 383, 384
  information center 380, 381
  other links 382
  standalone documents 381, 382
  Worldwide IBM ECM community 384
**document lifecycle 195**
**document lifecycle policy 252**
**DocumentLifecyclePolicy property 252**
**Document Management Alliance.** *See* **DMA**
**document properties**
  about 356
  restriction indicators 357
**Documents Under Control.** *See* **DUCk**
**Domain**
  components 95
  GCD 94
  topology levels 98
**domain-level items**
  AddOn 102
  AddOns 95
  content cache 109
  content configuration 105, 106
  exploring 100, 101
  FCD 103
  marketing sets 96
  Server Cache configuration 103, 104
  trace logging 106, 107
  trace logging, organizing 108
**Domain Name Service.** *See* **DNS;**
**Domain Specific Languages.** *See* **DSLs**
**DUCk 343**
**Duck project 371-373**
**DUCk solution**
  annotation subclass 364
  audit logging configuration 365, 366
  CE metadata changes 363
  code module, modifying 368-370
  custom document properties 364
  custom events 364, 365
  debug logging 370, 371
  Duck project 371-373
  DuckRQB project 367, 368
  Duck.war, deploying 374
  Duck.war, exporting 374
  event handler code module, configuring 366
  new code module 368
**Duck.war**
  deploying 374
  deployment descriptor 375
  exporting 374

JSF runtime, selecting 376
role mapping, configuring 377
WAS, deploying to 376
**duplicate suppression.** *See* **deduplication feature, IBM Content Connector (ICC)**
**dW ECW Zone**
URL 384
**Dynamic Referential Containment Relationship (DRCR) 205**
**dynamic security inheritance**
about 252
folders, as adapters 259
inheritable depth 253
object-valued properties (OVPs) 253
parent and child security objects 253
project team, adapters 257, 258, 259
project team, example 256, 257
roles and adapters 256
SecurityProxyType property 254
system-defined inheritance 255

# E

**EAR file deployment 156**
**Eclipse**
CE Java API 329, 330
**ECM**
about 8, 9
add-ons 14
compliance management 297
Enterprise interoperability 14
extensibility 14
features 12
not CMS 20
not database 20
notifications 15
not SCM 20
partner ecosystem 14
platform support 13
safe repository 13
scalability 14
standards 16
strong APIs 15
strong security features 13
traditional document management features 15, 16
triggers 15
use cases 9
vendor 14
**ECM, standards**
about 16
AIIM 17
CMIS 19
JCR 19
WebDAV 18
**ECM widgets 327**
**ECM Widgets.** *See* **IBM Enterprise Content Management Widgets**
**eDA 302**
**eDiscovery (eD)**
IBM eDiscovery Analyzer (eDA) 302
IBM eDiscovery Manager (eDM) 303
**eDM 303**
**EJB transport 317**
**Electronic Discovery.** *See* **eDiscovery (eD)**
**ElementSequenceNumber 190**
**Email**
ICC for 304
**end-user view, design**
about 345, 346
common login screen 346
documents, finding 347, 348
**Enterprise Content Management.** *See* **ECM**
**enterprise directories 239**
**Enterprise JavaBean transport.** *See* **EJB transport**
**enterprise mandates, DUCk application 354**
**Entry Templates**
about 172
creating 172
**environmental component configuration**
about 33
DB2, installing 40
directory, using 54
group accounts 34, 35
Red Hat Enterprise Linux 36
Tivoli Directory Server, installing 52
user 34, 35
WAS 45
**environmental components**
about 25
application servers 30
configuring 33

[ 418 ]

database components, using 28
databases 30
directory components, using 28
directory servers 30
hardware requirements 29, 30
installation guides 30
operating sytems 30
software requirements 29, 30
storage devices 30
tailored planning 30

**environmental components, CM**
DB2 Workgroup Server Edition 9.5, for FileNet Content Manager 4.5.1 297
WebSphere Application Server 6.1 and 7.0, for FileNet Content Manager 4.5.1 296

**event** 216, 217
**EventActionHandler interface** 220
**event handler code module, DUCk solution**
code module, modifying 368-370
debug logging 370, 371
deploying 366
DuckRQB project 367, 368
new code module 368

**event handlers** 220
**Event object** 219

# F

**FCD** 103
**FCDs** 283
**FCP** 380
**federation** 283
**FEM** 32, 83, 93
about 127, 165
CE configuring, for CSE 136
Object Store, configuring 138-141
P8 Domain, configuring 137, 138

**FileNet**
history 22, 23

**FileNet Certified Professionals.** See FCP
**FileNet Content Federation Services 4.5.1** 295
**FileNet Enterprise Manager.** See FEM; See FEM

**file systems**
ICC for 304

**Fixed Content Devices.** See FCD

**fix packs**
about 391, 392
installing 393

**fix packs, installing**
CE 4.5.1.4 clients 401, 402
CE 4.5.1.4 server 395, 396
CM components 394
CSE 4.5.1.1 client 396
CSE 4.5.1.1 server 397, 398
supporting components 393, 394
updated CE server, redeploying 398-400
XT 1.1.4.8 402-404

**folders and containment**
about 204
containment names 207
filling 205, 206
referential containment 204, 205

**freezing, document version** 193
**functional tier deployments**
CE 272
database 272
diagram 270
PE 272
session state 271, 272
web browser 270, 271
web server 271, 272

# G

**GCD**
about 94, 272
components 95
configuration objects 96
Domain 94
domain-level items 95
pointers to components 96
properties 95

**GetContent servlet** 349
**Global Configuration Database.** See GCD
**groupOfNames class** 60
**guest access** 236

# H

**High Availability (HA)** 285
**hypothetical scenario**
business requirements 263, 264
implementation 265, 266

players 263
strategy 265
test 267

# I

IBM Classification Module. *See* ICM
IBM Content Analytics. *See* ICA
IBM Content Collector. *See* ICC
IBM Content Integrator 8.5.1 295
IBM developerWorks (dW) 384
IBM documents
  environment, planning 27
  environment, preparing 27
  Fix Pack Compatibility Matrix 28
  infocenter 26
  P8 documents 26
IBM ECM Widgets. *See* IBM Enterprise Content Management Widgets
IBM eDiscovery. *See* eDiscovery (eD)
IBM eDiscovery Analyzer. *See* eDA
IBM eDiscovery Manager. *See* eDM
IBM Enterprise Content Management Widgets 309
IBM Enterprise Records (IER) 298
IBM FileNet Application Engine 4.0.2 and WorkPlace XT 1.1.4 295
IBM FileNet Business Process Framework 308
IBM FileNet Business Process Manager (BPM)
  about 141, 308
  IBM Enterprise Content Management Widgets 309
  IBM FileNet Business Process Framework 308
IBM FileNet Capture and Datacap 310
IBM FileNet Connector
  for SharePoint Web Parts V2.2 296
IBM FileNet Content Engine 4.5.1 294
IBM FileNet Content Manager (CM) system 379
IBM FileNet Content Search Engine 4.5.1 294
IBM FileNet Image Services (IS) 309
IBM FileNet Integration for Microsoft Office 1.1 and IBM FileNet Application Integration 295
IBM FileNet Process Engine 4.5.1 294
IBM FileNet Services
  for Lotus Quickr 1.1.0 296
IBM FileNet System Monitor 309
IBM Redbooks 383, 384
IBM's business partners 380
IBM System Dashboard for ECM (SD)
  about 162
  configuration 162
ICA 311
ICC
  about 303
  deduplication feature 305
  for Email 304
  for file systems 304
  for Micosoft SharePoint 304
  task connectors 304
ICM 305, 306
IDE 22
Id property 208
IETF 18, 279
ImmediateSubclassDefinitions properties 210
impersonation 237
implicit rules
  object owner 246
  object store administrator 246
  special query right 247
Information On Demand (IOD)
  about 387
  conference 387
  IOD Global Conference 387
  Regional IOD conference 387
infrastructure, Smart Archive Strategy 307
ingestion, Smart Archive Strategy 307
inheritable depth 253
InheritableDepth property 253
installing
  CE 75
  FEM 83
Installing Tivoli Directory Server. *See* TDS
instance subscription 217
Integrated Development Environment. *See* IDE
Integrated Windows Authentication (IWA) 342

interim fixes 389, 390
Internet Engineering Task. *See* IETF
Internet Engineering Task Force. *See* IETF
intersection mode 200
IOD Global Conference 387
IsolatedRegionNumber property 220
isolation 410, 411
IsSystemOwned property 211

## J

JAAS context 319
JAAS Subject 154
Java Archive (JAR) 220
Java Authentication and Authorization Service (JAAS) 227, 228
Java clients
  with CEWS 232
Java compatibility layer 324
Java Database Connectivity (JDBC) 202
Java Runtime Environment (JRE) versions 320
JavaServer Faces (JSF) 371
JOIN construct 201

## K

K2 Dashboard
  used, for configuring CSE 134, 136
Keyword Search 182

## L

LDAP
  configuring 152, 153
LDAP directory server (Tivoli) 127
Least Recently Used. *See* LRU
Lightweight Directory Access Protocol (LDAP) 239
Lightweight Third Party Authentication. *See* LTPA
LRU 289
LTPA
  about 154
  keys, exporting 154

## M

management, Smart Archive Strategy 307
mandatory access control 240
many-to-many relationships 214
Marking.ConstraintMask property 261
marking-controlled property 259
Marking.MarkingValue property 260
marking set
  about 259, 260
  example 261, 262
merged scope query 200
Message Transmission Optimization Mechanism. *See* MTOM
metadata, Object Store-level items
  about 114
  Choice Lists node, selecting 115, 116
  classes 116
  Property Template 114, 115
  subclassing example 117-124
Micosoft SharePoint
  ICC for 304
Microsoft Management Console. *See* MMC
MIME 322
MimeType property 190, 208
MMC 84
Model-View-Controller (MVC) framework 151
model-view-controller (MVC) web applications 328
Modification Access Required (MAR) 247, 248
MTOM 322
multi-factor authentication 227
multiple content elements 189
Multipurpose Internet Mail Extensions. *See* MIME

## N

Name property 208
navigational overview, DUCk application 354, 355
Network Deployment (ND) edition 29
network security

configuring 278
firewalls 279
SSL 278
TLS 278
**Network Time Protocol.** *See* **NTP**
**NTP** 37

## O

**OASIS** 19
**object owner** 246
**ObjectStore** 72
**object store administrator** 246
**Object Store-level items**
  auditing 111
  cache configuration 113
  Checkout Type 111
  ContentAccessRecordingLevel property 110, 111
  exploring 110
  metadata 114
  Object Browse 124
  Query 124, 125, 126
  repository objects 109
  Text Index Date Partitioning 112
**Object Stores**
  partitioning 277, 278
**ODMA** 18
**online support resources**
  about 385
  fix central 386
  personalized notifications 386
  PMRs and APARs 385
  support portal 385
  technotes 385
**Open Document Management API.** *See* **ODMA**
**ORB uniqueness** 160
**Organization for the Advancement of Structured Information Standards.** *See* **OASIS**
**Owner property** 246

## P

**P8 Domain** 94
**P8 platform architecture**
  about 70

Application Engine (AE) 73
Content Engine 71
Content Search Engine (CSE) 74
Process Engine (PE) 74
Rendition Engine (RE) 74
**parallel environments, building**
  development environment 274, 275
  domains, requiring 275, 276
  multiple Domains, using 276
  pre-production environment, need for 274
**parent and child security objects** 253, 254
**Parent property** 255
**PDF** 26
**PE** 74, 172
**PE APIs** 326
**PE client software** 157
**Permissions property** 249
**PersistenceType property** 211
**PE server**
  about 220
  CE client, installation 146, 147
  CE configuration 150
  client software 151
  configuration 147-149
  connections, testing 150
  database configuration 143
  DB2 client software 144, 145
  DB2 Database and Tablespaces 143
  DB2 user permissions 144
  installation 145, 146
  installing, steps 142
  shared memory 149
  users and groups 142, 143
**pointers to components, GCD**
  Content Cache Areas 96
  Fixed Content Devices 96
  ObjectStores 96
  PE Connection Points and Isolated Regions 96
  Text Search Engine 96
**Pointers to components, GCD**
  Rendition Engines 96
**Portable Document Format.** *See* **PDF**
**Problem Management Report (PMR)** 385
**Process Designer (PD)** 221
**Process Engine.** *See* **PE**
**Process Engine server.** *See* **PE server**

product releases  387, 389
project team
  about  256, 257
  adapters  257, 258
properties, GCD
  database schemas  95
  Name and ID  95
  permissions  95
PropertyDefinition.ModificationAccessRequired property  248
PropertyDefinitionObject.TargetAccessRequired property  249
property definitions
  properties  210-212

## Q

queries
  manual TDS queries  64

## R

Rational Application Developer (RAD)  329
RE
  about  74, 198, 163
  installation  164
  use cases  163
Red Hat Enterprise Linux
  about  36
  file storage area  38
  firewalls  39
  network addresses  37
  system clocks  37
  unwanted ports  39
referential containment  204
ReferentialContainmentRelationship object  255
Referential Containment Relationship (RCR)  205
ReflectivePropertyId  212
Regional IOD conference  387
releases and fixes
  about  387
  fix packs  391, 392
  interim fixes  389, 390
  product releases  387, 389
Rendition Engine. *See* RE
rendition support  198

Representational State Transfer. *See* REST
RequiredClassId  211, 212
resources  379
REST  272
restricted circulation (RC) documents  345
  about  352
  access control  359
  access logging  358, 359
  access, request for  359, 360
restricted quantity (RQ) documents  344
  about  361
  issues  361, 362
RetrievalName file extension  190
RetrievalName property  190
RHEL  393
role objects  256
run-as  237

## S

SCM  21
scope  200
scripts
  down.sh  66
  up.sh  65
SD. *See* IBM System Dashboard for ECM (SD)
search
  about  199, 200
  JDBC provider  202
  merge mode  200
  property searches  201, 202
  searchable property  201
  search templates (ST)  203
  selectable property  201
  stored searches (SS)  203
  text searches  201, 202
Search Designer (SD)  183
searches, CM
  about  180
  advances searches  182, 183
  Keyword Search  182
  Search Template (ST)  183, 184
  simple search  181
  Stored Search (SS)  183, 184
Search Templates (ST)  203
Secure Sockets Layer. *See* SSL

SecurityFolder property 255, 259
security model 356
SecurityParent property 255
security policy
  and document lifecycle policy 250
  and security templates 251
SecurityPolicy property 251
SecurityProxyType property 253, 254
SELECT clause 201
server components, CM
  IBM FileNet Content Engine 4.5.1. 294
  IBM FileNet Content Search Engine 4.5.1 294
  IBM FileNet Process Engine 4.5.1 294
Settability property 211
single-instance storage. *See* deduplication feature, IBM Content Connector (ICC)
single sign-on. *See* SSO
Smart Archive Strategy
  about 306
  infrastructure 307
  ingestion 307
  management 307
SOAP 323
Source Code Management. *See* SCM
source document 198
SSL 278
SSO 157, 235, 236, 328
sticky sessions 284
Storage Areas, content storage
  CFS 283
  Database Storage Area 282
  FCDs 283
  File Storage Area 282
Stored Searches (SS) 203
Structured Query Language (SQL) 199
Subscribable.raiseEvent(CustomEvent) method 217
subscription
  about 217
  asynchronous subscription 218
  synchronous subscription 218
su command 65
SuperclassDefinition properties 210
supported platforms
  factors, considering 280

synchronous subscription 218
System Dashboard. *See* IBM System Dashboard for ECM (SD)
System Dashboard for Enterprise Content Management 4.5.1 295
system-defined Inheritance 255

# T

Tagged Image Format Files. *See* TIFF
target 198
Target Access Required (TAR) 248
target environment
  about 31
  hardware component, requirements 33
  software component, requirements 31
Task connectors 304
TDS
  about 52, 393
  events, listing 53
  installer, launching 52
  installing 52
  Server Instance Administration Tool 53
thick EJB clients 231
TIFF 170, 213
TLS 278
topology levels, Domain
  Domain 98
  servers 99
  sites 98
  using 100
  viewing 98
  virtual servers 99
trace logging 410
traditional document management features
  auditing 16
  history 15
  metadata 16
  navigation 16
  reporting 16
  search 16
  versioning 15
  workflow integration 16
transport 316
Transport Layer Security. *See* TLS
transport-specific coding 319
troubleshooting

about 404
authentication 407-409
initial configuration 406, 407
performance 409
WAS bootstrap information 409
**troubleshooting, performance**
about 409
database tuning 411, 412
isolation 410, 411
trace logging 410
**troubleshooting, preventing**
backups 405
configuration control 404
snapshots 405
**tunneling 234**
**typical distributed deployment**
remote application and CE tier configuration 292
Remote Application Tier 291

# U

**union mode 200**
**unrestricted documents 344**
**use cases, ECM**
Central Document Repository 9, 10
compliance 10, 11
document-centric workflow 11
governance 10, 11
**userPassword attribute 62**
**user tokens 157**
**UserTransaction 318**

# V

**versioning**
about 176-191
InProcess (value 2) 194
Released (value 1) 194
Reservation (value 3) 194
Superseded (value 4) 194
**version series 191**
**VersionSeries.Versions 191**
**Victoria Electronic Records Strategy (VERS) 298**
**VS C# Express**
CE .NET API 337

# W

**WAS 393**
**WAS, environmental component configuration**
and DB2 51
performance tweaks 50
ports 46, 47
process attributes 48-50
profiles 46, 47
**WAT 151, 328**
**Web Application Toolkit.** *See* **WAT**
**WebDAV Server 296**
**Web Services Extensible Authentication Framework (WS-EAF) 234**
**Web Services Extensions.** *See* **WSE**
**Web Services Interface.** *See* **WSI transport**
**WebSphere Application Developer (WSAD) 329**
**WebSphere Application Server.** *See* **WAS, environmental component configuration**
**WebSphere Application Server 6.1 and 7.0**
for FileNet Content Manager 4.5.1 296
**WHERE clause 201**
**WjcFormat property 119**
**WjcWorkOfLiterature.Permissions property 248**
**WorkFlo 22**
**workflow**
content, integrating with 281
**WorkflowDefinition 221**
**workflow interactions**
about 172
Fixed Approval Workflow 175
one-time Isolated Region Setup 173, 174
XT, tasks 175
**Workplace Application Engine UI Service.** *See* **AE UIS**
**Workplace XT.** *See* **XT**
about 166, 167
documents, adding 168-170
documents, viewing 170, 171
Entry Templates 172
folders, adding 167, 168
properties 179, 180
security 179, 180

[ 425 ]

**Workplace XT.** *See also* **XT**
**worldwide IBM ECM community  384**
**WSE  85**
**WSI transport  317**

**XT**
  about  127, 151
  deploying  158, 159
  installation process  152
  installer, running  155, 156
  LDAP, configuring  152, 153
  LTPA  154
  pre-deployment configuration  157, 158
  running  160, 161
  trust relationship  154
**XT 1.1.4.8  402-404**
**XT, deploying**
  classloader configuration  159
  ORB uniqueness  160
  special subjects, mapping  160

# Z

**ZeroClick technology  298**

# [PACKT] enterprise
PUBLISHING
professional expertise distilled

## Thank you for buying
## Getting Started with IBM FileNet P8 Content Manager

## About Packt Publishing

Packt, pronounced 'packed', published its first book "Mastering phpMyAdmin for Effective MySQL Management" in April 2004 and subsequently continued to specialize in publishing highly focused books on specific technologies and solutions.

Our books and publications share the experiences of your fellow IT professionals in adapting and customizing today's systems, applications, and frameworks. Our solution based books give you the knowledge and power to customize the software and technologies you're using to get the job done. Packt books are more specific and less general than the IT books you have seen in the past. Our unique business model allows us to bring you more focused information, giving you more of what you need to know, and less of what you don't.

Packt is a modern, yet unique publishing company, which focuses on producing quality, cutting-edge books for communities of developers, administrators, and newbies alike. For more information, please visit our website: www.packtpub.com.

## About Packt Enterprise

In 2010, Packt launched two new brands, Packt Enterprise and Packt Open Source, in order to continue its focus on specialization. This book is part of the Packt Enterprise brand, home to books published on enterprise software – software created by major vendors, including (but not limited to) IBM, Microsoft and Oracle, often for use in other corporations. Its titles will offer information relevant to a range of users of this software, including administrators, developers, architects, and end users.

## Writing for Packt

We welcome all inquiries from people who are interested in authoring. Book proposals should be sent to author@packtpub.com. If your book idea is still at an early stage and you would like to discuss it first before writing a formal book proposal, contact us; one of our commissioning editors will get in touch with you.

We're not just looking for published authors; if you have strong technical skills but no writing experience, our experienced editors can help you develop a writing career, or simply get some additional reward for your expertise.

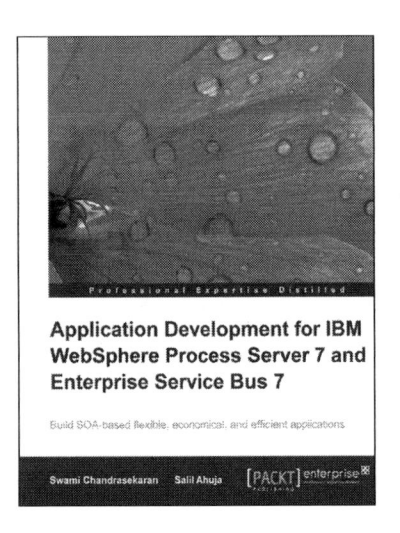

## Application Development for IBM WebSphere Process Server 7 and Enterprise Service Bus 7

ISBN: 978-1-847198-28-0     Paperback: 548 pages

Build SOA-based flexible, economical, and efficient applications

1. Develop SOA applications using the WebSphere Process Server (WPS) and WebSphere Enterprise Service Bus (WESB)
2. Analyze business requirements and rationalize your thoughts to see if an SOA approach is appropriate for your project
3. Quickly build an SOA-based Order Management application by using some fundamental concepts and functions of WPS and WESB

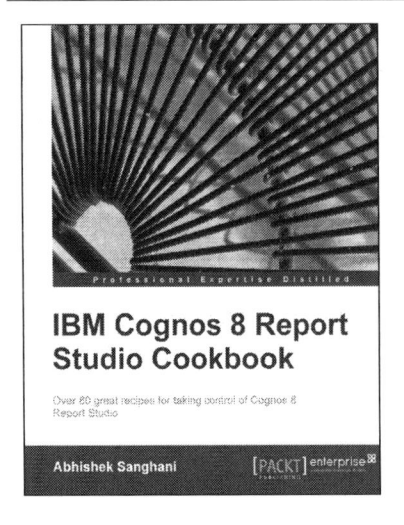

## IBM Cognos 8 Report Studio Cookbook

ISBN: 978-1-849680-34-9     Paperback: 252 pages

Over 80 great recipes for taking control of Cognos 8 Report Studio

1. Learn advanced techniques to produce real-life reports that meet business demands
2. Tricks and hacks for speedy and effortless report development and to overcome tool-based limitations
3. Peek into the best practices used in industry and discern ways to work like a pro
4. Part of Packt's Cookbook series-each recipe is a carefully organized sequence of instructions to complete the task as efficiently as possible

Please check www.PacktPub.com for information on our titles

## IBM Lotus Notes 8.5 User Guide

ISBN: 978-1-849680-20-2        Paperback: 296 pages

A practical hands-on user guide with time saving tips and comprehensive instructions for using Lotus Notes effectively and efficiently

1. Understand and master the features of Lotus Notes and put them to work in your business quickly
2. Contains comprehensive coverage of new Lotus Notes 8.5 features
3. Includes easy-to-follow real-world examples with plenty of screenshots to clearly demonstrate how to get the most out of Lotus Notes

## IBM Cognos 8 Planning

ISBN: 978-1-847196-84-2        Paperback: 424 pages

A practical guide to developing and deploying planning models for your enterprise

1. Build and deploy effective planning models using Cognos 8 Planning
2. Filled with ideas and techniques for designing planning models
3. Ample screenshots and clear explanations to facilitate learning
4. Written for first-time developers focusing on what is important to the beginner
5. A step-by-step approach that will help you strengthen your understanding of all the major concepts

Please check **www.PacktPub.com** for information on our titles

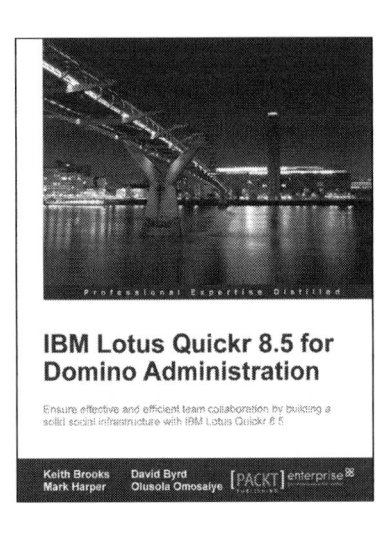

## IBM Lotus Quickr 8.5 for Domino Administration

ISBN: 978-1-849680-52-3　　　　Paperback: 250 pages

Ensure effective and efficient team collaboration by building a solid social infrastructure with IBM Lotus Quickr 8.5

1. Gain a thorough understanding of IBM Lotus Quickr 8.5 Team Collaboration, Repository, and Connectors
2. Recommended best practices to upgrade to the latest version of IBM Lotus Quickr 8.5
3. Customize logos, colors, templates, and more to your designs without much effort

## IBM Lotus Sametime 8 Essentials: A User's Guide

ISBN: 978-1-849680-60-8　　　　Paperback: 284 pages

Mastering Online Enterprise Communication with this collaborative software

1. Collaborate securely with your colleagues and teammates both inside and outside your organization by using Sametime features such as instant messaging and online meetings
2. Communicate with other instant messaging services and users, such as AOL Instant Messaging, Yahoo Instant Messaging, and Google Talk and know how someone's online status can help you communicate faster and more efficiently

Please check www.PacktPub.com for information on our titles

# [PACKT] enterprise
### professional expertise distilled

## IBM InfoSphere Replication Server and Data Event Publisher

ISBN: 978-1-849681-54-4  Paperback: 344 pages

Design, implement, and monitor a successful Q replication and Event Publishing project

1. Covers the toolsets needed to implement a successful Q replication project
2. Aimed at the Linux, Unix, and Windows operating systems, with many concepts common to z/OS as well
3. A chapter dedicated exclusively to WebSphere MQ for the DB2 DBA
4. Written in a conversational and easy to follow manner

## WS-BPEL 2.0 for SOA Composite Applications with IBM WebSphere 7

ISBN: 978-1-849680-46-2  Paperback: 644 pages

Define, model, implement, and monitor real-world BPEL 2.0 business processes with SOA-powered BPM

1. Develop BPEL and SOA composite solutions with IBM's WebSphere SOA platform
2. Detailed explanation of advanced topics, such as security, transactions, human workflow, dynamic processes, fault handling, and more—enabling you to work smarter

Please check **www.PacktPub.com** for information on our titles

Made in the USA
Lexington, KY
22 July 2012